Sex, Race, and Merit

# Sex, Race, and Merit

## Debating Affirmative Action in Education and Employment

*Faye J. Crosby and Cheryl VanDeVeer, Editors*

*Ann Arbor*

THE UNIVERSITY OF MICHIGAN PRESS

Copyright © by the University of Michigan 2000
All rights reserved
Published in the United States of America by
The University of Michigan Press
Manufactured in the United States of America
⊚ Printed on acid-free paper

2003   2002   2001   2000      4   3   2   1

*A CIP catalog record for this book is available
from the British Library.*

Library of Congress Cataloging-in-Publication Data applied for
ISBN 0-472-09734-2 (cloth: alk. paper)
ISBN 0-472-06734-6 (pbk.: alk. paper)

*To the memory of Clara Mayo*

FC

*and*

*To my coworkers Henrietta Brown, Judy Burton, Zoe Sodja,*
*Joan Tannheimer, and Nona Williams*

CV

# Contents

# Acknowledgments

Thanks go to many individuals. Judy Yung deserves a big thank-you for her leadership and inspiration on the prototype of this book. We are grateful for Abigail Stewart and Heidi Freund's belief in the project and for their good comments on how to shape the work. Our editor at the University of Michigan Press, LeAnn Fields, earned our respect and appreciation for her hard insights and soft delivery. Also important were two anonymous readers to whom the Press sent the book for review. Joan Larson and Marilyn Patton worked long and hard on manuscript preparation as did Zoe Sodja. Most of all, we thank Sirinda Sinchareon, the talented graduate student who kept everything on track through all phases of the work. Her contributions were simply extraordinary.

To two institutions, we also say thank you: the University of California and the University of Michigan. Research funds were made available to Faye Crosby at the University of California that enabled the work to be done. Then the Press had faith in our work and advanced to us the funds that allowed us to continue to go forward.

All of the published materials have been reprinted with permission. The acknowledgments for all pieces appear with the selections themselves. What we would like to note, however, are the kindness and helpfulness of many staff people working for many publishers throughout the United States. In this arena, where so many are wont to seek enemies, we only found friends.

# Introduction

Education is the bedrock of democracy. For any democracy to flourish, its citizens must be educated about important issues. The more citizens are informed and thoughtful about public and social policies, the stronger the democracy.

Sometimes to become informed is no simple matter, even with topics of pressing national concern. On certain issues, it is not easy for the ordinary citizen to learn about the facts at hand. In such cases, even people with a great deal of formal education may have difficulty deciding how to match the opinions of politicians and statesmen against reality.

Affirmative action poses a good example of an issue on which it is easy to hear a lot of opinions but difficult to learn the facts. Virtually all contenders for major political office in the United States today declare either strong support for or opposition to affirmative action. The controversies are both hot and noisy. When political and other public figures debate affirmative action, it is tempting to canonize one side and demonize the other. Each side sees itself as the special champion of justice in the United States. Ideology builds high fences.

If the debate were really between "good guys" and "bad guys," then it should be possible to distinguish easily between the opponents and the proponents of affirmative action on issues of discrimination and the appropriate remedies. If either the opponents of affirmative action or the proponents of it were the only ones with a seat on the freedom train, then it should be child's play to recognize the actual authors of the following statements A through D.

> **Statement A.** "Most of us think of ourselves as fair-minded people. We want an equitable and inclusive society. We want to stamp out racial and gender discrimination." *Who said this?*
>
> 1. President Bill Clinton (proponent of affirmative action)
> 2. Former California governor Pete Wilson (opponent)

3. Mr. Ward Connerly, regent of the University of California and architect of California's Proposition 209 (opponent)

4. Harvard Law School professor Christopher Edley, master planner of President Clinton's policy to save affirmative action (proponent)

**Statement B.** "More than 30 years ago, the Kerner Commission said we were becoming two Americas, one white, one black, separate and unequal. Today we face a different choice: Will we become not two, but many Americas, separate, unequal and isolated? Or will we draw strength from all our people and our ancient faith in the quality of human dignity . . . to lift the burden of race and redeem the promise of America?" *Who said this?*

1. President Bill Clinton (proponent)

2. Supreme Court justice Clarence Thomas (opponent)

3. Former president of Princeton University William Bowen (proponent)

4. Dr. Shelby Steele, author of *Content of Our Character* (opponent)

**Statement C.** "Two wrongs don't make a right. Illegal discrimination includes reverse discrimination; reverse discrimination is discrimination, and it is wrong." *Who said this?*

1. U.S. representative Charles Canady (opponent)

2. Professor Christopher Edley (proponent)

3. The Heritage Foundation announcement (opponent)

4. Former U.S. representative Pat Schroeder (proponent)

**Statement D.** "It is critical that . . . we provide reassurance to all concerned of the University's unwavering commitment to the underlying original principle of affirmative action." *Who said this?*

1. Governor George W. Bush (opponent)

2. Regent Ward Connerly (opponent)

3. Former University of California, Berkeley, chancellor Tien (proponent)

4. Dr. Nancy Cantor, provost of the University of Michigan (proponent)

Even highly educated people typically have difficulty selecting the right answers. Only a tiny fraction of those tested could correctly identify the authors as Mr. Connerly (statements A and D), President Clinton (statement B), Professor Edley (statement C).[1] On our test where one correct answer would occur by chance alone, audiences typically score a one or two!

What does it mean that people cannot attribute the statements correctly? What it means, we feel, is that most people involved in the issue want to end discrimination and special privilege and to bring about true equity. Where people differ is not in their devotion to fairness but in their visions of how fairness is best achieved.

It is time now to step out of the ideological morass with its patches of liberals and conservatives. If we take as our starting point the observation that we all want fairness, with an end to special privileges, we can begin to address the more crucial questions around issues of sex, race, and merit. We can ask: what constitutes merit? How are we to measure it? Should opportunities for improved living come about only as rewards to individuals for their proven merit, or are opportunities to be distributed according to some other principles? If so, what are they, and how shall they operate?

The purpose of *Sex, Race, and Merit* is to help move the debate beyond empty rhetoric. Its selections are aimed at letting people know both about affirmative action and its operation and about the principled debates it evokes among the people of the United States. We argue neither in favor nor against affirmative action. Our aim is, instead, to help educate on and off college campuses around the United States.

**Affirmative Action**

What is affirmative action? The most basic and comprehensive meaning is this: affirmative action occurs whenever an organization goes out of its way to make sure that there is no discrimination against people of color, against white women, against people with disabilities, or against veterans. When an organization goes out of its way to make sure that nonveteran, able-bodied white males are not victims of discrimination, we may applaud the organization, but we would not apply the label affirmative action. Similarly, if an organization does not intentionally discriminate against people of color, white women, disabled people, or veterans, we commend the organization, but when its policies involve only a passive or reactive stance on discrimination, we do not apply the label affirmative action.

An example makes clear the principles. Imagine that there are three companies: A, B, and C. Company A is a horrid place where prejudiced white managers go out of their way to block the opportunities of black people while promoting their own white cronies who have less talent than the black workers. In Company B, such behavior is not tolerated. In Company B if a black worker comes to management with a complaint of race discrimination, the complaint is taken seriously and investigated. Company C does not wait for the workers to come forward with a complaint. In Company C, one of the managers tracks the progress of all workers and takes notice of whether black workers and white workers are advancing in equal proportions and at equal rates. In Company C, if the vigilant manager notices that, say, black workers are not promoted as rapidly as similar white workers, an investigation into the reasons is begun even without anyone lodging a complaint. Company C is the affirmative action organization, while Companies A and B are not. But note that Company B desires fairness as much as Company C and they both wish for racial justice much more than Company A.

Affirmative action found its way into the U.S. political scene in the 1960s, the decade of the civil rights movement. Partially (but only partially) in response to pressure from groups of African American citizens, President Lyndon Johnson was looking for ways to implement his ideal of the Great Society. The Great Society would be one in which all people would have access to opportunities for self-improvement and in which the chasms between rich and poor would begin to diminish. Johnson hit upon the idea of dangling the carrot of government contracts to foster social change. Firms that wanted to make money by providing services or goods to the government would have to play by a new set of rules. If they objected to the rules, they did not have to play. Nobody was forced to seek or accept a government contract, but any organization that did had to have an affirmative action plan. This plan had to have two essential components: first, a method of monitoring employment patterns and, second, a plan for correcting imbalances that the monitoring revealed. Johnson's scheme appealed to the business community because it was pragmatic and because it relied on the kind of accounting practices that lies at the heart of modern business.

Only after several years did affirmative action come to be associated with higher education as well as business. Given the current focus on affirmative action in education, where it has been a much more controversial policy than it has been in business, it may come as a surprise to realize that most of the developments around affirmative action have been in the realm of employment.

In employment, affirmative action today can take a few forms. The most common form is to monitor hiring and promotion in a manner similar to what is depicted in Company C. When proactive monitoring reveals a problem, typically the organization hunts for and then dismantles whichever of its practices have been having discriminatory consequences. Often, when a problem has been identified, hiring or promotion goals are instituted. In classical affirmative action programs (where the employer monitors to make sure that qualified people are hired and promoted) the goals are derived from close study of the organization and are based on realistic appraisals of the labor market. Another form of affirmative action concerns construction work. In some locations municipalities, counties, or states set aside a percentage of the money budgeted for, say, construction work and award the set-aside money to contracts reserved for minority-owned businesses, even when those businesses do not submit the lowest bid on a proposed job. Yet another form of affirmative action in the construction industry has been to compensate firms (via adjustments of work bids) who subcontracted work to minority-owned or women-owned businesses.

In education contemporary affirmative action policies also have several faces. Some colleges and universities have had a practice of reserving a fixed number of spaces for qualified minority applicants. Other schools have numerically adjusted the scores of minority and majority applicants, in essence giving "bonus points" to the ethnic minorities or women who seek admissions. Still other schools have expended time and money (sometimes in the form of scholarships) on outreach to underrepresented populations but have not spent the same resources to recruit students from the mainstream.

How many Americans are affected directly or indirectly by affirmative action? Government figures indicate that one in four U.S. workers is employed by an organization that has a mandatory or voluntary affirmative action plan involving monitoring. These organizations include all government units, federal contractors, and many subcontractors. Several thousand additional workers are affected by set-aside programs and incentive programs in construction. Millions of U.S. employees have a direct stake in the future of affirmative action. Affirmative action programs in higher education touch fewer lives than in employment, but the numbers are still impressive. If we consider that all college students — whether they are women or men, people of color or white — have an interest in what their colleges and universities do, then we would have to conclude that over one million Americans are actively affected by affirmative action programs in higher education.

## Debating Affirmative Action

Criticisms of affirmative action policies pertaining to employment have come from both the political left and right. For left-wing critics, affirmative action is a problematic economic program. First, it only applies to people who are already part of the economic system, having employable skills and being available to work. Some commentators worry about affirmative action driving a wedge between employable poor and hard core poor, with the latter left to rot in inner cities while the former ride the affirmative action bus to the suburbs. There is another leftist challenge of affirmative action. By focusing on the match (or mismatch) between available talent and utilized talent, classic affirmative action policies seem to valorize the concept of talent, which, in turn, could be interpreted as simply an underhanded way to justify the status quo.

Against the left-wing criticisms, supporters of affirmative action policies in employment note that evolutionary change is often better than revolutionary change. Acknowledging that affirmative action does little, for example, to help welfare mothers or illiterate adults or addicted youth, they retort that no single economic program can cure all social ills. They also claim that no statistics support the allegation that affirmative action contributes to the plight of the inner city by causing employable poor to divide themselves from hard core poor.

More complex are criticisms from the right. Conservatives who dislike affirmative action take issue with an economic policy that forces people to pay attention to gender and race, either because of set-asides or because of monitoring categories. By seeing people in terms of categories and not as individuals, say the critics, affirmative action violates the Fourteenth Amendment of the Constitution and indeed runs counter to the core U.S. value of individual liberty. Affirmative action appears to erect roadblocks impeding the United States' journey toward becoming a race-blind and gender-blind society. Indeed, by allowing people to infer that a man of color or a woman has been hired to fill a quota rather than through merit, affirmative action creates self-doubt among its intended beneficiaries and fuels the very racial prejudice it is meant to curb.

In response, the supporters of affirmative action propose that historically and still today if one wishes to be racially fair, one cannot be racially blind, and if one wishes to be gender fair, one cannot be gender blind. Racial prejudice predates affirmative action, and it will not go away simply by ending hiring goals. If we wish to infer ability from performance, say the supporters, we must have a gauge of how other factors might affect performance. When we know that a woman has succeeded in a man's world, for example, we infer great ability to her; but knowing that a man has succeeded with all the cards stacked in his favor does not allow us to infer ability. If you want to hire a baseball player with a great batting swing, say the supporters, you need to know not only who ran across home plate but also which base that person was on when the ball was hit.

The debate about affirmative action in education is no less passionate, but it takes a slightly different form. Race-sensitive and gender-sensitive admissions policies have been the subject of intense debate, especially among professors and college administrators. One justification for affirmative action in admissions revolves around diversity. Diversity is a time-honored and deep educational value in the United States. For decades admissions officers in private schools have thought it more important to create cohorts of competent students that come from different regions of the United States than to create cohorts of wildly outstanding students who all come from Long Island. In support of their point of view, the educators have also pointed out the imperfections of standardized test scores and even of high school grades as predictors of achievements during and after college.

Not all educators think that there is more benefit in having a class of A and B students who come from all walks of life than there is in having a class of A students from one very narrow and homogeneous background. Some educators claim that race-sensitive or gender-sensitive admissions create two classes of students — those who were admitted on their merit and those who received special privilege. The sight of some students receiving special privilege, claim the opponents of affirmative action, angers those not so privileged and undermines the supposed beneficiaries. Besides, race-conscious programs differ from the older programs that paid attention to students' regional origins: the former appear to violate the Fourteenth Amendment of the Constitution, while the latter do not.

Recognizing the demoralizing effects on everyone of special privilege, some advocates of affirmative action apply to the case of race- and gender-conscious admissions the same logic that they apply to race- and gender-conscious policies in employment. They see affirmative action not as a type of special privilege for the underdog but rather as a means of dismantling the special privileges of those who have been at the top of the social heap. According to these analysts, when, for example, a disproportionately small number of students of color attend a university, it behooves the university to discover what subtle mechanisms may be at play. Are talented students of color being ill advised in their course selections? Are individual students of color being penalized by a system of calculations that gives extra points to advanced placement classes that their schools lack? These commentators sometimes note the sense of threat that comes to those who have been wearing "the invisible backpack of privilege" and who understand at some level that affirmative action means an erosion of their former position.

Even when people agree, as most Americans do, that it is desirable to reward merit and that it is good to end special privilege, affirmative action can be a lightning rod for deep ideological divisions. How are we to recognize the existence of special privilege? And what, after all, are we to consider most meritorious? Who has more talent — the B+ captain of the swim team who plays the French horn in a symphony orchestra? The B student with perfect SAT scores who organizes inner city youth into productive drug-free work teams? Or the A+ student who plays no sport or instrument and never participates in civic or other extracurricular activities? And how after all are we to value the ways of our own tribe without devaluing the ways of others?

**The Book**

When people argue about the need for affirmative action, about its effectiveness or its fairness, they often assume an understanding of the laws and policies. The first task of this book, therefore, is to provide basic information about the policy of affirmative action and its legal structure.

Parts 1 and 4 of *Sex, Race, and Merit* present factual materials. The first selection in Part 1 is a neutral explanation of affirmative action, focusing on how the program works in employment. The second selection in Part 1 presents an outline of the political controversy surrounding affirmative action as it developed in California, where Proposition 209 was passed by a majority of voters. The passage of Proposition 209, which legally abolished "preferential treatment" to individuals based on categorical memberships, is generally regarded as a watershed in the affirmative action landscape of the United States today.

Part 4 brings together relevant legal documents from the three branches of federal government — the executive branch (president), the legislative branch (Congress), and the judicial branch (especially the Supreme Court) — to show the changing contours of affirmative action's policy status. Particular attention should be paid to Lyndon Johnson's Executive Order 11246, which established the system of monitoring the utilization of talent as measured against its availability. Limitations of space have forced us to include only excerpts of a selection of court decisions, usually from the Supreme Court. The aim is to let nonlegal readers see for themselves how the various points of law are established. Access to primary sources is often difficult, even when the primary sources are legal documents open to the public. By bringing the primary sources into an anthology with published papers from the media and from academe, we aim to enhance readers' abilities to evaluate for themselves the merits of various popular and academic arguments about merit, ethnicity, gender, and affirmative action.

The strategy of *Sex, Race, and Merit* is to present two types of opinions and analyses sandwiched between the factual portions of the book. In Part 2 are newspaper articles arranged in chronological order. Over the last few years, media coverage of affirmative action has been enormous. Two types of stories predominate. First there are stories in which the reporters recount what has happened in a vote or in a Supreme Court decision or in a lawmaking session. These stories tend to portray the world in polarized terms, and they consist primarily of tallies in which are totted up the victories and defeats of either side. Second are the more reflective pieces, sometimes written by public figures such as Lani Guinier or Ward Connerly but more often written by journalists. Interestingly, the reflective pieces in the media are now making a strong effort to represent the complexities of affirmative action. More than the politicians (of course) and even more than academic writers, journalists have begun to avoid simplistic divisions into saints and devils.

Part 3 of the book presents essays by university faculty, divided into those who argue against affirmative action and those who argue in favor of it. As with the media accounts, the academic pieces are arranged within each subsection in chronological order. The selections in Part 3 are all excerpts of much longer works, and they have all been edited because of space constraints. For each selection, we have made every attempt to preserve the flow of the authors' arguments.

Looking at Part 3 an observant reader may notice among the "pro–affirmative action pieces" an excerpt from a book cowritten by Faye Crosby. For over a decade Crosby has been known in some academic circles as a vociferous supporter of affirmative action. How, one may wonder, can a book such as *Sex, Race, and Merit* purport to be neutral if one of the editors has unquestionably thrown her hat in the ring on behalf of affirmative action?

The question goes to the heart of academic inquiry. The answer has three parts. First, even when a scholar may not typically generate an argument (as Crosby would not generate arguments against affirmative action), the scholar ought to be able to recognize a good argument. Second, one can be a proponent of a concept without being a radical or fanatic adherent. No system is perfect, and if an authority like Crosby is going to be a true friend of affirmative action, she must be willing to listen to the arguments against it and the problems with it. Otherwise, how can she — or anyone — help improve it? Finally, the fact that Crosby can sometimes argue strongly in favor of the concept of affirmative action does not prevent her from, at other times, simply describing what affirmative (action) is. In fact, an orally presented version of the first selection in Part 1 of the anthology, also written by Crosby, has been praised for its objectivity by both the Reverend Mr. William Gray, a passionate advocate of affirmative action and head of the United Negro College Fund, and by Mr. Ward Connerly, architect of California's Proposition 209.

**A Final Note**

As Americans, we seek justice. But what exactly justice entails — especially in the controversial areas of gender and ethnicity — has been, is, and will be a matter for debate. Our system of government works best when those who enter the debates are well educated. When ordinary citizens have a strong grasp of complicated and important issues like affirmative action, society is well served. This book aims to educate people about the specific issues involved in affirmative action and to enlighten people about the broader national debates over sex, race, and merit. The complexity of the issues and their enormous importance mean that this book cannot please everyone entirely. One reader may wish for more detailed discussion of the court cases, another for more thorough treatment of the perils of affirmative action, yet another for more extensive news coverage. It is our conviction, however, that if the list of omissions is varied and if it does not cleave along party lines, much will be gained. Indeed, if *Sex, Race, and Merit* helps to lift discussions out of the unthinking swamps and backwaters of ideology and onto the higher grounds of principled and logical reflection, then all the effort that has gone into this volume will be more than amply repaid.

## NOTE

1. Answers: Statement A. 3. Mr. Connerly said this in an editorial in the *San Francisco Chronicle* on May 3, 1995. Statement B. 1. President Clinton said this at the University of California, San Diego, commencement speech on June 16, 1997. Statement C. 2. Professor Edley was coauthor of a report to the president on affirmative action. This statement appeared on page 3. Statement D. 2. Mr. Connerly again! He said this in a letter to his fellow regents dated July 5, 1995.

# Part 1: Basics

The two selections presented here provide a quick introduction to affirmative action and to the political and legal controversies surrounding it.

"Words Worth of Wisdom: Toward an Understanding of Affirmative Action" explains how affirmative action operates in employment. Currently, it is estimated that 25 percent of the U.S. labor force is covered directly or indirectly by affirmative action. In education, affirmative action operates in a similar way as in employment. Numbers are monitored, and when they are found to be lacking, actions are taken.

The excerpt from Lydia Chávez's book gives a chronology of major events concerning the battle over affirmative action, up to the moment when Proposition 209 was passed by the voters of California.

*Faye J. Crosby and Diana I. Cordova*

# Words Worth of Wisdom: Toward an Understanding of Affirmative Action

Controversy and clear thinking do not always go hand in hand. Sometimes, loud disagreements derive primarily from people having different interpretations of the same words. But when people become very attached to one point of view or another, they can refuse to clarify what the words mean.

About affirmative action, there has been a great deal of controversy, but very little clear exposition. One cannot read a newspaper today without coming across the words "affirmative action." Impassioned statements of sentiments — both opposing and supporting affirmative action — seem thick on the ground. Much less frequent are precise explanations of what exactly affirmative action entails. For instance, in a recent survey of three leading U.S. newspapers — *The New York Times, Washington Post,* and *USA Today* — we found that there were 176 articles on affirmative action published during the months of June–August of 1995. Of these, fewer than 6% offered a definition.

The existence of controversy is even officially recognized. Currently there are a number of governmental documents that deal with affirmative action. Virtually all of these documents acknowledge that the words have come to have different meanings in different contexts. A 1995 report prepared by the Congressional Research Service, for example, opens with the following observation:

> Affirmative action in employment is a highly controversial public policy. The controversy encompasses the very definition of the term itself. One complicating factor is that of the meaning of obligations imposed on employers. (Bruno, 1995, p. 1)

Similarly, the review ordered by President Clinton and submitted in July 1995 by Special Counsel Christopher Edley notes on its first page that

*Journal of Social Issues* 52, no. 4 (winter 1996): 33–49. Reprinted with permission from the Society for the Psychological Study of Social Issues.

" 'Affirmative action' enjoys no clear and widely shared definition. This contributes to the confusion and miscommunication surrounding the issue" (Stephanopoulos & Edley, 1995, p. 1).

In this article, we first define what affirmative action is, in both its classical and its additional forms. . . . [We concentrate on affirmative action in employment. Similar arguments can be made for education.]

## Defining Affirmative Action

Affirmative action is a national policy, albeit a controversial one. Various plans implement the policy. One can disapprove of any given affirmative action plan even if one endorses the policy. At the level of policy, we can differentiate two general meanings of the term "affirmative action." The first, which we call the Classical Definition, underlies the laws that have been in existence since the Johnson presidency. The second definition has more recently gained prominence.

### Classical Definition
The term "affirmative action" has been traced to Franklin Roosevelt's presidency when many policymakers acknowledged that steps needed to be taken to diminish racist business practices (Bruno, 1995; Clayton & Crosby, 1992; Taylor, 1989). It was not until the mid–1960s, however, that the term emerged from obscurity. Executive Order 11246, signed by President Johnson in 1965, included the words "affirmative action" and set the parameters for the classical definition.

According to the classical definition, affirmative action occurs whenever people go out of their way (take positive action) to increase the likelihood of true equality for individuals of differing categories. Whenever an organization expends energy to make sure that women and men, people of color and White people, or disabled and fully abled workers have the same chances as each other to be hired, retained, or promoted, then the organization has a policy of affirmative action in employment. By the same token, whenever an organization expends energy to make sure that females and males, people of color and White people, or disabled and fully abled students have the same chances as each other to be educated, then the organization has a policy of affirmative action in education. A far greater number of regulations and programs concern employment than education; but the concept is the same for both.

### Practical Implementation of the Traditional Policy
The most established affirmative action program has been in existence since 1965. Lyndon Johnson's Executive Order 11246 mandated that any organiza-

tion receiving a federal contract in excess of a certain figure (currently $50,000) with more than a certain number of employees (currently 50) should have a written plan that documents how closely the utilization of people of certain categories (e.g., women) matches the availability of qualified people in that category. When utilization falls short of availability (e.g., a university employs few women faculty in the social sciences despite a large available pool of women with Ph.D.'s in the social sciences), the organization must articulate its plans for improved performance. The plan might include special recruitment efforts, giving preference points to applicants from designated groups, temporary use of set-asides, or just simply closer scrutiny of one's current practices with an eye to eliminating any that have disparate impact on various groups of people. The Office of Federal Contract Compliance Programs (OFCCP) is charged with enforcement of the policy. The OFCCP requires that contractors make a good faith effort, with documentable practices, to meet their goals for improved utilization of targeted groups; but failure to meet goals is not in and of itself punishable.

According to OFCCP figures, approximately a quarter of the American work force is employed by federal contractors or subcontractors (U.S. Department of Labor, 1995). This means that about 26 million people are covered by mandatory affirmative action programs. Voluntary affirmative action programs are adopted by numerous other firms.

In contrast to the large scope of the coverage is the small size of the staff. With a total staff of about 800 people, the OFCCP has one national, 10 regional and many additional subregional offices. Offices primarily respond to requests for technical assistance, especially from new affirmative action employers. The OFCCP will, for example, help an employer calculate the availability of women, of people of color, of Vietnam era veterans, and of disabled people for various types of jobs.

The OFCCP also conducts compliance reviews. Yearly, the OFCCP conducts over 4000 compliance reviews and investigates 800 companies. When the review turns up problems, a conciliation agreement is developed. If conciliation efforts prove unfruitful, the OFCCP seeks administrative enforcement through the Office of the Solicitor. Theoretically, unsuccessful resolution can lead to debarment. In the last decade, five firms have been debarred.

*Additional Meanings*
In recent years, affirmative action has taken on a new meaning. It has come to mean unjustified set-asides or preferential treatment. Whereas the classical affirmative action policy insists on rigorous monitoring to make sure that preferences are not being arbitrarily given, some new programs specifically utilize arbitrary preferences. Whereas the classical affirmative action

policy always involved matching utilization and availability, and setting reasonable goals so that utilization could be brought into line over a certain timetable, some of the new programs rely on goals that are not based on availability figures.

How common is the new type of affirmative action policy? How often do organizations, including federal, state, and local governments, have set-aside programs in which a certain percentage of jobs or contracts or budgetary dollars goes to, say, minority applicants or women? How often do organizations have programs in which one classification of applicant (e.g., women) is automatically given preference over another (e.g., men) without regard to either qualifications or the availability/utilization ratio?

The answer seems to be: not very often. No one has conducted a census of current business practices, but the use of automatic preference and of quotas are not practices that would survive review by the OFCCP. According to the published rules of the Employment Standards Administration, the unit of the Department of Labor that includes the OFCCP,

> Affirmative action is *not* preferential treatment. It does *not* mean that unqualified persons should be hired or promoted over other people. What affirmative action does mean is that positive steps must be taken to ensure equal employment opportunity for traditionally disadvantaged groups. (U.S. Department of Labor, 1995, p. 1, emphasis in original)

Thus, if the organization is a federal contractor — as about a quarter of a million American businesses are — it is not likely to have practices that stray far from the availability/utilization model.

Concerning governmental programs, we have more direct knowledge. Although no review has been conducted of state and local programs, a thorough study, commissioned by Senator Robert Dole, has been conducted by Attorney C. V. Dale in the Congressional Research Service (CRS) of the federal laws and regulations establishing affirmative action goals or other preferences based on race, gender, or ethnicity (Dale, 1995). The review listed 170 federal laws and regulations (169 in addition to Executive Order 11246) identified by computerized searches (LEXIS/ NEXIS and WESTLAW) of legal databases and grouped, to the extent possible, according to governmental agency and subject matter.

Most of the entries are of a nondirective sort in which sentiments are expressed, but implementation is left unspecified. In the area of agriculture, for example, one regulation encourages financial management systems maintained by state agencies to use minority- and women-owned banks, while another encourages the use of minority-owned banking services by "applicants for certain FmHA community facility loans" (Dale, 1995, p. 6). In the area of commerce, to take some other examples, one regulation is summarized thus: "Grantees and subgrantees of certain grants and cooperative agreements to state and local government are encouraged to use minority banks (a bank which is owned at least 50 percent by minority group members)" (Dale, 1995, p. 9) while another "directs contracting officers of the Commerce Department to identify potential women-owned small businesses" (Dale, 1995, p. 10).

Of the 170 entries in the document prepared for Senator Dole, how many mention quotas, preferential treatment, or set-asides? How many (aside from Executive Order 11246) specifically mention monitoring? Do any refer to quotas?

According to Senator Helms, who introduced an anti affirmative action bill into the Senate on March 3, 1995, all of the listings are "preference programs" (*Congressional Record*, 1995). Helms would have us believe that quotas are the main means by which affirmative action operates.

Scrutiny of the document prepared by the CRS reveals quite a different story than the one put forward by Senator Helms. Never once in the entire 32 page document does the word "quota" appear. By one count, four laws or regulations designate that it is permissible or desirable to give preference to one group over another, and 17 mention set-asides. Thus, about 2% of the federal regulations and laws allow for preferential treatment while 10% provide for set-asides. In contrast, 14% explicitly mention monitoring in the fashion of Executive Order 11246 (Crosby, 1995). Thus, even today, most federal laws and regulations tacitly use the classical definition of affirmative action, and do not use the new definition of affirmative action as set-asides or arbitrary preferential treatment. Of course, it is possible that some organizations misapply the policy and enact plans that are closer to Helm's characterization than one might wish.

**Affirmative Action and Equal Opportunity**

How does affirmative action, using the Classical Definition, differ from a simple policy of equal opportunity? What is the difference between an affirmative action employer and an equal opportunity employer? This question is an important one (Crosby, 1994).

Affirmative action differs from simple equal opportunity in a number of ways. First and foremost, a policy of affirmative action means more than simply ending discriminatory practices. Organizations that are so-called equal opportunity employers can adopt a passive stance. They prohibit intentional discrimination, but they do not require anyone to discover whether certain practices are producing unintended discriminatory effects.

In contrast, the policy of affirmative action requires that an organization be proactive and not simply reactive. Affirmative action employers, for instance, need to take measures to assure themselves that they are actually achieving the desired goal of equality and opportunity.

From the one basic difference flow several other differences. An organization that adopts a policy of affirmative action recognizes that there can be and often is a slip between intentions and achievements. An organization can, for example, intend to treat women as well as it treats men, but it might discover that some of its programs have the unintended consequence of favoring one gender over the other.

The distinction between intent and effect is not foreign to either the business or the legal communities. One reason businesses track their products closely is, for instance, that they recognize that the expected effects of certain measures (e.g., product improvements, new marketing strategies, and so on) are uncertain. Measures sometimes backfire. Similarly, the legal system differentiates between "disparate treatment" and "disparate impact," acknowledging that policies that appear neutral can in fact affect, say, women and men differently.

While the distinction between intent and effect makes good business sense and good legal sense, it is not always an easy distinction to accept interpersonally. From childhood, we are taught that prejudice is the root of all discrimination. It is an easy, if unfortunate, leap to assume that by curing ourselves of prejudice we will instantly cause equality to occur. It is hard to appreciate that even those who have no prejudice can, through thoughtlessness or unfamiliarity, make life more difficult for some people than for others.

An example may illustrate how discrimination can exist without prejudice. Imagine that you are a 50-year-old White male teaching in a business school. Your rank is that of Full Professor. Virtually all of the senior staff is male, but among the younger, more junior professors, there are quite a few women. Like other baby boomers, you have had experience in the civil rights movement, and you firmly believe in both gender and race equity. In all your personal dealings you attempt to be fair. You are very devoted to your students, and you try to promote their career opportunities.

Imagine, further, that your school has traditionally been able to pay for its students to attend meetings of the Academy of Management. As a well-known person in the field, you make sure during the Academy meetings that you introduce promising students from your school to prominent faculty members at other schools. The face-to-face contacts, you know, help your students when they are on the job market.

Now imagine that your school has had budgetary constraints and has suspended the policy of paying for accommodations at the Academy meetings. You pay for your hotel room from a federally funded grant and, out of kindness, you invite a student to share your accommodations free. You are willing to put up with the inconvenience of having a roommate in order to help out a talented young person.

Given that you are a 50-year-old male, what is the likelihood that you share your hotel room with a female graduate student? And given that most of the senior faculty are male, do the female students at your school have the same chance to get to the meetings as the male graduate students? Has the unequal treatment of males and females in our example come about as the result of some prejudiced person intentionally discriminating against women? Obviously not.

Once one accepts that discrimination can occur in the absence of prejudice — that is, without it being intended — one can see the justification for systems that allow one to detect the persistence of inequities. So-called equal opportunity policies need have no detection devices. In the classical definition of affirmative action, monitoring is crucial.

The most efficient way to detect problems in one's procedures is to look at results. When people in specified categories are excluded from employment or from advancement, a problem exists. Monitoring the extent to which people in different categories are included in organizations is the traditional mode of operation for any classical affirmative action policy.

To monitor, one must be able to measure. Measuring means counting. Without categories, one cannot count. These simple observations bring us to the last — and particularly thorny — difference between a classical affirmative action policy and the policy of equal opportunity (Crosby, 1996; Ozawa, Crosby, & Crosby, 1996). While "equal opportunity" does not call for classification according to gender, ethnic grouping, or physical abilities group, affirmative action does. Any organization that has an affirmative action policy must notice whether its employees are male or female, people of color or White people, Vietnam era veterans or not, and disabled or fully abled. An affirmative action employer cannot pretend to be gender blind or race blind.

For many Americans today the very act of noticing gender or ethnicity seems itself to be a sign of sexism or racism. If we are going to treat everyone the same, goes the reasoning, why should we care if they are female or male; and why should we care what their ethnic background or skin tincture is (Carter, 1991)? There is too long a history of prejudice in America, say some, for people to be able to notice gender and ethnic differences without assigning differential values.

While recognizing how problematic it can be in some situations to call attention to gender and ethnicity, proponents of the classical affirmative action policy contend that race and gender blindness are not always synonymous with race and gender fairness (Clayton & Tangri, 1989). There are two ways in which race and gender fairness can be enhanced by taking into account whether a person is male or female and whether a person is White or an ethnic minority. First, equal treatment is the greatest when circumstances are custom tailored. If we want all employees to be equally comfortable in their uniforms, we need to tailor the uniforms to the body sizes of the employees and not expect the six-footer to squeeze into the same outfit as someone who is a foot shorter. If we want female employees to feel as safe as male employees, we need to make sure the parking lot is well lit at night.

The second way in which a cognizance of demographic characteristics can help promote gender and race fairness involves evaluation. Valid assessments of individual merit sometimes require one to take into account the gender, ethnicity, and other demographic characteristics of the person being evaluated. Sometimes, to judge accurately the qualifications or merit of a person, we need to take into account "background" characteristics of the person being evaluated.

Again, an example may help clarify the point. The example was provided to one of us by a retired officer in the Marines who had had responsibility for certain matters concerning aviation. According to the officer, some branches of the military had tested the ability of some female flyers to adapt to gravity loss in the hopes of seeing whether women might be qualified to pilot some expensive strategic aircraft. The women were tested in the same simulators that the men had been tested in. They were also tested in the same specialized gravitational suits that the men had used. The specialized suits were designed to help the body compensate rapidly for the loss of consciousness by, in effect, pushing blood back to the head and so had to be fitted to the contours of the body. Apparently, none of those responsible for the tests had remembered that the female and male bodies are typically proportioned differently, such that at any given height, a woman's legs are longer than a man's. When the women flyers took longer than men to recover consciousness after gravity loss, the problem was assumed to lie in the physiology of the female and was not recognized, as it ought to have been, to also be the result of the relatively ill-fitting body suit.

In many ways, the differences between affirmative action and equal opportunity are differences of method and of orientation. Both affirmative action (in its classical form) and equal opportunity strive to reward individual merit, and both conceive of the rewarding of merit as fair. The policies differ in whether they assume that our world operates in such a way that merit is automatically recognized and rewarded or operates with certain biasing tendencies.

*Lydia Chávez*

# Key Dates in the Battle over Affirmative Action Policy

1964. President Lyndon Johnson signs the Civil Rights Act of 1964. It prohibits discrimination in employment and education on the basis of race, color, religion, sex, or national origin.

1965. President Johnson signs an executive order requiring federal contractors to "take affirmative action" to ensure that applicants are employed and that employees are treated equally without regard to race.

1969–72. The Department of Labor under Presidents Johnson and Nixon begins requiring federal contractors to keep track of their workforce and to set goals and timetables for ending the underrepresentation of minorities and women.

1971. In *Griggs* v. *Duke Power,* the U.S. Supreme Court approves a statistical approach to discrimination law.

1978. In *Regents of the University of California* v. *Bakke,* the U.S. Supreme Court rules against quotas but, to foster diversity in education, approves the consideration of race and ethnicity as a "plus factor" in admissions.

1979. In *United States Steelworkers* v. *Weber,* the U.S. Supreme Court rules against a white steelworker's claim of reverse discrimination and holds that employers have an "area of discretion" to employ minority preferences to eliminate imbalances in their workforce.

1988. Thomas E. Wood, a 1975 Ph.D. recipient from Berkeley's philosophy department, fails to find a tenure-track teaching job and begins to believe that affirmative action was part of the problem.

1988. A group of professors form the National Association of Scholars to "reclaim the academy" from multiculturalism and affirmative action

From *The Color Bind: California's Battle to End Affirmative Action* by Lydia Chávez (Berkeley: University of California Press, 1998), 261–67. Reprinted with permission from The Regents of the University of California.

programs that they believe result in the hiring of unqualified faculty and the admission of unqualified students.

1989.    In *Richmond* v. *Croson,* the Supreme Court narrowly restricts the ability of state and local governments to use preferences in contracting.

1988–90.    Glynn Custred, a tenured professor at the California State University, Hayward, helps to organize the California Association of Scholars, a chapter of the National Association of Scholars.

1991.    Tom Wood and Glynn Custred meet through the California Association of Scholars.

1993.    Under pressure to diversify the Board of Regents, Governor Pete Wilson appoints Ward Connerly, a financial contributor to the governor's campaigns and an African American.

October 1993.    Custred and Wood file the California Civil Rights Initiative with the state attorney general for the first time but fail to collect enough signatures to put it on the ballot.

August 1994.    University of California regent Ward Connerly questions the fairness of affirmative action at hearings held by the assembly's judiciary committee.

November 1994.    The Republicans sweep Congress, and pollsters begin writing about the white male voting bloc. On the strength of this bloc and the popularity of the anti-immigrant Proposition 187, California Governor Pete Wilson comes from behind to beat challenger Kathleen Brown.

December 1994.    Wood and Custred name a campaign team that includes Joe Gelman, Arnie Steinberg, and Larry Arnn.

January 1995.    Connerly questions the fairness of affirmative action at the mid-January University of California regents meeting.

January 1995.    Members of the opposition to the California Civil Rights Initiative begin meeting and polling.

February 1995.    Governor Wilson reverses his earlier support for affirmative action and comes out in support of the California Civil Rights Initiative.

February 1995.    President Clinton calls for a review of all federal affirmative action programs.

March 1995.    Senator Dole, the leading Republican presidential challenger, reverses his long-time support of affirmative action.

March 1995.    Governor Pete Wilson announces that he has a "duty" to explore the possibility of running for president.

April 1995.    President Bill Clinton attends the California Democratic Party's convention, where he says he supports affirmative action but asks minorities and women to recognize that "this is a psychologically difficult time for a lot of white males."

May 1995.   The opposition to the California Civil Rights Initiative splits into two groups. One group, led by Eva Jefferson Paterson in the north, pursues an alternative initiative strategy. The other group in the south, led by Katherine Spillar of the Feminist Majority, plans to confront the initiative straight on.

June 1995.   In *Adarand Constructors* v. *Peña* the Supreme Court rules that "all racial classifications" are "inherently suspect and presumptively invalid."

June 1995.   Jack Kemp says he opposes the Republican stand against affirmative action.

July 1995.   President Clinton defends affirmative action and calls for a policy of "mend it, don't end it."

July 1995.   Led by Governor Pete Wilson and Ward Connerly, the U.C. regents vote to end affirmative action at the University of California.

July 1995.   Wilson jumps in the polls and has his most successful fundraiser to date.

July 1995.   Senator Dole introduces legislation in the Senate to end federal affirmative action.

August 1995.   For the second time, Custred and Wood file the California Civil Rights Initiative with the state attorney general.

September 1995.   Wilson, failing to attract financial backing, drops out of the campaign for president.

October 1995.   The northern California opposition files an alternative initiative — Equal Opportunity without Quotas — with the attorney general's office.

October 1995.   Unable to pay its bills, the California Civil Rights Initiative campaign halts its signature drive.

December 1995.   The northern California opposition drops the alternative initiative after the legislative analyst's office concludes that it will eliminate magnet schools and programs for minority students.

December 1995.   Ward Connerly takes over as chair of CCRI; Wilson's fundraising effort for the California Republican Party pours nearly $500,000 into the campaign, and the signature drive resumes.

January 1996.   The opposition to CCRI regroups while CCRI struggles to collect enough signatures before its February deadline.

February 1996.   The CCRI campaign turns in more than a million signatures to the attorney general's office.

February 1996.   The Feminist Majority assumes leadership of the state-wide coalition to oppose CCRI and hires Patricia Ewing to run the campaign.

February 1996.   The presidential primary season begins, with every Republican presidential candidate running against affirmative action.

March 1996.   In the week before the California primary Ward Connerly refuses to attend any press conference with Pat Buchanan, a contender in the Republican primary and an early supporter of CCRI.

March 1996.   Dole plans and then fails to give a major policy address on affirmative action, but he endorses CCRI.

March 1996.   In *Hopwood* v. *Texas,* the U.S. Circuit Court of Appeals in New Orleans strikes down an admissions policy at the University of Texas law school giving preferences to blacks and Hispanics, saying that public universities may not justify affirmative action programs based on the benefits of diversity.

May 1996.   General Powell makes his first public statements attacking the California Civil Rights Initiative.

June 1996.   House Speaker Newt Gingrich questions the wisdom of eliminating affirmative action.

June 1996.   Dole pulls back in his opposition to affirmative action.

July 1996.   CCRI is given a ballot number, Proposition 209.

July 1996.   Attorney General Dan Lungren issues a title and summary for Proposition 209 that omits the initiative's impact on affirmative action.

August 1996.   Sacramento County Superior Court Judge James T. Ford orders the attorney general to rewrite the ballot language because the omission of "affirmative action" is misleading.

August 1996.   Judge Ford's decision is overturned on appeal.

August 1996.   Dole chooses Kemp as his vice-presidential running mate. Kemp comes out in support of Proposition 209.

August 1996.   The Feminist Majority and NOW are forced out of the anti–Proposition 209 coalition.

September 1996.   Former Klansman David Duke visits California State University at Northridge to speak in favor of Proposition 209.

October 1996.   Falling in the polls, Dole decides to launch a major media campaign in California and to run commercials in support of Proposition 209.

October 31, 1996.   President Clinton visits Oakland, California, and makes his first public statement about 209.

November 3, 1996.   Racial discrimination at Texaco becomes front-page news.

November 5, 1996.   Voters in California approve Proposition 209, 54.6 percent to 45.4 percent.

November 6, 1996.   The anti–Proposition 209 coalition files suit in the U.S. District Court for Northern California, alleging that the proposition violates the Equal Protection Clause of the Fourteenth Amendment.

December 23, 1996.   Chief U.S. District Judge Thelton Henderson grants a preliminary injunction preventing the state from implementing Proposition 209 until the conclusion of a trial or a final ruling from a higher court.

April 8, 1997.   A three-judge panel of the U.S. Court of Appeals for the Ninth Circuit overturns Henderson.

June 1997.   In the first year after Wilson and Connerly led the battle to end affirmative action at the University of California, the university's Boalt Hall School of Law announces that only one African American and eighteen Latinos plan to enroll in the incoming class of 270 students for Fall 1997.

August 21, 1997.   The U.S. Court of Appeals for the Ninth Circuit reaffirms its earlier ruling that Proposition 209 is constitutional.

September 4, 1997.   The U.S. Supreme Court refuses to block enforcement of Proposition 209 but postpones the decision of whether to take up the opposition's appeal until the fall.

September 9, 1997.   Governor Pete Wilson asks the California legislature to remove or amend thirty state statutes that he says grant illegal race or gender preferences.

November 3, 1997.   Without comment, the U.S. Supreme Court lets stand the decision by the U.S. Court of Appeals for the Ninth Circuit that upholds Proposition 209.

November 4, 1997.   Houston voters reject an initiative to end the city's affirmative action program by a vote of 55 to 45 percent.

November 6, 1997.   The House Judiciary Committee kills federal legislation to end affirmative action.

# Part 2: Newspaper Articles

Thousands of newspaper and magazine articles have been written about affirmative action in the last decade, and only a small sample can be presented here. We have tried to present a variety of points of view, to reveal how journalists and commentators have approached the topic from many different angles. Articles that are simply inflammatory, in which one side tried to demonize the other, were avoided. Most of the articles are from major newspapers such as the *New York Times*. We looked for articles that were clearly written and as a result included more than the usual number of "invited columns" or "op ed" pieces. The selections by public figures such as Ward Connerly, Chang-Lin Tien, Nicholas Katzenbach and Burke Marshall, Lani Guinier, and Gerald Ford (former president of the United States) all contributed significantly to the media discussion of affirmative action. The text of each article is reprinted as it appeared but without pictures and sidebars.

*Ward Connerly*

# U.C. Must End Affirmative Action

One cannot evaluate the merits of affirmative action at the University of California without placing them in some overall context, which I will briefly attempt to do. Affirmative action comes in many forms. If its objective is to expand opportunities for all, few will disagree with that. If its objective is to take appropriate steps to ensure that minorities and women have equal access to jobs, contracts and public education, the majority of Americans will agree.

Our nation even accepted the premise that the blight of slavery and segregation were so devastating to Americans of African descent that a degree of preference in their favor could be justified for a period of time.

It has often been necessary for individuals such as Abraham Lincoln, Martin Luther King Jr., John F. Kennedy and Lyndon B. Johnson (and many others of all colors who have been less visible publicly) to summon the call for us to do what was right. But often some of us did not hear or listen to the call without considerable repetition, and even some pain along the way. In the final analysis, most Americans have accepted the proposition that all of us are entitled to fair and equal treatment and opportunity. In this nation, no leader, no matter how forceful or compelling, can make the people do that which a majority of us reject.

This brings me to another kind of affirmative action, the kind that I believe the overwhelming majority of Americans find offensive. This is the concept of quotas, or "goals" as the term is more euphemistically used. Although the use of this term pushes the hot button of supporters, it is deceptive to try to honestly discuss the issue without acknowledging that the ultimate goal of most affirmative action practices is the attainment of numerical parity.

In the University of California system, when our administrators and faculty talk about "under-represented minorities," they are saying that

*San Francisco Chronicle*, May 3, 1995. Reprinted with permission of Ward Connerly.

certain groups do not have sufficient numbers of their group included in the mix.

When the argument is then made that our goal is to achieve diversity and equal representation, it seems to me that the logical conclusion one can draw from this is that we want to achieve some measure of parity, and the only way I can see this being achieved is by the use of quotas.

Although this argument is viewed as hitting below the belt by affirmative action proponents, they cannot escape the reality of their goal: numerical parity based on gender, race and ethnicity.

It is important for us to remember that affirmative action was not intended to be a permanent method for allocating public resources, including admission to UC. We cannot have a public university built on the premise that Latinos get a certain percentage of the slots, blacks a certain percentage, Asians a certain percentage, whites a certain percentage, etc.

There is fierce competition between America's colleges and universities for black and Latino students. We all want "diversity," as well we should. But, I am afraid that all of us in the higher education community have gotten so caught up in the game of "mirror, mirror on the wall, who's the most diverse of all" that we have become indifferent to the consequences that our actions are generating.

I fear that we are discriminating against non-affirmative-action-eligible students. I fear that our admissions policies have lost credibility among a growing segment of the public, and that decreasing credibility is causing the public to increasingly question the quality of our institutions. Affirmative action at UC and throughout the nation has become entrenched. It is not a method of achieving a goal. It has become the goal. It is breeding hostility among the races.

Most of us think of ourselves as fair-minded people. We want an equitable and inclusive society. We want to stamp out racial and gender discrimination. We want to expand opportunities and we want those opportunities to be equally accessible to all. Affirmative action has become a major detour in our journey to a fair and equitable society. We need to give affirmative action, as a system of preferences, a decent burial, and the digging should start at the University of California.

*Steven A. Holmes*

# Defining Disadvantage up to Preserve Preferences

**W**ho's left?

That's the question that follows the Clinton Administration's recent announcement that it is considering a proposal to make it easier for whites to qualify for contracting preferences that had been reserved almost exclusively for racial and ethnic minorities. The proposal is part of a trend in which supporters of affirmative action seeking to widen the policy's political base, pushed by a 1995 Supreme Court ruling that made it difficult to operate programs based solely on race, have steadily broadened the definition of oppressed groups whose members qualify for special help.

Conceived as a policy to help blacks, many affirmative action programs have, over the years, been stretched to cover Hispanic people, Asians, Native Americans, Hawaiian Polynesians and women of any color or creed. Now, the Administration is contemplating rule changes that would open the affirmative action door to more whites, including white men.

While arguably legally necessary, the proposed change raises a number of uncomfortable questions. At what point have the benefits of affirmative action been scattered so broadly that they actually diminish rather than enhance opportunities for blacks, the group the policy was originally designed for? What is the justification for recent immigrants, who came to the United States voluntarily and may or may not have suffered from discrimination, to share the fruits of a policy meant to help the descendants of slaves who were forcibly brought here? At what point does "socially disadvantaged" become defined so broadly that the only ones not included are Donald Trump and Bill Gates?

"We have reached the point where Hasidic Jews are eligible, immigrants from India are eligible, white women are eligible," said Gerald Reynolds, president of the Center for New Black Leadership and a fervent

*Los Angeles Times,* August 24, 1997. Copyright © 1997 *Los Angeles Times.* Reprinted by permission.

opponent of affirmative action for anyone. "We've gone so far from the original idea that I believe it's time to reassess the whole approach."

## A Different Purpose

As the beneficiaries of affirmative action have increased, its moral rationale has changed. Supporters now speak as much of achieving diversity in a work force or on a college campus as they do of making up for past racism or preventing current discrimination. But while diversity may be a noble goal, it does not necessarily mesh with the original idea of affirmative action: helping to overcome the vestiges of slavery and Jim Crow.

"The concern that I have about the rhetoric of diversity is that it doesn't have any moral bite to it," said Glen C. Loury, a professor of economics at Boston University. "You end up with a kind of touchy-feely policy where you've lost the thread of why you were looking to treat people specially in the first place."

The latest step in the trend toward affirmative action catholicism came Aug. 14, when the Small Business Administration proposed changes in requirements for companies to qualify as "small disadvantaged" businesses. The new rules would cover companies that want to be enrolled in special programs that provide technical help and eligibility for certain Federal contracts set aside for them. The rules also cover companies that, if signed up as subcontractors, give larger prime contractors bonus points when they bid on Federal contracts.

Under the proposal, the owner of a small company would be considered economically disadvantaged if he or she had a personal net worth of less than $250,000, excluding equity in a home — a criterion that more than 90 percent of Americans could meet. Applicants would also have to show that they were socially disadvantaged, meaning that they have been the victims of some kind of chronic discrimination. Blacks, Hispanic people, Asians and members of other racial minorities are presumed to meet this criterion, while whites, both men and women, would have to make a showing of past bias.

While the proposed new rules would make it generally easier for whites to make a case, Federal officials say white men will still have difficulty establishing that they have suffered from discrimination. "This is not opening the floodgates for people who might not qualify," said Aida Alvarez, the S.B.A. administrator.

Perhaps not yet. But the Federal courts could very well toss some banana peels on what is already a slippery slope. Last month, Federal District Judge John L. Kane Jr. in Denver ruled that the white owner of a construction company had been the victim of bias — and therefore was socially disadvantaged — because he lost out on a government contract as a result of an affirmative action program that the Supreme Court later ruled unconstitutional. The ruling is not binding beyond Colorado, but it lays down a new legal principle: whites who could prove they have been unfairly treated by affirmative action programs.

"Judge Kane's ruling draws a circle around this program and puts everyone inside," said William Perry Pendley, the Denver lawyer who represented the white contractor.

The question of widening eligibility is vexing to black supporters of affirmative action. More beneficiaries could mean more support for a policy that is under growing attack in the courts and in the political arena. But more beneficiaries also means diluted benefits. In 1987, when they were first included in a Department of Transportation program that set aside contracts for "disadvantaged" businesses, companies owned by women earned 20.4 percent of dollars in the program. By 1996, the percentage had climbed to 41.4 percent.

"That's why it's such a dilemma," said Anthony W. Robinson, president of the Minority Business Enterprise Legal Defense and Education Fund. "You do need that kind of political support to try to preserve the policy. But sometimes you wonder whether you're cutting your own throat at the same time."

*Chang-Lin Tien*

# In Defense of Affirmative Action

When the debate over affirmative action in higher education exploded, my open support surprised many. My personal view about using race, ethnicity, and sex among the factors in student admissions has put me at odds with many, including the majority of the Regents of the University of California who govern my campus.

With California voters having decided in November, 1996, to end all state-sponsored affirmative action programs, silence would seem to be a far more prudent course for me to take. Educators already have enough battles to fight — declining public funding, controversy over the national research agenda, and eroding public support for America's academic mission.

Why did I take on the explosive issue of affirmative action? My participation in the debate is inspired both by my role in higher education and my experience as an immigrant of Chinese descent. As chancellor of the University of California, Berkeley, I had seen the promise of affirmative action come true. Today, no ethnic or racial group constitutes a majority among the university's 21,000 undergraduates. Berkeley students enter better prepared and graduate at the highest rate in our history. Through daily interaction in classrooms, laboratories, and residence halls, they develop a deep understanding of different cultures and outlooks.

As an immigrant, I know the U.S. is the land of opportunity. Unlike any other nation in history, America has taken pride in being built by immigrants and allows foreign-born people like me to participate in the world's greatest democracy.

In 1956, I came here for graduate studies, a virtually penniless immigrant from China with a limited grasp of the language and customs of the U.S. A teaching fellowship was my income. To stretch my frugal budget, I walked across town to eat at the least expensive restaurants and scouted out the lowest-cost washing machines and dryers.

*USA Today* (magazine) 126, no. 2630 (1997): 58–60. Copyright © 1997 Society for the Advancement of Education. Reprinted with permission.

As a result of the wonderful educational opportunities I have enjoyed, I have contributed to America. My research in heat transfer has enhanced our engineering expertise in many critical technologies, including nuclear reactor safety, space shuttle thermal design, and electronic systems cooling. My former students teach and conduct research in America's top universities and industries. I was privileged to head the university with the largest number and highest percentage of top-ranked doctoral programs in the nation.

Yet, along with opportunity, I have encountered the harsh realities of racial discrimination that are part of America's legacy. Like it or not, this history of racial division is linked with the debate over affirmative action. Although the U.S. has made great strides, race still divides our society. It is part of the debate over how we afford equal opportunities to everyone.

My first months in the U.S. reflect how opportunity and racial intolerance can be linked. I served as a teaching fellow for a professor who refused to pronounce my name and only referred to me as "Chinaman." One day, the professor directed me to adjust some valves in a large laboratory apparatus. When I climbed the ladder, I lost my balance and instinctively grabbed a nearby steam pipe. It was so hot, it produced a jolt of pain that nearly caused me to faint, but I did not scream out. I stuffed my throbbing hand into my coat pocket and waited until the class ended. Then I ran to the hospital emergency room, where I was treated for a burn that completely singed the skin off my palm.

My response seems to fit the Asian model minority myth: Say nothing and go about your business. My silence had nothing to do with stoicism, though. I simply did not want to endure the humiliation of having the professor scold me in front of the class.

Today, after four decades of major civil rights advances, members of racial and ethnic minorities like me no longer are intimidated into silence. Still, serious racial divisions remain. Those of us who are of Asian, Latino, or Middle Eastern heritage have become accustomed to having passersby tell us, "Go back to your own country." More typical is the politic query: "What country do you come from?" It makes no difference if you are first-generation or fifth-generation. If you have Asian, Latino, or Middle Eastern features or surname, many Americans assume you were born in another country. The ancestors of a professor in the university's School of Optometry left China to work in California during the 1850s. Even though his roots run far deeper than those of the vast majority of Californians, people invariably ask him where he was born.

Our nation can not afford to ignore the racial strife that continues to divide America. Nor should we forget that the U.S. is a great democracy built by diverse peoples. It is critical to attack the problem of racial division and build on national strengths. The finest hope for meeting this challenge will be America's colleges and universities.

These institutions launched affirmative admissions programs to open their doors to promising minority students who lacked educational and social opportunities. Over time, the composition of America's college students has changed. Campuses are more diverse than at any time in history.

Critics of continuing race or ethnicity as a consideration in student admissions argue that affirmative action unfairly discriminates against white and Asian-American applicants who worked hard in high school and received top grades. They further maintain that it no longer is needed to provide opportunities. Although I agree that affirmative action is a temporary measure, the time has not yet come to eliminate it. Educational opportunities vary dramatically in U.S. public schools.

The inner-city student can find illegal drugs more readily than computer labs and after-school enrichment courses. In contrast, the more affluent suburban student is hooked into the Internet, enrolled in honor classes, and looking forward to summer instruction.

Given this reality, it is fair and equitable to consider race and ethnicity as one factor among many — including test scores and grade-point averages — in admitting qualified youths to highly competitive universities. Such an approach remains the most effective way to make sure America does not turn into a two-tiered society of permanent haves and have-nots.

Assisting promising students is not the only reason for preserving affirmative action. The diversity of students, faculty, and staff that it inspired is one of the most exciting and challenging phenomena in American higher education today. All students stand to gain, whether they are whites, Asian-Americans, or traditionally underrepresented minorities.

I believe students on campuses that lack diversity can gain just a limited, theoretical understanding of the challenges and opportunities in a highly diverse nation. A lecture on Toni Morrison's novels or the theater of Luis Valdez is not enough.

No career or profession will be untouched by the rapid sociodemographic change. For instance, consider how America's diversity will affect those in U.S. colleges and universities. Education students will teach many youngsters born in different countries. Medical students will treat many patients with beliefs and attitudes about medicine that differ from the Western outlook. Students of engineering and business will work for major corporations, where they will be expected to design, develop, and market products that sell not just in the U.S., but in markets around the world. Law students will represent clients whose experience with the judicial system in their neighborhoods and barrios is distinctive from the way middle America regards the law.

## A Matter of Diversity

Diversity in colleges and universities benefits all students, not just the underrepresented minorities. Our experience at Berkeley shows the promise of affirmative action. Every time I walk across campus, I am impressed by the vibrant spirit of our diverse community. Nowhere do you see this better than teeming Sproul Plaza, where dozens of student groups set up tables representing a wide range of social, political, ethnic, and religious interests.

At Berkeley, undergraduates are about 40% Asian-American; 31% non-Hispanic Caucasian; 14% Hispanic; six percent African-American; and one percent Native American, with the rest undeclared. About one-quarter of freshmen come from families earning $28,600 a year or less; another quarter from families that earn more than $90,000. The median family income reported for 1994 freshmen was $58,000.

Young people from barrios, comfortable suburbs, farm towns, and the inner city come together at Berkeley to live and study side by side. Not surprisingly, they find first-time interactions with students of different backgrounds occasionally fraught with misunderstanding and tension.

As chancellor, I made it a point to listen and talk with students. Casual conversations as I walked the campus to meetings, dropped in at the library after work, and sat in on classes gave me greater insight into the day-to-day lives of Berkeley students. They told me about the practical challenges of moving beyond the stereotypes and learning to respect differences.

Some African-Americans and Latinos confided they sometimes believed their professors and white classmates considered them to be inferior academically. This made them feel isolated from the general campus community. Some whites told me they felt like they had been pushed out by less-deserving blacks and Latinos. They also believed that overachieving Asians were depriving them of educational opportunities.

The views of Asian-Americans differed. Some were disturbed by the "model minority" stereotype. They complained that it pits them against other minorities and masks the problem of discrimination they still face. Others were concerned about issues such as affirmative action. They believed it is fair to base admissions on academic qualifications alone — which would open the door to more Asian-Americans.

These differing outlooks are not cause for alarm. Instead, they reflect the views held in society at large. It is important that students of all racial and ethnic groups told me they valued the opportunities on our campus to come together with people of diverse backgrounds. I believe it is this attitude our campus must reinforce as we help them to address differences.

The residence halls are the first place students come together. Because we understand the challenges associated with living together with those who have different values and outlooks, we run programs that encourage students to discuss racial and cultural differences openly.

Our campus tradition of academic freedom is critical. When issues arise where students are divided by race, they don't ignore the matter. We encourage all members of the campus community to air differences freely in forums, seminars, and rallies. Whether the topic is affirmative action, enforcement of the successful California ballot measure that would ban illegal immigrants from public schools, or the organization of ethnic studies, students and faculty passionately debate the pros and cons.

Let me cite an example. In 1995, the longstanding conflict between Israelis and Palestinians led to fiery exchanges between Jewish and Muslim students on our campus. During rallies and counter-protests, an Israeli flag was ripped apart, while Muslim students alleged they were being demonized.

We addressed the issues directly. The campus held meetings to denounce "hate speech," while open debate was encouraged. My top objective was to make sure that discussions on this charged issue did not degenerate into racial epithets. I decided to forego an invitation from President Clinton to attend a White House meeting so I could meet with students who were central to the debate and help them hammer out their differences.

It is this tradition of study and debate that makes American higher education so valuable. Colleges and universities are a haven for open discussion. Only by addressing differences directly can students reach a deeper understanding of the real meaning of diversity.

Today, our campus faces a major new challenge. The University of California Regents have voted to end the use of race, ethnicity, and sex as a factor among many others in student admissions at its nine campuses in 1998. At first, the Regents' decision stunned me. I questioned whether we could preserve the diversity which is so important to our campus after losing an important tool for achieving student enrollments that reflect California's wide-ranging population.

Yet, I quickly realized the importance of the Regents' reaffirmation of their commitment to diversity even though they discarded affirmative action. So, I decided to take the Chinese approach to challenge. In Chinese, the character for crisis actually is two characters: One stands for danger and the other for opportunity. For me, times of crisis present both challenges and opportunities.

The end of affirmative action at the University of California gave us the impetus for trying new approaches to improving the eligibility rates of high school students traditionally underrepresented in higher education. At Berkeley, we set to work right away to turn challenge into opportunity. We realized our efforts would be doomed unless we worked even more closely with the public schools. Within weeks of the affirmative action decision, I joined the superintendents of the San Francisco Bay Area's major urban school districts to announce our new campaign to diversity: The Berkeley Pledge.

The announcement made it clear that our campus would not shirk its commitment to diversity. Instead, we pledged to step up the drive to support the efforts of disadvantaged youth to qualify for admission and preserve access to higher education. I committed $1,000,000 from private gifts, and we are seeking additional private support to fund this innovative approach.

America has come a long way since the days of Jim Crow segregation. It would be a tragedy if our nation's colleges and universities slipped backward, denying access to talented, but disadvantaged, youth and eroding the diversity that helps to prepare the leaders of the 21st century.

I find one aspect of the debate over affirmative action to be especially disturbing. There seems to be an underlying assumption that if it is eliminated, the nation will have solved the problems associated with racial division. Nothing could be further from the truth. It is critical for America to address the issue of how people from diverse backgrounds are going to study, work, and live in the same neighborhoods together in harmony, not strife.

This is the challenge in higher education. It demands the collaboration of students, faculty, staff, and alumni at universities and colleges across America. All must work together to maintain the diversity that is essential to excellence.

*Ethan Bronner*

# Study of Doctors Sees Little Effect of Affirmative Action on Careers

In a report certain to fuel the debate over affirmative action, an extensive study of doctors trained at the University of California at Davis over a 20-year period found that those admitted with special consideration for factors like race or ethnic origin had remarkably similar postgraduate records and careers to those admitted on academic merit alone.

The report, published in the *Journal of the American Medical Association,* found that students receiving admissions preferences — not all of them members of minorities — performed less well in the basic science courses of the first two years of training, were less likely to graduate with honors and more likely to repeat the certification examination to become doctors.

But the two groups graduated at essentially the same high rate and, following graduation, they followed parallel paths, completing residency training at the same rate, receiving similar evaluations by residency directors, selecting their specialties in the same percentages and establishing practices with almost the same racial mixes.

The research was undertaken by two professors of medicine at the Davis campus following the California Regents decision two years ago to bar any consideration of race or ethnicity in admitting students. In its decision, the Regents cited concerns about the quality of students admitted under affirmative-action programs, a fixture in higher education since the Supreme Court's landmark 1978 Bakke case, which originated at the Davis medical school.

Advocates of affirmative action praised the findings as proof that those who were given admission preferences have careers similar to those who were not.

"This is a highly significant study, what I would call a landmark study, which shows we should do more with applicants from special circumstances who are not quite optimal tickets in their grade point averages and test scores," said Dr. William Jacott, head of the family practice department at the University of Minnesota medical school and a trustee of the American Medical Association.

Opponents of affirmative action remained unimpressed, pointing out that if the two graduating groups ended up practicing on a similar ethnic mix, one major argument put forward in favor of affirmative action — that minority populations will be better served by such graduates — loses its power.

The study was conducted by Dr. Robert C. Davidson of the Department of Family and Community Medicine at the Davis campus and Dr. Ernest L. Lewis, associate dean for student affairs and a member of the department of urology at Davis. Both have served for many years on the school's admissions committee and were granted access to school records for the admissions in question, those for students who began their studies between 1968 and 1987. They also wrote to the graduates' residency programs and directors as well as to the graduates themselves to assess postgraduate careers.

Their data contain several ambiguities because of the circumstances of admission over the years. For example, in the group admitted under special consideration, only 53.5 percent were members of minority groups. The rest were beneficiaries of such consideration because of experiences like volunteering in the community or serving in the Peace Corps, or previous careers like teaching or nursing. These students were admitted even though their undergraduate grades and test scores were below the standard required by the medical school.

In addition, 4 percent of the students admitted without preferences were members of minority groups.

"The thrust of the article is to blur the distinction between racial differences and special consideration," remarked Stephan Thernstrom, a professor of history at Harvard and coauthor, with his wife, Abigail, of a new book, *Black and White: One Nation Indivisible* (Simon and Schuster). "It is sloppy or slippery of them to suggest that this program has been highly successful without making a distinction between the population that receives special consideration for racial as opposed to nonracial reasons."

The study coincides with growing concern over the value, effectiveness and fairness of affirmative action nationwide. This is especially true in California, where, two years ago, the Board of Regents banned the use of race and ethnic origin in university admissions and where last year a referendum, Proposition 209, barred race and gender considerations in state hiring and promotion.

It was a 1978 case from the Davis medical school, Regents of the University of California *v.* Bakke, that laid out the United States Supreme Court's criteria for taking race into account in admissions.

In that case, Alan Bakke, a white medical school applicant, was denied admission because the school kept certain slots for minority members. The court ruled that such a policy was unconstitutional but added that race could be one of a number of factors considered for in admissions.

The Regents' 1995 decision effectively invalidated the Bakke ruling for California schools.

An editorial in the *Journal of the American Medical Association* commenting on the study hailed the data as evidence that medical schools across the country must not be affected by the current political climate and should pursue affirmative action in their admissions.

The author of the editorial, Dr. Michael J. Scotti Jr., a vice president of the American Medical Association, said that medical schools had agreed through a partnership program to enroll 3,000 minority medical students by 2000, and had been making progress toward that goal. But since 1994, there has been a regression, he said, because of the climate created by legal challenges and the fear of further challenges. Dr. Davidson, the study's co-author, said that part of the problem was a perception among those applying to medical school that California campuses are no longer receptive to them since the 1995 Regents decision. He said that applications to Davis from minority group members plummeted in 1996, recovering only slightly last year.

He said he was certain that he would find that higher percentages of minority graduates were serving underserved populations when he undertakes a study to break down the special admissions beneficiaries between minorities and others.

Dr. Davidson and Dr. Lewis acknowledged that their study will not stop the debate over affirmative action, but stated, "We have shown that a special consideration admissions process with a major emphasis on cultural diversity in the student population at one school of medicine has been very successful in selecting students with the academic capability to succeed in medical school and provide a student population with broad cultural diversity."

*June Kronholz*

# Scholarship Program for Whites Becomes a Test of Preferences

A few years ago, a federal judge concluded that Alabama's state universities still were largely segregated and ordered them to do more to bring diversity to their campuses.

That's how it happens that Jessie Thompkins, a black man who grew up attending segregated schools, is suing Alabama State University, a historically black university that was founded by freed slaves, over its $1 million–a–year scholarship program. A program, as it turns out, that is open only to whites.

To Mr. Thompkins, the issue is a simple one: "They said I have to be white and I can't be." But as the courts and public opinion force affirmative action into steady retreat, America's dialogue about preferences is anything but simple. It ricochets from the inviolability of merit to the benefits of diversity, and from the desire to right old wrongs to the fear of creating new ones.

In Washington state, a white woman who comes from a one-parent household, worked her way through community college and earned a master's degree sued when she says she was denied a place in law school because preferential admission was given to blacks. But in California and Texas, minority applications and admissions to law school have plummeted since preferences were ended this fall; new classes suddenly are overwhelmingly white.

In Prince George's County, Md., black parents are suing the school district because it reserves seats, at magnet schools with a majority of black students, for white children. In Buffalo, white parents are suing the school district because it reserves seats, at an honors school that already has a lot of white students, for black children.

It's illegal for a university that gets public funding to discriminate by race. But what about historically black public universities, which have been

Reprinted with permission from *The Wall Street Journal,* December 23, 1997.

an avenue to success for generations of African-Americans? Can they be required to integrate themselves out of their historical mission? That, in part, is at issue in lawsuits in Georgia, Mississippi and Alabama.

## Sign of the Times

Indeed, few cases put affirmative action in as stark a light as does the Jessie Thompkins case. In a state where "whites only" signs hung over public facilities only a few decades ago, a whites-only scholarship turns history on its head. "It's strange," says Mr. Thompkins. "You have a historically black institution giving scholarships to whites to remedy discrimination."

That remedy that Mr. Thompkins is challenging had its start in 1981, when Clarence Thomas — then at the Department of Education's Office of Civil Rights and now a leading opponent of affirmative action on the Supreme Court — concluded after a long investigation that "vestiges" of segregation remained at the state's universities. Almost no one was surprised.

In 1963, Alabama's flagship university, the University of Alabama, was integrated with the help of federal troops in one of the most dramatic confrontations of the civil-rights movement. But two decades later, the state's 13 historically white public universities still were largely white — and continued to house the state's professional schools and most of its graduate programs. The two historically black universities still were overwhelmingly black.

In 1985, with the support of the Justice Department, a group of Alabama State students sued Alabama in an effort to force it to devote more money, and to direct new programs, to the black schools. After a decade of litigation, a federal judge did that and more: In an effort to attract more whites to Alabama State and Alabama A&M University, the judge ordered each to spend $1 million a year in new state funding on scholarships for whites.

A General Accounting Office study in 1994 found that, nationwide, about 5% of all undergraduate grants were so-called minority-targeted or race-exclusive scholarships. But almost always, the race has been African-American, Hispanic, Pacific Islander or Native American — not white.

Alabama State was founded as Abraham Lincoln Normal School in 1867 for training black teachers, and for the first 100 years of its existence, it was prevented by state law from enrolling whites. But more than that kept the school segregated: only one master's-degree program, and it was chronically short of money.

Alabama State was convinced that its future depended on enrolling more whites — otherwise, it risked a merger with a nearby historically white campus — so it decided to make the scholarship program even broader than ordered by the court. It added $229,000 of its own money, and offered scholarships even to out-of-state white students. In the 1996–1997 school year, after a year of struggling to get the program running, the university awarded 40% of its budget for academic grants to whites. That provided for 671 scholarships — one for almost every white on the campus of 5,419 students.

**Taking Exception**

Mr. Thompkins, who is 38 years old, wasn't even born yet when Rosa Parks made Montgomery the epicenter of the civil-rights movement in 1956 by refusing to move to the back of a Montgomery bus. Still, he speaks of growing up in fear of the Ku Klux Klan; of the racial ugliness that accompanied the integration of Alabama's high schools; of the time his family fled their home in Marion, Ala., because of tensions over a visit to town by Ralph Abernathy, the civil-rights leader.

Small and wiry, Mr. Thompkins had the fastest time in the nation among high-school hurdlers in the 400-meters in his senior year, and went on to the University of South Alabama, a predominantly white college, on an athletic scholarship. In 1991 — after graduating from South Alabama, getting a master's degree in sports coaching, running on the track team of a gym-shoe manufacturer, and student teaching for a year — Mr. Thompkins enrolled in Alabama State's graduate program in education.

The university gave him graduate assistantships for three years and promised him, he says, that the scholarship would continue until he graduated. When he went to apply for the grant in 1995, though, Mr. Thompkins says he was told the only scholarships available were reserved for whites. His recollection of the incident: "I said, 'Ma'am?' She said, 'You can apply, but you won't get it.' I said, 'Well!' "

Almost as galling, he says, was that the whites-only scholarships paid for tuition, books, fees, and room and board — about $6,400 a year — and also included $900 a year for "incidentals." In return for his grants, which varied from $3,500 to $5,000 a year, Mr. Thompkins says he helped coach the university track teams and clerked at the school tennis courts.

To qualify for some of the white scholarships, moreover, students need only a C average, and don't even necessarily have to have a high-school diploma — a GED certificate, for General Education Development, is acceptable, too. Brandon Tanksley II, editor of the university newspaper, talks of campus disquiet over the scholarships with the very words that conservatives are using to decry affirmative action at predominantly white universities. "It's not that they're minority students" — by which he means whites — "it's that they're not competitive," says Mr. Tanksley.

William Hamilton Harris, the president of Alabama State, won't talk about Mr. Thompkins' scholarship applications except to say that "he has had more scholarships than anybody, ever, in the history of Alabama State." (A lawyer for Mr. Thompkins says, "That doesn't matter. He was denied this scholarship because of his race.") And the academic qualifications of the whites are irreproachable, he adds. The university even hints it may compare the grades of its white and black students in court.

Without a scholarship, Mr. Thompkins dropped out of school in 1995 and took a job sorting packages at United Parcel Service to support his wife and four young sons. In 1996 and 1997, he returned as a part-time student, applied for scholarships again, and again was rejected. A dozen black lawyers whom he contacted about filing a discrimination case all had been involved in the 1985 suit that ultimately produced the whites-only scholarships, and they turned him away because of conflicts of interest, he says.

Last summer, the Center for Individual Rights finally filed a suit on his behalf and three other Alabama State students. The conservative law group earlier forced the University of Texas law school to drop racial preferences in its admissions; it also filed the University of Washington case and a similar challenge to affirmative action at the University of Michigan. Mr. Thompkins compares himself to Cheryl Hopwood, the plaintiff in the Texas case, even though she was a white woman seeking admission to a predominantly white school. "We were bumped aside, regardless of our qualifications, because of our race," he says.

**Begging to Differ**

Alabama State's president, Mr. Harris, agrees with Mr. Thompkins on the irony of white scholarships in a state long given to black exclusion. "It's a twist, a reversal," he says. But any agreement he has with Mr. Thompkins ends there.

Tall and elegant, Mr. Harris is a historian, has written three books on blacks in the labor force, and served as the president of two other colleges before coming here. Even so, he talks of his fear of being stopped some night on a traffic violation and finding his reputation and academic standing subsumed by racial stereotypes. "It's still there in our country," he says, "that meanness about color."

Civil-rights groups suggest that a common thread in recent federal-court rulings on affirmative action is that three decades of such remedies as preferences and diversity plans have overcome prejudice in schools, in contracting and on the job, so now they can be abandoned. But Mr. Harris sees less progress toward racial equity than do the courts — "I grew up in a segregated era in the South; I know," he says. He argues that if the country needs doctors and lawyers of every race, then it also needs affirmative action to help some of them get there.

No small part of his resolve to defend the white scholarships is the fear that if they are ruled unlawful, then minority scholarships at other schools could be vulnerable, too. "The need for set-asides for blacks hasn't run its course," he says. But there are other subtler benefits of the grants: Bringing whites and blacks together on campus "will broaden the quality of education and the quality of life at Alabama State," he says.

Joseph King, a white student, perhaps proves the point. After his florist shop burned down, he enrolled at Alabama State, wanting to fulfill his lifelong dream of becoming a teacher. Only after he had been admitted did he learn of the scholarships. He applied and got one, noting that "only a fool would turn down money."

Mr. King, 34, graduated with a 3.98 grade-point average and now has applied for another scholarship to attend graduate school at Alabama State. "I made a lot of friends that I wouldn't have met otherwise," he says. He did his student teaching at an all-black elementary school, and if a job came open at another black school, well, "race doesn't matter," he says.

In his modest home just off the Alabama State campus, Mr. Thompkins clings to the same notion — that race doesn't matter — to argue the other side of the affirmative-action debate. "We don't need race-based quota," he says. "I don't want anyone telling my children they're the wrong color. If you want something, you work for it; you just work for it."

Mr. Thompkins expects to graduate from Alabama State this spring as a specialist in education, the highest education degree the university offers. His case, tied up in motions, still is a long way from trial. Next, he says, he's thinking of going to law school.

*Nicholas deB. Katzenbach and Burke Marshall*

# Not Color Blind: Just Blind

Few African-American students are likely to enter the great public law schools of California and Texas in the fall. That is the direct, foreseeable consequence of a California referendum and a Texas Federal court decision. So concerned were civil rights groups about the popular and legal doctrine that led to this result that they joined together to deny the U.S. Supreme Court the opportunity to decide an apparently definitive affirmative action case involving teachers in Piscataway Township, N.J. Do such events — especially Piscataway — foretell the end of affirmative action, or have we simply lost sight of our long-term vision of a color-blind society?

In 1989, the Piscataway school board, faced with the need to lay off a single teacher, chose to lay off a white while retaining an African-American of equal seniority and qualifications. The board gave racial diversity, citing its affirmative action policy, as the sole reason for the choice. Its decision was rejected by a Federal judge who found the board in violation of the 1964 Civil Rights Act. That ruling was upheld by a Federal Appellate Court. The school board appealed to the Supreme Court. Late last year, with financial assistance from civil rights groups, the board settled the case and withdrew its appeal.

The settlement has since become a kind of raw shorthand in the national debate about affirmative action because its facts serve to make clear the core of that debate. The seeming baldness of the facts plainly told the civil rights groups' leaders that the case should not be permitted to remain in the Supreme Court, and that it would be prudent to use their funds to avoid its doing so. This may be the first time that money has been used directly to take an important public policy issue off the Court's docket.

All this arose because the case was framed to portray person-to-person competition for a job in which race alone was the decisive factor. This aspect fitted neatly with the notion, widespread among opponents of

*New York Times,* February 22, 1998. Reprinted with permission from Nicholas deB. Katzenbach.

affirmative action, that it creates a zero-sum game in which there is a loser for every winner and that the game is won and lost on the basis of race. Thus it obscures the larger goal of finding and preserving room for blacks in all aspects — economic, political, educational, social — and at all levels of society.

In addition, the case involved a layoff — the loss of a specific, known job — instead of a positive general decision as to what kind and mix of people are needed in a work force or in a faculty or student body. The facts fitted in not only with some legal learning — that an affirmative action program should not "unnecessarily trammel" the expectations of those not included in the program — but also more importantly with the personalization of the controversy into one in which whites are individually hurt by being deprived of their deserved opportunities, by deliberate and explicit efforts to include blacks.

These aspects of the Piscataway litigation appeared perfect for opponents of affirmative action and a legal land mine for its defenders. The former believed that the facts of the case would lead a majority of the Supreme Court to say, about affirmative action in general, that the case showed its injustices and the malevolent consequences of permitting the use of race as a factor, certainly as a decisive one, in allocating any scarce resources, like jobs or admissions to great universities. Strangely enough, the latter group — the important civil rights organizations and their lawyers, as well as the Clinton Administration — saw the case in the same way. Thus all concerned either hoped or feared that the Court, when faced with the rejected white teacher, would say: "Enough of this. It has gone on too long already. This is the end of affirmative action for any purpose, as far as the law is concerned."

Is affirmative action really the unfair black "preference," or "reverse discrimination," policy that its critics claim and that Piscataway seems to present so starkly? Have we in fact lost sight of the larger goal of integrating blacks into our society? Or have we been so successful in achieving a "color blind" society about which Martin Luther King dreamed that the larger goal need no longer concern us?

Those who oppose affirmative action programs do not make such broad claims. They affirm the goal of an integrated society and do not contend we have yet achieved it. Critics simply argue that it is morally and constitutionally wrong to seek its achievement through race-based programs that give a "preference" to African-Americans. Such programs, they maintain, are essentially wrong for the same reasons that it is wrong for whites to discriminate against blacks. It denies "equal opportunity" to whites and is antithetical to awarding jobs or promotions or college admissions on the basis of "merit."

There is no longer any dispute that overt, provable racial bias against blacks in employment or education should be unlawful. The disputed question is whether overt and provable bias is the only form of racial bias with which our society should — or can lawfully — be concerned. Certainly that bias — state supported in the Deep South and rampant throughout the country — was the immediate and most important target of the civil rights laws of the 1960s. Equally, the white majority in this country, despite deep-seated feelings of racial superiority, committed itself to achieving an integrated society. That happened, we believe, for the simple reason that it did not seem possible, then or now, for this country to maintain its democratic principles unless we could achieve Dr. King's dream. Is the elimination of overt bias all we need to do to accomplish that end?

The term "affirmative action" was first officially used in 1961 when President Kennedy strengthened an existing executive order prohibiting racial discrimination by government contractors in their employment practices. It was a natural, not a provocative, term to use. In the early '60s, blacks were essentially excluded from every level and every desirable institution of society. In many places they could not enter theaters, restaurants, hotels or even parts of public libraries, courtrooms and legislatures. How could that condition possibly have been changed — and the nation as a whole have decided that it should be changed — without taking action affirmatively, positively, deliberately, explicitly to change it?

So it was that there was no real controversy at the national level over the basic idea of acting affirmatively about race, although debate started soon enough, as it should have, over the details of particular steps. But at that time the country saw problems of race as problems to be faced and dealt with as the racial problems they were. The label "affirmative action" became popular perhaps because it suggested that we were at long last dealing with our oldest and most difficult problem. It was applied beyond the Kennedy executive order to a variety of race-based programs, private and public, voluntary as well as legally coerced, that sought to guarantee the employment — or, in the case of educational institutions, the admission — of qualified African-Americans. It preceded the Civil Rights Acts of the 1960s and was consciously aimed at racial bias at a time when individuals could not yet sue private employers. But companies' employment of qualified African-Americans to insure eligibility for government contracts was measured not individual by individual but by success in achieving reasonable numbers over time.

The technique of setting goals for minority employment is important because of its capacity to deal with all forms of potential bias — overt, concealed or even inadvertent. Most national corporations have adopted employment goals. They appreciate the economic advantages of expanding and integrating the work force and they understand the need to press hard if the overall goal of inclusion is to be obtained.

The natural inclination of predominantly white male middle managers is to hire and promote one of their own. Most of the time the decision honestly reflects their judgment as to the best candidate without conscious appreciation of how much that judgment may have been conditioned by experience in the largely segregated society we still live in. To hire or promote an African-American is often viewed as risky. Will he or she be accepted by fellow workers? A white may be praised for his independence; a like-minded black is seen as not a "team player." If corporations set reasonable hiring and promotion goals and reward management for their achievement, the integration process is speeded up. Public and private policies coincide.

Critics of affirmative action in employment see it not as an effort to create a reasonably integrated work force but as a system for favoring a less-qualified African-American over a better-qualified white — a system of "preference" rather than "merit." There are three difficulties with their argument.

First, critics seek to reduce what is administered as a flexible system of hiring and promoting numbers of people into a measurement of one individual against another. Affirmative action programs deal with numbers of people at various times and seek to examine flexibly the results in numbers, not whether individual A is better than B. Such a program does not examine or re-examine each decision or demand precise achievement of numerical goals; it does not require a "quota," like a sales quota. It thus encourages personnel judgments, tolerating individual mistakes whether a white or a black is the victim.

Second, the critics assume that it is possible precisely to define and measure "merit." The best person for one job may not be the best for another, and vice versa; how does one square individual differences, or the "overqualified" candidate, with merit and the requirements of a particular job? Assuming that we are selecting from a pool of candidates who all meet whatever objective criteria are applicable to job performance, selection of the "best qualified" becomes a matter of subjective judgment by the employer — a judgment that involves weighing such intangibles as personality, leadership ability, motivation, dependability, enthusiasm, attitude toward authority. If critics are claiming that affirmative action has resulted in a less-competent work force because of the hiring and promotion of less-qualified blacks, neither evidence nor experience supports that conclusion.

Third, to argue that affirmative action constitutes a "preference" for African-Americans is simply to argue that it distorts what would otherwise be a more efficient and fair system. Since the premise of the argument is that affirmative action constitutes a "preference" for blacks, it is fair to assume that proponents believe a "color blind" system would result in fewer blacks being employed. Why? If the pool of qualified applicants is 10 percent African-American, then a color-blind system or an affirmative action program would result in about 10 percent black representation in the work force.

Thus, the word "preference" as critics use it is an effort to convert a broad employment effort into a series of individual choices or comparisons, as in Piscataway, with the additional innuendo that the fact of "preference" means a less-qualified African-American will always prevail. That is a serious distortion of affirmative action.

Put differently, opponents of affirmative action in employment believe either that today the playing field is level for all races or that, absent overt racial bias, we should act as if it were. By contrast, most African-Americans and many whites believe that bias still exists, though not always overtly, and that affirmative action is simply a guarantee that the playing field is not tilted.

Laws forbidding racial discrimination were relatively easy to administer when the bias was overt and widespread. The more that bias goes underground or, worse yet, is unconscious on the part of the decision maker, who believes his decision is uninfluenced by race, the more difficult and controversial that administration becomes. To label and punish unconscious bias as though it wore a hood may well be offensive. Programs of affirmative action avoid that problem while promoting the integrated society we seek. They minimally interfere with discretion in making particular choices and give management a desirable latitude in exercising particular judgments.

The other use of affirmative action most commonly criticized is in college admission. Educational institutions usually create a pool of applicants who meet objective tests designed to determine if the applicant is capable of performing successfully. Tests can reasonably predict first-year performance and do not claim to do more. But selection from the pool is not confined to rank on test scores, and applicants with lower scores are admitted for many reasons. Some applicants are admitted on the basis of judgments about potential and predictions about future performance not unlike those used in employment decisions. A student from a poor school who qualifies may be seen, despite a lower score, as having great motivation and aptitude. In other cases, "merit" is measured by other abilities, like musical or athletic talent. In still others, admissions may be determined by geography, financial ability, relationship to graduates or relationship to people important in other ways to the institution. And finally, race and national origin may be taken into account and labeled "affirmative action."

If race cannot be taken into account and admission is based on test scores alone, far fewer African-Americans will qualify. That was the predictable result in California and Texas, where state institutions were forbidden to take race into account. Again, the word "preference" is unfortunate because critics use it to imply that some kind of racial bias is used to reject better-qualified whites. Most of the students admitted are in fact white, hardly a demonstration of a bias in favor of blacks, and certainly not one that can be equated with past denials of admission to blacks to our best universities.

What proponents of affirmative action in college admissions urge is simply an institutional need for qualified African-Americans on the grounds that a diverse student body contributes to educational excellence and to the preparation of students to live in an integrated society. Critics do not question the educational advantage of diversity — though their prescriptions would make its achievement virtually impossible. Further, those African-Americans who can qualify for the institutional admissions pool would probably not be as successful as they are without superior motivation and determination — qualities most Americans would associate with merit.

Colleges and professional schools serve as gatekeepers to professional and business careers. If African-Americans can successfully do the academic work, they will importantly contribute to the public goal of an integrated society. Studies support the contention that some blacks perform better academically than some whites with better test scores and that African-Americans successfully compete for employment at a comparable level with whites upon graduation.

The arguments against this "preference" are similar to those in other affirmative action programs: it is anti-merit and discriminates against whites with higher scores on admissions tests. That argument is not really worth consideration unless one is prepared to argue that all admissions should be measured exclusively by test scores. No one is prepared to go that far. The plea for fairness based on "merit" as measured by test scores appears to be confined to race — a plea that in our society should be regarded with some skepticism.

Affirmative action programs, whether to avoid present bias or to remedy the effects of three centuries of discrimination against African-Americans, are race-based. The problems they seek to cure are and always have been race-based. They stem from history — the political, economic and social domination of blacks by a white majority that regarded blacks as inferior. Undoubtedly there are blacks who are biased against whites and who, given the power to do so, would discriminate against them. Of course, given the power, it would be as morally wrong for them to do so as it has been for whites. But discrimination by blacks against whites is not America's problem. It is not the problem that predominantly

white legislatures, businesses and universities seek to solve through affirmative action programs.

To speak of these white efforts as though they were racially biased
against whites and to equate them with the discriminatory practices of the
past against African-Americans is to steal the rhetoric of civil rights and
turn it upside down. For racial bias to be a problem, it must be accompanied by power. Affirmative action programs are race-based not to show
preference for one race over another but to resolve that problem. Only if
one ignores that purpose and states the matter in Piscataway terms—
preferring one individual over another for no reason other than race—does
there even appear to be room for argument. If problems of race are to be
solved, they must be seen as the race-based problems they are.

It is this aspect of the controversy that recent decisions of the Supreme
Court have brought into question. The Equal Protection Clause of the 14th
Amendment was designed to insure that former slaves and their descendants were entitled to the same legal protection as white citizens. Like the
13th Amendment abolishing slavery and the 15th guaranteeing the right to
vote regardless of race, it was clearly and unequivocally aimed at racial
problems—in today's terminology "race-based." The Equal Protection
Clause has never been viewed as preventing classification of citizens for
governmental reasons as long as the legislative classification was "reasonable" in terms of its purpose.

Where that classification involved race, however, the Court determined that it must be given "strict scrutiny." In other words, given our
history both before and after the passage of the amendment, the Court
understandably thought it was wise to regard any racial classifications by
overwhelmingly white legislatures with skepticism. When it was satisfied
after strict scrutiny that the classification did not have the purpose or effect
of discriminating against African-Americans or other ethnic minorities, the
Court found legislation to be consistent with the amendment. In the context of both our history and that of the amendment, this simply forbade
abuse of white political superiority that prejudiced other races or ethnic
minorities.

More recently, however, a majority has edged toward pronouncing the
Constitution "color blind," coming close to holding legislation that uses
any racial classification unconstitutional. Reading the Equal Protection
Clause to protect whites as well as blacks from racial classification is to
focus upon a situation that does not and never has existed in our society.
Unfortunately, it casts doubt upon all forms of racial classification, however benign and however focused upon promoting integration. If such a
reading is finally adopted by a majority of the Court, it would put a constitutional pall over all governmental affirmative action programs and even put

similar private programs in danger of being labeled "discriminatory" against whites and therefore in violation of existing civil rights legislation — perhaps the ultimate stupidity.

The Court has, in short, never accepted as a national priority — in its terms "a compelling state interest" — the necessary race-based efforts, private and public, to include blacks in the institutional framework that constitutes America's economic, political, educational and social life. Its recent decisions on the distribution of political power through districting outcomes have precluded race as a major factor while permitting incumbency, party affiliations, random geographic features and boundaries drawn for obsolete historical reasons. Other lines of cases have similar outcomes for university admissions (as against unfair and educationally irrelevant factors like family ties, athletic prowess and geography) and employment choices. It is very nearly as if this Court has simply mandated that what is the country's historic struggle against racial oppression and racial prejudice cannot be acted upon in a race-conscious way — that the law must view racial problems observable by all as if oppression and prejudice did not exist and had never existed. The Court's majority, in other words, has come very close to saying — and the hope and fear about the Piscataway case was that it would finally say at last — that courts cannot be permitted to see what is plain to everybody else.

*Wall Street Journal*

# Defining Affirmative Action

Most people, if asked, will probably say they are "for" affirmative action. The big question at the moment is, just what exactly is it that most people are for?

In the broadest sense, what most people likely support is the belief that somehow, somewhere, a lot of black Americans got the short end of the stick. Whether it was slavery, the obvious pathologies of inner-city life or the crummy schools, it seems obvious that some sort of extra effort across the broad spectrum of American life would be necessary to start the cycle of upward mobility.

That said, we obviously have entered an era in which efforts are under way — ballot initiatives, lawsuits — to stop a lot of the official, public, formal programs flying under the affirmative-action banner. We've never thought this was racism, but it's clearly a backlash. Where has it come from?

Last week's D.C. Appeals Court overturned the Federal Communication Commission's minority hiring requirements, and its decision offers an insight into this contentious subject.

For starters, the case's alleged transgressor against affirmative action was the Lutheran Church — Missouri Synod, a group not normally associated with turning back the clock. Further, the violating activity was done by the church's radio stations, whose programs combine Lutheran religiosity and classic music broadcasting from the campus of Concordia Seminary.

The NAACP filed a petition to deny license renewal and the FCC agreed that the stations' minority hiring practices were deficient. What followed in the appeals court's decision, in more detail than we can accommodate here, was a journey through the arcana and hair-splitting that is the reality of being on the right side or wrong side of "affirmative action." For being wrong, the Lutherans were fined $25,000 and risked loss of their stations.

The church said it had minority employees. The FCC said there

*Wall Street Journal,* April 20, 1998.

weren't enough of them. But the FCC also said that it has recently downplayed its reliance on statistics, instead emphasizing an overall effort to achieve something called "diversity." Even so, the Lutherans were presumably found in some sort of definable violation.

The court's decision has drawn a lot of attention for saying the FCC's current policy doesn't survive the "strict scrutiny" standard of the Supreme Court's recent *Adarand* decision. But we find more interesting the court's effort to make clear that the FCC's guidelines weren't about any sort of broadly supported good-faith efforts at outreach, but are in fact about getting the numbers right, as subject to FCC interpretation, or risking federal legal action.

"As a matter of common sense," the court wrote, "a station can assume that a hard-edged factor like statistics is bound to be one of the more noticed screening criteria. The risk lies not only in attracting the Commission's attention, but also that of third parties. 'Underrepresentation' is often the impetus (as it was in this case) for filing a petition to deny which in turn triggers intense review." The court added that, "In sum, under both its current and past practice, the commission has used enforcement to harden the suggestion already present in its EEO program regulations."

Put differently, just how and when is it possible to know you've got the right number of angels dancing on the head of this particular pin? This is not about some country club's total ban on blacks, Jews and Italians. It's about employers like the Lutheran Church hiring some blacks, Hispanics, Asian-Pacific Islanders or American Indians, the categories of minority status noted in the decision — but not "enough" of them.

Affirmative action's most ardent proponents think the private sector can't be trusted to make "enough" hires without the raised club of federal law enforcement. But that club creates cases like this one, which explains why, increasingly, there is indeed a growing backlash against something called "affirmative action."

The United States is not Northern Ireland or Bosnia. The tension around affirmative action is not about some irredeemable historical animosity. What we suspect it is about, after three decades of positive effort, is finding a way to rediscover the good faith that overwhelming numbers of Americans ultimately brought to the task of enhancing the status of blacks in the nation's life, while recognizing that there has to be a better way of continuing that good faith than letting the federal police decide when Lutheran radio stations are committing crimes against conscience.

*Lani Guinier*

# An Equal Chance

Now that the results are in, some opponents of affirmative action are having second thoughts. One year after California passed a referendum banning the use of race and ethnicity in public college admissions, the number of blacks, Hispanics, and American Indians admitted to the University of California's two top campuses has dropped precipitously, leading to concern about the resegregation of higher education.

But while the news from California is dismaying, a different, more encouraging story is being written in Texas, a state with political leaders who see diversity as a rich resource that benefits everyone, not only people of color.

Last year, a Federal court outlawed consideration of race in higher-education admissions in Texas. At the time, the state had been using high school grades and Scholastic Assessment Test scores along with affirmative action criteria to decide admissions.

After the ruling, a panel of professors and community activists joined a group of Hispanic and black lawmakers to persuade the State Legislature to adopt what has come to be called the 10 percent plan.

This eliminated the use of S.A.T. scores for Texas students in the top 10 percent of their high school class and automatically admitted them to the two most selective public schools, the University of Texas at Austin and Texas A & M University.

At first, some critics objected that S.A.T. scores were indispensable measures of future success. But, as the advisory group of professors and activists pointed out, the best way to predict how a student will do in college is by measuring classroom performance in high school. This was borne out when achievement tests administered to the thousands of minority students admitted through the program showed that only a handful needed remedial education.

So far the Texas plan has produced many winners. As of March of this year, 7 percent more black and 21 percent more Mexican-American applicants were eligible for enrollment under this system than under the old affirmative action guidelines. And access to public education has increased for white high school graduates in rural parts of Texas — students who also tend not to do well on the S.A.T. and so had been refused admission to the most competitive public colleges under the old system.

No wonder a number of moderate white legislators joined the coalition in supporting the plan. As State Representative Irma Rangel pointed out, the 10 percent plan treats all groups equally, giving them "the respect they deserve." Similarly, when Gov. George Bush, a Republican, signed the bill, he declared, "We want all our students in Texas to have a fair shot at achieving their dreams, and this legislation gives them that fair shot."

Texas officials recognize that there is more to be done beyond rethinking college admissions policy. They have also formulated new ideas for improving primary schools. Schools and districts are now required to report test scores, attendance and dropout rates by race, ethnicity and economic standing. Each school is then rated according to the performance of the various ethnic and economic groups. This means more attention is paid to every student, and the entire class benefits.

As a result, black, Hispanic and economically disadvantaged students are closing the achievement gap. On a national math test given in 1996, Texas fourth graders in various categories — white, black and poor students — all ranked first in the country. By contrast, California, where politicians have demonized issues of race, education and immigration, saw its fourth graders, including white students, finish near the bottom, ahead of those in only two other states.

Texas's innovative approaches, and its less polarized environment, are helping to shift an increasingly narrow debate over affirmative action into a wider public discussion on education. This also sends the message that access and diversity are not the enemy of excellence.

*Michael A. Fletcher*

# For Asian Americans, a Barrier or a Boon?

In many ways, John I. Yam embodies the paradox that affirmative action poses for Asian Americans.

While contractors were working on Yam's dream home, a 5,000-square-foot contemporary overlooking sparkling Lake Washington, the dust and noise from the construction set off a dispute with a neighbor that quickly took on racial tones. "He told me to go back to Hong Kong," said Yam, a doctor who has established a booming suburban practice since coming to the United States three decades ago. That brief bout with bigotry reminded Yam that Asian Americans need action as much as any minority because, whatever their accomplishments, they are often seen as outsiders.

But other times, Yam is convinced that affirmative action unfairly holds Asian Americans back. His son, Garrett, has been rejected by more than 20 medical schools without so much as an interview, despite a 3.5 grade point average and above-average medical board scores. Yam suspects that his son would be readily admitted were Asian Americans not already overrepresented in medical school: They account for nearly a fifth of the nation's 67,000 medical students, but only 4 percent of the overall population.

"I feel Asian Americans lose their competitive edge because of affirmative action," Yam said. "We're not competing on equal footing with whites or other races because so many Asian youngsters score high on tests and do well in school."

As the debate over affirmative action has intensified into perhaps the nation's most contentious racial issue, it often has been cast as a contest between blacks and whites. Yet it is Asian Americans who are about to play a central role in the next big battle over affirmative action.

If early public sentiment holds, Washington state will become only the second place in the nation to abolish race-based programs. Patterned after

California's Proposition 209, which was approved by voters in 1996 and took effect last year, Washington's Initiative 200 would bar the consideration of race or sex in hiring, government contracting and admissions to public colleges and universities. So far, polls suggest that more than two-thirds of voters support the ban. With their relatively broad political reach and status as one of the state's largest minority groups, Asian Americans enjoy unusual visibility here and a central question developing in the ongoing debate is whether affirmative action helps or hurts them. It is a question that leaves many Asian Americans ambivalent.

"With blacks and whites, this issue is a lot more simple. Blacks benefit from affirmative action and whites don't," said Arthur Hu, a Seattle engineer and a leader in the Initiative 200 effort. "But Asians basically break the rules."

Asian Americans often are depicted as the nation's model minority, whose self-reliance, educational achievement and financial success offer irrefutable evidence not only of America's vast promise but also of its declining emphasis on race.

Asian Americans' median family income of $43,000 and 42 percent college completion rate surpass those of any other racial or ethnic group in the country, including whites. They have an impressive record of entrepreneurship and their devotion to family stability, as measured by the percentage of children from two-parent households, is unmatched.

But Asian American activists are quick to add that their success is not all that it seems. There are huge educational and economic gaps within the diverse Asian American community, with Chinese and Japanese Americans generally better off than those with roots in Southeast Asia.

Also, they note, Asian Americans as a group tend to be better paid because they are better educated. A more careful perusal of the data, for example, shows Asian Americans with a college degree earn less than whites with equal educational credentials.

And despite their high educational achievement, Asian Americans comprise only 0.3 percent of the senior level managers in Fortune 1000 companies, receive a tiny share of government contracts and are underrepresented in a range of jobs, from journalist to college professor.

Many Asian Americans see those disparities as the modern legacy of the discrimination they have faced in this country, including the Chinese Exclusion Act, which prevented Chinese immigration to the United States for decades; laws banning Japanese ownership of farm land; and the forced detention of Japanese Americans during World War II.

"It is clear that we still need affirmative action," said Akemi Matsumoto, a community college counselor and leader in the No! 200 campaign. "Our hard work doesn't always pay off."

The battle over Initiative 200 comes at a critical time in the anti–affirmative action debate. While race-based programs have suffered key defeats in the courts, repeated efforts to roll them back by state legislatures, by Congress or by voter initiative have almost uniformly failed.

Which is why the simmering dispute in Washington state marks a pivotal moment in the years-long struggle over the issue, and why it is being so closely watched. The initiative has received strong support not only from the state's Republican Party but also from deep-pocketed national groups intent on abolishing affirmative action. Backers of the initiative have received $178,000 — almost half their overall funding — from the American Civil Rights Institute, a group formed by Ward Connerly, who led the effort to abolish affirmative action in California.

A February survey by an independent polling firm found that 69 percent of registered voters were inclined to support the measure across the state, which has an 83 percent white population. But where Asian Americans stand on the issue is harder to ascertain because there is no reliable polling data analyzing their sentiment.

Most of the state's Asian American elected officials, including its Chinese American governor, Gary Locke (D), have come out against the initiative. And a coalition of Asian American civil rights and cultural groups is working to defeat the measure.

"There are a lot of myths about Asian Americans and affirmative action," said Seattle City Council member Martha Choe (D), a vocal opponent of Initiative 200. "There has been an attempt to use us as a wedge, but the fact is that we are direct beneficiaries of affirmative action."

Yet however deep the support for affirmative action is among the Asian American political leadership, the level of backing among the rank and file is far less certain.

Albert Ting graduated from high school in suburban Seattle in 1988 with a 3.9 grade point average and an impressive 1370 on his Scholastic Achievement Test. But when he applied to the engineering program at the University of California at Berkeley, Ting was initially enrolled only in the school's extension program, which prevented him from living and taking classes on campus. He questions whether he would have been kept out had Berkeley not used race as a factor in admissions. On a campus where Asians score higher than any other group, the bar for those students ends up being raised in the name of racial diversity.

"There were a lot of Asian students in the extension program," said Ting, 27, who eventually graduated from Berkeley's engineering school and now works as a programmer for Microsoft Corp.

As Ting considers Initiative 200, that experience looms large in his mind. "Affirmative action should be about getting people to a level where they can compete," he said. "We are all kind of hurt because of the focus on fixing symptoms, rather than the root causes of problems. The answer is not to have people who are more qualified not admitted to schools."

It is a message that others have used in an effort to rally Asian American opposition to affirmative action. Near the end of his unsuccessful 1996 presidential campaign, former Sen. Robert J. Dole (R) broke his silence on the issue by delivering a speech in support of California's Proposition 209 before a largely Asian American audience.

Ultimately, the effort to build Asian American support for California's Proposition 209 was largely unsuccessful: As many as 61 percent of the state's Asian Americans voted against the measure, according to exit polls. Yet, by some gauges, Asian Americans appear to have benefited from the measure, at least when it comes to college admissions.

In the huge University of California system, there have been steep drops in the number of black and Hispanic undergraduates admitted for next fall, but the number of Asian American admissions has remained steady. Meanwhile, there have been sharp increases in the number of Asian Americans admitted to the university system's top professional schools while admissions for other minorities plummeted.

"In many ways, Asians under affirmative action as it has been practiced for the last 25 or 30 years are becoming as victimized by quotas as Jews were in the '20s, '30s and '40s," said John Carlson, chairman of the Initiative 200 campaign.

On the sprawling, tree-lined campus of the University of Washington, the state's premier public university, Asian Americans make up 22.1 percent of the student body. And many of them believe they had to meet a higher standard than other minorities to get in.

But some also write off such hurdles as the price one pays to ensure broad racial diversity.

"It is unusual to see people of color in positions of authority here, which can be discouraging," said Kieu-Anh King, a Vietnam-born student who graduated last week. "Holding everybody to equal standards is something everyone is in favor of on one level. . . . But looking at the classroom climate and the lack of diversity here, you see the need for affirmative action."

After taking a year off, King hopes to attend graduate school in public policy at Princeton, Harvard or the University of California at Berkeley. For that, he credits more than his own hard work. He says Connie So, one of his few Asian American professors, not only cajoled him to apply, but steered him to a minority fellowship program that will pay the bill.

*Brent Staples*

# When a Law Firm Is Like a Baseball Team

The state of Washington followed California earlier this month when it voted to eliminate state-sponsored affirmative action in education and government contracts. But the nation as a whole has moved in the opposite direction since California's Proposition 209 raised fears of a national movement that might resegregate higher education and the professions, deepening racial divisions.

Faced with the prospect of civic disaster, even hard-line conservatives have taken a more moderate stance, seeking ways to limit affirmative action instead of killing it. The new tack among conservatives is to frown on race-sensitive policies in most contexts, while endorsing them in the municipal services and in public colleges on the premise that publicly financed institutions should be racially representative to keep taxpayer support.

Abigail Thernstrom presented a troubling variation on this theme last month in *The Wall Street Journal.* Ms. Thernstrom argued that African-Americans who attended middling and "allegedly dead-end colleges" had done so well professionally that they had no need of access to first-tier institutions like Harvard, Duke or the University of Chicago. In the Thernstrom theory, elite universities could re-segregate with no foreseeable harm to African-Americans — as long as middling colleges continued to provide broad access.

This view is noxiously classist and historically naïve. Studies of workforce integration show that African-Americans are routinely required to have far more impressive credentials than whites, even when competing for the same jobs. For whites, elite university degrees are a nice enhancement. But for African-Americans, those same degrees are required just to get in the door.

The "black superstar" effect was first documented in, of all places, professional baseball. The sport portrays itself as the ultimate meritocracy and pats itself on the back for hiring Jackie Robinson at a time when other sports still barred African-Americans. But 10 years ago, a study of lifetime pitching and batting averages by sports sociologists at Northeastern University showed that black players had to out-hit and out-pitch their white counterparts by substantial margins to win and keep their jobs. Baseball managers who had come of age when the game was all white had difficulty recognizing baseball talent when it came with a black face. Mere journeymen could have long and profitable careers — as long as they were white. But among African-Americans, only stellar and above-average players would do.

These inequities are rooted in the logic of slavery and are based on the myth that blacks are intellectually inferior. As a consequence of this myth, black people face substantially higher barriers to employment than whites — especially in the elite professions where whiteness has historically served as an unstated job requirement.

Elite law firms today are roughly analogous to professional baseball teams 50 years ago. The old-money firms are notoriously clubby and overwhelmingly white, and have only in recent decades dropped policies that excluded women and African-Americans. Residual racism finds fertile ground in an interview process that makes less than it should of objective qualifications — and far too much of subjective judgments about an applicant's personality and suitability to the "culture" of the firm.

The Harvard University legal scholar David Wilkins is researching these problems in a national project. He published some of his early reflections in a 1996 article in the *California Law Review*. Mr. Wilkins notes that black law firm applicants with average grades are less likely to be hired than whites with the same transcripts. Black partners are far more likely than whites to have attended Harvard or Yale.

The "black superstar" effect is especially pronounced at the top-rated law firms. A partner at the Chicago firm of Sidley & Austin told researchers that law firms set "higher standards for minority hires than for whites. . . . If you are not from Harvard, Yale or the University of Chicago, you're not adequate. You're not taken seriously."

Critics of race-sensitive admissions policies argue that black students who come from mediocre public schools could enhance their transcripts and professional opportunities by attending less competitive universities where they could more easily excel. That option is open to whites — who get hired and reach partner status with degrees from middling law schools. But black students who pursue such a course are locked out of elite firms.

This process has been best documented in law, but related studies show it at work well across the corporate spectrum.

The Thernstrom theory—that African-Americans can achieve equal professional access without attending Harvard, Yale, Princeton or the University of Chicago—is wrong on its face. The country may yet get there, but we have a long way to go.

*Edward Blum and Marc Levin*

# Racial Profiling: Wrong for Police, Wrong for Universities

The recently publicized incident of police brutality in New York City has brought the issue of racial profiling to the forefront of national debate. Attorney General Janet Reno has condemned racial profiling and Rep. John Conyers Jr. (D-Mich.) has introduced legislation that would require the Justice Department to collect racial and ethnic data about police stops from law enforcement agencies across the country. Conyers has stated that "stopping our citizens to be searched on account of their race is an unacceptable activity on the part of law enforcement."

He's right.

The critics of racial profiling by police officers are correct in their analysis: using race as a proxy for criminality is wrong. It offends the very meaning and purpose of the Constitution and an entire body of civil rights laws. Skin color and ethnicity are meaningless qualities within the American judicial system. Equal protection under law is built on colorblind principles.

It is baffling, however, that so many of the critics of police racial profiling encourage schools and universities to engage in the very same racial stereotyping when it involves admissions and curriculum. In this case, the racial advocacy groups argue that skin color is paramount, nearly primordial. In fact, they contend that the cultural differences between the races are so enormous that race is virtually synonymous with identity.

Apparently, the civil rights groups decrying police profiling by race believe that it is "bad" stereotyping, but when universities profile applicants by race, that is "good" stereotyping. Well, they can't have it both ways. Either skin color tells us something about how a person should be treated in society or it doesn't.

This should force Jesse Jackson to rethink his absurd claim that "to ignore race and sex is racist and sexist." Jackson wants the cops to ignore it, but not the admissions committee.

*Washington Times,* May 17, 1999. Copyright © 1999 News World Communications, Inc. Reprinted with permission of the *Washington Times.*

Joe Hicks, a former Black Panther from Los Angeles, has reconsidered his views on race: "I reject race. I challenge the idea that racial identity should define how you view the world." Right on.

Many academics continue to argue that racial classifications and preferences to achieve "diversity" are simply benign forms of profiling. After all, they say, blacks bring a unique life perspective to the classroom. Is this true? What personality characteristics and life experiences do all black students have that are not to be found in their white classmates? Are there distinct personality characteristics and life experiences that are found in all Hispanics? All Jews? All Asians? If there are, what are they?

Obviously, these claims are patently false; they are the delusions of the "race matters" crowd who make contradicting arguments about the nature and importance of skin color. Skin color is merely an accident of birth. It does not mean someone is smart or ignorant, hard working or lazy, sensitive or unfeeling, artistic or athletic, reads novels or *TV Guide*. In the final analysis, people are individuals, whose identity is shaped by innumerable characteristics and experiences, of which race is the least important. All policies that classify people and then treat them differently based on race are inescapably a form of intolerable stereotyping.

After racial preferences were struck down and minority enrollment shrank at the University of Texas School of Law, a professor remarked that it was unimaginable that he may be forced to teach civil rights law to a class that had only one or two African Americans. Why is this? Did the professor believe that white law students were unable to learn and appreciate civil rights laws without a black student in the class with them? His premise would make it necessary to have Jews in a classroom to learn about the Holocaust and Latinos to learn about Cinco de Mayo.

A few years ago, Jesse Jackson told an audience that when he walks alone at night in inner-city neighborhoods, he is relieved when the footsteps he hears behind him are from whites, rather than from blacks. His implication was abundantly clear: whites are less prone to criminal behavior than blacks. The media jumped all over this remark and Rev. Jackson was forced to "clarify" his statement the following day. In truth, Rev. Jackson was caught in the same act of "racial profiling" as many police forces are today.

The use of skin color as a feature of importance in public policy has led to some grave consequences, the most insidious being the demand for racial proportionality in all areas of American life. For example, a George Washington University Law professor has called on black jurors to acquit nonviolent black defendants, even if the evidence against them is irrefutable. He believes that the number of blacks in prison should match their percentage in the overall population. A few years ago, former California

Assembly Speaker Willie Brown proposed legislation for high schools to graduate minority students at the same rate as majority students, regardless of their grades.

Current university "affirmative action" policies incorrectly make race a proxy for victimization and disadvantage, just as some police departments make race a proxy for probable criminality. Both are wrong. We cannot get beyond race as a country by continuing to base our policies on it. We cannot end discrimination by continuing to practice it. Most importantly, we cannot achieve a colorblind 21st century unless we eliminate racial profiling in every part of our society.

*Gerald R. Ford*

# Inclusive America, under Attack

$O$f all the triumphs that have marked this as America's century—breathtaking advances in science and technology, the democratization of wealth and dispersal of political power in ways hardly imaginable in 1899—none is more inspiring, if incomplete, than our pursuit of racial justice. The milestones include Theodore Roosevelt's inviting Booker T. Washington to dine at the White House, Harry Truman's desegregating the armed forces, Dwight Eisenhower's using Federal troops to integrate Little Rock's Central High School and Lyndon Johnson's electrifying the nation by standing before Congress in 1965 and declaring, "We shall overcome."

I came by my support of that year's Voting Rights Act naturally. Thirty years before Selma, I was a University of Michigan senior, preparing with my Wolverine teammates for a football game against visiting Georgia Tech. Among the best players on that year's Michigan squad was Willis Ward, a close friend of mine whom the Southern school reputedly wanted dropped from our roster because he was black. My classmates were just as adamant that he should take the field. In the end, Willis decided on his own not to play.

His sacrifice led me to question how educational administrators could capitulate to raw prejudice. A university, after all, is both a preserver of tradition and a hotbed of innovation. So long as books are kept open, we tell ourselves, minds can never be closed.

But doors, too, must be kept open. Tolerance, breadth of mind and appreciation for the world beyond our neighborhoods: these can be learned on the football field and in the science lab as well as in the lecture hall. But only if students are exposed to America in all her variety.

For the class of '35, such educational opportunities were diminished by the relative scarcity of African-Americans, women and various ethnic groups on campus. I have often wondered how different the world might have been in the 1940's, 50's and 60's — how much more humane and just — if my generation had experienced a more representative sampling of the American family. That the indignities visited on Willis Ward would be unimaginable in today's Ann Arbor is a measure of how far we have come toward realizing, however belatedly, the promises we made to each other in declaring our nationhood and professing our love of liberty.

And yet. In the last speech of his life, Lyndon Johnson reminded us of how much unfinished work remained. "To be black in a white society is not to stand on level and equal ground," he said. "While the races may stand side by side, whites stand on history's mountain and blacks stand in history's hollow. Until we overcome unequal history, we cannot overcome unequal opportunity."

Like so many phrases that have become political buzzwords, affirmative action means different things to different people. Practically speaking, it runs the gamut from mandatory quotas, which the Supreme Court has ruled are clearly unconstitutional, to mere lip service, which is just as clearly unacceptable.

At its core, affirmative action should try to offset past injustices by fashioning a campus population more truly reflective of modern America and our hopes for the future. Unfortunately, a pair of lawsuits brought against my alma mater pose a threat to such diversity. Not content to oppose formal quotas, plaintiffs suing the University of Michigan would prohibit that and other universities from even considering race as one of many factors weighed by admission counselors.

So drastic a ban would scuttle Michigan's current system, one that takes into account nearly a dozen elements — race, economic standing, geographic origin, athletic and artistic achievement among them — to create the finest educational environment for all students.

The eminently reasonable approach, as thoughtful as it is fair, has produced a student body with a significant minority component whose record of academic success is outstanding.

Times of change are times of challenge. It is estimated that by 2030, 40 percent of all Americans will belong to various racial minorities. Already the global economy requires unprecedented grasp of diverse viewpoints and cultural traditions. I don't want the future college students to suffer the cultural and social impoverishment that afflicted my generation. If history has taught us anything in this remarkable century, it is the notion of America as a work in progress. Do we really want to risk turning back the clock to an era when the Willis Wards were isolated and penalized for the color of their skin, their economic standing or national ancestry?

To eliminate a constitutional affirmative action policy would mock the inclusive vision Carl Sandburg had in mind when he wrote: "The Republic is a dream. Nothing happens unless first a dream." Lest we forget: America remains a nation with have-nots as well as haves. Its government is obligated to provide for hope no less than for the common defense.

# Part 3: Scholars Write on Affirmative Action in Education and Employment

Many public discussions of affirmative action enflame without instructing. Part 3 reprints a number of excerpts from scholarly books and articles. Half of the selections argue against affirmative action, and half argue for it. The pieces presented give a very complex, if abbreviated, introduction to the tangle of issues at hand. All parties agree on certain fundamental points. Clearly, everyone wants to

reward merit;

achieve diversity;

end discrimination;

avoid or eliminate special privilege.

We must not lose sight of how much consensus about matters of principle exists among all parties to the debate on affirmative action.

To acknowledge the consensus is to help us move to a more satisfactory discussion of differences than has been possible in the past. In reading the various selections, you might wonder: How does one define and measure merit? What dimensions of diversity — including sex and race — are important in employment and education? What are fair and effective ways to end discrimination? How can we know if special privilege exists?

Space limitations forced us to edit all of the selections. Ellipses (. . .) denote missing text. If a whole paragraph or more has been omitted, the ellipses appear at the left margin. If a portion of the text within a paragraph has been omitted, the ellipses appear within the text. In all cases, we have tried to preserve the sense and clarity of the authors' arguments.

It was not apparent to us how best to arrange the excerpts presented here. Three schemes seemed viable. A simple chronological order, as in Part 2, would have played havoc with the internal consistency of the packet of arguments offered by scholars who question the worth of affirmative action and might also have diminished the force of the group of "pro" arguments. Having decided to keep in a cluster the "pro" arguments and the "anti" arguments, we were left to wonder which should go first in the anthology: pro or anti. In an attempt to achieve impartiality, we tossed a coin. The result of that coin toss was to place the pro arguments first.

*Patricia J. Williams*

# From *The Alchemy of Race and Rights*

I have decided to attend a Continuing Education of the Bar course on equal-employment opportunity. Bar-style questions are handed out for general discussion. The first question reads:

Question One: X and Y apply for the same job with firm Z. X and Y are equally qualified. Which one should get the job?

I panic. What exactly is meant by Question One? But apparently this is supposed to be a throwaway question. On the blackboard the instructor writes:

Right Answer: Whichever one you like better.

As usual I have missed the point and am busy complicating things. In my notebook I write:

Wrong Answer: What a clear, graspable comparison this is; it is like choosing between smooth pebbles. X, the simple crossing of two lines, the intersection of sticks; Y, the cleaned bones of a flesh-and-blood referent. There is something seductive about this stone-cool algebra of rich life stories. There is something soothing about its static neutrality, its emotionless purity. It is a choice luxuriantly free of consequence.

   At any rate, much of this answer probably depends on what is meant by "equal qualifications." Rarely are two people absolutely equally qualified (they both went to Harvard, they graduated in the same class, they tied for number one, they took all the same classes, etc.) so the judgment of equality is usually pretty subjective to begin with (a degree from Yale is as good as one from Harvard, a degree in philosophy is as useful as a degree in political science, an editor of the school paper is as good as the class president) and usually overlooks or fills in a lot of information that may in fact distinguish the candidates significantly (is it the same to be number one in a small class as in a huge class; is the grading done by some absolute standard, or on a strictly enforced bell curve; did X succeed by taking only standardized tests in large lecture courses; does Y owe his success to the individualized attention received in small seminars where he could write papers on subjects no one else knew or cared about?). All such differentiations are matters of subjective preference, since all such "equality" is nothing more than assumption, the subjective willingness not to look past a certain point, or to accept the judgments of others (the admissions director of Harvard, the accuracy of the LSAT computer-grader).

The mind funnels of Harvard and Yale are called standards. Standards are concrete monuments to socially accepted subjective preference. Standards are like paths picked through fields of equanimity, worn into hard wide roads over time, used always because of collective habit, expectation, and convenience. The pleasures and perils of picking one's own path through the field are soon forgotten; the logic or illogic of the course of the road is soon rationalized by the mere fact of the road.

But let's assume that we do find two candidates who are as alike as can be. They are identical twins. They've had exactly the same training from the same teachers in a field that emphasizes mastery of technique or skill in a way that can be more easily calibrated than, say, writing a novel. Let's say it's a hypothetical school of ultra-classical ballet — the rules are clear, the vocabulary is rigid, artistry is judged in probably far too great a measure by mastery of specific placements and technical renderings of kinetic combinations. (The formal requirements of the New York City Rockettes, for example, are that a dancer must be between 5 feet 5½ inches and 5 feet 8 inches tall precisely and be able to do twenty eye-level kicks with a straight back.) I could probably hire either one, but I am left with the nagging wonder as to my own hypothetical about whether I want either one of these goody-two-shoed automatons. I wonder, indeed, if the fact that the "standard" road is good may obscure the fact that it is not the only good road. I begin to wonder, in other words, not about my two candidates, but about the tortoise-shell nature of a community of employees that has managed to successfully suppress or ignore the distinguishing variegation of being human. (Even if we were talking about an assembly line, where the standard were some monotonous minimal rather than a rarefied maximum, my concern holds that certain human characteristics are being dishonored as irrelevant — such as creativity, humor, and amiability.)

I wonder if this simple but complete suppression of the sterling quirks and idiosyncrasies of what it is that makes a person an individual is not related to the experience of oppression. I wonder if the failure to be held accountable for the degree to which such so-called neutral choices are decided on highly subjective, articulable, but mostly unarticulated factors (the twin on the left has a higher voice and I like high voices) is not related to the perpetuation of bias.

By the time I finish writing this, the teacher is well along into discussion of the next question, this time a real one:

Question Two: X and Y apply for the same job with firm Z. X and Y are equally qualified. X is black and Y is white; Z is presently an all-white firm. Which one should get the job?

It feels almost blasphemous to complicate things like this. I feel the anger in the challenge to the calm neatness of the previous comparison; it seems to me that this is a trick question, full of labyrinthian twists and illusion. Will I be strong enough to cut my way through the suggestions and shadows, the mirror tricks of dimensionality? I hold my breath as the teacher writes on the blackboard:

Right Answer: Whichever one you like better, because race is irrelevant. Our society will impose no rules grounded in preference according to race.

In my notebook I write:

Left Answer: The black person should get the job. If the modern white man, innocently or not, is the inheritor of another's due, then it must be returned. I read a rule somewhere that said if a thief steals so that his children may live in luxury and the law returns his ill-gotten gain to its rightful owner, the children cannot complain that they have been deprived of what they did not own. Blacks have earned a place in this society; they have earned a share of its enormous wealth, with physical labor and intellectual sacrifice, as wages and as royalties. Blacks deserve their inheritance as much as family wealth passed from parent to child over the generations is a "deserved" inheritance. It is deserved as child support and alimony. It is ours because we gave birth to it and we raised it up and we fed it. It is ours because our legal system has always idealized structuring present benefit for those who forbore in the past.

But, then, I'm doing what I always seem to do—mistaking the rules of fraud and contract for constitutional principles. How's this: It's important to hire the black person because the presence of blacks within, as opposed to without, the bell jar of a given community changes the dynamic forever.

As I write, a discussion has been raging in the room. One of the course participants growls: "How can you force equality down the throats of people who don't want it? You just end up depriving people of their freedom, and creating new categories of oppressed, such as white men."

I think: the great paradox of democratic freedom is that it involves some measure of enforced equality for all. The worst dictatorships in history have always given some freedom: freedom for a privileged some at the expense of the rest is usually what makes oppression so attractively cost-effective to begin with. Is freedom really such a narrowly pluralistic concept that, so long as we can find some slaves to say they're happy with the status quo, things are fine and free? Are they or the rest of the slaves less enslaved by calling enslavement freedom?

The tension voiced by the growler seems to be between notions of associative autonomy, on the one hand, and socialized valuation of worth — equality and inequality notions — whose foundations are not in view and go unquestioned. Categorizing is not the sin; the problem is the lack of desire to examine the categorizations that are made. The problem is not recognizing the ethical worth in attempting to categorize with not only individual but social goals in mind as well. The problem is in the failure to assume responsibility for examining how or where we set our boundaries.

Privatized terms so dominate the public discourse that it is difficult to see or appreciate social evil, communal wrong, states of affairs that implicate us whether we will it or not. Affirmative action challenges many people who believe in the truism that this is a free country. For people who don't believe that there is such a thing as institutional racism, statements alleging oppression sound like personal attacks, declarations of war. They seem to scrape deep from the cultural unconscious some childish feelings of wanting to belong by forever having others as extensions of oneself, of never being told of difference, of not being rent apart by the singularity of others, of the privilege of having the innocence of one's most whimsical likes respected. It is a feeling that many equate with the quintessence of freedom; this powerful fancy, the unconditionality of self-will alone. It is as if no others exist and no consequences redound; it is as if the world were like a mirror, silent and infinitely flat, rather than finite and rippled like a pool of water.

The "it's a free country" attack on affirmative action is also an argument, however, that is profoundly inconsistent with the supposed rationale for the imposition of "standards," however frequently the arguments are paired. The fundamental isolationism of individual preference as an arbiter is quite different from the "neutrality," the "blindness," and the "impersonality" used to justify the collectivized convenience of standardized preference. I wonder what a world "without preference" would look like anyway. Standards are nothing more than structured preferences. Preferential treatment isn't inherently dirty; seeing its ubiquity, within and without racial politics, is the key to the underground vaults of freedom locked up in the idea of whom one likes. The whole historical object of equal opportunity, formal or informal, is to structure preferences for rather than against — to like rather than dislike — the participation of black people. Thus affirmative action is very different from numerical quotas that actively structure society so that certain classes of people remain unpreferred. "Quotas," "preference," "reverse discrimination," "experienced," and "qualified" are con words, shiny mirror words that work to dazzle the eye with their analogic evocation of other times, other contexts, multiple histories. As a society, we have yet to look carefully beneath them to see where the seeds of prejudice are truly hidden.

. . .

My dispute is perhaps not with formal equal opportunity. So-called formal equal opportunity has done a lot but misses the heart of the problem: it put the vampire back in its coffin, but it was no silver stake. The rules may be colorblind, but people are not. The question remains, therefore, whether the law can truly exist apart from the color-conscious society in which it exists, as a skeleton devoid of flesh; or whether law is the embodiment of society, the reflection of a particular citizenry's arranged complexity of relations.

All this is to say that I strongly believe not just in programs like affirmative action, but in affirmative action as a socially and professionally pervasive concept. This should not be understood as an attempt to replace an ideology controlled by "white men" with one controlled by "black women" — or whomever. The real issue is precisely the canonized status of any one group's control. Black individuality is subsumed in a social circumstance — an idea, a stereotype — that pins us to the underside of this society and keeps us there, out of sight/out of mind, out of the knowledge of mind which is law. Blacks and women are the objects of a constitutional omission that has been incorporated into a theory of neutrality. It is thus that omission becomes a form of expression, as oxymoronic as that sounds: racial omission is a literal part of original intent; it is the fixed, reiterated prophesy of the Founding Fathers. It is thus that affirmative action is an affirmation; the affirmative act of hiring — or hearing — blacks is a recognition of individuality that includes blacks as a social presence, that is profoundly linked to the fate of blacks and whites and women and men either as subgroups or as one group. Justice is a continual balancing of competing visions, plural viewpoints, shifting histories, interests, and allegiances. To acknowledge that level of complexity is to require, to seek, and to value a multiplicity of knowledge systems, in pursuit of a more complete sense of the world in which we all live. Affirmative action in this sense is as mystical and beyond-the-self as an initiation ceremony. It is an act of verification and vision, an act of social as well as professional responsibility.

*Susan D. Clayton and Faye J. Crosby*

# From *Justice, Gender, and Affirmative Action*

Opposition to affirmative action has been based largely on whether or not it works. Our argument in favor of affirmative action stems from a conceptually prior issue: whether or not it is needed. Other policies and procedures in the United States function at a less than optimal level. Voting, for example, is supposed to be the process through which citizens elect politicians who will represent their point of view, yet voter turnout is dropping, distrust of politicians is increasing, and most people agree that elections have become too much like popularity contests where the candidates try not so much to express their own positions to the voters as to say whatever is most likely to win them votes. Few would advocate abolishing elections, though, because voting is necessary to our democratic system. We believe that affirmative action is necessary. The question then is not whether or not our society should have affirmative action but how to make it work most effectively.

Affirmative action is apparently designed to respond to an economic condition and to have an economic effect: improving the financial position of women and of men of color by overcoming their segregation in low-status, low-paying jobs. On a deeper level, however, it also responds to a psychological and sociological condition, which is the perception that members of these groups are second-class citizens in the United States.

. . .

In this country, at this time, the existence of discrimination against women is treated more or less as a truism. Talk show hosts discuss it, newspapers do series of articles on it, introductory-level college textbooks acknowledge it, and scholarly volumes from staid presses announce it in their titles (Rhode 1989). In Crosby's (1982) study of working men and women, 97 percent of the sample acknowledged that women as a group

From *Justice, Gender, and Affirmative Action* by Susan D. Clayton and Faye J. Crosby (Ann Arbor: University of Michigan Press, 1992), 3–4, 67–69, 71–74, 79–81, 127–28.

earned less than men, and 80 percent blamed "the system." When Huckle (1983) asked male and female midlevel managers in 1973 and in 1983 to comment on the low representation of women in higher levels of government, the 1983 group was more likely than their colleagues to attribute the lack of women to discrimination and less likely to attribute it to sex differences in career goals.

The cognitive precondition for women to experience collective relative deprivation is in place, and it seems that women do perceive sex discrimination. Recently, a *New York Times* poll found that 67 percent of women agreed that the United States "continues to need a strong women's movement to push for changes that benefit women" (Dionne 1989, A1). Fifty-five percent said that most men don't take women seriously at work (Belkin 1989), and when asked what the most important goal of women's organizations should be, the most common response was job equality, chosen by 27 percent of the women surveyed (Dionne 1989).

But has the increased recognition of sex discrimination led individual women to understand that they, personally, are likely to suffer from the inequities that affect others? By and large, the answer is no. Feelings of personal deprivation are distinguishable from feelings of group deprivation. An understanding of collective discrimination does not mean that a woman will feel personally affected; an objective situation of personal disadvantage may not be experienced as a gender-related issue.

Here we review evidence showing the dissociation, under many conditions, of personal and group deprivation. We look at the reasons why people have difficulty perceiving individual instances of discrimination, even when they are personally involved. Taken together, the cognitive and emotional factors that interfere with the perception of discrimination are numerous — so much so that an examination of them leads us to wonder how they are ever overcome.

**The Phenomenon of Denial**

Crosby (1982, 1984) studied working women in Newton, Massachusetts, to examine a paradox: while many studies had demonstrated that women were disadvantaged in the labor market, other studies had found women to be no more dissatisfied with their jobs than were men. Replicating these earlier findings, Crosby found that women were no more likely than men to feel that they were the victims of job discrimination, although they earned significantly less than comparable men in the sample. They were, however, concerned about the position of working women in general.

Crosby was surprised by this discrepancy between working women's awareness of sex discrimination, on the one hand, and their apparent lack of sensitivity to their own disadvantage, on the other. Common sense had provoked the expectation that women would be more likely to complain about their own individual situations than about the situation of women in general. After all, self-interest is commonly considered more potent a force than altruism. The findings of the Newton study could have been a fluke.

Some evidence existed even at the time to suggest that the findings of the Newton study were neither a fluke nor an artifact of how the study had been conducted. The same pattern had also been found among Franco-phones in Canada (Guimond and Dubé 1983) and gay men in America (D'Emilio 1983). Other, informal corroboration came during the year or two following publication of the Newton study's results. Each time Crosby gave a colloquium on the study, she preceded her talk with a survey among the scholarly audience. She asked her listeners to respond yes or no to a series of questions about the existence of sex discrimination in the country, in academia, in the college or university where she was giving her talk, and in specific departments. Representative of the results she obtained on the many occasions when she gathered data were figures obtained in 1983 at the Simone de Beauvoir Institute in Montreal, where approximately thirty female scholars were among the audience. When asked if they believed that women were discriminated against in the North American labor force, fifteen responded yes. When asked if this was true throughout academia in North America, twelve responded yes. When asked if there was discrimination at their own university, eleven responded yes; in their own department, five responded yes. None of the women, however, saw herself as being currently the victim of sex discrimination. Although they could truly have been the lucky exceptions, an anecdote described by Jesse Bernard suggests otherwise. At a conference in 1973, only a few women said they had been victims of discrimination, reported Bernard. "But one woman in the audience . . . pointed out on the basis of what the women themselves had said, the numerous examples of discrimination they had experienced" (in foreword to Theodore 1986, x).

During the last decade, this phenomenon has also been reported among working women in Canada (Hafer and Olson 1989), gay men in England (Birt and Dion 1987), black lesbian women throughout the United States (Mays and Cochran 1986), and black MBAs in the United States (Ford 1988), all of whom reported higher dissatisfaction with the situation of their group than with their own personal situations. Typical are the findings of David L. Ford, Jr., who interviewed 181 MBA graduates who were minority group members, mostly black, about their career progress relative to white colleagues. While 5 percent perceived their progress as being slower, 68 percent thought it was the same and 27 percent thought it was faster. Overall, the interviewees reported being quite satisfied with their jobs. When compared with an equivalent white sample, however, Ford found that the black respondents were disadvantaged both in rate of promotion (70 percent of blacks and only 27 percent of whites were still in the first level of management) and in mean salary increase since being hired ($1,508 for blacks compared to $2,100 for whites). He commented that "their perceptions of their own progress vis-à-vis that of their white counterparts appeared to be out of touch with reality" (68).

. . .

Denial . . . seems to be the norm for most Americans. National polls in the last two years have found that respondents typically believe things are worse in general than for themselves personally. Thus, 69 percent of a national sample disapproved of Congress in general, but only 30 percent disapproved of their own congressional representatives; 84 percent believed pollution to be a serious problem, but only 42 percent found it serious in their own area; and 51 percent felt the police in big cities were racially biased, but only 20 percent felt this was true of their own communities (Holmes 1991). Wegener (1990) described it this way: "All those members of a society who have, objectively, below-average positions will have the deceptive impression that they stand 'somewhere in the middle' " (77). The denial of personal disadvantage is a general tendency, with recognition of discrimination proving to be the exception rather than the rule. Contrary to commonsense notions, it seems to be the case that people would rather hide from injustice than expose it, even when the exposure could result in increased benefits for the self.

### Explanations

Many of the explanations proposed for the denial of personal disadvantage refer to some emotional or motivational state on the part of the individual. Indeed, the very word "denial" connotes Freudian images of a motivated refusal to accept what the mind at some level already knows. Before exploring such possibilities, however, it is important to consider a more straightforward explanation.

*Cognitive Factors*
The victim of discrimination may be honestly unaware of the problem, even subconsciously. Despite the fact that she is objectively disadvantaged relative to a comparable man, a woman may not perceive that gender-based distinctions are being made. There are a number of reasons why this might be the case. First, it is more difficult to observe things that don't happen than to observe things that do. A woman may notice if she is fired

or subjected to overt sexual harassment, or even if a more junior man is promoted before she is. But for her to fail to get promoted year after year, or to receive suboptimal raises, is a nonoccurrence. It is difficult to identify a particular incident and say, "This thing happened because I was discriminated against." In addition, a female employee may not have information about the "comparable man." Ours is a culture in which talking about one's salary or other benefits, or about one's qualifications for a particular job, is considered impolite except in certain restricted contexts.

Added to the general prohibition against discovering relevant salary information is another barrier: that of cross-gender comparisons. Women may be less likely to choose men to compare themselves to because men are less similar, and thus less useful sources of information, than are other women. Evidence of this gender barrier was found in a study in which 97 percent of a group of male and female students chose to obtain comparative information from a group of the same sex rather than the opposite sex (Zanna, Goethals, and Hill 1975). Subjects, who had taken a subset of the Miller Analogies Test (a test used to measure vocabulary and intellectual ability), were told either that women tended to do better on the test or that men tended to do better. Even when the opposite sex was supposed to do better, subjects chose a member of their own sex as a comparison first and only secondly chose to receive comparative information about a group of the opposite sex. A similar pattern occurred in Newton, Massachusetts. About 94 percent of men and 86 percent of women in low-prestige jobs identified a same-sex other as their principal referent. Even women in high-prestige jobs chose other women 60 percent of the time, despite the fact that men might be expected to set the standard in those positions (Zanna, Crosby, and Loewenstein 1987).

Given the constraints on comparisons, a woman may never find out that a man in the same job position earns more than she does, received a higher bonus, or has a more direct line of communication to the boss. One of us, in her second year on a job, was informed by a graduate student that the male faculty got together for poker every other Thursday. She had never been invited to join the game and was not even aware of its existence. The other one of us came by a similar route to find out that she was paid 85 percent of the salary of a male colleague, hired the same year as she, even though she had a Ph.D. and several publications while he had neither a Ph.D. nor any publications to his name.

Even when a woman does obtain comparative information about salaries, the information is often impossible to interpret in the absence of corresponding information about qualifications. Perhaps his higher salary reflects longer training, higher productivity, or stronger evaluations from his students or his manager. People are often very private about their accomplishments — or lack thereof. It is easy for people to imagine that others possess qualifications in proportion to their rewards (Lerner 1971).

When numerous qualifications are examined, furthermore, even quite complete comparative information may not suffice. Two employees are never exactly alike. If the man's greater outcomes (or rewards) can be attributed to his superiority on just one qualifying characteristic, no attribution to gender is necessary. Perhaps he is paid more even though his seniority is lower; this may be due to the fact that his degree is from a more prestigious university. Or if his educational background is less high in status, maybe he has done some extra assignments or committee work. Or if he works shorter hours than the woman, maybe he nonetheless manages to be more brilliant during those hours. One of the women we interviewed about discrimination faced this problem of explaining the difference, when the man who was hired to replace her during a pregnancy leave was paid more than she. Although she first stated, "I was discriminated against," she retreated during the interview, saying, "Well, he had a Ph.D. [which the respondent did not]." Because the difference between a man and a woman in salary can almost always be attributed to some difference between them other than gender, it is difficult to make a claim of discrimination in a particular case — not impossible, but difficult.

. . .

People may have ideas about what discrimination "looks like." They may feel, for example, that discrimination only occurs when there is the intention to discriminate, or when a man earns much more than an equally qualified woman. Deviations from the implicit prototype may not be recognized as sex discrimination. Susan D. Clayton (1989) set out to examine what happens when discrimination is not prototypical. Using materials similar to those employed by Crosby, Clayton, Hemker, and Alksnis (1986), Clayton gave students five cases in which a complaining employee and a comparison employee were compared on education, motivation, productivity, seniority, and salary. In each of the cases, the complaining employee (employee A) could be said to be receiving a salary that was too low, but the difference might also be explained away. Cases varied in the size of the difference in salary and the size of the difference in qualifications. Subjects were asked to rate the unfairness of employee A's salary compared to employee B's. An analysis of the mean ratings for each case found that the cases were rated as significantly different in unfairness and that this difference was almost completely accounted for by the size and the direction of the salary difference. That is, cases in which employee B made much more money than employee A were considered to be the most unfair; the case in which employee A made more money than employee B was considered to be the least unfair. There was no evidence that qualifications were considered at all in judging unfairness.

Participants in Clayton's study had distinct ideas about what did and did not constitute a typical case of discrimination. Asked what led them to consider a particular case fair or unfair, 40 percent of those who considered the situation fair explained their evaluation by stating that the situation did not fit the criteria for being considered unfair: the salary difference was too trivial, it was probably unintentional, it was due to random fluctuations, or "it can't be unfair because A makes more than B." Thus to be considered to be unfair to employee A, a company did not just have to pay less compensation than was deserved; it had to do so deliberately, and employee A had to make less than the comparison employee. In real life, a woman may feel safe from discrimination if she is sure that her bosses are well-intentioned or if she makes more than the most available comparison male, regardless of whether or not her salary advantage reflects her qualifications and her bosses' good intentions.

The cognitive factors that make it difficult to perceive gender asymmetries affect everyone, women and men, those who run organizations and those who are at the bottom of the ladder. Good intentions will not necessarily enable a person to perceive unfairness in the absence of aggregate data nor to be free of the effects of prototypic thinking. Cognitive biases that obscure justice affect people regardless of education level or experience on the job, just as visual illusions affect everyone regardless of aesthetic training and artistic inclination. That is why aggregating information, which is mandated by affirmative action, is absolutely critical if we are to continue to promote gender equity in the workplace.

. . .

*The Future of Affirmative Action*
Slowly, the context of affirmative action is changing. Rather than being seen as a favor or "hand up" that is given to women and to men of color, it is perceived by some as a way in which the company or institution is helping itself: making sure it doesn't miss out on a group of qualified people through discriminatory recruiting practices or lose some of its qualified employees because institutionalized racism or sexism prevented them from working to their full potential. As Avon CEO James Preston put it, "managing diversity is not something we do because it's nice but because it's in our best interest" (quoted in Hernandez 1990, 18). Thomas (1990) suggested that good and effective programs should be designed to benefit "us" (the company, including all its employees) as opposed to "them" (a target group, implicitly isolated and made competitive by such thinking). Still

more slowly, a recognition is developing that all people have race and all people have gender; diversity does not imply a norm from which some groups deviate but a collection of different people, each with some differences and some similarities and each with valuable skills to offer.

Affirmative action is a policy that contains the seeds of its own dissolution. When the goals of true equality have been reached, when the "protected classes" are fully integrated into the educational and occupational life of America, affirmative action will be unnecessary. We have not yet reached such a happy state of being. Sexism and racism are still strong forces in American society, and both hostility toward and stereotypes about women and people of color influence decisions on the job. Yet we are often as intellectually incapable of perceiving single instances of injustice as we are emotionally averse to countenancing them. And so, even after substantial progress has been made, affirmative action is necessary to ensure that records are kept, data are aggregated, and companies are forced not only to assume that their practices are nondiscriminatory but to test that assumption. The hard work is not yet over.

*Barbara R. Bergmann*

# From *In Defense of Affirmative Action*

Some who favor the aims of affirmative action but worry that it cannot survive the growing political and legal attack from the right are pushing a substitute: "Just help people from disadvantaged backgrounds." The foes of affirmative action say, "Just enforce the laws against discrimination." Here we look at the strengths and weaknesses of some proposed alternatives to affirmative action. Some of these alternatives have value and should be used, whether affirmative action lives or dies. The question, though, is whether any of them, or any combination of them, would be sufficient to accomplish the difficult job of achieving fairness in the labor market if affirmative action does die.

**Help to the Disadvantaged**

The growing agitation against affirmative action has triggered a hunt for substitutes that would help the African American community but be more widely accepted than affirmative action. Some are suggesting programs that would single out for help people from disadvantaged backgrounds, regardless of their race or sex.[1] Since African Americans suffer from high rates of poverty, those promoting this strategy hope that such a program would help many of the same people who are targeted by affirmative action. Some white males would presumably be included in the program, perhaps making it less unpopular than affirmative action.

In practice, a black person might get a job that a white person might have had in the absence of such a program. However, that displacement of white for black would be done in the name of helping the disadvantaged rather than helping blacks. It might therefore pass muster with those who claim their opposition to affirmative action is based on abhorrence of any program that makes use of people's racial or ethnic identification.

Working out the details of such a program might be difficult. Certifying the background of those qualified to participate could be cumbersome and subject to fraud. Further, a majority of the poverty-stricken population is white non-Hispanic; African Americans constitute 28 percent of the poor.[2] African Americans might not get even 28 percent of the slots made available by such a program if there were no element of race-based selection. If these slots were valuable opportunities, white males might vie for them and win almost all of them unless care were taken to avoid such an outcome. There is a name for that kind of care: affirmative action. Whites already win most of the well-paying jobs that go to low-skilled people of modest backgrounds — over-the-road truck drivers, house painters, and the like. To prevent the program from freezing out blacks, formal or informal quotas for blacks in the program would have to be set up. But if that happened, the program would become race-based.

There is a more fundamental reason why a program for the disadvantaged would be a poor and inadequate substitute for affirmative action, which acts specifically to end segregation by race and sex. A program based on disadvantaged status would leave much discrimination-caused segregation intact. Consider the large law firm, with no active affirmative action program, that has never hired a woman or a black person as a lawyer. If it already has some white male lawyers who grew up in poverty, then presumably it has fulfilled its obligation under a program of helping the disadvantaged and would not feel a need to desegregate by race and sex. If it has no lawyers from a disadvantaged background, then it could take on some. If they all turned out to be white males, no complaint could be made on that score, provided no overt discrimination had been practiced.

A program to give special help to the disadvantaged might accomplish some good. While it would not do the job that affirmative action is designed to do, it would be a worthwhile comparison program.

### Enforcing the Laws against Discrimination

If we have laws to protect us against discrimination, what do we need affirmative action for? The answer, of course, is that the laws that prohibit something do not always do a good job of protecting us against it. Many people engage in practices forbidden by law — selling and using illegal drugs, being delinquent in child support payments — despite the laws against them. Laws alone are ineffective when the behavior that they forbid is not confined to a small part of the population, when the behavior goes on behind closed doors, when violations are difficult and expensive to prove, and when the penalties are not easy to apply.

All of these difficulties hobble the application of the laws against discrimination. The practices that result in a high degree of segregation by job are ingrained: they seem natural and right to many people. Many of them are sins of omission, such as a failure to include women and African Americans in the pool of people being considered for a job.

Whether discrimination has actually occurred in any particular case, and the extent of the damages suffered, have to be determined by filing a lawsuit in a federal court. The lawsuit can be brought by the injured workers or by the Equal Employment Opportunity Commission (EEOC). The EEOC has had the resources to bring to court only a tiny fraction of the thousands of complaints that are filed with it each year. The agency receives sixty-three thousand complaints of employment discrimination a year and brings suit in fewer than five hundred cases. During the years of the Reagan and Bush presidencies, the EEOC further limited its effectiveness by concentrating on suits on behalf of individuals. The agency generally avoided filing class action suits, in which the discrimination claims of large groups of employees are addressed in a single suit. Class action suits are the only ones that can cause employers adjudged to have discriminated under the Civil Rights Act to suffer substantial financial loss. They generate more publicity, lend themselves to statistical evidence, and also make it difficult for the employer to base a defense on the alleged bad behavior, incompetence, or peculiarities of those bringing the complaint.

Antidiscrimination lawsuits are not easy for plaintiffs to win, and even those who do win may wait many years before receiving redress. Court cases can drag on for decades without final resolution. In one case started in 1973, a group of women employees sued the U.S. Navy, claiming they had been discriminated against in pay and promotion because of their sex.[3] It took eight years before the federal judge in charge of the case made a decision, ruling in favor of the complainants. However, some issues remained to be ruled on, and that took five more years. It took still another five years for damages of $670,000 to be determined and awarded to the women by the court. However, even then the damages were not paid because the navy appealed the judgment to a higher court.

. . .

A lawsuit, if successful, may result, after a decade or more, in restitution of lost wages for individuals who have been discriminated against, reimbursement of legal expenses, and possibly punitive damages. However, such monetary awards cannot repair much of the harm that discrimination and the lawsuit itself cause to the individuals involved. If the company contests the charge, it will dig up anecdotes that will put the complainant's performance and behavior in the worst light. Given the ordeal involved, people who feel they have been discriminated against are well advised to avoid lawsuits, and most do. Very seldom is the person reinstated to a position with the original employer commensurate with the position he or she would have held had the discrimination not occurred and the lawsuit not been brought. Nor can unclouded relations between the parties be restored. A sum of money cannot begin to compensate for the bitterness that being the object of discrimination engenders or for the loss of the opportunity to do more interesting work, develop one's talents, supervise others, or gain the self-esteem that comes from a smoothly developing career. Nor does the damage award compensate for the anxiety and time demands of being involved in a lawsuit with an uncertain outcome that will go on for a long and indeterminate period.

Lawsuits may have little direct effect on the employer's hiring, assignment, and promotion practices. The judge will not require the employer to discipline individuals who have been responsible for discriminatory acts, even egregious ones; such individuals may continue to play a major role in personnel decisions. When the complainant is an individual who no longer has a job with the employer and is represented by a private lawyer rather than an antidiscrimination agency of the government, no pressure will be brought to bear on the employer to make changes. Such a complainant, usually having left his or her job with the employer, no longer has a direct interest in changing the employer's personnel practices and is unlikely to expend time, money, and energy asking the judge to order systemic changes.

Even if lawsuits were much cheaper, quicker, and easier than they are, there would still be good reasons not to depend on them as a way to remove discriminatory practices from the workplace. The vast majority of people who are discriminated against have no way of knowing that this has happened to them. In most situations, rejected job applicants have no information that would enable them to judge whether their qualifications are better than those of the candidates selected. Those who have been hired but assigned to dead-end segregated positions, or passed over for promotion on account of their race or sex, are unlikely to pursue complaints unless they have a superior position outside the company lined up to go to and frequently not even then. Many employees are not even aware that segregation by race or sex on the job is wrong or illegal.

Finally, most people are not of a disposition to embark on a crusade for their rights; most are absorbed in everyday concerns about making a living, keeping their job, and having a reasonably pleasant relationship with bosses and coworkers. They know that accusations of discrimination would poison their relations with their employer, and with good reason they fear being blacklisted with other employers. For all of these reasons, it would be futile to depend on lawsuits to do the job of eliminating discrimination in our society.

Antidiscrimination lawsuits do have their uses. They have served to test the definition of what constitutes discrimination under the law and what does not. The courts have declared sexual harassment to be discriminatory. They have disallowed seemingly neutral tests that disproportionately screen out minority persons and women unless such tests are rigorously job-related. They have told employers they are discriminating when they exclude all women on the grounds that the "average woman" is in some respect inferior to the "average man," and when they exclude all blacks on the grounds that the "average black" is inferior to the "average white." Occasionally, a class action lawsuit brought on behalf of a sizable group of employees results in a large damage payment by an employer, alerting other employers to avoid the conduct that brought on the suit.

However, employers would make progress at a snail's pace if they moved only in response to lawsuits, opened up jobs only to those proven in a court of law to have been discriminated against, and changed only those procedures proven discriminatory in court proceedings.

**Education and Training**

Some of those who deplore affirmative action have argued that the way to solve the race problem in this country is to improve the qualifications of African Americans through training programs, in part by improving the schools black children attend. When blacks' qualifications are as good as those of whites, employers will want to hire them and the problem will end, according to this line of argument.

The disparity in educational and training opportunities for blacks and whites does need to be redressed. But those who advocate training instead of affirmative action ignore the fact that even now blacks and women with good qualifications do not do as well as white men in the labor market. Women college graduates earn little more on average than males with only a high school diploma.

Representing the education-improvement strategy as a solution that does away with the necessity for affirmative action puts off making improvements in the job situation for blacks until an indefinite future that may never come. It derails the drive to make employers hire more black people for jobs they can do well right now. Hundreds of billions of federal dollars have been spent on training programs for the disadvantaged over the last thirty years, but the results in terms of increased earnings for the trainees have not been impressive.[4]

Improving the qualifications of blacks will have limited effect unless employers treat equally qualified blacks and whites equally. The Urban Institute testing study and many studies based on census data show that blacks and whites with similar qualifications are not being treated equally by employers right now. The education-improvement approach ignores the fact that it is difficult to motivate young people to undergo training and take education seriously if they have little hope of getting a good job at the end of it. It also ignores the fact that blacks and women are largely excluded from much of the work for which unskilled persons are hired and given on-the-job training. Apprenticeship programs, which could provide an excellent way to integrate crafts occupations by sex and race, continue to be egregious offenders in restricting their benefits to white males.[5]

Better education should be part of our program for reducing racial and sexual disparities, and so should on-the-job training programs with slots reserved for blacks and women. Nevertheless, however well they augment programs to reduce discrimination, training and education programs cannot replace them.

**Testing Programs**

"Testing"—sending out carefully matched pairs of people of different races or ethnicities to apply for the same job—has been used to diagnose the extent of discrimination in the labor market. Programs of this type might be used also for enforcement purposes, to provide evidence against individual employers. A similar program has already been used in the housing field. Matched pairs have been sent to apply for apartments, and their disparate treatment has provided considerable evidence of discrimination. This evidence has formed the basis of successful legal moves against landlords who discriminate.[6] In the employment field, because repeated tests would be required to show that any particular employer was discriminating, the technique could be used only against employers with a sizable stream of vacancies. Testing of employers is a highly promising strategy against discrimination. It is no substitute for affirmative action but complements it. Affirmative action is the procedure that employers need to put in place to ensure that if they are tested, they are shown not to be discriminating.

**Just Pray**

The foes of affirmative action do not say, but certainly imply, that we should give up the effort to decrease labor market segregation by race and sex. They imply that everything is already fair enough. Those groups who currently do badly in the job market would presumably get the same consideration and have the same success as white males if they improved their qualifications and their behavior. At a recent Princeton University public policy conference, three panel members — a representative of the conservative Heritage Foundation, an African American foe of affirmative action, and a Clinton White House adviser — agreed on another strategy to improve the position of the disadvantaged. They all said that an increase in religious devotion on the part of the historically subordinate groups could provide an answer to America's social problems.

Some foes of affirmative action do not hold out much hope that even more prayer could improve matters. They tell us that no matter what African Americans do, they will always lag behind because their genes are of poor quality.[7] There is a large market for this kind of news; Herrnstein and Murray's *The Bell Curve* has sold hundreds of thousands of copies.

The evidence on the extent of segregation of jobs by race and sex shows that there are problems of discrimination in the labor market. If we attack those problems directly, we will be improving the incentive for young people — the ones now left out — to behave prudently and to get an education. If we do not, the exhortations to young people to be good and to study will continue to fall on many deaf ears. Prayer has never taken us very far in solving this country's race and poverty problems. Only an activist policy — with affirmative action as a prime ingredient — will do that.

## NOTES

1. Such a substitution is consonant with the ideas of William J. Wilson, who has suggested that the problems of the African American community derive mainly from a high rate of poverty rather than from racial discrimination. See *The Truly Disadvantaged* (Chicago: University of Chicago Press, 1987).

2. U.S. Bureau of the Census, *Income, Poverty, and Valuation of Non-cash Benefits: 1993*, Current Population Reports Series P60-188 (Washington, D.C.: U.S. Government Printing Office, 1995), p. xvi.

3. Material on this case and the USIA and DuPont cases is derived from Joan Biskupic, "After Nineteen Years, Racial Job-Bias Case Isn't Over Yet," *Washington Post,* November 23, 1992, pp. 1, 12.

4. See U.S. Senate, Committee on Labor and Human Resources, *Federal Job Training Programs: The Need for Overhaul: Hearings before the Committee on Labor and Human Resources,* statement of James J. Heckman, January 1–12, 1995, pp. 260–72. These programs cost the federal government $24.8 billion in 1994; only 11 percent of them conducted studies of their effectiveness. See also *The Harassed Staffer's Guide to Employment and Training Policy* (Baltimore: Johns Hopkins University, Sar Levitan Center for Social Policy Studies, June 1995).

5. A 1993 *Wall Street Journal* article praised an apprenticeship program run by a modest-sized Virginia manufacturer of chain saws, lawn trimmers, and blowers.

Starting in the late 1970s, the program turned thirty-six people into skilled crafts workers. Only two of the trainees were black; not a single one was a woman. Kevin G. Salwen, "The Cutting Edge; German-Owned Maker of Power Tools Finds Job Training Pays Off," *Wall Street Journal,* April 19, 1993, p. 1. A 1993 *Smithsonian* magazine story on apprenticeship mentioned in the text thirty-one trainees and trainers; not a single one was a woman. All of the several dozen people in the accompanying photographs were white. One picture did show one woman apprentice being taught pattern-making for women's clothes by a woman. E. Krester, "Germany Prepares Kids for Good Jobs; We Are Preparing Ours for Wendy's," *Smithsonian* 23 (March 1993): 44–50.

6. Sharon LaFraniere, "Testers to Probe Bias by Landlords," *Washington Post,* November 5, 1991, p. A19.

7. Richard J. Herrnstein and Charles Murray, *The Bell Curve: Intelligence and Class Structure in American Life* (New York: Free Press, 1994).

*Christopher Edley, Jr.*

# From *Not All Black and White: Affirmative Action, Race, and American Values*

This essay is about hard choices and how to think about them, not just about my conclusions or those of a President for whom I worked. I believe that thoughtful people seeking a deeper understanding of what affirmative action is all about, deciding for themselves how America ought best to achieve racial justice, will profit from a rigorous effort to think about the hard choices and first principles, in much the same way that President Clinton and his advisors did during 1994 and 1995. By thoughtful people, I certainly mean anyone who is reading this; I also mean people who believe that one need not embrace absolutism in order to be principled, and need not avoid strong value commitments in order to be tolerant.

From classrooms to boardrooms, from dinner tables to Capitol corridors, when our values are in doubt or in conflict, we often shrink from the hard work of understanding each other, of searching for the truth in what each side believes and moving toward something shared. The doubts and conflicts concerning race in America are many and deep. It has ever been so. Still, now and again the earth moves, and then the possibilities of the moment — today's moment — are at once exciting and frightening.

. . .

I have a relative who is a self-described "gun nut." An African-American psychiatrist, he strikes me as borderline paranoid when he talks about the importance of keeping semiautomatic weapons "just in case." Then I think about the Michigan Militia and its sister organizations, some with their militant white supremacy. Suppose the Black Panthers in 1967 had 15,000 armed and trained adherents, as the militias claim today? If they had preached Jesus and religious fundamentalism instead of Maoism and Pan-Africanism? There are reasons why the Panthers' kind of radicalism might

Excerpts from *Not All Black and White: Affirmative Action and American Values* by Christopher Edley, Jr. (New York: Hill and Wang, 1996), xi, 3 4, 220–24, 278. Reprinted by permission of Hill and Wang, a division of Farrar, Straus and Giroux, LLC.

not rise again, but there are also reasons why it might, though too few of us appreciate the peril. No one has said it better than James Baldwin with his apocalyptic phrase "The Fire Next Time."

In the past two years I've struggled to understand better that peril which America faces, first working as Special Counsel to President Clinton, managing the White House review of affirmative action, and then writing this. The peril is that the many sharp differences between the races, expressed along hardened political and social battle lines, may be precursors for an escalating racial conflict and, ultimately, conflagration. This process is already at work, and accelerating. Clever preachers of hate have forever been a threat to free societies, but they are now in the ascendancy in black and white communities throughout the United States, even on the Mall and the steps of our nation's Capitol.

I am very clear in my own mind about the needed response. The peril must be an impetus for self-conscious projects to build bridges among communities. The preachers of hate can be turned out of the temples and replaced by preachers who know that progress comes not from war but from the hard work of building community. Not from isolation and fear but from dreams, hope, and reason. Those are not merely words. They are a prescription for a kind of activism and advocacy that differs from much now practiced on both the left and the right.

So, for me, the agony of observing and living the contemporary problem of race in America is just this: to hold simultaneously the fear of war and the dream of community. Each day's news, each season's book list, every major political campaign, assaults us with upsetting evidence about society's pain and about the gathering storm clouds but brings, too, the glimmerings of something better. Which signs to believe? How to act? And where to find the strength to invest oneself in caring?

. . .

## Affirmative Action and Theories of Social Transformation

The common criticism of affirmative action that it has benefited only a few blacks, principally so-called elite ones, seems sweeping and inaccurate. It is admittedly difficult to separate out the effects of anti-discrimination measures and other affirmative action measures in, say, blue-collar employment. Yet it is fair to say that among the most dramatic consequences of affirmative action has been the desegregation of many (far from all) elite centers of social, economic, and political power. Increasing numbers of African, Hispanic, and Asian Americans — and of women — are found in corporate boardrooms, prestigious university facilities, and media editorial offices, holding high political appointments, and so forth. In what sense is this a meaningful kind of progress, given the continuing misery of the underclass?

There are several elements embedded in this issue — including the wisdom of investing scarce political capital in this particular strategy. But the two key concerns are these: From *the left:* Isn't the effect of affirmative action to give select individuals a stake in preserving the fundamental elements of "the system," when they might otherwise become an effective, militant leadership cadre pressing for more radical changes in capitalism and in American politics? Call this the "Band-Aid" critique. And from *the right:* Aren't the elite blacks who benefit most dramatically from affirmative action somehow not truly deserving, their gains ill-gotten by trading on white guilt about or empathy for the underclass? Call this the "racial spoils" critique.

The "Band-Aid" critique has an element of truth, and no doubt identifies one reason for the lack of leadership in the national African-American community. The "racial spoils" critique also has an element of truth, but it is substantially blunted by several considerations. First, it is not accurate to say, for example, that a middle-class black being considered for a corporate promotion has faced no race-based disadvantages. Certainly the disadvantages are less than those faced by less fortunate blacks, and certainly class-based disadvantages faced by less fortunate individuals of *any* ethnicity are considerable. But in the United States today, *any* black man or woman is likely to face continuing, serious disadvantages because of race, relative to white peers. (Then there's a separate argument about whether those disadvantages are serious enough to warrant a given form of affirmative action, but that's a different discussion.) Second, there are important reasons other than remediation to engage in affirmative action in a given setting. A particular institution and the nation may both have a strong interest in inclusiveness in order to help that institution be more successful on its own terms and for the general benefits to society. Third, the individual benefited by affirmative action may be able to do something for other blacks as a result of his or her new position. We have black entrepreneurs employing African-American workers, black teachers serving inner-city students, and black government officials working to shift public priorities when previously the government paid scant attention to the black underclass.

Oddly, what the two critiques share is a skepticism about the conception of social transformation which we might term "trickle-up incrementalism," in contrast to structural upheaval. The contrast is descriptively important because it determines whether, for example, you see the incremental gains from affirmative action as meaningful, hopeful, and a harbinger of greater progress to come, or as limited, trivial, or even counterproductive. And the contrast is important prescriptively, because it tells us whether those who would be change agents ought to focus on more sweeping and necessarily confrontational strategies.

So one can consider the isolated, sometimes solitary beneficiaries of affirmative action as the vanguard elements of a slowly rising mass. More will follow. It just takes time. It takes a while for people to rise past the obstacles. Twenty-five years of stop-and-go, here-and-there affirmative action and advances in civil rights may not be enough to judge the potential of the trickle-up strategy. On the other hand, one can see the few who have "made it" as destined to be isolated exceptions, believing that only some deeper, more thorough upheaval can transform society enough to help those stuck below the barriers created by race and class. The trickle-up strategy may work but will take too many generations and cost too much misery and wasted human potential.

Where the left and right differ is in their prescriptions for the kind of transformative change required. The conventional left thinks of class struggle and the end of capitalism as we know it. The new conservatives think of a militant orthodoxy of values and culture — stressing personal responsibility, self-help, individualism, the overthrow of state-sponsored welfare dependency, and the virtual extirpation of public altruism. (I have an opinion about this.)

I cannot choose between trickle-up reformism and radical transformation as strategies for racial justice or, for that matter, any other kind of justice. Much depends upon what time frame you believe is relevant and how patient you are, and our brand of democratic capitalism seems flexible enough to reinvent itself when social and political forces require. As the New Deal reformers saw it, for example, the creation of big government — what we now variously call the administrative state or the welfare state — was a shrewd maneuver to protect capitalism from the Depression-fed global wildfires of totalitarianism, fascism, and illiberal collectivism. A brilliant example, you might say, of the evolutionary imperative that one must adapt or die. The dramatic civil rights gains of 1954–68 are perhaps comparable. (And the burst of environmental protectionism may also fit this pattern: it was needed in order to save the planet from capitalism and hence save capitalism from itself.)

But consider these interesting implications of the two schools of thought:

> Trickle-up theory will work only if one optimistically believes that the changes required of the system are within its evolutionary grasp, that the impediments to change that will bring greater justice to the underclass can all be overcome in time. But for a racial pessimist, who considers the distance between the races to be so great and the very

core of our politics so poisoned as to make good solutions unattainable, this trickle-up theory is a snare and a deception.

For a left-leaning racial pessimist, the prescription for class-based transformative upheaval is just as unappealing as trickle-up strategies are, because the poison of racial division undermines the class solidarity needed for successful struggle. A left-leaning racial optimist would simply have to be satisfied that a preferable alternative to democratic capitalism really exists. (I myself have not seen it.)

The right-leaning prescription for salvation, a conservative values-oriented revolution, makes sense if you accept the basic conservative analysis of the situation: that race is not the problem, social pathology is. As a host of conservatives have put it, if you eliminated discrimination and racism tonight, not one person in the black underclass would be better off tomorrow. (And therefore we shouldn't bother to try?) So this conservative presentation for social transformation, like the leftist prescription based on class struggle, is premised on a judgment that race matters, *but not much.*

If this presentation of the various implications is correct, the choice is easy: none of them has much going for it a priori. So the way to choose is to be pragmatic. What seems achievable today, next month, this decade? Some people have a revolutionary vision — what Louis Farrakhan and Pat Buchanan have in common deserves its own book — but most of us know no better than to march, and sometimes run, by putting one foot in front of the other, again and again.

Why am I suspicious of the radicals on the left, even when I share so many of their values? For one, they assert a need for deep structural upheaval but only vaguely define it. Not only is the institutional detail lacking, even the aspiration is uncertain. How much of the order of things must change? Capitalist relations and institutions? Religious orderings of social life? Gender roles? Family structure? And we are to replace these with what? How?

To my mind, the question whether the pillars of capitalism or other major institutions must be brought down should be answered consequentially. If the goal is emancipation of all peoples, how is that most likely to be brought about? To me, thinking as a "race man," this is not in the first instance an ideological inquiry (though an answer requires interpretation, prediction, and hence subjectivity reflecting inchoate ideological presumptions) but, rather, a matter of policy analysis, social empiricism, and trial and error. Plenty of error.

We don't have a good alternative to appropriately reformed democratic capitalism, and we don't have proof that a sweeping transformation is required to achieve racial justice. (We should apply Occam's razor to keep our revolutionary ambitions modest.) And there's certainly no reason to believe that sweeping change would be more achievable than conventional reform. Thus it seems entirely true that the prospects for American racial justice are bound up in the prospects for American democratic capitalism. I fleetingly had other views in my youth, but now I think: Mend it, don't end it.

. . .

Finally, we come to the question of when to end affirmative action. Thomas Sowell has noted that his review of affirmative action in several countries failed to identify a single instance in which it had been dismantled, and he doubted that its proponents would ever willingly let it end here in America.

When will affirmative action end in the United States? If we mean "end entirely and for all situations," the answer is simple: it should end when the justification for it no longer exists, when America has achieved racial justice in reality. Some critics doubt the good faith of those who promise that affirmative action is only temporary and transitional. But it is no more disingenuous or fantastic to promise that affirmative action is temporary than to promise that racial justice is achievable.

President Clinton said it well: "Mend it, don't end it." Affirmative action will remain controversial, and we should expect it to, like any policy addressing an intractable and painful problem. The cure for America's color problem surely can be no easier than the solution to problems of welfare and poverty, environmental protection, or labor-management relations. The continuing controversy—whether flames or embers—is about values and vision. What does America want to see in the mirror? What kind of communities do we want for our children? What dreams will nourish the spirits of the least among us?

We have a history of division, but for the most part it is division based on our perspectives, not our dreams. There is division between the good America and the other America, and almost every heart understands it is a division that impoverishes and, I fear, imperils us all. Faced with that peril, each generation must decide whether to dig defensive trenches or build bridges, and each of us must choose whether to participate in that decision or just let others decide for us and for our children.

I have a child. And I know what kind of America I want for him. I cannot imagine choosing to be a bystander.

Barbara F. Reskin

# From *The Realities of Affirmative Action in Employment*

## Comparisons of Affirmative Action and Nonaffirmative Action Employers

Quantitative and qualitative studies that compared firms with and without affirmative action procedures suggest positive outcomes of affirmative action for women and minorities. For example, recent surveys of employers in Los Angeles, Atlanta, Boston, and Detroit indicate that firms that reportedly considered affirmative action in hiring were ten percent more likely to have hired white women and 20 percent more likely to have hired African-American men than firms that did not practice affirmative action, net of other factors that affected hiring decisions (Holzer and Neumark 1999; Turner 1996, p. 22). There was, however, no effect for African-American or Hispanic women (Holzer and Neumark 1998).

Studies of minorities' and women's representation across jobs in specific firms and industries also point to affirmative action's effectiveness in preventing employment discrimination. For example, women made considerable inroads into nontraditional jobs in industries that the OFCCP had targeted or in which leading firms were subject to court orders, including the banking and steel industries (Deaux and Ullman 1983; Reskin and Roos 1990; Blair-Loy 1996, p. 22). Also, women's representation among managers and officials in Cleveland's five largest banks climbed by more than 20 percent after the OFCCP reviewed the banks' employment practices in 1978 (U.S. Department of Labor 1996, p. 6).

The presidential executive order requiring affirmative action, along with pressure from the EEOC, precipitated sharp gains in African Americans' representation in South Carolina's textile industry (Heckman and Paynor 1989). Xerox Corporation's voluntary affirmative action program

From *The Realities of Affirmative Action in Employment* by Barbara F. Reskin (Washington, DC: American Sociological Association, 1998), 51–58, 75–79.

increased minorities' share of jobs from three percent to 27 percent between 1964 and 1996 (Rand 1996). Affirmative action seniority overrides in
AT&T that stemmed from its 1972 consent decree with the EEOC reduced
job segregation by sex by 14 percent in six years (Northrup and Larson
1979). Merck & Co., by treating its affirmative action efforts like any other
business objective, increased women's representation among employees
and among managers by five percentage points (Bureau of National Affairs
1986, p. 124). During the same period, stimulated by a 1973 discrimination
suit, General Motors's "aggressive affirmative action plan" increased
women's and minorities' share of managerial jobs by four to five percentage points (Bureau of National Affairs 1986, pp. 115–16). A discrimination
suit also spurred the BankAmerica's affirmative action activities. Their
results can be seen in minorities' and women's overrepresentation in management at BankAmerica relative to the industry. In 1985, minorities' and
women's representation in managerial jobs at the bank exceeded industry
averages by eight to 12 percentage points (Bureau of National Affairs 1986,
pp. 103–4).

Affirmative action was also instrumental in curtailing race and sex
discrimination in public law enforcement. Between 1970 and 1990, the
numbers of minority and female police officers in the U.S. increased ten-
fold: from less than 10,000 to 97,000 minorities and from less than 2,000 to
more than 20,000 women (Bendick 1997). Both court-ordered and voluntary affirmative action plans led to less discriminatory hiring, but the effect
of court-ordered plans was greater, presumably because such plans included goals and monitoring (Martin 1991, p. 495). During the 1970s and
1980s — a period during which courts ordered about 40 percent of police
departments to engage in affirmative action because they had systematically discriminated against minorities and women in hiring, and another 42
percent of police departments adopted voluntary plans — minorities' representation among police officers shot up from seven percent to 22.5 percent,
and women's share rose from two to nine percent (Martin 1991).

### Declines in Occupational Segregation

Pervasive job segregation exists and reflects minorities' and women's virtual exclusion from many lines of work. If affirmative action has curtailed
the race and sex discrimination in access to jobs that gave rise to race and
sex segregation, we should see declines in sex and race segregation over the
last quarter century. Segregation indices for 1970, 1980, and 1990 capture
changes in the levels of sex and race segregation during this period.[1] In
1970, the index of occupational segregation by sex was 67, indicating that
about two-thirds of all women would have had to have changed occupa-

tions for the sexes to be similarly distributed across occupations. In 1980, the index was 60, and in 1990 it was 53. After 60 years of fluctuating between 65 and 70 (Gross 1968), the sex segregation index dropped by 20 percent in two decades. The index of occupational segregation for African Americans and whites dropped from 37 in 1970 to 29.5 in 1980, and 27 in 1990 (calculated from U.S. Bureau of the Census 1972, 1983, 1992).[2] This 27-percent decline in occupational segregation by race signals the inroads African Americans made into predominantly white occupations between 1970 and 1990.

Occupational desegregation opened to minorities and women desirable jobs from which they had been excluded. African-American men made particular gains in the skilled crafts. In 1960, one in ten held such jobs, compared with 20.9 percent of white men; by 1970, 15.4 percent of African-American men worked in skilled crafts, compared with 21.9 percent of whites (U.S. Bureau of the Census 1963, table 25, 1973, table 2).[3] African-American women made the greatest headway in clerical occupations.[4] In 1960, 7.4 percent held such jobs, compared with 26 percent in 1990 (U.S. Bureau of the Census 1963, table 3).[5] White women's greatest gains were in managerial and administrative jobs: 5.5 percent were managers and administrators in 1960; 27 percent were managers and administrators by 1990.[6] The proportions of African-American women and men in management rose from two and four percent, respectively, in 1970 to 18.6 and 13.3 percent, respectively, in 1990 (U.S. Bureau of Labor Statistics 1971, 1991). Although many factors have contributed to women's and minorities' increased representation in these jobs, the findings summarized above suggest that, by preventing discrimination, affirmative action has opened thousands of jobs to women and minorities that discrimination had formerly closed to them.

Declining job segregation has helped to narrow the pay gap between white men and men and women of color. For example, in 1969 African-American women who worked full time year round earned only 46 percent of what white men earned; in 1996, they earned 60 percent as much (Browne 1998, table 1). African-American men averaged 70 percent of white men's earnings in 1969; by 1996 the disparity had narrowed to 75 percent. While significant wage disparities persist, the research evidence shows that they have narrowed.

### Are Targets of Affirmative Action Adversely Affected?

In assessing the effectiveness of affirmative action, we must consider whether it adversely affects its beneficiaries by fostering in them or their co-workers the belief that they are not qualified for their jobs (e.g., Steele

1990; O'Neill and O'Neill 1992, p. 103). In a society that subscribes to a meritocratic ideology, people may find it demeaning to get a job because of their sex or race. This section reviews research on whether affirmative action induces self-doubt in members of target groups and on whether others assume that the beneficiaries of affirmative action are unqualified.

### Self-Doubt by Targets

If benefiting from affirmative action leads women and minorities to doubt their abilities, then it defeats its objective of enhancing equal opportunity. According to Shelby Steele (1990), "The effect of preferential treatment — the lowering of normal standards to increase African-American representation — puts African Americans at war with an expanded realm of debilitating doubt, so that the doubt itself becomes an unrecognized preoccupation that undermines their ability to perform." What do the data show?

The beneficiaries of affirmative action should doubt their abilities only if (1) they believe that they obtained a position because of affirmative action, and (2) obtaining a position through affirmative action leads them to question their ability. Available research indicates that seven to eight percent of white women and 20 to 30 percent of African Americans think that they have benefited from affirmative action (Moore 1995; Hochschild 1995, p. 101; Molyneux 1996, p. 17; Verhovek 1997, p. 32).[7] Thus, while some minorities and women are potentially subject to self-doubt that results from believing affirmative action benefited them, most members of the targeted groups should be immune to this source of self-doubt because most do not think that affirmative action has helped them get a job or promotion.

According to laboratory experiments, only women who believe that they were selected for a leadership role entirely on the basis of their sex (almost no research has examined the effect of affirmative action based on race; Crocker and Major 1989; Kravitz, Harrison, Turner, Levine, Chaves, Brannick, Denning, Russell, and Conard 1997, p. 34) suffer adverse psychological effects. Female college students who served as experimental subjects tended to devalue their abilities more when they were told that they were selected solely on the basis of their sex than when they were told that they were selected on the basis of merit (Heilman, Simon, and Repper 1987; Heilman, Block, and Lucas 1992; Heilman 1994; Turner, Fix, and Struyk 1991; for a review, see Kravitz et al. 1997, pp. 33–5).[8] Female managers who believed that they had been promoted mainly because of their sex were less satisfied with their jobs than other women (Nacoste 1990). However, women who believe that sex as well as merit was among the criteria for their selection suffered no negative psychological effects (Major, Feinstein, and Crocker 1994, pp. 133–5; Turner and Pratkanis

1994, p. 63). Importantly, since OFCCP regulations and Supreme Court rulings insist that qualifications be the primary basis for selecting candidates, beneficiaries of affirmative action are selected primarily on the basis of merit.

Further evidence that benefiting from affirmative action does not have serious negative consequences comes from a comparison of the job attitudes of minorities and women whose employers engaged in affirmative action and those whose employers did not. African-American women, African-American men, and white women whose employers practiced some form of affirmative action were as satisfied with their jobs as their counterparts whose employers did not engage in affirmative action, according to a 1990 national survey of Americans (Taylor 1994). This finding is consistent with the laboratory experiments cited above that showed no adverse effects of being chosen partly on the basis of merit as well as sex.

*Stigmatization by Others*
Both experimental studies in which undergraduate students are subjects and surveys of actual workers indicate that people often assume that women and minorities who purportedly got their jobs because of affirmative action are less competent than other women and minorities. For example, managers who lacked information on a hypothetical female worker's performance rated women labeled as "affirmative action hires" as less competent than those not so labeled (Heilman et al. 1992, p. 541). These negative effects suggest that affirmative action and equal employment policies lead to the presumption that standards have been relaxed.

However, according to a 1995 Gallup poll, just eight percent of white women, 19 percent of African-American women, and 29 percent of African-American men have *ever* felt that their colleagues at work *or* school questioned their abilities or qualifications because of affirmative action (Crosby and Herzberger 1996, p. 62). In addition, although African-American male survey respondents employed in affirmative action firms described their evaluations as less positive than African-American men employed in nonaffirmative action firms, the opposite pattern held for African-American women (Taylor 1994).

Thus, the data indicate that stigmatization by others is not widespread. Although some members of target groups feel stigmatized by affirmative action, they are in the minority, in part because few members of target groups think that affirmative action has affected them. For instance, a survey of female top executives revealed that 22 percent felt that affirmative action had both positive and negative effects on their careers, but just one percent felt that affirmative action's effects had been entirely negative (Catalyst 1996, p. 55).

Importantly, the tendency of some people to stigmatize members of groups targeted for affirmative action does not necessarily mean that affirmative action is the real cause of the stigmatization. Sex and race stereotypes in combination with the sex and race labeling of jobs foster a presumption that white men obtain customarily-male jobs because they are the most qualified, although most obtain their jobs partly through personal contacts. The cultural devaluation of women and minorities seems to give these groups, but not white men, the burden of proving that they are qualified for jobs that white men usually perform.

In contexts in which discrimination continues to restrict minorities' and women's access to jobs and stereotypes cast doubt on their abilities, female and minority workers who challenge exclusionary practices may find themselves in a lose-lose situation: Either they are excluded because of discrimination with the attendant psychological and economic costs, or affirmative action prevents discriminatory exclusion but introduces the risk of stigmatization. Eliminating affirmative action would prevent the second kind of cost, while raising the likelihood of the first.[9] Fortunately, affirmative action employers can minimize the stigmatization of members of targeted groups by taking steps to ensure that all employees understand that qualifications are the primary consideration in all job assignments and promotions.

### Other Effects on Members of Targeted Groups

By opening jobs to minorities and women from which they have been excluded, affirmative action allows them to acquire skills and experience that will enhance their productivity and add to the nation's stock of human capital. Moreover, the existence of affirmative action programs raises minorities' and women's aspirations. According to a large body of research, people's perceptions of opportunity affect their aspirations. Just as people respond to blocked opportunities by lowering their aspirations, they pursue opportunities that are open to them (Kanter 1977; Reskin and Hartmann 1986; Markham, Harlan, and Hackett 1987; Jacobs 1989; Cassirer and Reskin 1998). By convincing minorities and white women that employers will not discriminate against them, affirmative action encourages minorities and women to pursue jobs formerly closed to them (Pettigrew and Martin 1987, p. 51; Reskin and Roos 1990).

. . .

**Affirmative Action and American Commerce**

Does affirmative action curb productivity, as some critics have charged? On the one hand, affirmative action could impede productivity if it forces employers to hire or promote marginally qualified and unqualified workers, or if the paperwork associated with affirmative action programs is burdensome. On the other hand, employers who assign workers to jobs based on their qualifications rather than their sex or race should make more efficient use of workers' abilities and hence should be more productive than those who use discriminatory employment practices (Becker 1971; Leonard 1984a; Donohue 1986). Affirmative action could also increase profitability by introducing varied points of view or helping firms broaden their markets (Cox and Blake 1991; Watson, Kumar, and Michaelson 1993).

*Effects on Productivity*
There is no evidence that affirmative action reduces productivity or that workers hired under affirmative action are less qualified than other workers. In the first place, affirmative action plans that compromise valid educational and job requirements are illegal. Hiring unqualified workers or choosing a less qualified person over a more qualified one because of their race or sex is illegal and is not condoned in the name of affirmative action (U.S. Department of Labor, Employment Standards Administration n.d. (b), p. 2). Second, to the extent that affirmative action gives women and minority men access to jobs that more fully exploit their productive capacity, their productivity and that of their employers should increase.

Although many Americans believe that affirmative action means that less qualified persons are hired and promoted (Verhovek 1997, p. 32), the evidence does not bear this out. According to a study of more than 3,000 workers hired in entry-level jobs in a cross-section of firms in Atlanta, Boston, Detroit, and Los Angeles, the performance evaluations of women and minorities hired under affirmative action did not differ from those of white men or female or minority workers for whom affirmative action played no role in hiring (Holzer and Neumark 1998). In addition, Columbus, Ohio, female and minority police officers hired under an affirmative action consent decree performed as well as white men (Kern 1996). Of nearly 300 corporate executives surveyed in 1979, 72 percent believed that minority hiring did not impair productivity ("Labor Letter," 1979); 41 percent of CEOs surveyed in 1995 said affirmative action improved corporate productivity (Crosby and Herzberger 1996, p. 86).[10]

Of the handful of studies that address the effect of affirmative action on productivity, none suggests a negative effect of the employment of women or minorities on productivity. First, the increasing representation of female and minority male workers between 1966 and 1977 and between 1984 and 1988 did not affect firms' productivity (Leonard 1984a; Conrad 1995). Second, in the context of policing, the proportions of minority or female officers are unrelated to measures of departments' effectiveness (Lovrich, Steel, and Hood 1986, p. 70; Steel and Lovrich 1987, p. 67). Third, according to a sophisticated analysis of 1990 data on establishments' and workers' characteristics, there is no relationship between firms' employment of women and their productivity in smaller plants, but in plants with more market power (and hence the capacity to discriminate), the more women plants employed, the better the firms' performance (Hellerstein, Neumark, and Troske 1998).

Studies assessing the effect of firms' racial makeup on their profits also show no effects of affirmative action on productivity. An analysis of 100 of Chicago's largest firms over a 13-year period found no statistically significant relationship between the firms' share of minority workers and their profit margins or return on equity (McMillen 1995). This absence of an association is inconsistent with companies using lower standards when hiring African-American employees. Finally, according to a study that compared the market performance of the 100 firms with best and worst records of hiring and promoting women and minorities, the former averaged an 18-percent return on investments, whereas the latter's average returns were below eight percent (U.S. Department of Labor, OFCCP, Glass Ceiling Commission 1995, pp. 14, 61).[11]

*Costs to Business*
Estimates of the price tag of affirmative action range from a low of hundreds of millions of dollars to a high of $26 billion (Brimelow and Spencer 1993).[12] More realistic estimates put enforcement and compliance costs at about $1.9 billion (Leonard 1994, p. 34; Conrad 1995, pp. 37–8). According to Andrew Brimmer (1995, p. 12), former Governor of the Federal Reserve Board, the inefficient use of African Americans' productive capacity (as indicated by their education, training, and experience) costs the economy 70 times this much: About $138 billion annually which is about 2.15 percent of the gross national product. Adding the cost of sex discrimination against white women would substantially increase the estimated cost of discrimination because white women outnumber African-American men and women in the labor force by about three to one. The more affirmative action reduces race and sex discrimination, the lower its costs relative to the savings it engenders.

The affirmative action that the Federal executive order requires of Federal contractors adds to their paperwork. Companies with at least $50,000 in Federal contracts that employ at least 50 employees must provide written affirmative action plans that include goals and timetables, based on an annual analysis of their utilization of their labor pool. They must also provide specified information to the OFCCP and keep detailed records on the composition of their jobs and job applicants by race and sex. In response to an OFCCP survey soliciting their criticisms of the program, about one in eight Federal contractors complained about the paperwork burden (Stephanopoulos and Edley 1995, section 6.3). Keeping the records required by the OFCCP encourages bureaucratization of human resource practices. As noted, informal employment practices, while cheaper in the short run, are also more subject to discriminatory bias and hence cost firms efficiency. Thus, implicit in the logic of the OFCCP's requirements is the recognition that formalizing personnel practices helps to reduce discrimination.

*Business Support*
U.S. business has supported affirmative action for at least 15 years. The Reagan administration's efforts to curtail the contract compliance program in the early 1980s drew strong opposition from the corporate sector (Bureau of National Affairs 1986). Among the groups that went on record as opposing cutbacks in Federal affirmative action programs was the National Association of Manufacturers, a major organization of U.S. employers ("Groups at Odds," 1995, p. AA-2). All but six of 128 heads of major corporations indicated that they would retain their affirmative action plans if the Federal government ended affirmative action (Noble 1986, p. B4). A 1996 survey showed similar levels of corporate support for affirmative action: 94 percent of CEOs surveyed said that affirmative action had improved their hiring procedures, 53 percent said it had improved marketing, and — as noted above — 41 percent said it had improved productivity (Crosby and Herzberger 1996, p. 86). The business community's favorable stance toward affirmative action is also seen in the jump in stock prices for firms recognized by the OFCCP for their effective affirmative action programs (Wright, Ferris, Hiller, and Kroll 1995, p. 281).

Perhaps the most telling sign of business support for affirmative action is the diffusion of affirmative action practices from Federal contractors to noncontractors. As noncontractors have recognized the efficiency or market payoffs associated with more objective employment practices and a more diverse workforce, many have voluntarily implemented some affirmative action practices (Fisher 1985).

**Affirmative Action and Other Stakeholders**

The consequences of affirmative action reach beyond workers and employers by increasing the pools of skilled minority and female workers. When affirmative action prompts employers to hire minorities or women for positions that serve the public, it can bring services to communities that would otherwise be underserved. For example, African-American and Hispanic physicians are more likely than whites and Anglos to practice in minority communities (Komaromy, Grumbach, Drake, Vranizan, Lurie, Keane, and Bindman 1996). Graduates of the Medical School at the University of California at San Diego who were admitted under a special admissions program were more likely to serve inner-city and rural communities and saw more poor patients than those admitted under the regular procedures (Penn, Russell, and Simon 1986).

Women's and minorities' employment in nontraditional jobs also raises the aspirations of other members of excluded groups by providing role models and by signaling that jobs are open to them. Some minorities and women do not pursue jobs or promotions because they expect to encounter discrimination (Mayhew 1968, p. 313). By reducing the perception that discriminatory barriers block access to certain lines of work, affirmative action curtails this self selection (Reskin and Roos 1990, p. 305). In addition, the economic gains provided by better jobs permit beneficiaries to invest in the education of the next generation.

## NOTES

1. For a definition of the segregation index, see Chapter 2 [in the original book].

2. Between 1970 and 1990 the index of race segregation declined from 38.3 to 28.6 among men and from 36.6 to 25.3 among women. During the same period, the index of sex segregation fell from 67.9 to 51.9 among African Americans and from 67.6 to 60.2 among whites (Reskin, Hickey, and Wheeler 1998).

3. African-American and white women have made little headway in the skilled trades. Only 0.8 percent of African-American women and one percent of white women held craft occupations in 1970; twenty years later, their representation had inched up to 2.3 and 2.1 percent (U.S. Bureau of the Census, 1972, 1992).

4. In 1980, the U.S. Census Bureau renamed clerical occupations "administrative support" occupations. The administrative-support category largely comprises clerical occupations.

5. During the same period, the percentage of black men employed in clerical occupations rose from 5 to 9 percent (U.S. Bureau of the Census, 1963, table 3).

6. Smith and Welch (1984) speculated, based on data for federal contractors, that employers reclassified some customarily female jobs as managerial to give the impression of more advancement for female employees.

7. These rates are consistent with the modest effects of affirmative action reported above.

8. Male research subjects who were told that they were chosen for a leadership role solely on the basis of their sex disregarded this information. Their failure to express any ill effects at having been selected entirely because of their sex may stem from the fact that they rejected this as implausible (Heilman et al. 1987; Major et al. 1994, p. 138). Other experimental research suggests that believing that one's

selection was based entirely on preference has negative psychological consequences for experimental subjects with low self-esteem (Heilman et al. 1990).

9. Unfortunately, experimental studies have not compared the psychological effects of selection-based merit plus sex or race with the effects of sex- or race-based rejection, which remains the most likely alternative.

10. No data were provided on the proportion who believed that affirmative action hampered productivity.

11. Although firms' stock prices fall after the media report a discrimination suit, they rebound within a few days (Hersch 1991; Wright et al. 1995).

12. The $26 billion estimate includes the budgets of the OFCCP, the EEOC, other Federal agencies' affirmative action related activities, and private firms' compliance costs estimated at $20 million for each million of public funds budgeted for enforcement (Brimelow and Spencer 1993). Arguably, the EEOC's budget — indeed all enforcement costs — should be chalked up to the cost of discrimination, not the cost of affirmative action.

*William G. Bowen and Derek Bok*

# From *The Shape of the River: Long-Term Consequences of Considering Race in College and University Admissions*

Stretching from St. Paul to New Orleans, Mark Twain's Mississippi winds for twelve hundred miles through fog, rapids, slow eddies, sand-bars, bends, and hidden bluffs. Drawing upon his own experiences on the Mississippi, Twain created an image of the river as both physically central to the United States and symbolically central to the progress of the country. The image of the river is also central to the story of our book, which is concerned with the flow of talent—particularly of talented black men and women—through the country's system of higher education and on into the marketplace and the larger society.

The image most commonly invoked in discussions of this process is the "pipeline." We often hear of the importance of keeping young people moving through the "pipeline" from elementary school to high school to college, on through graduate and professional schools, and into jobs, family responsibilities, and civic life. But this image is misleading, with its connotation of a smooth, well defined, and well understood passage. It is more helpful to think of the nurturing of talent as a process akin to moving down a winding river, with rock-strewn rapids and slow channels, muddy at times and clear at others. Particularly when race is involved, there is nothing simple, smooth, or highly predictable about the education of young people.

While riverboat pilots on the Mississippi navigated "point to point"—only as far as they could see into the next bend—they had to know every depth, every deceptive shoal, and every hidden snag of the river. Moreover, since the boats ran throughout the night, in high water and low, and both up the river and down it, these pilots had to know the river's features in every imaginable condition, and from either direction. Even though they could only steer through what they saw in front of them, they had to understand how the bend that they were navigating at any moment fit into the shape of a twelve-hundred-mile river.

The college admissions process and the educational experience that follows it are similarly complex. Most recently, debate about the use of race as a criterion has centered on the question of who "merits" or "deserves" a place in the freshman class. At this one bend in the river, prior grades and numerical test scores offer a tempting means of defining qualifications, since they are easily compiled and compared. But what do they really tell us, and what are we trying to predict? Much more, surely, than first-year grades or even graduation from one college or another. It is the contributions that individuals make throughout their lives and the broader impact of higher education on the society that are finally most relevant.

. . .

## The Nature of This Study

Many Americans are uncomfortable about the use of race as a factor in admitting students to selective colleges and professional schools. Critics have attacked the policy on several grounds. They maintain that it is wrong for universities to exclude white applicants with high grades and impressive test scores while accepting minority applicants with lower grades and scores. They point out that admissions officers sometimes accept minority applicants who are not disadvantaged but come from wealthier, more privileged homes and better schools than some applicants who are rejected. They claim that all such policies accentuate racial differences, intensify prejudice, and interfere with progress toward a color-blind society. They assert that admitting minority applicants with lower grades and scores may stigmatize and demoralize the very students that the policy attempts to help, by forcing them to compete with classmates of greater academic ability.

Defenders of race-sensitive admissions respond with arguments of their own. They insist that such policies are justified to atone for a legacy of oppression and to make up for continuing discrimination in the society. They point out that admissions officers have long deviated from standardized test scores and prior grades to favor athletes, legacies, and other applicants with special characteristics that are deemed desirable. They argue that admitting a diverse class gives students of all races a better preparation for living and working in an increasingly diverse society.

Until now, the debate has proceeded without much empirical evidence as to the effects of such policies and their consequences for the students involved. We seek to remedy this deficiency by drawing on an extensive study of students from a number of academically selective colleges and universities — places where the debate over race-sensitive institutions has been played out in "real time." We are concerned primarily with the performance, in college and after college, of black and white students admitted to these schools.

In setting forth the "facts," as best we can discern them, we recognize that all data of this kind are subject to many interpretations. Moreover, even considering such questions can antagonize people on both sides of the argument who believe that the "right principles" are so compelling that no amount of evidence can change their minds. Plainly, data take us only so far in considering this subject. Individuals who agree on "the facts" may still end up disagreeing about what should be done because of overriding differences in values. As a result, we have no expectation that the analyses presented in this study will resolve complex issues to everyone's satisfaction. But we do hope that our research can inform the debate by framing questions carefully and presenting what we have learned about outcomes.
. . .

**The College and Beyond Database**

Much of the new content in this study derives from exploitation of a rich database called College and Beyond (C&B). This database was built by The Andrew W. Mellon Foundation over nearly four years (from the end of 1994 through 1997) as a part of the Foundation's broader interest in supporting research in higher education. . . . In brief, the part of the database used in this study contains the records of more than eighty thousand undergraduate students who matriculated at twenty-eight academically selective colleges and universities in the fall of 1951, the fall of 1976, and the fall of 1989. Created on the explicit understanding that the Foundation would not release or publish data that identified either individual students or individual schools, it is a "restricted access database."

The "in-college" component of the database was compiled from individual student records in collaboration with the participating colleges and universities. For each entering student (except those few cases where records had been lost or were incomplete), the database contains information available at the time the student was admitted, including race, gender, test scores, rank in high school class, and, for many students, information about family background. It also includes records of academic performance in college, compiled mainly from transcripts, which have been linked to the admissions data. Each student record was coded to indicate graduation status (when and if the student graduated), major field of study, grade point average, and whether the student participated in athletics or other time-intensive extracurricular activities.

For many of these same matriculants, we also have extensive survey data describing their subsequent histories (advanced degrees earned, sector of employment, occupation, earned income and family income, involvement in civic activities, marital status and number of children).

. . .

In the fall of 1976, eight of the twenty-eight C&B schools had average combined SAT scores of more than 1250 (before the recentering of the scores by ETS which has raised all the scores). Nationally, we estimate that there were only twenty schools in this category, and the eight C&B schools enrolled 40 percent of all freshmen entering these extremely selective colleges and universities. Another thirteen of the C&B schools had average scores of 1150 to 1250; nationally, there were fifty-three schools in this range, and the thirteen C&B schools enrolled 34 percent of all their freshmen. The remaining seven C&B schools had average SAT scores in the 100–1149 range, and they enrolled 7 percent of all freshmen who entered the 241 schools with SAT scores in this range.[1] In short, the C&B student population contains a sufficiently large fraction of the total number of matriculants at the most selective colleges and universities that we are reasonably confident that our findings apply generally to this set of institutions and especially to those with average scores above 1150.

. . .

Until now, there has been little hard evidence to confirm the belief of educators in the value of diversity. Our survey data throw new light on the extent of interaction occurring on campuses today and on how positively the great majority of students regard opportunities to learn from those with different points of view, backgrounds, and experiences. Admission "on the merits" would be short-sighted if admissions officers were precluded from crediting this potential contribution to the education of all students.

Imposition of a race-neutral standard would produce very troubling results from this perspective: such a policy would reduce dramatically the proportion of black students on campus — probably shrinking their number to less than 2 percent of all matriculants at the most selective colleges and professional schools. Moreover, our examination of the application and admissions files indicates that such substantial reductions in the number of black matriculants, with attendant losses in educational opportunity for all students, would occur without leading to any appreciable improvement in the academic credentials of the remaining black students and would lead to only a modest change in the overall academic profile of the institutions.[2]

**Addressing Long-Term Societal Needs**

Virtually all colleges and universities seek to educate students who seem likely to become leaders and contributing members of society. Identifying such students is another essential aspect of admitting "on the merits," and here again race is clearly relevant. There is widespread agreement that our country continues to need the help of its colleges and universities in building a society in which access to positions of leadership and responsibility is less limited by an individual's race than it is today.

The success of C&B colleges and universities in meeting this objective has been documented extensively in this study. It is helpful to "look back up the river" from a slightly different vantage point. Some of the consequences of mandating a race-neutral standard of admission can be better understood by constructing a rough profile of the approximately 700 black matriculants in the '76 entering cohort at the C&B schools whom we estimate would have been rejected had such a standard been in effect. Our analysis suggests that:[3]

Over 225 members of this group of retrospectively rejected black matriculants went on to attain professional degrees or doctorates.

About 70 are now doctors, and roughly 60 are lawyers.

Nearly 125 are business executives.

Well over 300 are leaders of civic activities.

The average earnings of the individuals in the group exceeds $71,000.

Almost two-thirds of the group (65 percent) were *very* satisfied with their undergraduate experience.

Many of these students would have done well no matter where they went to school, and we cannot know in any precise way how their careers would have been affected as a result. But we do know that there is a statistically significant association, on an "other things equal" basis, between attendance at the most selective schools within the C&B universe and a variety of accomplishments during college and in later life. Generally speaking, the more selective the school, the more the student achieved subsequently. Also, we saw that C&B students as a group earned appreciably more money than did the subgroup of students in our national control with mostly As, which suggests that going to a C&B school conferred a considerable premium on all C&B students, and probably an especially high premium on black students. Black C&B students were also more likely than black college graduates in general to become leaders of community and social service organizations. These findings suggest that reducing

the number of black matriculants at the C&B schools would almost certainly have had a decidedly negative effect on the subsequent careers of
many of these students and on their contributions to civic life as well.

Even more severe effects would result from insisting on race-neutral
admissions policies in professional schools. In law and medicine, all schools
are selective. As a consequence, the effect of barring any consideration of
race would be the exclusion of more than half of the existing minority student
population from these professions. Race-neutral admissions policies would
reduce the number of black students in the most selective schools of law and
medicine to less than 1 percent of all students. Since major law firms and
medical centers often limit their recruitment to the most selective schools,
this outcome would deal a heavy blow to efforts to prepare future black
leaders for the professions.

But what about the other students (most of them presumably white)
who would have taken the places of these retrospectively rejected black
students in selective colleges and professional schools? There is every reason
to believe that they, too, would have done well, in school and afterwards,
though probably not as well as the regularly admitted white students (who
were, after all, preferred to them in the admissions process). Still, on the
basis of the evidence in this study, the excluded white male students might
have done at least as well as their retrospectively rejected black classmates,
and probably even better in terms of average earnings.[4] On the other hand,
fewer of the "retrospectively accepted" white women would have been employed, and those who were employed would have earned about the same
amount of money as the retrospectively rejected black women. Fewer of the
additional white students, women and men, would have been involved in
volunteer activities, especially in leadership positions.

Would society have been better off if additional numbers of whites and
Asian Americans had been substituted for minority students in this fashion? That is the central question, and it cannot be answered by data alone.

Fundamental judgments have to be made about societal needs, values,
and objectives. When a distinguished black educator visited the Mellon
Foundation, he noted, with understandable pride, that his son had done
brilliantly in college and was being considered for a prestigious graduate
award in neuroscience. "My son," the professor said, "needs no special
consideration; he is so talented that he will make it on his own." His
conclusion was that we should be indifferent to whether his son or any
of the white competitors got the particular fellowship in question. We
agreed that, in all likelihood, all of these candidates would benefit from
going to the graduate school in question and, in time, become excellent
scientists or doctors. Still, one can argue with the conclusion reached by the
parent. "Your son will do fine," another person present at the meeting said,

"but that isn't the issue. *He may not need us, but we need him!* Why? Because there is only one of him."

That mild exaggeration notwithstanding, the relative scarcity of talented black professional is all too real. It seemed clear to a number of us that day, and it probably seems clear to many others, that American society needs the high-achieving black graduates who will provide leadership in every walk of life. This is the position of many top officials concerned with filling key positions in government, of CEOs who affirm that they would continue their minority recruitment programs whether or not there were a legal requirement to do so, and of bar associations, medical associations, and other professional organizations that have repeatedly stressed the importance of attracting more minority members into their fields. In view of these needs, we are not indifferent to which student gets the graduate fellowship.

Neither of the authors of this study has any sympathy with quotas or any belief in mandating the proportional representation of groups of people, defined by race or any other criterion, in positions of authority. Nor do we include ourselves among those who support race-sensitive admissions as compensation for a legacy of racial discrimination.[5] We agree emphatically with the sentiment expressed by Mamphela Ramphele, vice chancellor of the University of Cape Town in South Africa, when she said: "Everyone deserves opportunity; no one deserves success."[6] But we remain persuaded that present racial disparities in outcomes are dismayingly disproportionate. At the minimum, this country needs to maintain the progress now being made in educating larger numbers of black professionals and black leaders.

Selective colleges and universities have made impressive contributions at both undergraduate and graduate levels. To take but a single illustration: since starting to admit larger numbers of black students in the late 1960s, the Harvard Law School has numbered among its black graduates more than one hundred partners in law firms, more than ninety black alumni/ae with the title of Chief Executive Officer, Vice President, or General Counsel of a corporation, more than seventy professors, at least thirty judges, two members of Congress, the mayor of a major American city, the head of the Office of Management and Budget, and an Assistant U.S. Attorney General. We have documented more systematically the accomplishments of the nearly 1,900 black '76 matriculants at the twenty-eight C&B schools, and the evidence of high achievement is overwhelming—there is no other word for it. These individuals are still in their late thirties, having entered college just over twenty years ago. We shall be very surprised if their record of achievement is not magnified many times as they gain seniority and move up various institutional ladders.[7] If, at the end of the day, the question is whether the most selective colleges and universities have succeeded in educating sizable numbers of minority students who have already achieved considerable success and seem likely in time to occupy positions of leadership throughout society, we have no problem in answering the question. Absolutely.

There is a need to make clear choices. Here is perhaps the clearest choice. Let us suppose that rejecting, on race-neutral grounds, more than half of the black students who otherwise would attend these institutions would raise the probability of acceptance for another white student from 25 percent to, say, 27 percent at the most selective colleges and universities. Would we, as a society, be better off? Considering both the educational benefits of diversity and the need to include far larger numbers of black graduates in the top ranks of the business, professional, governmental, and not-for-profit institutions that shape our society, we do not think so.[8]

. . .

## How Fast Are We Heading Downstream?

Final questions to ponder concern a longer sweep of the river. What is our ultimate objective? How much progress has been made? How far do we still have to go? Along with many others, we look forward to a day when arguments in favor of race-sensitive admissions policies will have become unnecessary. Almost everyone, on all sides of this debate, would agree that in an ideal world race would be an irrelevant consideration. As a black friend said almost thirty years ago: "Our ultimate objective should be a situation in which every individual, from every background, feels *unself-consciously included.*"

Many who agree with Justice Blackmun's aphorism, "To get beyond racism, we must first take account of race," would be comforted if it were possible to predict, with some confidence, when that will no longer be necessary. But we do not know how to make such a prediction, and we would caution against adopting arbitrary timetables that fail to take into account how deep-rooted are the problems associated with race in America.

At the same time, it is reassuring to see, even within the C&B set of institutions, the changes that have occurred between the admission of the '76 and '89 cohorts. Over that short span of time, the average SAT scores of black matriculants at the C&B schools went up 68 points—a larger gain than that of white matriculants. The overall black graduation rate, which was already more than respectable in the '76 cohort (71 percent), rose to 79 percent. Enrollment in the most highly regarded graduate and professional schools has continued to increase. The '89 black matriculants are even more active in civic affairs (relative to their white classmates) than were the

'76 black matriculants. Appreciation for the education they received and for what they learned from diversity is voiced even more strongly by the '89 cohort than by their '76 predecessors.

Whatever weight one attaches to such indicators, and to others drawn from national data, the trajectory is clear. To be sure, there have been mistakes and disappointments. There is certainly much work for colleges and universities to do in finding more effective ways to improve the academic performance of minority students. But, overall, we conclude that academically selective colleges and universities have been highly successful in using race-sensitive admissions policies to advance educational goals important to them and societal goals important to everyone. Indeed, we regard these admissions policies as an impressive example of how venerable institutions with established ways of operating can adapt to serve newly perceived needs. Progress has been made and continues to be made. We are headed downstream, even though there may still be miles to go before the river empties, finally, into the sea.

## NOTES

1. Estimates of the number of institutions in each SAT interval are based on data provided by the Higher Education Research Institute at UCLA.

2. While it is, of course, possible for an institution to be so committed to enrolling a diverse student population that it enrolls unprepared candidates who can be predicted to do poorly, we do not believe that this is a consequential problem today in most academically selective institutions. Three pieces of evidence are relevant: (1) the close correspondence between the academic credentials of those students who would be retrospectively rejected under a race-neutral standard and those who would be retained; (2) the modest associations (within this carefully selected population) of the test scores and high school grades of black matriculants at the C&B schools with their in-college and after-college performance; and (3) the remarkably high graduation rates of black C&B students—judged by any national standard.

3. We first estimated how many black C&B matriculants within each SAT interval would have been "bumped" from each selectivity tier of C&B schools, and then used the "average" characteristics of each of the cells to estimate the numbers of retrospectively rejected students who are now doctors, and so on. Even more black students in the '89 cohort would have been retrospectively rejected, and a similar mode of analysis suggests that many of these recent matriculants are already making a mark in graduate schools and civic activities.

4. The fact that white male C&B graduates continue to command a modestly higher level of earnings than their black classmates who graduated with the same grades, majors, and so on, is worthy of much more study. At least as intriguing is the fact that black male graduates of C&B schools earn, on average, *more than twice* as much as black graduates nationwide. In short, the C&B earnings premium is much higher for black male matriculants than for whites. This striking finding has

led one commentator on our manuscript to suggest that C&B schools are underinvesting in talented black students, since the apparent value added is so high. We are reluctant to come to this strong a conclusion, since many factors need to be taken into account in explaining the differences in earnings premiums. But the extremely high black C&B premium is surely highly suggestive.

5. Justice Thurgood Marshall made such an argument in the *Bakke* case in urging his colleagues on the Supreme Court to uphold the racial quotas by the University of California, Davis, Medical School; in his view, such programs were simply a way "to remedy the effects of centuries of unequal treatment. . . . I do not believe that anyone can truly look into America's past and still find that a remedy for the effects of that past is impermissible" (438 U.S. at p. 402). Understandable as this argument may seem against a historical background of slavery and segregation, it did not prevail because the remedy is not precise enough to be entirely just in its application. Not every minority student who is admitted will have suffered from substantial discrimination, and the excluded white and Asian applicants are rarely responsible for the racial injustices of the past and have sometimes had to struggle against considerable handicaps of their own. For these reasons, a majority of justices in the *Bakke* case rejected Marshall's reasoning, although similar arguments continue to be heard.

6. Mamphela Ramphele, "Equity and Excellence — Strange Bedfellows? A Case Study of South African Higher Education." Paper presented at The Princeton Conference on Higher Education, March 21–23, 1996.

7. The widely perceived need for more black executives and professionals creates one danger that should be recognized explicitly: some black candidates may be "overpromoted" by firms or individuals too eager to "do the right thing" or even to "look good." No one benefits when this happens. Fortunately, this potential problem has been helped by the increase in the number of well-qualified black candidates and the experience gained by many institutions in judging people's abilities. The obverse problem — a reluctance to give black candidates a chance to succeed or fail in demanding positions — is probably still the more serious one.

8. This emphasis on the consequences of rejecting race-neutral policies will seem misplaced to some of the most thoughtful critics of affirmative action, who will argue that their objection to race-based policies is an objection in principle: in their view, no one's opportunities should be narrowed, even by an iota, by reference to the individual's race. We respect this line of argument. However, we do not agree, "in principle," that colleges and universities should ignore the practical effects of one set of decisions or another when making difficult decisions about who "merits" a place in the class. The clash here is principle versus principle, not principle versus expediency. In making admissions decisions, what is right in principle depends on how one defines the mission of the educational institution involved. For us, the missions of colleges and universities have strong educational and public policy aspects and do not consist solely of conferring benefits on particular individuals.

*Claude M. Steele*

# Expert Testimony in Defense of Affirmative Action

Standardized admissions tests such as the SAT, the ACT, and the LSAT are of limited value in evaluating "merit" or determining admissions qualifications of all students, but particularly for African American, Hispanic, and American Indian applicants for whom systematic influences make these tests even less diagnostic of their scholastic potential. The first part of this caution — that the test should not be relied upon too heavily in general admissions — is a standard recommendation of the companies that produce these tests, but is also based on extensive evidence documenting the limited predictiveness of these tests. This is not surprising given that these tests are not designed to measure innate ability nor mastery of a specified curriculum. Instead, standardized tests measure developed skills.

The second part of the caution with respect to standardized tests — that use of these tests with minority applicants is especially unreliable — is based on longstanding research, including work done in my own laboratory over the past 10 years, showing that experiences tied to one's racial and ethnic identity can artificially depress standardized test performance. Importantly, these effects go beyond any effects of socioeconomic disadvantage, affecting even the best prepared, most invested students from these groups who often come from middle-class backgrounds. Relying on these tests too extensively in the admissions process will preempt the admission of a significant portion of highly qualified minority students. In making this argument, I will address three issues: The nature of the mental capacity measured by these tests; how well these tests predict performance in higher education for all students; and reasons African American, Hispanic, and American Indian students are more likely to underperform on these tests.

Reprinted with permission from Elizabeth M. Barry, Associate Vice President and Deputy General Counsel, The University of Michigan.

## I. What Kind of Capacity Is Measured by Standardized Admissions Tests?

1. *How are the SAT, ACT, and LSAT designed?* To understand what these tests do and do not measure, it is important first to understand how they are constructed. In the first step, a group of professional item writers and content area experts generate a large pool of test items in the areas covered by the test. In this process, the test makers are guided by general guidelines about what skills and knowledge are critical to succeeding in a given area. But these guidelines are not derived from some clearly specified theory or knowledge of how to measure intelligence or scholastic aptitude in these areas. They are settled on, for the most part, by consensus among the item generators and the board of area experts who they consult.

Next, these items are given to a norming sample of people who are selected for either being a representative or a random sample of the population for whom the test is to be used. Roughly speaking, items that correlate with school grades in this norming sample are kept on the test and items that do not correlate well with grades in this sample are dropped from the test. For example, correct answers given on test items involving algebra by a student who received high grades in his or her algebra classes would be kept because they correlated positively with school success. In this way, items are identified that, for this population, are associated with school success, or in testing parlance, are "predictive" of school success. The resulting test can then be administered in this population with the feature that one's score on it will be somewhat predictive of the grades one will achieve. Like most standardized scholastic tests, the SAT, ACT, and LSAT are all constructed in this way.

2. *What do these tests measure?* The overriding implication of this construction procedure is that it is difficult to answer this question with a precise, conceptual definition. As has been classically said, "scholastic aptitude is what scholastic aptitude tests measure." The content of the test is not derived from a clear conception of the aptitude under test, and the inclusion of items on the test is decided empirically — by which items correlate with school grades in the norming sample. To develop a conceptual understanding of the mental capacities measured by the test, one would have to do what test researchers do: Work backwards by trying to discern through factor analysis of the items selected what underlying capacities they measure.

Two things about the nature of these tests that bear on their use in college and law school admissions can be said with certainty. First, based on this test construction methodology it is clear that the items on these tests measure what has to be substantially learned or "developed" skills and knowledge. Many factors including heredity may underlie scholastic aptitude, but even the highest estimates of hereditary influence allow for substantial influence of experiential factors. This means that one's performance on these tests can be influenced by one's experience, by one's cultural background, by one's access to schooling and the cultural perspectives, attitudes, and know-hows that might favor test performance, by the extent to which one's peers value school achievement, by the nature of one's dinner table conversation, and so on. This point will be important to my later discussion of the role of race and ethnicity in influencing performance on these tests. In addressing those issues, it is important to emphasize that the SAT, ACT, and LSAT are not tests of innate ability that are impervious to experiential influences. Quite the opposite is true.

The second point about test content that can be made with certainty is that, in addition to not measuring mental capacity, neither are they achievement tests: they are not constructed to test how much one has learned from a specifiable curriculum. Rather, they are described by their makers as "aptitude" tests. I have just explained how difficult it is to conceptually define the "aptitude" they measure (other than to say that it is a measure of test-taking aptitude). But it is not the case that, not measuring a specifiable aptitude, they do measure achievement or how much one has learned in school. Ours is the only nation in the world that uses aptitude tests in higher education admissions rather than tests that measure achievement — how much a person has learned in earlier schooling, which are typically better predictors of success in higher education than aptitude tests.

In sum, then, as the companies that make them acknowledge, the SAT, ACT, and LSAT measure a set of scholastic skills that are neither innate nor directly influenced by school curricula. Thus the value of these tests in informing admissions decisions depends not on assessing some well-defined talent or knowledge base, but solely on their empirically determined ability to predict college or law school grades. How well, then, do they predict these grades?

## II. How Good Are Standardized Admission Tests at Predicting Success in Higher Education?

The SAT is popularly assumed to measure such a singularly important component of academic merit as to mandate its centrality in the admissions process. Among the most common rationales for using it to make admissions decisions, in addition to the use of school grades, is that it taps a form of scholastic aptitude that is not dependent on the quality of one's high school curriculum — thus the idea that it measures an underlying, if not innate, aptitude. In contrast to most people's expectations, however, the SAT in fact measures only about 18% (ranging from 7% to 30%) of the factors that determine a person's freshman grades. And this figure holds even when controlling for the difficulty of the courses taken. (It also holds when the statistical problem of restriction of range is controlled for.) Moreover, the SAT adds hardly any predictive power in the prediction of freshman grades over what one gets from using high school grades alone. That is, using the SAT only increases one's prediction of freshman grades by about 3% or 4% (ranging from 0% to 7%) over what one could predict using high school grades alone. And as the criterion measures get farther away in time from when the SAT is taken—as for sophomore grades, graduation rates, and professional success—the correlations with the SAT get substantially smaller.

An important implication of this fact is that even large score differences on the SAT do not translate into very large differences in the skills that underlie grade performance. This is what is implied by the small relationship between scores on the test and subsequent grades: that relatively few of the skills critical to grades are measured by the tests. And this, in turn, means that a score difference between two people, or between two groups (for example, Blacks and Whites), that is as large as say, 300 points, a difference that can sound big, actually represents a very small difference in skills critical to grade performance.

Perhaps the limitations on the usefulness of these tests can be made clearer with an analogy. Suppose that you were confined to selecting a basketball team based on how many of 10 free throws a player hits. The first thing you'd worry about is having to select basketball players based on the single criterion of free-throw shooting, which you know is only a small portion of the skills that go into actual basketball playing. Even worse, you would know that you would never pick Shaquille O'Neal. Similarly, standardized tests tap only a small set of the skills that make a good student—approximately the 18% that I mentioned.

Another problem you would have selecting your basketball team would be how to interpret a player's scores. If a player hits 10 of 10 or 0 of 10 you would be fairly confident about making a judgment; the 10 of 10 guy you keep, the 0 of 10 guy you drop. But what about the player who hits 3, 4, 5, 6, or even 7? Middling scores like these could be influenced by many things other than underlying potential for free-throw shooting or basketball playing, such as the amount of practice involved, access to effective coaching, whether the player was having a good or a bad day. Roughly the same is true, I suggest, for interpreting standardized test scores: Extreme scores (though less reliable) might permit some confidence in a student's likelihood of success, but middling scores are more difficult to interpret as an indication of underlying promise. Are they inflated by middle-class advantages such as prep classes, private schools, and European Cathedral tours? Or are they deflated by race-linked experiences such as social segregation and being consistently assigned to the lower tracks in school?

Although test scores can be useful and do have the ability, however limited, to inform admissions decisions, the fact is that they simply do not capture any large portion of what makes up academic potential or merit. Grades depend on many things not measured by these tests, and admissions committees should use them with caution and only together with as much other information about candidates as can be obtained. This advice holds for students from any background. But there are reasons to believe that this advice is especially important in the case of minorities.

### III. Are There Significant Factors That Might Cause African American, Hispanic, and American Indian Students to Perform Less Well than Other Groups on These Tests?

The answer to this question is a resounding, "Yes." I describe here what I regard as the two most important such factors.

*Stereotype threat and test performance.* My research, and that of my colleagues, has isolated a factor that can depress the standardized test performance of minority students — a factor we call stereotype threat. This refers to the experience of being in a situation where one recognizes that a negative stereotype about one's group is applicable to oneself. When this happens, one knows that one could be judged or treated in terms of that stereotype, or that one could inadvertently do something that would confirm it. In situations where one cares very much about one's performance or related outcomes — as in the case of serious students taking the SAT — this threat of being negatively stereotyped can be upsetting and distracting. Our research confirms that when this threat occurs in the midst of taking a high stakes standardized test, it directly interferes with performance.

In matters of race we often assume that once a situation is objectively the same for different groups, that it is *experienced* the same by each group. This assumption might seem especially reasonable in the case of "standardized" cognitive tests. But for Black students, unlike White students, the experience of difficulty on the test makes the negative stereotype about their group relevant as an interpretation of their performance, and of them. Thus they know as they meet frustration that they are especially likely to be seen through the lens of the stereotype as having limited ability. For those Black students who care very much about performing well, this is an extra intimidation not experienced by groups not stereotyped in this way. And it is a serious intimidation, implying, as it does, that they may not belong in walks of life where the tested abilities are important, walks of life in which they are heavily invested. Like many pressures, it may not be fully conscious, but it may be enough to impair their best thinking.

To test this idea, Joshua Aronson and I asked Black and White Stanford students into our laboratory and, one at a time, gave them a very difficult 30-minute verbal test, the items of which came from the advanced Graduate Record Examination in literature. The bulk of these students were sophomores, which meant that the test would be difficult for them — precisely the feature that we reasoned would make this simple testing situation different for our Black participants than for our White participants. We told each student that we were testing ability.

Black students performed dramatically worse than White students on the test. As we had statistically equated both groups on ability level, the differences in performance were not because the Black students had weaker skills than the White students. Something else was involved. Before we could confirm that that "something else" was stereotype threat, we had to control for the possibility that the Black students performed worse than the White students because they were less motivated or because their skills could be somehow less easily extrapolated to the advanced material of this test. We concluded that if stereotype threat and not something about these students themselves had caused their poor test performance, then doing something that would reduce this threat during the test should allow their performance to improve, to go up to the level of equally capable White students. We devised a simple way to test this: We presented another group of Black and White sophomores, again statistically equated on ability level, the same test we had used before — not as a test of ability, but as a "problem-solving" task that had nothing to do with ability. This made the stereotype about Blacks' ability irrelevant to their performance on the task since, ostensibly, the task did not measure ability. A simple instruction, yes, but it profoundly changed the meaning of the situation. It told Black participants that the racial stereotype about their ability was irrelevant to their performance on this particular task. In the stroke of an instruction, the "stereotype spotlight," as psychologist Bill Cross once called it, was turned off.

As a result, Black students' performance on this test matched the performance of equally qualified Whites. With the stereotype spotlight on, Blacks performed dramatically worse than Whites; with it off, they performed the same. Thus, stereotype threat of the sort that we argue characterizes the daily experiences of Black students on predominantly White campuses and in a predominantly White society can directly affect important intellectual performances such as standardized test performance.

But it has broader effects too. Stereotype threat follows its targets onto campus, affecting behaviors of theirs that are as varied as participating in class, seeking help from faculty, contact with students in other groups, and so on. And as it becomes a chronic feature of one's school environment, it can cause what we have called "disidentification"; the realignment of one's self-concept and values so that one's self-regard no longer depends on how well one does in that environment. Disidentification relieves the pain of stereotype threat by breaking identification with the part of life where the pain occurs, which necessarily includes a loss of motivation to succeed in that part of life. When school is the part of life where stereotype threat is felt — as for women in advanced math or African Americans in all areas — disidentification can be a costly and life-altering adaptation.

In subsequent years, our research has revealed several important parameters of the effect of stereotype threat on standardized test performance. First, it can interfere with the test performance of any group whose abilities are negatively stereotyped in the larger society: Women taking difficult math tests; lower-class French students taking a difficult language exam; older people taking a difficult memory test; White male athletes being given a test of natural athletic ability; White males taking a difficult math test on which they are told "Asians do better"; as well as Hispanic students at the University of Texas being given a difficult English test. This research shows stereotype threat to be a very general effect, one that is undoubtedly capable of undermining the standardized test performance of any group negatively stereotyped in the area of achievement tested by the test.

We have also discovered that the detrimental effect of stereotype threat on test performance is greatest for those students who are the most invested in doing well on the test. As an intimidation, one might expect that it would affect the weakest students most. But this is not what happens. Across our research, stereotype threat most impaired students who were the most identified with achievement, those who were also the most skilled, motivated, and confident — the academic vanguard of the group more than the academic rearguard.

This fact had been beneath our noses all along in our data and even in our theory. A person has to care about a domain in order to be disturbed by the prospect of being stereotyped in it. So all of our earlier experiments had selected participants who were identified with the domain of the test involved — Black students identified with verbal skills and women identified with math. But we had not tested participants who were less identified with these domains. When we did, what had been beneath our noses hit us in the face. None of these disidentified students showed any effect of stereotype threat whatsoever. Nothing.

Now make no mistake, these disidentified students did not perform well on the tests. Like anyone who does not care, they would start the test, discover its difficulty, stop trying very hard and get a lower score. But their performance did not differ depending on whether they were at risk of being judged stereotypically — their performance was the same regardless of whether they had been told it was their ability we were testing.

This finding tells us two important things. The first is that the poorer standardized test performance of Black students may have two sources. One is more commonly understood: It is the poorer performance of some among this group who are not well prepared and perhaps not well identified with school achievement. The other, however, has not been well understood: The underperformance among strong, school-identified members of this group whose lower performance reflects the stereotype threat they are under.

But these findings make a point of some poignance as well: The characteristics that expose this vanguard to the pressure of stereotype threat are not weaker academic identity and skills, but stronger academic identity and skills. They have long seen themselves as good students, better than most other people. But led into the domain by their strengths, they pay an extra tax on their investment there, a "pioneer tax," if you will, of worry and vigilance that their futures will be compromised by the ways society perceives and treats their group. And it is paid everyday, in every stereotype-relevant situation. Recent research from our laboratory shows that this tax has a physiological cost. Black students performing a cognitive task under stereotype threat had elevated blood pressure.

This finding raises another point: Being a minority student from the middle-class is no escape from stereotype threat and its effect on standardized test performance or performance in higher education more generally. In the American mind we have come to view the disadvantages associated with being Black, for example, as disadvantages of social and economic resources and opportunity. This assumption is often taken to imply its obverse: That is, if you are Black and come from a home that has achieved middle-class status, your experiences and perspectives are no longer significantly affected by race. Our research shows quite clearly that this is not so. In fact, if being middle-class gave you the resources that helped you identify with school achievement, ironically, it may lead you to experience stereotype threat even more keenly. It is investment in the domain of schooling — often aided by the best resources and wishes of middle-class parents — that can make one, at the point of reaching the difficult items on the SAT, experience the distracting alarm of stereotype threat.

All of these findings then, taken together, constitute a powerful reason for treating standardized tests as having limited utility as a measure of academic potential of students from these groups. But there are other reasons as well.

*Different experiences.* The point here is that factors like race, social class, and ethnicity still shape the life trajectories and experiences of individuals in society and as a result can have profound effects on test performance. For example, consider what being African American, even from the middle-class, can predispose a person to experience: Assignment to lower academic tracks throughout schooling; being taught and counseled with lower expectations by less skilled teachers in more poorly funded schools; attending school in more distressed neighborhoods or in suburban areas where they are often a small, socially isolated minority; living in families with fewer resources; and having peers who — alienated by these conditions — may be more often disinterested in school. Clearly these race-linked experiences are enough to lead students from this group to have lower scores on the SAT at the point of applying to college without any reference to innate ability. A similar scenario could be described for many Hispanic groups in this society and for American Indians (especially those living on reservations).

If one thinks of all the relationships, experiences, and motivations that underlie good test performance as a river or confluence of influences, it is clear that some groups will have more access to this river than others. Accordingly, those with less access, by dint of the weaker academic and test performance skills this causes, will have lower test scores and thus more limited access to higher education. Of course, to the extent that the skills they lack are critical to success in school, this limitation of access is appropriate under the ideal of sending the most qualified students on to higher education. But it is important to stress, even here, that for these students, their lower test scores may reflect their limited access to the critical confluence of experiences as much as any real limitation in potential for higher education.

Again the free-throw analogy might be helpful. The part of this analogy most relevant to the present point is how to interpret the performance of people who, for sociocultural reasons, have had little exposure to free-throw shooting. They are not likely to hit many shots. But the problem is how to interpret their poor performance vis-à-vis their potential to play basketball. Their poor free-throw shooting could reflect problems that would make them very poor basketball players, or it could reflect a lack of experience that could be easily overcome, or even an orientation that while hurting free-throw shooting might *help* basketball playing. It would be difficult to know. And this is the fundamental ambiguity surrounding the interpretation of low SAT scores among students from backgrounds without significant access to the culture represented on the test. Their lower scores are more difficult to interpret.

## Conclusion

In recent years the media has made a great deal of the fact that minority students on a college campus often have lower average SAT scores than Whites and Asians on the same campus. The clear implication, presumably taken up by the public, is that SAT gaps of this size reflect that the minorities being admitted are "less qualified" than the White and Asian students. My testimony, I hope, has put these gaps in a different light: Gaps of this size actually represent only a tiny difference in the real skills needed to get good college or law school grades and they reflect the influence of a complex of factors tied to race in our society that, for reasons unrelated to real academic potential, depress minority student test scores. Furthermore, this gap is almost never caused by there being a lower admissions threshold for Blacks than for Whites or Asians. It reflects the fact that there is a smaller proportion of Blacks than Whites and Asians with very high SAT scores. Thus, when you average each group's scores, the Black average will be lower than the White and Asian averages. Why there is a smaller proportion of Blacks with very high scores is, of course, a complex question with multiple answers involving, among other things, the effects of race on educational access and experience, as well as the processes dwelt on in this document. The point, though, is that Black test score deficits are taken as a sign of their being underprepared when, in fact, virtually all Black students on a given campus have tested skills completely "above threshold" within the range of the tested skills for other students on the campus, and in this sense, have skills up to the competition.

Having made these arguments, I hope to have provided a better understanding of minority students' underperformance on standardized tests and of what that underperformance means with regard to their ability to succeed in higher education. It is simply the case that we have no single, or even small, set of indicators that satisfactorily captures "merit" or "potential" for academic success and a contributing life.

*Faye J. Crosby, Bernardo M. Ferdman, and Blanche R. Wingate*

# From "Addressing and Redressing Discrimination: Affirmative Action in Social Psychological Perspective"

How investigators approach their research reveals a great deal about their assumptions regarding the phenomena of interest. In the case of affirmative action, some researchers (e.g., Heilman, 1996; Nacoste, 1994) have made pronouncements about affirmative action's potentially deleterious effects on the basis of results from experiments in which participants reacted to either merit-based or category-based selections of people for tasks and rewards. The persistent juxtaposition of merit-based versus category-based selection is based on the assumption that one cannot simultaneously pay attention to both merit and group membership. Yet most identity-conscious affirmative action programs do exactly that. Some experimental designs assume, in other words, that selecting individuals for positions in a group-conscious fashion necessarily means that merit cannot be considered. But as Konrad and Linnehan (1999) point out, research designs that ask participants to consider both qualifications and group membership would more closely parallel actual affirmative action practices. If they are to avoid bias, researchers must not expect their participants to assume that anyone selected for a job will be qualified except for persons from underrepresented groups, such as men and women of color, or White women. The term "qualified minority" or "qualified woman" carries many associations, including the implication that these associations are not commonly expected. In the United States, however, we do not usually see — in the context of selection for jobs — the term "qualified majority group member."

. . .

From *Intergroup Processes.* Vol. 4, *Blackwell Handbook in Social Psychology,* edited by Rupert Brown and Samuel Gaertner (Oxford: Blackwell, forthcoming).

*Affirmative Action and Self-Doubt*

Shelby Steele (1990) and others (Carter, 1991; Heilman, 1996) have proposed that affirmative action can stigmatize its intended beneficiaries. Steele has voiced the related idea that the Black people who endorse and rely on affirmative action are those with damaged pride. Similar ideas are often repeated in the media (e.g., Connerly, 1995). Meanwhile, other scholars (e.g., Branscombe & Ellemers, 1998) have proposed that opposition to affirmative action among members of disadvantaged groups may indicate that the target has internalized society's stigma so that he or she can only bolster self-esteem and personal status by alienation from the in-group.

What does the empirical evidence show? Although not voluminous, it shows that most women and most men of color do not feel diminished by affirmative action policies. A 1995 Gallup poll asked 708 White women and minority group members the question, "Have you ever felt that your colleagues at work or school privately questioned your abilities or qualifications because of affirmative action or have you never felt this way?" (Gallup Short Subjects, 1995). Results showed that only 8% of White women, 19% of African American women, and 29% of African American men answered yes.

While most disadvantaged people feel undermined when told that they received benefit through special privilege instead of merit (Arthur, Doverspike, & Fuentes, 1992; Heilman, 1994, 1996; Nacoste, 1994; for a review, see Kravitz, Harrison, Turner, Levine, Chaves, Brannick, Denning, Russell, & Conard, 1997), only a minority of society's disadvantaged confuse affirmative action with special privilege. In an early study (Ayers, 1992), a small sample of women of color reported on their reactions to being selected through affirmative action for honors, awards, or jobs. One young woman was angered to have been chosen as the "best Black" student, but the older women expressed gratitude for being given an opportunity to show their value. A very senior administrator articulated the opinion that White people's distrust of an affirmative action candidate is simply White people's contemporary "acceptable" form of racism, a form that is less detrimental than previous forms. A recent in-depth study of 800 women of color in U.S. corporations conducted by Catalyst (1998) echoes the results of Ayers's study: most women of color see affirmative action as a set of practices which enhance, and do not displace, the true reward of merit.

The positive effect is not limited to women. Taylor (1994) studied the responses of 319 White women, 40 Black women, and 32 Black men who were employed by companies that either did or did not have an affirmative action policy in place. Taylor found no evidence of affirmative action's supposed deleterious effects. Instead, she found strong positive effects for workplace affirmative action policies. For example, Black men employed by firms that utilized affirmative action reported more occupational ambition and less cynicism than those who worked for companies without affirmative action policies. One might wonder how (tiny) self-doubt that may arise from participating in an affirmative action program compares to the (enormous) self-doubt that arises from unemployment.

Nor do students appear undermined in their self-esteem by affirmative action policies. In one survey (Truax, Cordova, Wood, Wright, & Crosby, 1998), 351 undergraduate students were asked their reactions to affirmative action and also whether they wondered if their peers and professors thought that they had been admitted to college because of their ethnicity and not their intellectual abilities. Few of the White and Asian American students but a great majority of the African American, Hispanic, and Native American students felt that others doubted their ability in this way. These students also felt that their academic abilities were judged on the basis of ethnic stereotypes. Yet they overwhelmingly endorsed affirmative action. Support for affirmative action and worry about the perceptions of Whites were positively although marginally correlated.

Schmermund, Sellers, Mueller, and Crosby (1998) extended Truax et al.'s work by administering surveys to 181 Black students at five institutions in Western Massachusetts. Although Truax et al. could infer from the pattern of their data that students of color had not internalized what Major, Feinstein, and Crocker (1994) call "suspicion of inferiority," they had no direct evidence of students' academic self-esteem. The students in Schmermund et al.'s study also strongly endorsed affirmative action and often claimed that their fellow students and professors viewed them with suspicion. While approximately 60% of the students thought other students doubted their competence and 50% thought professors did, less than one-third of the sample admitted that they sometimes doubted their own academic merit. Interestingly, there was a marginally significant negative association between self-doubt and endorsement for affirmative action: students who disliked affirmative action felt more academically insecure than those who liked the policy. This relationship is the opposite of what Shelby Steele (1990) or some others (e.g., Heilman, 1996) would predict.

Data exist for samples even younger than college students. Miller and Clark (1997) asked 161 U.S. high school students about their faith in the American Dream. The students endorsed the dream, but Black students agreed less than Hispanic, Asian, or White students with the concept that the United States provides equal opportunities for all races and classes. For these students, concluded Miller and Clark, outreach programs and other forms of affirmative action were essential for the preservation of hope.

. . .

**Expanding the Conversation**

Affirmative action practices share two goals, but not always in equal measure. First, affirmative action exists to enhance diversity in specified groups such as undergraduate students or corporate managers. Second, affirmative action exists to achieve fairness for all. Affirmative action's road to fairness rests on two underlying assumptions. The first is that fairness requires an explicit effort, especially given the unfair discrimination and oppression of yesterday and oftentimes, of today. The second assumption is that fairness to individuals within categories is aided by taking cognizance of those categories. Thus, for example, if we are to assure the fair treatment of women and men, we must first notice who is male and female and note the treatment of people in each category. In this view, justice involves treating the whole group equally, not only selected individuals (Ferdman, 1997).

The importance of noting categorical information is probably greatest when previously monolithic groups embark on the quest for diversity (Dass & Parker, 1999; Ferdman & Brody, 1996; Thomas, 1990). But as organizations, and indeed society as a whole, come to embrace diversity, number counts will need to give way to more sophisticated analyses. Assessment of group representation purely in terms of numbers often tends to be framed from an assimilationist perspective (see Ferdman, 1997; Jones, 1998; Miller & Katz, 1995). When psychologists come to value truly diverse ways of thinking and acting, and when even the privileged White people see diversity as being in their own self-interest (Potts, 1994; Wheeler, 1994, 1995), we can help assure that affirmative action goes beyond addressing and redressing discrimination toward diversity and inclusion. If we are thoughtful about affirmative action, we may come to consider not only the problems but also the opportunities created by intergroup distinctions.

*Richard Rodriguez*

# From *Hunger of Memory: The Education of Richard Rodriguez*

Minority student — that was the label I bore in college at Stanford, then in graduate school at Columbia and Berkeley: a nonwhite reader of Spenser and Milton and Austen.

In the late 1960s nonwhite Americans clamored for access to higher education, and I became a principal beneficiary of the academy's response, its programs of affirmative action. My presence was noted each fall by the campus press office in its proud tally of Hispanic-American students enrolled; my progress was followed by HEW statisticians. One of the lucky ones. Rewarded. Advanced for belonging to a racial group "underrepresented" in American institutional life. When I sought admission to graduate schools, when I applied for fellowships and summer study grants, when I needed a teaching assistantship, my Spanish surname or the dark mark in the space indicating my race — "check one" nearly always got me whatever I asked for. When the time came for me to look for a college teaching job (the end of my years as a scholarship boy), potential employers came looking for me — a minority student.

Fittingly, it falls to me, as someone who so awkwardly carried the label, to question it now, its juxtaposition of terms — minority, student. For me there is no way to say it with grace. I say it rather with irony sharpened by self-pity. I say it with anger. It is a term that should never have been foisted on me. One I was wrong to accept.

. . .

In a way, it was true. I was a minority. The word, as popularly used, did describe me. In the sixties, *minority* became a synonym for socially disadvantaged Americans — but it was primarily a numerical designation. The word referred to entire races and nationalities of Americans, those numerically underrepresented in institutional life. (Thus, without contradiction, one

---

From *Hunger of Memory* by Richard Rodriguez (Boston: D.R. Godine, 1981), 143, 146–47, 148–53. Reprinted by permission of David R. Godine, Publisher, Inc. Copyright © 1982 by Richard Rodriguez.

could speak of "minority groups.") And who were they exactly? Blacks — all blacks — most obviously were minorities. And Hispanic-Americans. And American Indians. And some others. (It was left to federal statisticians, using elaborate surveys and charts, to determine which others precisely.)

I was a minority.

I believed it. For the first several years, I accepted the label. I certainly supported the racial civil rights movement; supported the goal of broadening access to higher education. But there was a problem: One day I listened approvingly to a government official defend affirmative action; the next day I realized the benefits of the program. I was the minority student the political activists shouted about at noontime rallies. Against their rhetoric, I stood out in relief, unrelieved. *Knowing:* I was not really more socially disadvantaged than the white graduate students in my classes. *Knowing:* I was not disadvantaged like many of the new nonwhite students who were entering college, lacking good early schooling.

Nineteen sixty-nine. 1970. 1971. Slowly, slowly, the term *minority* became a source of unease. It would remind me of those boyhood years when I had felt myself alienated from public (majority) society — *los gringos*. *Minority. Minorities. Minority groups.* The terms sounded in public to remind me in private of the truth: I was not — in a *cultural* sense — a minority, an alien from public life. (Not like *los pobres* I had encountered during my recent laboring summer.) The truth was summarized in the sense of irony I'd feel at hearing myself called a minority student: The reason I was no longer a minority was because I had become a student.

. . .

It is important now to remember that the early leaders of the northern civil rights movement were from the South. (The civil rights movement in the North depended upon an understanding of racism derived from the South.) Here was the source of the mistaken strategy — the reason why activists could so easily ignore class and could consider race alone a sufficient measure of social oppression. In the South, where racism had been legally enforced, all blacks suffered discrimination uniformly. The black businessman and the black maid were undifferentiated by the law that forced them to the rear of the bus. Thus, when segregation laws were challenged and finally defeated, the benefit to one became a benefit for all; the integration of an institution by a single black implied an advance for the entire race.

From the experience of southern blacks, a generation of Americans came to realize with new force that there are forms of oppression that touch all levels of a society. This was the crucial lesson that survived the turbulence in the South of the fifties and sixties. The southern movement gave impetus initially to the civil rights drives of nonwhite Americans in the

North. Later, the black movement's vitality extended to animate the liberation movements of women, the elderly, the physically disabled, and the homosexual. Leaders of these groups described the oppression they suffered by analogy to that suffered by blacks. Thus one heard of sexism — that echo of racism, and something called gray power. People in wheelchairs gave the black-power salute. And homosexuals termed themselves "America's last niggers." As racism rhetorically replaced poverty as the key social oppression, Americans learned to look beyond class in considering social oppression. The public conscience was enlarged. Americans were able to take seriously, say, the woman business executive's claim to be the victim of social oppression. But with this advance there was a danger. It became easy to underestimate, even to ignore altogether, the importance of *class.* Easy to forget that those whose lives are shaped by poverty and poor education (cultural minorities) are least able to defend themselves against social oppression, whatever its form.

In the era of affirmative action it became more and more difficult to distinguish the middle-class victim of social oppression from the lower-class victim. In fact, it became hard to say when a person ever *stops* being disadvantaged. Quite apart from poverty, the variety of social oppressions that most concerned Americans involved unchangeable conditions. (One does not ever stop being a woman; one does not stop being aged — short of death; one does not stop being a quadriplegic.) The commonplace heard in the sixties was precisely this: A black never stops being black. (The assertion became a kind of justification for affirmative action.)

For my part I believe the black lawyer who tells me that there is never a day in his life when he forgets he is black. I believe the black business executive who says that, although he drives an expensive foreign car, he must be especially wary when a policeman stops him for speeding. I do not doubt that middle-class blacks need to remain watchful when they look for jobs or try to rent or when they travel to unfamiliar towns. "You can't know what it is like for us," a black woman shouted at me one day from an audience somewhere. Like a white liberal, I was awed, shaken by her rage; I gave her the point. But now I must insist, must risk presumption to say that I do not think that all blacks are equally "black." Surely those uneducated and poor will remain most vulnerable to racism. It was not coincidence that the leadership of the southern civil rights movement was drawn mainly from a well-educated black middle class. Even in the South of the 1950s, all blacks were not equally black.

All Mexican-Americans certainly are not equally Mexican-Americans. The policy of affirmative action, however, was never able to distinguish someone like me (a graduate student of English, ambitious for a college teaching career) from a slightly educated Mexican-American who lived in a barrio and worked as a menial laborer, never expecting a future improved. Worse, affirmative action made me the beneficiary of his condition. Such was the foolish logic of this program of social reform: Because many Hispanics were absent from higher education, I became with my matriculation an exception, a numerical minority. Because I was not a cultural minority, I was extremely well placed to enjoy the advantages of affirmative action. I was groomed for a position in the multiversity's leadership class.

Remarkably, affirmative action passed as a program of the Left. In fact, its supporters ignored the most fundamental assumptions of the classical Left by disregarding the importance of class and by assuming that the disadvantages of the lower class would necessarily be ameliorated by the creation of an elite society. The movement that began so nobly in the South, in the North came to parody social reform. Those least disadvantaged were helped first, advanced because many others of their race were more disadvantaged. The strategy of affirmative action, finally, did not take seriously the educational dilemma of disadvantaged students. They need good early schooling! Activists pushed to get more nonwhite students into colleges. Meritocratic standards were dismissed as exclusionary. But activists should have asked why so many minority students could not meet those standards; why so many more would never be in a position to apply. The revolutionary demand would have called for a reform of primary and secondary schools.

To improve the education of disadvantaged students requires social changes which educational institutions alone cannot make, of course. Parents of such students need jobs and good housing; the students themselves need to grow up with three meals a day, in safe neighborhoods. But disadvantaged students also require good teachers. Good teachers — not fancy electronic gadgets — to teach them to read and to write. Teachers who are not overwhelmed; teachers with sufficient time to devote to individual students; to inspire. In the late sixties, civil rights activists might have harnessed the great idealism that the southern movement inspired in Americans. They might have called on teachers, might have demanded some kind of national literacy campaign for children of the poor — white and non-white — at the earliest levels of learning.

But the opportunity passed. The guardians of institutional America in Washington were able to ignore the need for fundamental social changes. College and university administrators could proudly claim that their institutions had yielded, were open to minority groups. (There was proof in a handful of numbers computed each fall.) So less thought had to be given to the procession of teenagers who leave ghetto high schools disadvantaged, badly taught, unable to find decent jobs.

I wish as I write these things that I could be angry at those who mislabeled me. I wish I could enjoy the luxury of self-pity and cast myself as a kind of "invisible man." But guilt is not disposed of so easily. The fact is that I complied with affirmative action. I permitted myself to be prized. Even after publicly voicing objections to affirmative action, I accepted its benefits. I continued to indicate my race on applications for financial aid. (It didn't occur to me to leave the question unanswered.) I'd apply for prestigious national fellowships and tell friends that the reason I won was because I was a minority. (This by way of accepting the fellowship money.) I published essays admitting that I was not a minority—saw my by-line in magazines and journals which once had seemed very remote from my life. It was a scholarship boy's dream come true. I enjoyed being—not being—a minority student, the featured speaker. I was invited to lecture at schools that only a few years before would have rejected my application for graduate study. My life was unlike that of any other graduate student I knew. On weekends I flew cross country to say—through a microphone—that I was not a minority.

Someone told me this: A senior faculty member in the English department at Berkeley smirked when my name came up in a conversation. Someone at the sherry party had wondered if the professor had seen my latest article on affirmative action. The professor replied with arch politeness, "And what does Mr. Rodriguez have to complain about?"

You who read this act of contrition should know that by writing it I seek a kind of forgiveness—not yours. The forgiveness, rather, of those many persons whose absence from higher education permitted me to be classed a minority student. I wish that they would read this. I doubt they ever will.

*Shelby Steele*

# From *The Content of Our Character: A New Vision of Race in America*

Racial representation is not the same thing as racial development, yet affirmative action fosters a confusion of these very different needs. Representation can be manufactured; development is always hard-earned. However, it is the music of innocence and power that we hear in affirmative action that causes us to cling to it and to its distracting emphasis on representation. The fact is that after twenty years of racial preferences, the gap between white and black median income is greater than it was in the seventies. None of this is to say that blacks don't need policies that ensure our right to equal opportunity, but what we need more is the development that will let us take advantage of society's efforts to include us.

I think that one of the most troubling effects of racial preferences for blacks is a kind of demoralization, or put another way, an enlargement of self-doubt. Under affirmative action the quality that earns us preferential treatment is an implied inferiority. However this inferiority is explained — and it is easily enough explained by the myriad deprivations that grew out of our oppression — it is still inferiority. There are explanations, and then there is the fact. And the fact must be borne by the individual as a condition apart from the explanation, apart even from the fact that others like himself also bear this condition. In integrated situations where blacks must compete with whites who may be better prepared, these explanations may quickly wear thin and expose the individual to racial as well as personal self-doubt.

All of this is compounded by the cultural myth of black inferiority that blacks have always lived with. What this means in practical terms is that when blacks deliver themselves into integrated situations, they encounter a nasty little reflex in whites, a mindless, atavistic reflex that responds to the color black with alarm. Attributions may follow this alarm if the white cares to indulge them, and if they do, they will most likely be negative — one such attribution is intellectual ineptness. I think this reflex and the attributions that may follow it embarrass most whites today, therefore, it is usually quickly repressed. Nevertheless, on an equally atavistic level, the black will be aware of the reflex his color triggers and will feel a stab of horror at seeing himself reflected in this way. He, too, will do a quick repression, but a lifetime of such stabbings is what constitutes his inner realm of racial doubt.

The effects of this may be a subject for another essay. The point here is that the implication of inferiority that racial preferences engender in both the white and black mind expands rather than contracts this doubt. Even when the black sees no implication of inferiority in racial preferences, he knows that whites do, so that — consciously or unconsciously — the result is virtually the same. The effect of preferential treatment — the lowering of normal standards to increase black representation — puts blacks at war with an expanded realm of debilitating doubt, so that the doubt itself becomes an unrecognized preoccupation that undermines their ability to perform, especially in integrated situations. On largely white campuses, blacks are five times more likely to drop out than whites. Preferential treatment, no matter how it is justified in the light of day, subjects blacks to a midnight of self-doubt, and so often transforms their advantage into a revolving door.

Another liability of affirmative action comes from the fact that it indirectly encourages blacks to exploit their own past victimization as a source of power and privilege. Victimization, like implied inferiority, is what justifies preference, so that to receive the benefits of preferential treatment one must, to some extent, become invested in the view of one's self as a victim. In this way, affirmative action nurtures a victim-focused identity in blacks. The obvious irony here is that we become inadvertently invested in the very condition we are trying to overcome. Racial preferences send us the message that there is more power in our past suffering than our present achievements — none of which could bring us a *preference* over others.

When power itself grows out of suffering, then blacks are encouraged to expand the boundaries of what qualifies as racial oppression, a situation that can lead us to paint our victimization in vivid colors, even as we receive the benefits of preference. The same corporations and institutions that give us preference are also seen as our oppressors. At Stanford University minority students — some of whom enjoy as much as $15,000 a year in financial aid — recently took over the president's office demanding, among other things, more financial aid. The power to be found in victimization, like any power, is intoxicating and can lend itself to the creation of a new class of super-victims who can feel the pea of victimization under twenty mattresses. Preferential treatment rewards us for being underdogs rather than for moving beyond that status — a misplacement of incentives that, along with its deepening of our doubt, is more a yoke than a spur.

But, I think, one of the worst prices that blacks pay for preference has to do with an illusion. I saw this illusion at work recently in the mother of a middle-class black student who was going off to his first semester of college. "They owe us this, so don't think for a minute that you don't belong there." This is the logic by which many blacks, and some whites, justify affirmative action — it is something "owed," a form of reparation. But this logic overlooks a much harder and less digestible reality, that it is impossible to repay blacks living today for the historic suffering of the race. If all blacks were given a million dollars tomorrow morning it would not amount to a dime on the dollar of three centuries of oppression, nor would it obviate the residues of that oppression that we still carry today. The concept of historic reparation grows out of man's need to impose a degree of justice on the world that simply does not exist. Suffering can be endured and overcome, it cannot be repaid. Blacks cannot be repaid for the injustice done to the race, but we can be corrupted by society's guilty gestures of repayment.

Affirmative action is such a gesture. It tells us that racial preferences can do for us what we cannot do for ourselves. The corruption here is in the hidden incentive *not* to do what we believe preferences will do. This is an incentive to be reliant on others just as we are struggling for self-reliance. And it keeps alive the illusion that we can find some deliverance in repayment. The hardest thing for any sufferer to accept is that his suffering excuses him from very little and never has enough currency to restore him. To think otherwise is to prolong the suffering.

Several blacks I spoke with said they were still in favor of affirmative action because of the "subtle" discrimination blacks were subject to once on the job. One photojournalist said, "They have ways of ignoring you." A black female television producer said, "You can't file a lawsuit when your boss doesn't invite you to the insider meetings without ruining your career. So we still need affirmative action." Others mentioned the infamous "glass ceiling" through which blacks can see the top positions of authority but never reach them. But I don't think racial preferences are a protection against this subtle discrimination; I think they contribute to it.

In any workplace, racial preferences will always create two-tiered populations composed of preferreds and unpreferreds. This division makes automatic a perception of enhanced competence for the unpreferreds and of questionable competence for the preferreds — the former earned his way, even though others were given preference, while the latter made it by color as much as by competence. Racial preferences implicitly mark whites with an exaggerated superiority just as they mark blacks with an exaggerated inferiority. They not only reinforce America's oldest racial myth but, for blacks, they have the effect of stigmatizing the already stigmatized.

I think that much of the "subtle" discrimination that blacks talk about is often (not always) discrimination against the stigma of questionable competence that affirmative action delivers to blacks. In this sense, preferences scapegoat the very people they seek to help. And it may be that at a certain level employers impose a glass ceiling, but this may not be against the race so much as against the race's reputation for having advanced by color as much as by competence. Affirmative action makes a glass ceiling virtually necessary as a protection against the corruptions of preferential treatment. This ceiling is the point at which corporations shift the emphasis from color to competency and stop playing the affirmative action game. Here preference backfires for blacks and becomes a taint that holds them back. Of course, one could argue that this taint, which is, after all, in the minds of whites, becomes nothing more than an excuse to discriminate against blacks. And certainly the result is the same in either case—blacks don't get past the glass ceiling. But this argument does not get around the fact that racial preferences now taint this color with a new theme of suspicion that makes it even more vulnerable to the impulse in others to discriminate. In this crucial yet gray area of perceived competence, preferences make whites look better than they are and blacks worse, while doing nothing whatever to stop the very real discrimination that blacks may encounter. I don't wish to justify the glass ceiling here, but only to suggest the very subtle ways that affirmative action revives rather than extinguishes the old rationalizations for racial discrimination.

In education, a revolving door; in employment, a glass ceiling.

I believe affirmative action is problematic in our society because it tries to function like a social program. Rather than ask it to ensure equal opportunity we have demanded that it create parity between the races. But preferential treatment does not teach skills, or educate, or instill motivation. It only passes out entitlement by color, a situation that in my profession has created an unrealistically high demand for black professors. The social engineer's assumption is that this high demand will inspire more blacks to earn Ph.D.'s and join the profession. In fact, the number of blacks earning Ph.D.'s has declined in recent years. A Ph.D. must be developed from preschool on. He requires family and community support. He must acquire an entire system of values that enables him to work hard while delaying gratification. There are social programs, I believe, that can (and should) help blacks *develop* in all these areas, but entitlement by color is not a social program; it is a dubious reward for being a black.

It now seems clear that the Supreme Court, in a series of recent decisions, is moving away from racial preferences. It has disallowed preferences except in instances of "identified discrimination," eroded the precedent that statistical racial imbalances are *prima facie* evidence of discrimination, and in effect granted white males the right to challenge consent degrees that use preference to achieve racial balances in the workplace. One civil rights leader said, "Night has fallen on civil rights." But I am not so sure. The effect of these decisions is to protect the constitutional rights of everyone rather than take rights away from blacks. What they do take away from blacks is the special entitlement to more rights than others that preferences always grant. Night has fallen on racial preferences, not on the fundamental rights of black Americans. The reason for this shift, I believe, is that the white mandate for absolution from past racial sins has weakened considerably during the eighties. Whites are now less willing to endure unfairness to themselves in order to grant special entitlement to blacks, even when these entitlements are justified in the name of past suffering. Yet the black mandate for more power in society has remained unchanged. And I think part of the anxiety that many blacks feel over these decisions has to do with the loss of black power they may signal. We had won a certain specialness and now we are losing it.

But the power we've lost by these decisions is really only the power that grows out of our victimization — the power to claim special entitlements under the law because of past oppression. This is not a very substantial or reliable power, and it is important that we know this so we can focus more exclusively on the kind of development that will bring enduring power. There is talk now that Congress will pass new legislation to compensate for these new limits on affirmative action. If this happens, I hope that their focus will be on development and anti-discrimination rather than entitlement, on achieving racial parity rather than jerry-building racial diversity.

I would also like to see affirmative action go back to its original purpose of enforcing equal opportunity — a purpose that in itself disallows racial preferences. We cannot be sure that the discriminatory impulse in America has yet been shamed into extinction, and I believe affirmative action can make its greatest contribution by providing a rigorous vigilance in this area. It can guard constitutional rather than racial rights, and help institutions evolve standards of merit and selection that are appropriate to the institution's needs yet as free of racial bias as possible (again, with the understanding that racial imbalances are not always an indication of racial bias). One of the most important things affirmative action can do is to define exactly what racial discrimination is and how it might manifest itself within a specific institution. The impulse to discriminate is subtle and cannot be ferreted out unless its many guises are made clear to people. Along with this there should be monitoring of institutions and heavy sanctions brought to bear when actual discrimination is found. This is the sort of affirmative action that America owes to blacks and to itself. It goes after the evil of discrimination itself, while preferences only sidestep the evil and grant entitlement to its *presumed* victims.

But if not preferences, then what? I think we need social policies that are committed to two goals: the educational and economic development of disadvantaged people, regardless of race, and the eradication from our society — through close monitoring and severe sanctions — of racial, ethnic, or gender discrimination. Preferences will not deliver us to either of these goals, since they tend to benefit those who are not disadvantaged — middle-class white women and middle-class blacks — and attack one form of discrimination with another. Preferences are inexpensive and carry the glamour of good intentions — change the numbers and the good deed is done. To be against them is to be unkind. But I think the unkindest cut is to bestow on children like my own an undeserved advantage while neglecting the development of those disadvantaged children on the East Side of my city who will likely never be in a position to benefit from a preference. Give my children fairness; give disadvantaged children a better shot at development — better elementary and secondary schools, job training, safer neighborhoods, better financial assistance for college, and so on. Fewer blacks go to college today than ten years ago; more black males of college age are in prison or under the control of the criminal justice system than in college. This despite racial preferences.

The mandates of black power and white absolution out of which preferences emerged were not wrong in themselves. What was wrong was that both races focused more on the goals of these mandates than on the means to the goals. Blacks can have no real power without taking responsibility for their own educational and economic development. Whites can have no racial innocence without earning it by eradicating discrimination and helping the disadvantaged to develop. Because we ignored the means, the goals have not been reached, and the real work remains to be done.

*Stephen L. Carter*

# From *Reflections of an Affirmative Action Baby*

## V

I begin at the beginning. Given the logic of all that I have said, I often feel that I should oppose all racial preferences in admission to college and professional school. But I don't. When the law school admission season rolls around during the winter, I find myself drawn to the folders of applicants who are not white, as though to something rare and precious. Those folders I give an extra bit of scrutiny, looking, perhaps, for reasons to recommend a *Yes*. I am not trying to get the numbers right and I do not believe that the standards applied by colleges or professional schools are racist; rather, I find myself wanting others to have the same leg up that I had. The question is whether I can square this instinct with what I have said about the damage that preferences do. One of the principal mistaken emphases (or perhaps a public relations problem) of the modern diversity movement is that it often seems in its rhetoric to press toward circumventing or eradicating standards, rather than training us and pushing us until we are able to meet them. There is an important distinction between this modern approach and the more traditional understanding of affirmative action as a program that would help a critical mass of us gain the necessary training to meet the standards of our chosen fields rather than seeking to get around them. Not the least of the difficulties is that the more time we spend arguing that various standards for achievement are culturally inappropriate, the more other people are likely to think we are afraid of trying to meet them.

My own view is that, given training, given a chance, we as a people need fear no standards. That is why I want to return the special admission programs to their more innocent roots, as tools for providing that training and that chance for students who might not otherwise have it. A college or university is not fulfilling its educational missions if it fails to take a hard look at the applicant pool to be sure that it is not missing highly motivated students—some of them people of color, some of them not—who might not be "sure things" but who show good evidence of being positioned to take advantage of what the school can offer. This means taking risks, but that is what higher educational institutions ought to be doing—not to fill a quota or to look good on paper or to keep student activists quiet, and certainly not to bring into the student body a group of students who will thereafter be called upon to represent the distinctive voices of oppressed people (imagine the brouhaha were a professor to take this idea seriously in calling on students in class discussion), but because the purveying of knowledge, the reason universities exist, is a serious enterprise, and one professors should undertake joyfully, even when it isn't easy and even when there is a risk of failure.

. . .

When a person admitted because of membership in a special category does not succeed, that lack of success is often attributed to others in the same category. The stereotype of the dumb jock exists because of the widespread perception (a correct one) that athletes are frequently admitted on paper records for which other students would be rejected. When people of color are admitted in the same fashion, the damage is worse, because the double standard reinforces an already existing stereotype, and because the stereotype, like the program, sorts explicitly according to race. Consequently, if our success rate at elite colleges turns out to be lower than that of white students (as, thus far, it is), we can scarcely avoid having the fact noticed and, in our racially conscious society, remembered as well.

This risk is a predictable consequence of double standards and cannot be avoided. It can, however, be reduced. The best way to reduce the risk would be to eliminate racial preferences, and over time, as the competitive capacity of people of color continues to improve. A more immediate solution is for those students who are admitted as a consequence of affirmative action, while on the college campus and while in professional school and while pursuing their careers—in short, *for the rest of their professional lives*—to bend to their work with an energy that will leave competitors and detractors alike gasping in admiration. The way to turn this potential liability into a powerful asset is to make our cadre of professionals simply too good to ignore.

. . . [T]he first thing that an opportunity-based affirmative action must do is to abandon the pretense that it will in any significant way compensate for present educational disadvantage. Programs of preferential admissions will not wipe away the lingering effects of struggling through the inner-city public schools about which the nation long ago ceased to care. To bring onto college campuses students whose academic abilities have been severely damaged by the conditions in which they have been forced to learn would be a recipe for failure. At best, affirmative action can take those students of color who have already shown the greatest potential and place them in environments where their minds will be tested and trained, the campuses of elite colleges and professional schools.

. . .

There is common agreement, however, that a principal difficulty is the high cost, especially at the nation's most exclusive universities, which makes alternative career choices more attractive. This is why preferential financial assistance (for all its obvious problems) might actually be a more logical and efficient solution than preferential admission. As this manuscript was being completed, a debate erupted over the decision (subsequently modified) by the United States Department of Education to deny federal funds to schools offering preferential financial aid packages on the basis of race.[1] This decision, defended on the ground that federal aid should be administered in a color-blind manner, created a dilemma for colleges interested in keeping both minority recruitment and academic standards at high levels. If one argues that affirmative action is impermissible, then schools are left with only the market mechanism — money — as a tool for enticing onto their campuses excellent students who are not white. A genuine believer in market solutions should allow participants in the market to bid for scarce resources — and by all accounts, first-rate students of color are such a resource. One might want to argue that this bidding is not fair, but if colleges can rely on neither preferential admission nor bidding to attract students who are not white, they plainly can do no more than pay lip service to the ideal of "minority recruitment."

## VI

With the proper goal in mind, then, a degree of racial consciousness *in college and perhaps professional school admission* can plausibly be justified — but just a degree, and just barely. The educational sphere is the place for action because the proper goal of all racial preferences is opportunity — a chance at advanced training for highly motivated people of color who, for whatever complex set of reasons, might not otherwise have it. So justified, the benefit of a racial preference carries with it the concomitant responsibility not to waste the opportunity affirmative action confers. What matters most is what happens *after* the preference.

I call this vision of professional achievement and racial preference the affirmative action pyramid, and it works much as the name implies: The role of preference narrows as one moves upward. And although I do not want to say arbitrarily *This is the spot,* what is clear is that as one climbs toward professional success, at some point the preferences must fall away entirely. Possibly a slight preference is justified in college admission, not as a matter of getting the numbers right, and certainly not as a matter of finding the right set of hitherto excluded points of view, but as a matter of giving lots of people from different backgrounds the chance — only the chance — to have an education at an elite college or university. But when that opportunity has been exercised, when the student has shown what he or she can do, the rationale for a preference at the next level is slimmer. So an even slighter affirmative action preference for professional school admission, while possibly justified on similar grounds, is less important, and a little bit harder to defend, than a program at the college level.

And when one's training is done, when the time comes for entry to the job market, I think it is quite clear that among professionals,[2] the case for preference evaporates. The candidate has by this time had six or seven or eight years of training at the highest level; it is a bit silly, as well as demeaning, to continue to insist that one's college and professional school performance is not a very accurate barometer of one's professional possibilities. The time has come, finally, to stand or fall on what one has actually achieved. And, of course, as one passes the point of initial entry and moves up the ladder of one's chosen field, all of the arguments run the other way; the time for preference has gone, and it is time instead to stand proudly on one's own record. The preferences cannot go on forever. Sooner or later, talent and preparation, rather than skin color, must tell.

The question of the ability of people of color to meet professional standards should be distinguished from the separate question of the fairness of the standards themselves. Naturally, one must be wary of attributing fairness or neutrality to any particular set of professional standards simply because the standards exist; it is all too easy to suppose that those whom the standards fence out are excluded because they deserve to be and those whom the standards allow in have earned their places. As the British historian J. R. Pole has demonstrated, it has long been a feature of the American character to justify whatever social and economic lines happen to exist as fair and perhaps natural, even as the line drawers, and the lines themselves, have shifted over time.[3] Recent years, moreover, have seen increasing documentation of the connection between attitudes toward race and much of the original impetus (and original design) for drawing lines to measure intellect.[4]

For the committed professional, however, an argument of this kind can quickly become moot. The professions, after all, are in a sense defined by their standards, and most professionals of whatever color are far too busy proving themselves to spend time quibbling over the fairness of standards for medical board certification or law firm partnership. True, the standards for academic tenure are currently under assault as embodying a bias against people of color, but away from the campuses, I doubt there are many black professionals for whom the satisfaction of "I forced them to change their standards to take account of my cultural background" can compete with the thrill of "They did their worst, and I beat them at their own game." The distinction has nothing to do with fairness or cultural identity or self-actualization; the point is to gain what might be called The Edge, what every professional driving toward the top of his or her chosen field wants to hold over all the others, the competition, who are grabbing for the same brass ring.

## VII

Any notion that we should demand to be treated just like anybody else also runs afoul of one of the great and frightening complexities of our age: standardized testing. On nearly every standardized test that one can name, whether for aptitude, achievement, admission, or employment, the median scores of black candidates lag well behind the median scores of white candidates.[5] On most tests, the gap has been narrowing, but it continues to exist. Given the multitudinous societal rewards that are distributed in part on the basis of standardized test scores, black people as a group will continue to run behind until our scores are raised.

America places greater emphasis on standardized testing than any other country in the world. Often, test results are misused, serving as a crutch, a single quantitative means for sorting applicants rather than one important factor in a mix of qualifications. And they are all too frequently misunderstood, treated as though they measure aptitudes that are innate rather than skills that are learned. Consequently, in a racially conscious society, it is scarcely surprising, but certainly frightening, that many people seem to think that the tests reveal racial differences in genetic inheritance.

For many civil rights advocates, the contemporary solution is to get rid of the tests and their quantitative evidence of the continuing disadvantage with which racism, with its brutal force, has burdened us. The term that has been coined to explain the difference in median test scores is "cultural bias"; in other words, the tests measure traits that some people, because of their backgrounds, are less likely to possess. The important question, however, is not whether the measured traits are culture-specific, but whether measuring them is useful to the tester.

Consider: If a test is not good at predicting job or professional school performance and is also racially exclusionary, getting rid of it is a very good idea, but the reason to get rid of it is not that it is racially exclusionary but that it is a poor predictor. This helps everybody, not just candidates who are black, because, as Derrick Bell has pointed out, it "increase[s] the likelihood that those selected, regardless of race, will fulfill the needs of the position."[6] That is what it means for a test (or any other qualification) to be job-related, which, although sometimes expensive to demonstrate, is all that the courts have required employers defending discrimination cases to show.

The trouble is that many of the tests on which black scores lag behind white ones are not poor predictors of the performance of black people — or rather, if they are poor predictors, black people are not disadvantaged by those poor predictions. Many standardized tests tend to *overpredict* the performance of people who are black; that is, the actual job performance or school performance is likely to be slightly *worse* on average than what one would expect, given the scores.

This fact, well supported by considerable and varied social science data, has led to some peculiar forms of argument. An example may be drawn from the National Research Council's very extensive study of the General Aptitude Test Battery, perhaps the most frequently used employment test. The report concluded that using the same formula to predict the job performance of both white and black candidates who sat for the test "would not give predictions that were biased against black applicants." On the contrary, "[i]f the total-group equation does give systematically different predictions than would be provided by the equation based on black employees only, it is somewhat more likely to over-predict than to underpredict."[7]

Does the report then conclude that the use of a single norm for the GATB does not discriminate against black candidates and, in fact, might even be helpful? Well, no, not exactly. One must be careful of the results, the report explains, because "there may be bias against blacks in the primary criterion measure used in the studies — supervisor ratings." Why? Because "[u]sually the supervisors were white."[8] The idea seems to be that the GATB predicts only supervisors' ratings, which, for black employees, might not be an accurate measure of job performance.

To their credit, the report's authors give the same careful attention to studies of supervisor bias that they do to studies of test bias. The difficulty with their thesis is that the empirical work does not clearly bear it out, leading to this awkward conclusion: "Although common sense suggests that evaluations of the performance of blacks or women might well be depressed to some degree by prejudice, it is difficult to quantify this sort of intangible (and perhaps unconscious) effect."[9]

The other possibility — the one that goes mysteriously unmentioned in the otherwise very comprehensive report — is that on this particular point, common sense is wrong. That there is a degree of racism is hardly a surprise, but in an era when highly skilled labor is at a premium, perhaps the supervisor bias is small. Perhaps it does not exist. Or perhaps the bias works the other way: perhaps white supervisors, deeply imbued with stereotypical notions of black laziness and stupidity, are so astonished when black employees turn in outstanding performances that the ratings are *higher* than they would be for similarly performing whites. There is, as far as I know, no empirical support for any of these explanations either; but if the guide is to be common sense, these are as sensible as anything else.

Besides, if one concludes that supervisor ratings are too biased to be used as a measure of job performance, one trembles at the edge of a precipice of paradox. When it is not possible to hire everybody, one must sort among the potential employees *somehow*. Ordinarily, the most sensible means is to try to guess something about the candidate's future — that is, to make a prediction. One might reasonably argue over whether a college or professional school should try to predict grades or future life performance.[10] But it is difficult to see how an employer has any choice but to try to predict job performance, for there is no other reason to hire an employee except to do the job. If an employer is suddenly to be told that for black employees, it is not legitimate to measure performance by either quantitative measures (standardized tests, said to be biased) or subjective measures (supervisor ratings, also said to be biased), there comes the question whether the performance of black employees can be evaluated based on *anything*. It does not seem to strike a blow for equality to argue to employers that after hiring black employees with lower test scores than white employees who are turned away, an employer may not rely on supervisor evaluations (or, evidently, anything else) in deciding how well they have done.

This is a problem on the campuses too, where in the more extreme rhetoric of the diversity movement, a strong undercurrent suggests that mainstream professors — the Eurocentric white males who run the place — are not qualified to evaluate the work of scholars of color who are bringing the voices of the oppressed into the debate. But such an argument is self-defeating. After all, if mainstream faculties are incapable of evaluating the work of these new faculty members, who ought to do the evaluations? Indeed, how can those of us who are black — relatively young and inexperienced scholars that most of us still are — tell whether our work is any good? I suppose we could limit our universe of discourse and ask only one another. But then perhaps white scholars should ask only one another about the quality of their work, too, and I'm not sure what basis we would have for objection. True, it might be protested that white scholars have been asking only one another for decades — but I have always thought that those of us who are not white are moving into academia to change that process, not justify it.

## VIII

In the long run, gaining The Edge we seek means beating the tests, too, and I am confident that we will. Ideally, a phaseout of affirmative action in professional employment should be accompanied by what Nathan Glazer has described as "vigorous attention to the elements in the education of blacks that lead to those test scores of all types that are at present a substantial barrier to black achievement."[11] In the meanwhile, even as we preserve temporarily a degree of racial preference in admission, our goal must be the creation of a cadre of black professionals who, by being too good to ignore, refute all the racist stereotypes. If affirmative action opens some doors at the level of college or professional school entry, fine; let us then be unembarrassed about it. Thereafter, our job — and it *is* a job, one we should undertake cheerfully on behalf of our people, for it is far more important in the long run than speaking the right words in the right voice — is to make the most of the opportunities affirmative action creates. And our strategy must be to insist, once the door is open, on being treated no differently than anybody else. Only then will we be able to look boorish interviewers and colleagues (and the genuinely racist ones, too) squarely in the eye and say in response to the qualification question, "Sure, I got into law school because I'm black    so what?"

The alternative is to pretend that the untrue dream that has haunted affirmative action is the reality. Rather than returning programs of racial preference to their simpler roots, we can instead continue our pretense that all black people are damaged in their competitive capacities by racism, and that the damage is something that will be undone if only we can get the casualties into the right school. We can continue to argue for a world in which there are two standards of achievement, the white and the black. We can continue to fight for the proposition that blackness is a good proxy for culture, and culture, in its turn, a good proxy for political opinions, so that our battle to integrate America becomes a struggle to make the authentic voices of our people heard in the corridors of power. And if we continue that fight, we necessarily continue to argue that there is a right way and a wrong way to represent the people, and that a black person in a position of power who presents the wrong views is betraying the birthright that blackness confers.

But if we travel down this less happy path, this path of accusation and avoidance, then we are not, after all, the beneficiaries of affirmative action: we are its victims.

NOTES

1. The compromise resolution was that schools may not use federal funds for racially preferential scholarships but may fund such scholarships from other sources.

2. I make no claim here about the propriety of affirmative action in labor markets demanding less in the way of educational credentials.

3. J. R. Pole, *The Pursuit of Equality in American History* (Berkeley: University of California Press, 1978).

4. See, for example, Stephen J. Gould, *The Mismeasure of Man* (New York: W. W. Norton, 1981).

5. The use of the word *median,* while frequently overlooked, is important. The scores of black candidates tend to be clustered around a lower point than the scores of white candidates, but this gives no information about the *actual* score of any particular candidate. A given black candidate might fall in the 99th percentile, even if most black candidates score far lower; and a given white candidate might fall in the 1st percentile, even if most white candidates score far higher.

6. Derrick Bell, "Whites Make Big Gains under Broadened Selection Criteria," *Los Angeles Daily Journal,* 1 September 1987, p. 4.

7. National Research Council, *Fairness in Employment Testing* (Washington, D.C.: National Academy Press, 1989), p. 185.

8. Ibid., p. 6. Another important report that tries to deal in similar ways with similar statistical difficulties is National Commission on Testing and Public Policy, *From Gatekeeper to Gateway: Transforming Testing in America* (Chestnut Hill, Mass.: National Commission on Testing and Public Policy, 1990). Although the National Commission on Testing report discusses racial differential in scoring in terms of cultural bias, it does not seriously defend an underprediction claim, choosing instead — correctly, in my judgment — to warn against an overreliance on scores alone in evaluating *all* candidates, not just those whose presence is said to lend diversity.

9. National Research Council, *Fairness in Employment Testing,* p. 186. This is not to suggest that race and other irrelevant characteristics play no role in any evaluations. On the contrary, the social psychology literature suggests that they frequently do, although predicting whether the role will be positive or negative is not easy. See, for example, John B. McConahay, "Modern Racism and Modern Discrimination: The Effects of Race, Racial Attitudes, and Context on Simulated Hiring Decisions," *Personality and Social Psychology Bulletin* 9 (1983): 551; Eve Spangler, Marsha A. Gordon, and Ronald M. Pipkin, "Token Women: An Empirical Test of Kanter's Hypothesis," *American Journal of Sociology* 84 (1978): 160.

10. For a thoughtful discussion of these "later-life" predictions, see Robert Klitgaard, *Choosing Elites* (New York: Basic Books, 1985), pp. 116–53.

11. Nathan Glazer, "The Future of Preferential Affirmative Action," in *Eliminating Racism: Profiles in Controversy,* ed. Phyllis A. Katz and Dalmas A. Taylor (New York: Plenum Press, 1988), pp. 329, 339.

*Dave M. O'Neill and June O'Neill*

# From "Affirmative Action in the Labor Market"

In this article, we first examine the impact of federal affirmative action policy on the relative economic status of those it is intended to help, and we try to distinguish this effect from the influence of other civil rights policies as well as that of other factors such as skill differentials.

. . .

**Empirical Evidence**

Two kinds of methodologies have been applied to study the effects of the affirmative action efforts of the Office of Federal Contract Compliance (OFCCP) on the relative economic status of women and minorities. One uses administrative data from firms reporting to the Equal Employment Opportunity Commission (EEOC) and the OFCCP and compares changes in the distribution of minority and gender groups among employees in contractor and noncontractor firms. However, it is not possible with administrative data to determine directly if wage effects have occurred. The second approach uses economywide data on changes in the relative earnings of minorities and women and compares these changes with changes in program enforcement.

**Studies Using Administrative Data**

. . .

A number of studies have used administrative data to analyze patterns of employment change across the thousands of individual reporting firms, both contractor and noncontractor. The principle again is to compare the

From Dave M. O'Neill and June O'Neill, "Affirmative Action in the Labor Market," *Annals of the American Academy of Political and Social Science* 523 (September 1992): 88–103. Copyright © 1992 by the American Academy of Political and Social Science. Reprinted by permission of Sage Publications.

experience of federal contractors and noncontractors with respect to changes in their relative employment of protected groups. These studies, however, use multivariate analysis and therefore control for firm size, industry, and other factors that might contribute to employment changes. . . . In general, the studies find that federal contractors have increased their employment of black men relative to white men, and they have done so by more than the noncontractor firms that report to the EEOC. However, the measured effects differ in magnitude from study to study[1] and, although statistically significant, are not large enough to have produced any noticeable impact on the average relative earnings of black men.

It is difficult to draw any definite conclusions from the studies of administrative data. The aggregate data . . . show a large relative increase in black male employment in the federal contractor sector, but only in the period prior to 1974, prior to the period of maximum OFCCP enforcement power. The results of the multivariate analyses of microdata are not uniform, but some find an effect for the 1974–80 period. They do not eliminate the possibility that affirmative action had a positive impact, but neither do they provide strong evidence in favor of that possibility. It must be reiterated that the administrative data measure only employment gains in the federal contractor sector since data on wage gains are unavailable. As Donohue and Heckman stress, there is no close link between these employment shifts and overall improvements in the relative earnings of minorities.[2]

### Studies Using Time-Series Data

The second set of studies has the advantage of focusing directly on the changes over time in the relative earnings of protected groups and white males. Its major drawback, however, is that many different factors can influence the movement of earnings ratios over time, and it is therefore difficult to isolate the net effect of a particular influence, such as the OFCCP's affirmative action effort.

Figures 1–3 show trends over the period 1955–90 in relative earnings ratios for three comparison groups: black men to white men; black women to white women; and all women to all men. Examination of Figure 1 reveals a dramatic increase in the earnings of black men relative to white men between 1964 and 1974. (The relative earnings of black women also rose significantly, but for them the change represented a continuation of an ongoing increase.) The Civil Rights Act of 1964 made discrimination in employment illegal, and the time-series data suggest that it had a strong positive effect on the relative economic status of black men. Econometric studies by Richard Freeman, James Heckman, and others support this conclusion.[3] These authors attempt to measure other factors that might

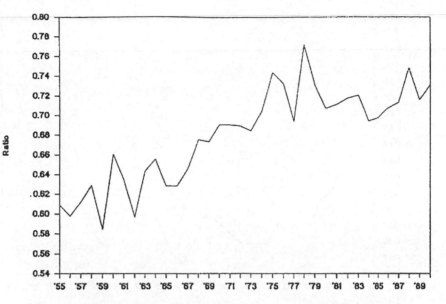

FIGURE 1 Black-white male earnings ratios: year-round full-time workers, 1955–90 (Data from U.S. Department of Commerce, Bureau of the
Census, Current Population Survey.)

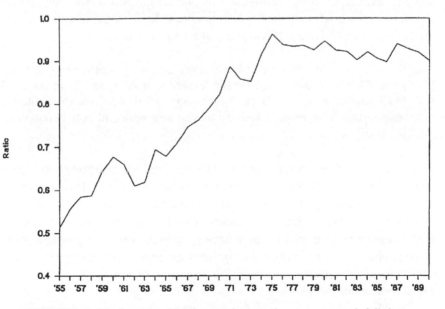

FIGURE 2 Black-white female earnings ratios: year-round full-time
workers, 1955–90 (Data from Bureau of the Census, Current Population
Survey.)

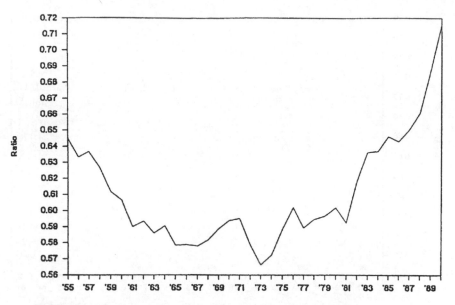

FIGURE 3 Female-male earnings ratios: year-round full-time workers, 1955–90 (Data from Bureau of the Census, Current Population Survey.)

have influenced earnings ratios such as business cycles, economic growth rates, and black-white education differences. In a study of employment trends in South Carolina, Heckman and Paynor conclude:

> Suddenly in 1964 blacks of both sexes became employed on a large scale. That year witnessed the implementation of Title VII of the 1964 Civil Rights Act. . . . Both the timing and the regression evidence suggest that government activity played an important role in integrating textiles.[4]

Some observers have taken this post-1964 increase in the ratio as evidence that the OFCCP's affirmative action program had a significant impact. However, both the timing of the effect — during the period 1964–74, during most of which the goals and timetables approach had not yet been implemented — and its concentration in the South[5] strongly suggest it was the passage of the Civil Rights Act itself that produced the large increase in relative earnings.

**Developments in the 1980s**

The enforcement efforts of the OFCCP likely diminished during the 1980s. Adjusted for inflation, federal budget expenditures for this office declined by 28 percent from 1979 to 1989. The question then arises of whether the reduction in resources — as well as the lack of enthusiasm on the part of the Reagan administration — had negative consequences for the minorities and women targeted for affirmative action.

Figures 1–3 again show how three groups fared. Roughly speaking, black-white earnings ratios for men (Figure 1) and for women (Figure 2) reached a peak in the mid-1970s and since then have fluctuated, showing a slight tendency to decline. The ratio of women's earnings to men's, by contrast, which had failed to increase throughout the 1960s and 1970s, despite the antidiscrimination efforts, rose significantly during the 1980s (Figure 3).

Both the lack of convergence in the black-white earnings gap among men and the strong rise in the earnings of women relative to men appear to be the result of factors unrelated to affirmative action. During the 1980s, there was a sizable increase in the wage differential between skilled and unskilled workers. Studies have shown that this structural shift in labor market demand can account for most of the trends in the racial earnings ratio since the mid-1970s.[6] Blacks, on average, are less skilled than whites and consequently suffer disproportionately from a shift in demand against low-skilled labor. Women's earnings rose relative to men's in the 1980s largely because women's skills increased relative to men's. Recent cohorts of working women are relatively more educated and have acquired more continuous years of work experience than was true of women in the past.[7]

### Is Affirmative Action Needed in the 1990s?

It is now almost thirty years since the passage of the Civil Rights Act. Although earnings differentials between blacks and whites have narrowed, they have by no means disappeared. Earnings differentials of varying sizes are still found between other groups as well — men and women, Hispanics and whites. The extent to which these differentials reflect underlying differences in work-related skills as opposed to discriminatory hiring and employment practices is clearly important in any debate over the need for such policies as affirmative action.

Table 2 summarizes recent data comparing the hourly earnings of black, Hispanic, and Asian workers to those of white non-Hispanic workers of the same gender. The observed patterns in the ratios suggest the complexity of the factors at work in the labor market. For example, Asian men, a group subjected to a considerable amount of prejudice and discrimination, actually have higher earnings than white men. But they also have more education. Within schooling categories, the earnings of Asian men are less than white men's, but not by much, especially considering the special language problems of recent Asian immigrants.

Strikingly different patterns are observed among women. The earnings of minority women are all very close to those of white women. Asian women's earnings actually exceed those of white women within education categories; this pattern is in sharp contrast to the situation among males.

The most serious concerns about the effects of labor market discrimination on earnings, however, relate to minority males, especially black males. Black-white earnings ratios within schooling categories are considerably higher than they were in 1964, but they are still significantly below parity. However, differences in the quality of schools attended and in family background result in differences in achievement among those who have completed the same nominal amount of schooling. Substantial differences between blacks and whites have been found in scores on tests measuring school achievement.[8] For example, at the same age and schooling level, black men score well below white men on the Armed Forces Qualification Test (AFQT). It has been demonstrated that the earnings of both blacks and whites are positively associated with AFQT scores.[9] It follows that, on average, blacks and whites with the same education level may not be viewed as equally productive by nondiscriminating firms.

How much of the racial differential in earnings between blacks and whites with the same educational level can be explained by the AFQT differential? Results derived from analysis of data on individual black and white male earners in 1987 show that after controlling for AFQT differentials by race — as well as years of schooling and region — the earnings ratio

TABLE 2  Ratios of Hourly Earnings of Black, Hispanic, and Asian Workers to Those of White Non-Hispanic Workers, by Years of School Completed and Gender, for Workers Aged 20–59 (1988–89)

| Years of Schooling | White | Black | Hispanic | Asian |
|---|---|---|---|---|
| Men | | | | |
| Total | 1.000 | .724 | .743 | 1.024 |
| 8–11 | 1.000 | .819 | .809 | .938 |
| 12 | 1.000 | .777 | .820 | .887 |
| 13–15 | 1.000 | .814 | .859 | .937 |
| 16 or more | 1.000 | .801 | .843 | .927 |
| Women | | | | |
| Total | 1.000 | .903 | .864 | 1.141 |
| 8–11 | 1.000 | .928 | .929 | 1.082 |
| 12 | 1.000 | .942 | .927 | 1.045 |
| 13–15 | 1.000 | .942 | .963 | 1.064 |
| 16 or more | 1.000 | 1.011 | .964 | 1.022 |

SOURCE: Calculated from the microdata files of U.S. Department of Commerce, Bureau of the Census, Current Population Survey, Mar. 1989; ibid., Mar. 1990.
NOTE: Hourly earnings ratios are averaged over calendar years 1988 and 1989.

increases from 83 percent to 90–96 percent.[10] Among those with college training, the ratio rises above 100 percent. These results suggest that deprivation related to school, home, and neighborhood are more serious obstacles to the attainment of black-white equality in earnings than current labor market discrimination.

**Concluding Comments and Implications**

We could find no good evidence that the federal program of affirmative action with numerical hiring goals, which reached its full force between 1974 and 1980, had a significant and lasting effect on the relative economic status of black men. This may seem an unlikely conclusion given the amount of controversy surrounding the program. If it had little effect, then why all the shouting? Our conjecture is that the program may have had significant effects on individual firms and workers even though its net effect in the aggregate was small.

For example, Jonathan Leonard has found that the OFCCP focused its compliance reviews on large firms with relatively large representations of black workers — in other words, on firms that were least likely to be discriminating.[11] Such a strategy, while generating highly visible enforcement activity, may not lead to significant increases in the relative economic status of black men.[12] Public perceptions of government programs are usually based on anecdotal evidence from newsworthy cases. Thus the complaints of a few individuals about reverse discrimination can shape public attitudes even if, in the aggregate, only a tiny percentage of qualified nonminority workers have been displaced by less qualified minority workers. Indeed, in a democracy like ours the possibility seems remote that an affirmative action program could force large numbers of private sector contractors to hire large numbers of unqualified minorities over a long period of time.

This does not mean that affirmative action bears no ill effects. The implementation of numerical goals and timetables by the OFCCP in the 1970s may have done little either to raise the relative economic status of black men or to lower the economic status of white men. Rather, its main impact may have been to generate divisiveness and ill will. A cost that is still harder to measure is the possibly negative impact that affirmative action may have had on the self-image of minority youths or on their incentives for self-help.[13]

NOTES

1. John J. Donohue, III and James Heckman, "Continuous versus Episodic Change: The Impact of Civil Rights Policy on the Economic Status of Blacks,"

*Journal of Economic Literature,* 29:1603–43 (Dec. 1991), pp. 1630–35, provides a review of the relevant studies, as does June O'Neill et al., *Economic Progress of Black Men in America,* Clearing House Publication 91 (Washington, DC: Commission on Civil Rights, Oct. 1986), pp. 100–109. Some of the individual studies frequently cited are Orley Ashenfelter and James Heckman, "Measuring the Effect of an Anti-Discrimination Program," in *Evaluating the Labor Market Effects of Social Programs,* ed. Orley Ashenfelter and James Blum (Princeton, NJ: Princeton University, Industrial Relations Section, 1976), pp. 46–84; Jonathan Leonard, "Impact of Affirmative Action on Employment," *Journal of Labor Economics,* 2(4): 439–63 (1984); Jonathan S. Leonard, "Employment and Occupational Advances under Affirmative Action," *Review of Economics and Statistics,* 66:377–85 (1984).

2. Donohue and Heckman, "Continuous versus Episodic Change," pp. 1630–35.

3. Richard B. Freeman, "Changes in the Labor Market for Black Americans, 1948–1972," in *Brookings Papers on Economic Activity,* ed. Arthur Okun and George Perry (Washington, DC: Brookings Institution, 1973), pp. 67–132; Donohue and Heckman, "Continuous versus Episodic Change," pp. 1603–43.

4. James Heckman and Brooks Paynor, "Determining the Impact of Federal Antidiscrimination Policy on the Economic Status of Blacks: A Study of South Carolina," *American Economic Review,* 79(1): 173 (Mar. 1989).

5. Donohue and Heckman, "Continuous versus Episodic Change," pp. 1637–40.

6. Chinhui Juhn, Kevin M. Murphy, and Brooks Pierce, "Accounting for the Slowdown in Black-White Convergence," in *Workers and Their Wages: Changing Patterns in the United States,* ed. Marvin Kosters (Washington, DC: American Enterprise Institute Press, 1991), pp. 107–45.

7. June O'Neill and S. Polachek, "Why the Gender Gap in Wages Narrowed in the 1980s," *Journal of Labor Economics,* 11(1): 205–228 (January 1993).

8. O'Neill et al., *Economic Progress of Black Men,* pp. 54–77; June O'Neill, "The Role of Human Capital in Earnings Differences between Black and White Men," *Journal of Economic Perspectives,* 4(4): 25–45 (Fall 1990), tab. 5, p. 41. Abigail Thernstrom, "The Drive for Racially Inclusive Schools," *The Annals of the American Academy of Political and Social Science,* 523:131–43 (Sept. 1992).

9. O'Neill, "Role of Human Capital," p. 43 and tab.

10. Ibid., tab. 5, p. 41.

11. Jonathan S. Leonard, "Affirmative Action as Earnings Redistribution: The Targeting of Compliance Reviews," *Journal of Labor Economics,* 3:363–84 (July 1985). Leonard labels the OFCCP targeting strategy as "leaning on open doors."

12. If firms subject to compliance reviews are not in fact discriminating, then relative gains by blacks can be made only at the expense of more qualified white workers. Such a situation would be difficult to force upon employers for any period of time or on a large scale.

13. See Glenn C. Loury, "Incentive Effects of Affirmative Action," *The Annals of the American Academy of Political and Social Science,* 523:19–29 (Sept. 1992).

*Harold Orlans*

# From "Affirmative Action in Higher Education"

*Selective Institutions*

The wisdom of special standards for black and Hispanic applicants has been much debated, especially at selective institutions.

Once, multiple-choice tests were said to make admission decisions fairer than subjective judgments based on essays, photographs, interviews, and family background that favored well-to-do and well-mannered applicants. Today, such tests are said to be biased against blacks and Hispanics, for whom greater reliance is placed on interviews, separately ranked test scores, extracurricular interests, and elusive or illusory factors like personal determination or the contribution of diversity to educational quality.

Critics say that admitting academically poor minorities is unfair to better-qualified applicants who are excluded. It can lead to high dropout rates, lower academic standards, remedial instruction, and a separate track with easier courses, grades, and degrees for below-par students. Those who need tutoring and grants and take longer to graduate are costly, per degree, so their retention is closely tied to money. Protests at callous revolving-door policies — when, to boost minority enrollment, colleges admit many students who soon drop out — are most cheaply met by promoting and graduating them.

It is charged that, at elite colleges, mediocre minority students are patronized and suffer anxiety and self-doubt they would not feel at less selective colleges and that lowered standards stigmatize able minority students who do not require them. Advocates of affirmative admissions respond that they prefer favorable to unfavorable discrimination. There have been special admission standards for the children of alumni, faculty, donors, politicians, celebrities, athletes, and local residents, and easy degrees

From Harold Orlans, "Affirmative Action in Higher Education," *Annals of the American Academy of Political and Social Science* 523, 144–58. Copyright © 1992 by the American Academy of Political and Social Science. Reprinted by permission of Sage Publications.

for students who buy term papers, cheat on exams, and take a gentleman's C with little study and much beer. Why not for blacks and Hispanics?

Elite colleges have social as well as academic functions. The inclusion of formerly excluded minorities among their graduates and, thereby, among our future leaders is a more important service than the preparation of more scholars and scientists. As blacks and Hispanics are a rising proportion of the population, their higher education is vital to social peace and to the quality of the work force and economy.

Eliminating special admissions would greatly reduce the number of blacks and Hispanics at selective colleges and raise it at state and community colleges, where they are already concentrated. It would revive the discarded idea of educating them only for jobs at the lower rungs of the economic and social ladder. It would restore the lily-white complexion of prominent colleges, exposing them to political and financial retribution.
. . .

*Asian Students*

The academic status of Asian Americans contrasts sharply with that of blacks and Hispanics. Though designated a minority and included in government minority statistics and policies, their academic qualifications usually equal or, in science, excel those of whites.

Yet many selective institutions admit proportionately fewer Asian than black and Hispanic applicants. Asians call that a quota or ceiling, as it must be; like whites, they must have their overrepresentation reduced if other groups are to have their underrepresentation raised.

In the early 1980s, the proportion of Asian applicants admitted to Harvard, Brown, Yale, Princeton, and Stanford was below the average for all applicants,[1] a plain case of discrimination against superior students. The proportion of applicants admitted from each ethnic group is seldom reported; for the class entering Amherst in September 1991, it was as follows: blacks, 55 percent; Hispanics, 53 percent; Asians, 31 percent; whites, 18 percent.[2]

At Berkeley, the admission chances of applicants with a 3.5 high school grade average and 1200 Scholastic Aptitude Test score were put at "nearly a hundred percent" for blacks and "about five percent" for whites or Asians.[3] As the University of Virginia admissions dean explained, " 'We take more in the groups with weaker credentials and make it harder for those with stronger credentials.' "[4]

The head of a Connecticut preparatory school tells the following story. Two of his students, both Californians, applied to Berkeley.

Student A was ranked in the top third of his class, student B in the bottom third. Student A had College Board scores totalling 1,290; student B's scores totaled 890. Student A had a record of good citizenship; student B was expelled . . . for breaking a series of major school rules. Student A was white; student B was black. Berkeley refused student A and accepted B.[5]

Determining fair and proper representation is an insoluble dilemma. Should a model college class reflect the ethnic composition of comparable colleges? of all or the best seniors in high schools from which the college recruits? of the present or future local, state, or national population? An Education Commission of the States report wants minority enrollment "at least proportionate to the minority population of each state."[6]

If affirmative efforts are to improve, not perpetuate, the educational status of blacks and Hispanics, colleges should raise their enrollment above present levels. To do so, they must dip deeper into their scholastic ranks. Blacks were 5 percent and Hispanics, 3 percent of the Massachusetts population yet 8 and 7 percent, respectively, of the fall 1990 entering class at Harvard, which may have sought targets closer to the 12 and 8 percent of the national population that blacks and Hispanics then constituted.

Of course, selective colleges cream the crop, leaving poorer students to crowded public colleges.

*Unselective Institutions*
Colleges need students as sawmills need logs. Since government student aid benefits the college as well as the student, a tacit collusion can arise whereby both share the money and neither cares overmuch about education — or even about attendance. . . .

. . .

**Affirmative Hiring**

About 1100 institutions with $50,000 or more in federal contracts must set numerical goals for hiring more women and minority faculty and other employees in areas where they are "underutilized," or not employed in proportion to their "availability."

. . .

*Women Faculty*
Historically, the proportion of faculty who were women has greatly exceeded the proportion of women among Ph.D. recipients. . . . Only in the early 1980s did the flood of women into graduate and professional schools change that situation. Women faculty and advanced-degree recipients have been concentrated in education, the humanities, and what have been called semiprofessions such as home economics, library science, nursing, and social work.

Women have also been concentrated in the lower faculty ranks and salaries, in teaching rather than research activities, and in two- and four-year colleges and universities with lesser reputations. Affirmative action has sought to change this distribution to resemble that of men and to produce more women Ph.D.s in predominantly male fields like the physical sciences, math, and engineering.

The dubious success of substantial resources devoted to this effort can be judged by comparing the degrees awarded to women in various sciences with those in professional fields (Table 3).

One might see the rise in the number of women's engineering Ph.D.s and the doubling of their physics Ph.D.s in the 1978–88 decade as a great success, but few degrees were actually awarded and the number in mathematics declined. The continued growth in the life sciences, traditionally the sciences of greatest interest to women, seems more significant.

The real revolution occurred in the professions, especially law and medicine. Including 24,600 master's of business administration degrees, the terminal business degree, which the Education Department does not regard as professional, women received four times more professional than doctoral degrees in 1988. From 1958 to 1989, the proportion of M.D.s awarded to women rose from 5 to 33 percent and the number, from 347 to 5,128; the proportion of law degrees, from 3 to 41 percent and the number,

**TABLE 3   Advanced Degrees Awarded to Women in Selected Sciences and Professions, 1978–88**

| Degree and Field | Number of Degrees Awarded | | | | Percentage Change 1978–88 | |
| | 1978 | | 1988 | | | |
| | Total | Women | Total | Women | Total | Women |
|---|---|---|---|---|---|---|
| Ph.D.* | 25,291 | 7,355 | 23,172 | 9,505 | −8.4 | 29.2 |
| Science and Engineering* | 13,086 | 2,792 | 12,847 | 4,114 | −1.8 | 47.3 |
| Physics | 804 | 29 | 721 | 57 | −10.3 | 96.6 |
| Math | 619 | 91 | 341 | 59 | −44.9 | −35.2 |
| Life sciences | 3,522 | 778 | 3,658 | 1,285 | 3.9 | 65.2 |
| Engineering | 1,261 | 30 | 1,778 | 178 | 41.0 | 493.3 |
| Professional* | 66,581 | 14,311 | 70,735 | 25,251 | 6.2 | 76.4 |
| Dentistry | 5,189 | 566 | 4,477 | 1,177 | −13.7 | 108.0 |
| Medicine | 14,279 | 3,069 | 15,358 | 5,080 | 7.6 | 65.5 |
| Law | 34,402 | 8,945 | 35,397 | 14,330 | 2.9 | 60.2 |

SOURCES: For Ph.D.s (to U.S. citizens only): *Science & Engineering Indicators—1989* (Washington, DC: National Science Board, 1989), p. 226; for professional degrees: *Digest of Education Statistics 1991* (Washington, DC: National Center for Education Statistics, 1991), pp. 280–81, and *Digest of Education Statistics 1980* (Washington, DC: National Center for Education Statistics, 1980), p. 128.
    *Including fields not listed below.

from 272 to 14,519: a genuine invasion and occupation of formerly male domains.

## The Asian-Black Contrast

Affirmative action was instituted for blacks but, in advanced degrees and faculty appointments, Asians have prospered.

The contrast between the relatively stable number of Ph.D.s awarded to and faculty positions held by blacks since the mid-1970s and the sharp increase in those of Asians is striking. The 1990 census reported four times as many blacks as Asians in the U.S. population; the 1980 census, eight times as many. Yet from 1975 to 1985, the number of full-time Asian faculty rose 9,300 and black faculty, 500. By 1990, there were more Asian than black faculty—24,250 and 23,225, respectively.

In 1987, six times more Asian than black scientists and engineers with Ph.D.s were engaged in academic research and development, a source of income beloved by academic administrators (Table 4). That helps to explain why, at Harvard in a recent year, six times more Asians than blacks held faculty appointments, including many postdoctoral training and research positions.[7]

**TABLE 4   Number of Black and Asian Scientists and Engineers with Ph.D.s Engaged in Academic Research and Development, 1987**

| Sciences | Total# | Blacks | Asians |
|---|---|---|---|
| Physical* | 22,407 | 192 | 2,179 |
| Mathematical† | 9,172 | 62 | 995 |
| Computer | 3,491 | . . . ** | 348 |
| Environmental‡ | 6,348 | 30 | 331 |
| Life | 51,918 | 736 | 4,456 |
| Biological | 34,138 | 459 | 2,857 |
| Agricultural | 7,040 | 97 | 347 |
| Medical | 10,740 | 180 | 1,252 |
| Engineering§ | 19,059 | 119 | 3,381 |
| Psychological | 13,012 | 230 | 319 |
| Social‖ | 29,179 | 736 | 1,834 |
| Total | 154,586 | 2,111 | 13,843 |

SOURCE: *Science & Engineering Indicators—1989* (Washington, DC: National Science Board, 1989), p. 320.

*Chemistry, physics, astronomy.
†Mathematics, statistics.
‡Earth and atmospheric science, oceanography.
§Aeronautical, chemical, civil, electrical, materials, mechanical, nuclear, systems, and so on.
‖Economics, political science, sociology, anthropology.
#Including whites, Hispanics, Native Americans.
**Less than 20.

The contrast in the academic record, credentials, and employment of these two minorities shows the folly of seeking identical employment patterns for groups whose social, economic, and educational experience differs so radically.

Many Asians received their early education in nations where schools provide academic preparation, not detention, entertainment, or a battlefield where teachers and students fight for attention and control. Asian Ph.D. and faculty statistics are magnified by foreign students who eventually remain. Of the 5,150 Asians awarded Ph.D.s in 1989, only 624 were citizens; 631 held permanent visas, and 3,877, temporary visas. Both foreign and American-born Asians come from intact families, study earnestly, and are not mocked or harassed for doing so. The longer they live here, the more they may relapse toward the American academic mean.

Many black students suffer the ills of distressed neighborhoods, turbulent schools, and broken homes. In 1989, 60 percent of those in higher education and 53 percent of those awarded Ph.D.s were women, compared to 29 percent of Asians and 41 percent of whites. Many men had left school for work, unemployment, the military, crime, and other nonacademic pursuits.

Asians have clustered in the sciences and engineering, where academic employment prospects remain good; blacks, in softer graduate fields. Historically, black graduates could find work in segregated colleges and school systems; education still accounted for 48 percent of the Ph.D.s earned by black citizens in 1989.

By margins as high as 6 to 1, blacks have preferred professional degrees in such fields as law, medicine, dentistry, and business to Ph.D.s. Who but universities trying to placate protesting students and labor inspectors can say they are wrong to choose the rewards of private practice over the aggravations of the academy?

NOTES

1. Sucheng Chan and Ling-chi Wang, "Racism and the Model Minority: Asian-Americans in Higher Education," in *The Racial Crisis in American Higher Education,* ed. Philip G. Altbach and Kofi Lomotey (Albany: State University of New York, 1991), p. 54.

2. *Amherst Student,* 3 Apr. 1991, pp. 1–2. Of the 973 students admitted 103, or 10.6 percent, were black; 102, or 10.5 percent, Hispanic; 146, or 15 percent, Asian; and 622, or 64 percent, white or unidentified.

3. As Ernest Koeningsburg, professor of business, who has served on Berkeley admission committees, is quoted in Dinesh D'Souza, "Illiberal Education," *Atlantic,* Mar. 1991, p. 54.

4. Quoted by Thomas Edsall and Mary Edsall, "Race," *Atlantic,* May 1991, p. 73.

5. Donald Werner, "College Admissions: Shaky Ethics," *New York Times,* 4 June 1988. Copyright 1988 by The New York Times Company. Reprinted by permission.

6. Mary Crystal Cage, "Government Officials Urged to Create Incentives for Colleges to Increase Minority Enrollment," *Chronicle of Higher Education,* 12 Dec. 1990, p. A17.

7. See John B. Williams, "Affirmative Action at Harvard," *The Annals of the American Academy of Political and Social Science,* 523, 207–220 (Sept. 1992).

*Terry Eastland*

# From *Ending Affirmative Action: The Case for Colorblind Justice*

One of the central and hard-won lessons of the fight for colorblindness, lasting more than a century and a quarter, was that distinctions drawn on the basis of race inevitably lead to racial discrimination. That is why the advocates of colorblindness sought the elimination of racial distinctions in the law. They sought to end the source, the raw material, of racial discrimination. The nation was the better for their efforts when, starting in the 1940s, our legal system was strengthened by the addition of a variety of antidiscrimination laws, culminating in the Civil Rights Act of 1964. Soon afterward, the founders of affirmative action, searching for ways to improve the material condition of black Americans and make amends for slavery and segregation, found the constraints of colorblind law inconvenient. They managed to loosen the colorblind strictures of the Civil Rights Act of 1964, and the federal judiciary failed to tighten them in turn. Once preferential treatment was made possible, it spread throughout the public and private sectors, and the targets of numerical affirmative action became more numerous, coming to include Hispanics, Asians, and women.

Defenders of the policy initially promised that it would be temporary—a position that implicitly recognized that it is better not to sort people on the basis of race, that colorblindness is a worthy guide. But with the first step away from colorblindness, further steps came more easily, and in time we heard less often the promise that someday we would renew our previous commitment.

Nonetheless, more than a quarter century of thinking by race and counting by race has served only to confirm and strengthen the case for colorblind law.

We now know that when government has the power to sort people on the basis of race, racial discrimination often results. Preferential treatment is never benign. Whoever would have been admitted to a school, or won the promotion or the contract, but for race, has suffered discrimination — and there is no good discrimination. The nation owes a debt of gratitude to people like Allan Bakke, Brian Weber, Randy Pech, and Cheryl Hopwood, who have brought lawsuits challenging preferential affirmative action. They have courageously kept alive the question of the legality and morality of preferential treatment, providing often lonely witness to the principle at the heart of colorblind law — that no one in America should be discriminated against on account of race.

We know, too, that the effort to regulate on the basis of race can have unanticipated consequences. Where the old advocates of colorblind law were pessimists about the very idea of racial regulation, the founders of affirmative action were optimists, confident of their ability to distinguish between benign and invidious racial classifications. They thought the world could be divided into good and bad people. The bad discriminated against blacks either intentionally or through seemingly neutral procedures that produced adverse effects. The good — and the founders of affirmative action included themselves in this category — sought to do well by blacks. They were pure in heart, and so they could be trusted not to harm blacks.

But now we know better. It was weak-minded and dangerously naive to think that taking race into account would produce unambiguously good results for those in whose behalf it was done. Many ostensible beneficiaries of affirmative action have testified that preferential treatment often leads to self-doubt, dependency, and entitlement. To be sure, affirmative action doesn't always do that. Sometimes it "works," though the paradox of affirmative action is that its "working" is a function of how soon the recipient quits it entirely and labors under the same rules as everyone else, a sign of genuine equality that is possible only among individuals. But, as the practice of affirmative action has shown, no one knows enough confidently to predict in advance of an act of preferential treatment which effects, for better or worse, it will have upon a given recipient. This negative experience of affirmative action does not constitute an unanswerable argument against it; patients do undergo risky operations. But we do have a choice in the matter; that is, we do not have to take the risk of affirmative action. And once free of it, those now eligible for it would be able to compete and achieve on the same terms as everyone else.

*Richard F. Tomasson*

# From "Affirmative Action in Education"

Affirmative action for designated race and ethnic categories in higher education is, at worst, patronizing, corrupting, and eventually demoralizing to its intended beneficiaries; at best, quite unnecessary in a country oversupplied with colleges and universities.

Actually, preferential undergraduate admissions has relevance for only a tiny, but very significant, proportion of colleges and universities, those that are able to be selective. Fewer than 5 percent of freshmen are enrolled in the twenty-five "top" universities and the twenty-five "top" small colleges.[1] The great majority enroll in institutions that require little more than graduating from high school along with some mild provisions regarding grades or test scores. Some state schools have no admission requirements at all beyond high school graduation; in a few states, law mandates admission to any graduate of a high school in the state. Community colleges admit anyone.

But to elite colleges and universities affirmative action is an obsessive concern. The most touted public reason is to achieve a diverse student body. The old reason, to compensate for past hurtful discrimination, has faded away as the clients of affirmative action have expanded beyond blacks to include other groups for whom the claim of past discrimination is less compelling, or not compelling at all. (Interestingly and revealingly, there is a virtual absence of gender-based affirmative action in higher education.)

There is another sort of preference, much less publicly celebrated by universities than that of achieving ethnic diversity. It is an affirmative action for the privileged. And it is used to justify race and ethnic preferences. If a college gives special treatment to the offspring of alumni, so goes the argument, is it not equally just to give similar treatment to minority

From *Affirmative Action: The Pros and Cons of Policy and Practice* edited by Richard F. Tomasson, Faye J. Crosby, and Sharon D. Herzberger (Washington, DC: American University Press, 1996).

applicants? Can one accept the former sort of preference and not the latter? Isn't there a *quid pro quid* here? If being an alumnus offspring is treated as a plus when applying to Dartmouth, fairness would seem to insist that being a minority person should also be treated as a plus. Justice Lewis Powell argued just this in his famous *Bakke* opinion of 1978, but, as John Jeffries, Jr., has written in his biography of the justice, he intended it to be only a temporary measure, maybe to last a decade. What the justice feared was that special admissions programs like those at Davis "would become entrenched bureaucracies, and minorities would come to regard them as perpetual entitlements. What Powell feared most was permanence. For him, racial preferences were a short-term response to a pressing need."[2]

At Harvard College in 1968 almost "half of alumni sons were being admitted"; this has declined in recent years to "approximately 40 percent of alumni children . . . against 14 percent of nonalumni applicants."[3] This preference is justified by the claim that alumni are one of the "constituencies important to the college." It really exists to encourage alumni to be generous with their pocketbooks.

Preferential treatment of "legacies" in elite colleges and universities has received little criticism.[4] It is a deplorable practice, more so than any preferential treatment of minorities and for which it provides perverse justification. Favoring legacies is a worse sin than favoring minorities because it lacks the altruistic, if misguided, intentions of affirmative action. It most directly discriminates against Asians, few of whom are legacies, and from whom it takes away places. Both forms of preference are violations of the universalistic and meritocratic standards that should be of bedrock importance to universities.

Presidents of major universities are among the most vocal Cassandras when contemplating the passing on of affirmative action. The president of the University of California, Chang-Lin Tien, has claimed that without affirmative action only about 2 percent of Berkeley undergraduates would be black. The president of the University of Texas at Austin, Robert A. Bergdahl, has lamented that without affirmative action only some 3 percent of those accepted to the university's law school would be black. Even if these estimates are on target, and they probably are, they should not be cause for alarm, nor a last-ditch argument for affirmative action in university admissions.

In a world without affirmative action, maybe only 2 percent of Berkeley undergraduates would be black, but maybe 15 percent of the undergraduates at nearby San Francisco State and San Jose State would be black. If only 3 percent of the entering students at the University of Texas Law School were black, maybe 10 percent of those at the state's somewhat less selective law school in Houston would be black. The most thoughtful reaction to such an unbalanced but discrimination-free system is, *So what!* The student — and faculty — composition of universities in our multi-ethnic country will always be unbalanced and in flux. Jews and Asians are more over-represented in selective colleges than blacks and Hispanics are underrepresented. About a quarter of Ivy League undergraduates are Jews; over 40 percent of recent freshman classes at Berkeley and UCLA have been Asian. It took Italian-Americans six or seven decades after their heaviest immigration to this country in the first decade of this century to achieve parity with the general population in higher education.[5]

Only in America do we find the practice of admitting students to upper tier schools by using, in addition to academic criteria — grades and test scores — such dubious, presumptive, and downright irrelevant criteria as potential for leadership, character, personality, unusual life experiences, extracurricular activities, charitable activities, athletic, musical and other talents, special qualities allegedly revealed by written essays, plus letters of recommendation and interviews. If all this subjectivism and departure from objectively measurable academic merit is allowable in the name of achieving the elusive diversity and a balanced entering class, why not race and ethnicity too?

No fewer than twenty-three diverse people make up the admissions staff at Harvard.[6] "We obviously want to get talented students from all backgrounds," says William R. Fitzsimmons, dean of admissions and financial aid at Harvard. He continues with a non sequitur, often unavoidable when attempting to defend what admissions people do: "One of the roles we've always played is to educate future leaders. Increasingly, African Americans are becoming more involved in the leadership of cities, states, and in Congress, and in that context we would be remiss if we weren't going out and getting talented people from every background." "To say that one person is more qualified for admission than another is tough to do," claims Karl M. Furstenberg, dean of admissions at Dartmouth.

There are no data anywhere to suggest that university admissions committees in highly selective institutions have any greater success in choosing successful entering classes, using all their subjective criteria, than if they went strictly by the numbers. Quite the contrary, since the publication more than four decades ago of Paul Meehl's *Clinical vs. Statistical Prediction,* the evidence is compellingly the other way: statistical prediction is better than clinical prediction in determining successful educational outcomes and successful job performance.[7]

Elite American colleges and universities would do well to admit students at all levels and in all programs solely on the basis of objective academic measures, just as is done in all western European universities except the colleges of Oxford and Cambridge. Universities, of all our institutions, should abhor discretionary and informal methods of selection when selection must be made. This includes law schools and medical schools. Law and medicine are both wide and varied fields in which there is scope for many different types of personality, many sorts of talent. Race and ethnicity — like being a so-called legacy or having had unusual life experiences or coming from Wyoming — should be irrelevant considerations.

Many people will argue that in such a coldly objective system narrow grade grubbers and successful test takers will beat out the erratic geniuses with wide interests, but less than stunning graders and test scores. But, again, *So what!* They can go to the University of Wisconsin instead of Yale.

This would be a great reform for American higher education. It would abolish the rampant subjectivism that now prevails in deciding who gains admittance to America's elite colleges, those that bestow extraneous status and career advantages.

The fairest, most efficient, and simplest system of admissions to our extraordinarily competitive colleges and universities would be a lottery system. Here is how it might work: A portion of an entering freshman class, say, a third, would be offered early admission only on the basis of grades and test scores. This means doing away even with interviews and letters of recommendation. These are the superbly qualified. The remaining two-thirds would be chosen by lottery from *all* those deemed qualified on the basis of the same measures used to choose the superbly qualified. These are the well qualified.

Not only would such a system remove the gratuitous discretion presently used in admissions to elite schools, it would make them a bit less elite, a move in the right direction for the world's most stratified system of higher education. It would produce a natural diversity instead of a contrived diversity.

A lottery system would not overcome the current over-representation of whites, most notably Jews and Asians, and the under-representation of blacks and Hispanics. *But it would lessen the over- and under-representation of the various groups because the net has been cast more widely.* More applications are in the pool. Chance would be a factor as it is in life. No more would there be stigmatized "affirmative action babies," and no more would there be the excessive dropout rate of black and Hispanic students along with the sad consequences.

Below the super-selective institutions there is a tier of more modestly selective institutions for those who don't quite make it to the major leagues. And let it be put up in neon lights that most American colleges and universities are hardly selective at all. There is more than enough room for everybody.

. . .

It is a subversive and dangerous practice to manipulate entrance requirements by race to achieve some allegedly desirable balance. Who is to decide what that balance should be? It is subversive because it is an assault on a merit-based ethic and on fairness to discrete individuals as opposed to a racial or ethnic category. This ethic is one of the fundamental values of modern democratic society, and it is being squeezed out by the new equality of group representation. Such social engineering is also socially dangerous because of its unintended consequences. Lowering entrance standards for blacks and Hispanics requires raising standards for whites and Asians. Within the selective institution this widens the gap between, on the one hand, whites and Asians, and blacks and Hispanics, on the other. In recent years the gap in SAT scores between whites and blacks has been an enormous 235 points at UCLA, 218 at Dartmouth, 206 at the University of Virginia, 171 at Stanford. Harvard has the lowest average difference in SAT scores among elite colleges, 95 points.[8] The 1994 national gap in scores was 198 points, 217 for males and 181 for females.

. . .

In no institutional sector is the balkanization of our society seen more clearly than in the universities.[9] In no sector will it be more difficult to phase out preferential affirmative action than in the universities.

## NOTES

1. Richard Harwood, "The New Elite in American Society," *Cosmos 1995,* pp. 13–19.
2. John C. Jeffries, Jr., *Justice Lewis F. Powell, Jr.* (New York: Charles Scribner's Sons, 1994), p. 471.
3. Robert Klitgaard, *Choosing Elites* (New York: Basic Books, 1985), p. 27; Jake Lamar, "Whose legacy is it, anyway?" *New York Times* (9 October 1991), p. A15.
4. Exceptions are Thomas Sowell, *Preferential Policies: An International Perspective* (New York: Morrow, 1990) and *Race and Culture: A World View* (New York: Basic Books, 1994) and Michael Lind, *The Next American Nation* (New York: Free Press, 1995), pp. 165–171.
5. Linda Chávez, *Out of the Barrio* (New York: Basic Books, 1991), p. 120.
6. From a picture of the staff in the *Chronicle of Higher Education,* vol. 41 (28 April 1995), p. A19. The quotations in this paragraph are from the article in which the picture appears, "Private Colleges Try to Keep a Low Profile," by Stephen Burd.
7. See the voluminous evidence for the superiority of statistical vs. clinical prediction in Richard J. Herrnstein and Charles Murray, *The Bell Curve; Intelligence and Class Structure in American Life* (New York: Free Press, 1994).

8. SAT scores are from various articles in the *Chronicle of Higher Education* under the rubric "Affirmative Action on the Line" (28 April 1995).

9. See John H. Bunzel, *Race Relations on Campus: Stanford Students Speak* (Stanford, CA: Stanford Alumni Association, 1992), for one such report.

*Madeline E. Heilman*

# From "Affirmative Action's Contradictory Consequences"

The potentially deleterious consequences of affirmative action for organizations and the people who work in them have been amply documented (see Heilman, 1994, for a review). The root of these negative consequences is the widespread belief that affirmative action entails preferential selection and treatment on the basis of group membership (Kravitz & Platania, 1993). The research indicates that when individuals have reason to discount the role of merit criteria in selection, when the other is perceived to be benefited not because of what he or she merits but because of what social group he/she belongs to, (1) the selected others can become tainted with a stigma of incompetence, (2) the nonbeneficiaries can feel cheated and become resentful and demotivated, and (3) the beneficiaries themselves can suffer in their self-evaluations and work attitudes and behavior. Each of these are [*sic*] discussed briefly below.

## Three Deleterious Consequences of Affirmative Action

### The Stigma of Incompetence
Results of several research investigations give credence to the idea that affirmative action can stigmatize its intended beneficiaries, causing inferences of incompetence. Thus, Garcia, Erskine, Hawn, and Casmay (1981) demonstrated that more unfavorable evaluations were made about the qualifications of minority applicants to a graduate school program when commitment to affirmative action was highlighted, and Jacobson and Koch (1977) demonstrated that a woman's leadership performance was devalued when she was appointed leader solely on the basis of her sex. In a series of investigations, my colleagues and I built upon this work (Heilman, Block, & Lucas, 1992). Inferences of incompetence were found to result from association with affirmative action regardless of whether research participants doing the evaluations were male or female, or whether they were

*Journal of Social Issues* 52, no. 4 (winter 1996): 105–8.

students or working people. These inferences were evidenced whether the target beneficiary was a woman or a member of a racial minority, or whether the association with affirmative action efforts was explicitly communicated or only assumed. Additional research (Heilman, Block, & Stathatos, 1997) has demonstrated the affirmative action stigma of incompetence to be very potent and to prevail even after on-the-job information is available; short of explicit and unequivocal evidence of performance effectiveness, it appears to dominate competence judgments.

*Reactions of Those Who Feel Unfairly Bypassed*
There is reason to believe, based on evidence in the literature (e.g., Kluegel & Smith, 1982; Nacoste, 1987, 1990), as well as reports in the public press (e.g., Brimelow, 1992; Henry, 1991), that by explicitly taking group membership of women and minorities into account and giving it favored consideration in decision making, those who traditionally would have been selected for jobs often feel they have been unfairly bypassed. The negative consequences of this experience of injustice have been documented in a recent study (Heilman, McCullough, & Gilbert, 1996). When the male subjects saw themselves as more (or even equally) deserving of a desired task role than the preferentially selected female beneficiary, there were costs in terms of motivation, negative affect, and work attitudes. And what is particularly striking about these results is the finding that this occurred even without information establishing deservingness; when preferential selection occurred, male nonbeneficiaries assumed themselves to be the more qualified and deserving of the desired task role. It also should be noted that all participants who were exposed to a preferential rather than a merit-based selection procedure demonstrated a greater reluctance to engage in helping behavior than those who were not.

*Beneficiaries' Self Views of Competence*
Early research by Nacoste (1985), using a role playing procedure, suggested that affirmative action may in fact harm those it was designed to benefit Subsequent investigations, conducted together with several of my colleagues, systematically explored this issue. A series of laboratory experiments during which subjects actually were selected for a desired task role (leader) either on the basis of merit or preferentially on the basis of their sex strongly supported the idea that preferential selection can trigger negative self-regard for women beneficiaries; they were found to rate their performance more negatively, to view themselves as more deficient in leadership ability, and to be more eager to relinquish their desirable leadership role (Heilman, Simon, & Repper, 1987; Heilman, Lucas, & Kaplow, 1990). The absence of similar findings for men, and results of an investigation directly

varying male and female subjects' degree of confidence in their ability to do the task (Heilman et al., 1990), indicated that this negativity was most likely to occur when individuals were uncertain about their competence, suggesting that those in today's organizations whose selection breaks new ground are particularly vulnerable to adverse consequences. Extending those ideas, another study (Heilman, Rivero, & Brett, 1991) looked beyond self-perceptions and attitudes to actual work-related behavior and demonstrated the tendency of preferentially selected women subjects to shy away from demanding tasks, choosing those that are less challenging and complex. Findings of harm to beneficiaries of affirmative action also had been reported by other investigators (Major, Feinstein, & Crocker, 1994; Turner, Pratkanis, & Hardaway, 1991).

## The Costs of Affirmative Action's Deleterious Consequences

How important are these potentially negative consequences of affirmative action when measured against its evident success in employment participation rates? The answer is, resoundingly, "very important." Despite its potential limitations on generalization to all affirmative action situations (it has primarily focused on women beneficiaries, been conducted in the laboratory, and involved "strong" forms of affirmative action in which group membership was given heavy weight in the selection decision), the consistent pattern of results found in my research, together with the corroborating findings of others using different samples and methods, compel serious questions about the ultimate effectiveness of affirmative action as a policy. These questions concern not only its potentially detrimental psychological consequences but also the likelihood of it achieving its original objective — the attainment of equality in the workplace.

The research findings suggest that, as currently construed, affirmative action policies can thwart rather than promote workplace equality. The stigma associated with affirmative action, as well as the increased salience of social categories produced by the very idea of affirmative action, are apt to fuel rather than debunk stereotypical thinking and prejudiced attitudes. Denying individuals the satisfaction and pride in knowing they have achieved something on their own merits can decrease their self-efficacy, fostering self-views of inferiority. The anger and/or frustration resulting from feeling unfairly bypassed for employment opportunities can aggravate workplace tensions and intergroup hostilities. Therefore, despite its apparent success in expanding employment opportunities for women and minorities, affirmative action has not necessarily moved us closer to the objective of creating a more equal workplace or a more equal society.

Is this a function of affirmative action as a concept or of affirmative action as it currently is implemented? Might not affirmative action be more successful in reaching all of its original objectives if it were enacted differently in the work setting? Although scholars have begun to address these questions (see, for example, Pratkanis & Turner, 1996), the answers are not yet clear. What is clear, however, is that the adverse psychological consequences of affirmative action rest on perceptions not on objective reality. Thus, combating them requires challenging and redefining current beliefs and assumptions about what, exactly, affirmative action is and what it means in actual practice. As long as it is thought to bring women and minorities into the organizational mainstream through preferential procedures based predominantly on group membership, it seems likely to continue to perpetuate the very conditions that gave rise to the problems it was designed to resolve.

So, where does this leave us? There is a need to maintain efforts to combat discrimination and promote equal opportunity in the workplace; without such efforts sexism and racism, unbridled, will no doubt poison the environment of work organizations even more than they currently do. Nonetheless, the message imparted so repeatedly by research results must be heeded: simply providing women and minorities access to jobs traditionally reserved for White men in our society does not necessarily further their cause. Access does not imply acceptance, and access does not guarantee advancement. On the contrary, affirmative action, unless it ceases to be associated with an absence of quality standards, seems as much a part of the problem as a part of the remedy.

Stephan Thernstrom and Abigail Thernstrom

# From *America in Black and White: One Nation, Indivisible*

In 1994, under pressure from the federal government, the University of California at San Diego agreed to pay $600,000 to twenty-seven men and women who had applied for jobs they didn't get. The school denied doing anything wrong; indeed, the assistant vice-chancellor for human resources, an African American, claimed not to have known the applicants' racial or ethnic identity. Color wasn't the issue, he said; the jobs required skills these applicants lacked.

That same year in that same city the Marriott Hotel promised to pay back wages totaling $627,000 to thirty-four black women, unsuccessful applicants for jobs. As part of the settlement with federal investigators, Marriott offered jobs to the women, established on-the-job training, and gave them credit for the vacation time and sick leave they might have had. It created a training program for managers and agreed to regular meetings with department heads to "review, update and reaffirm" Marriott's affirmative action policies. In addition, the hotel promised to keep careful track of its hiring record, so that members of staff assigned to interviewing prospective employees would know if members of designated minority groups were underrepresented in the relevant positions; in fact, managers were expected to justify the hiring of a white whenever the number of minorities in the position was disproportionately low.[1]

Why plead guilty if in fact the school and hotel were (as they claimed) innocent? Investigations into possible employment discrimination by those who do business with the federal government — most often undertaken in the absence of a single complaint against the suspect institution — are lengthy and, for those whom the government targets, arduous and expensive. Refusing to settle is costly, with part of the cost being the loss of lucrative contracts. On the other side of the ledger is the necessity not only to pay salaries and benefits that were not earned, but to engage in diversity training and race-based hiring — costs, indisputably, but most often viewed as less pricey than a fight.

These are not exceptional stories, and they are but one corner of a much larger picture. Affirmative action considerations now affect almost all federal and many state government contracts, as well as much employment, both public and private. Has the heavy hand of the government become too intrusive? Or is vigorous enforcement of racial equity in employment and government contracts essential to keep discrimination in check? Those who support preferential policies view them as vital to the economic well-being of blacks. They are seen as an essential life raft — the means by which many blacks stay economically afloat, the antipoverty program that really works, the only real guarantee against a resurgence of racism that will wipe out the economic progress made by African Americans.

Critics of preferential policies, of course, have a different view. Aside from philosophical opposition to programs in which skin color determines the beneficiaries and to inferring inequality of opportunity from statistical disparities, they note abuses — large and small. For instance, a September 1994 audit of fifty of the larger minority-owned firms that had been the beneficiaries of a federal set-aside for "small disadvantaged businesses" uncovered a startling fact. Thirty-five of the fifty owners had a net worth in excess of $1 million; five of them had personal residences valued at between $800,000 and $1.4 million.[2] Other levels of government have set-aside policies that are plagued by similar problems. In 1993 a controversy erupted over a minority business enterprise program that reserved 35 percent of Atlanta's contract work for blacks. The program, instituted by a black mayor in 1975, was supposed to help black entrepreneurs; instead, it became the means by which a handful of mostly white businessmen got rich through a system of kickbacks and bribery.[3]

Whatever the merits of these opposing arguments, one thing is clear: we have come a long way since the Civil Rights Act of 1964, which focused on stopping acts of intentional discrimination in the workforce. How we got from here to there: that is the main question we address here. We concentrate on the federal story, although we touch on affirmative action policies in state and local government and in the private sector as well.

. . .

## "Disadvantaged" Black Millionaires

The 8(a) program requires participants to be both socially and economically disadvantaged. Nevertheless, some participants are exceedingly well off, an SBA audit discovered. "Owners who receive high annual compensa-tions should be found ineligible for continued participation." But continu-ing participation was not the primary issue; how did anyone living in a million-dollar house qualify in the first place? As of early 1995, the list of 8(a) eligible firms included thirty-two of the top hundred black businesses in the country, and $440 million in federal dollars had gone to a single company.[4] Moreover, 1 percent of the 5,155 participants in the 8(a) pro-gram had received more than 25 percent of the $4.4 billion in contract dollars awarded in 1994.[5]

The problem of wealthy black businessmen benefiting from other sorts of set-asides became national news in the spring of 1995, when the Republican-controlled Congress repealed a Federal Communications Commission (FCC) program that allowed companies to defer paying taxes on profits from the sale of broadcast properties purchased by firms that were at least partially minority-owned. Frank Washington had designed the policy in 1978 when he was at the FCC as assistant to the chairman. In 1995 he headed up a partnership planning to purchase (for $2.3 billion) a cable television system owned by one of the world's largest entertain-ment-media conglomerates, Viacom. Had Congress not intervened, it would have been a fabulously lucrative deal for the California multimil-lionaire who — as an African American — qualified for the break he had invented; the tax deferral was worth about $600 million to Viacom, whose savings Washington and his partners would have shared by buying at a below-market price.[6] The long list of other prominent and prosperous African Americans who profited handsomely from the preferential treat-ment the FCC accorded members of minority groups included General Colin Powell, O. J. Simpson, Patrick Ewing, Bill Cosby, and Vernon Jordan.[7]

Other problems have plagued set-aside programs, many of them in-volving the difficulty in determining when the minorities involved in a particular business are only there as a front for others. The bribes and kickbacks that enriched white businessmen in Atlanta (mentioned previ-ously) were not an isolated instance. In May 1995 two brothers identified as Mafia members were arrested in New York, charged with creating compa-nies in which minorities were serving as a front in order to obtain contracts that were off-limits to whites. Having been certified by the state as minority business enterprises, those sham minority-owned companies had obtained about $5 million in city and state contracts for work in schools, hospitals, and the subway system, even though their bids were not the lowest submit-ted. The problems were not new; eleven years earlier a state investigation had labeled the entire set-aside program a failure.[8]

**Assessing the Evidence of Bias in Employment
and Contracting**

Whatever the problems, the civil rights community and the Democratic Party continue to argue, race-conscious employment and contracting programs remain essential. "There are those who say, my fellow Americans, that even good affirmative action programs are no longer needed," President Clinton said on 19 July 1995. But "let us consider" that "the unemployment rate for African Americans remains about twice that of whites. . . . in the nation's largest companies only six-tenths of 1 percent of senior management positions are held by African Americans. . . . Black home loan applicants are more than twice as likely to be denied credit as whites with the same qualifications. . . ."[9]

The issue the president raised is obviously serious and complicated, and those who have studied the evidence do not agree on either the level of discrimination in the economy or on the remedy for that which persists. If blacks are still unemployed at twice the white rate, affirmative action has not been putting people back to work, critics argue. If three decades of medicine hasn't cured the disease, why continue? they ask. Supporters, on the other hand, believe that traditional antidiscrimination policies, with their focus on invidious intent and their insistence on race-neutral hiring, will not do the trick. The problems are too systemic and too subtle; they require a certain measure of race consciousness. "Set-asides" in government contracts and specific hiring "goals and timetables" in both the private and public sector are at least a hedge against calamity.

How much discrimination? is obviously the first question. We start with the figures for annual income by race and sex for 1994, the most recent data currently available in sufficient detail for our purposes. In 1994 the incomes of black men averaged only 64 percent of those of non-Hispanic white men, while black women took in 90 percent as much as white women (Table 1).

These numbers alone, however, are insufficient to conclude that discrimination depresses the incomes of black males by 36 percent and the incomes of black females by 10 percent. We know, for instance, that earning power depends on education. Even if the labor market were perfectly fair, racial differences in educational qualifications would lead to differences in income. Although African Americans have made very impressive educational gains since World War II, in 1994, 27 percent of blacks aged twenty-five or over had no high school diploma, as compared with only 15 percent of whites. And nearly twice as many whites as blacks (24 percent versus 13 percent) were college graduates.[10] Since high school dropouts, whether white or black, typically earn a lot less than college graduates, the racial gap in education inevitably results in some racial gap in income as well.

Table 1 controls for this factor by looking at racial differences in income for people with roughly similar amounts of education. It shows that black women are pretty much on a par with white women who have had roughly equivalent schooling. Black women who never completed high school have lower incomes, but those with a high school diploma earned 3 percent more than similarly educated white women, and college-educated African-American women had a slightly bigger advantage. This does not prove that employers are discriminating against white women; the small difference could be the result of their working slightly shorter hours, of being a bit more concentrated in rural areas where wage levels are lower, or any one of a dozen other factors.

Racial differences in incomes for men are considerably larger, and controlling for education does less to eliminate them. Black male high school dropouts had incomes that were 69 percent of those of non-Hispanic whites with similar educations; for black men who had graduated from college, the percentage was not much higher—77 percent. In every educational category the income of black men was further behind that of white men than was the case for women.

Before concluding that discrimination against black men in the job market is still severe, however, we need to ask whether racial differences in educational achievement have been adequately measured. The educational categories are broad and crude, and thus they conceal differences that are relevant to earning power. The highest educational class listed is college

TABLE 1   Black Incomes as a Percent of Non-Hispanic White Incomes, by Sex and Education, Persons 25 or Older, 1994

|  | MEN | WOMEN |
| --- | --- | --- |
| All | 64 | 90 |
| Less than 9 yrs. of school | 71 | 87 |
| 9–12 yrs. but no high school diploma | 69 | 90 |
| High school graduate | 69 | 103 |
| Some college | 77 | 106 |
| College graduate | 77 | 107 |

SOURCE: U.S. Bureau of the Census, Current Population Reports, PPL-45. *The Black Population in the United States: March 1995* (Washington, D.C.: U.S. Government Printing Office, 1996), table 9. Note that the comparison here is between blacks and non-Hispanic whites, not all whites, the usual comparison made elsewhere in this book. Differences between blacks and non-Hispanic whites will be sharper than those between blacks and all whites, because many Hispanics are recent immigrants or the children of immigrants and pull down average incomes for whites as a whole. Since the Census Bureau has only recently tabulated the data in this form, analyses of trends over time will have to be done in terms of the simple white-black comparison. The necessary data to do that for 1994 have not been published. A few tabulations for whites are provided in *Black Population in the U.S.: 1995,* table 16, but no breakdown of incomes by education.

graduates, but we know that people who go on to attain advanced degrees in law, medicine, or computer science are likely to earn more than those with no more than a bachelor's degree. Since whites pursue graduate study at a higher rate than blacks, we can expect white "college graduates" (a group that includes those who have still higher degrees) to earn more than black "college graduates"; they are more likely to have the credentials necessary for certain occupations that are paid extremely well.

Moreover, knowing only that someone is a high school dropout or a high school graduate or a college graduate does not tell us very much about the skills he possesses. Measuring how well educated that person is by counting the number of years he spent in a classroom is like judging how well someone plays the violin by counting up the hours he has spent practicing. The hours may have been wasted, and, likewise, in judging the education of workers, it makes sense to look not at years in school, but at the level of cognitive skill they are able to display on standardized tests. The question, then, is not whether blacks and whites with exactly eleven years of education, say, have the same incomes. Instead, we should ask whether blacks and whites who read, write, and do math at the eighth-grade level or the twelfth-grade level have the same incomes — ignoring how many years of school it took for them to obtain that level of skill.

The National Assessment of Educational Progress (NAEP) and College Board tests show that African-American students, on the average, are alarmingly far behind whites in basic cognitive skills. A number of economists and sociologists investigating discrimination in the labor market have recently concluded that this is the principal reason why they don't have average incomes that are as high as those of whites. What looks like discrimination, this body of research suggests, is better described as rewarding workers with strong cognitive skills. Thus a study of men twenty-six to thirty-three years old who held full-time jobs in 1991 found that when education was measured in the traditional way (years of school completed), blacks earned 19 percent less than comparably educated whites. But when the yardstick was how well they performed on basic tests of word knowledge, paragraph comprehension, arithmetical reasoning, and mathematical knowledge, the results were reversed. Black men earned 9 percent *more* than white men with the same education — as defined by skill.[11]

Other research suggests much the same thing.[12] For instance, *Teaching the New Basic Skills* by economists Richard J. Murnane and Frank Levy has demonstrated the increasing importance of cognitive skills in our changing economy. Employers in firms like Honda now require employees who can read and do math problems at the ninth-grade level at a minimum. Their entry-level positions involve tasks that cannot be adequately performed without that foundation of elementary skills.[13] And yet the 1992 NAEP tests show that barely two out of five students at the end of their high school years could read that well; only three out of five had the requisite skills in math. Looking at the incomes six years after graduation of two national samples of high school seniors from 1972 and 1980, the authors found that their performance on reading and math tests in high school greatly affected their later earnings; moreover, the connection was even stronger for the class of 1980. The difference between the annual earnings of a man with no more than a high school education and weak basic math skills and those of a male employee with the same amount of schooling but strong math skills was striking. Those who had been seniors in 1972 and knew more math earned (six years later) $1,200 more; the more skilled group that had been in the twelfth grade in 1980 took in an additional $2,700. For young women the difference was even greater; in the 1980 group those who were stronger in math earned $3,400 a year (23 percent) more than women with a poor grasp of numbers.[14]

The implications of this analysis are obvious. Basic shifts in our economy have been placing an increased premium on cognitive skills, and scores on the best national tests given demonstrate that groups that perform better earn more. That is why racial differences in scores on tests of cognitive skill go a long way toward explaining racial differences in earnings. The 1992 NAEP math tests, for example, revealed that only 22 percent of African-American high school seniors but 58 percent of their white classmates were numerate enough for firms like Honda to consider hiring them. And in reading, 47 percent of whites in 1992 but just 18 percent of African Americans could handle the printed word well enough to be employable in a modern automobile plant. (By 1994, depressingly, the proportion of whites with this rather low level of reading skill had fallen by 4 points, and the figure for blacks had fallen even more — by 5 points, to just 13 percent.)[15] With racial differences of this magnitude in the cognitive skills many employers are increasingly demanding, one can only wonder why the racial gap in income is not larger than it is.

This body of evidence, based upon large, representative national samples of the workforce, obviously does not prove that employers never discriminate against African Americans. Nor does it prove that employers would not discriminate against blacks a good deal more in the absence of vigilant governmental oversight. It does, though, show that inferring racial bias from differences in incomes or earnings is too simple. It is necessary to control for education, and to control for education measured by a better yardstick than years spent in the classroom.

One other body of evidence relevant to this issue merits brief mention (see Table 2). In 1990 researchers from the Urban Institute, a Washington,

D.C., research center, attempted to assess employment discrimination in Washington and Chicago by having matched pairs of testers, male college students who (in theory) had identical qualifications but were of different races, apply for advertised jobs. A similar study was conducted in Denver in 1991. When a position was offered to the white rather than the black member of the pair, it was taken to be evidence of discrimination. Since some observers—including justices of the U.S. Supreme Court—have taken the results as powerful evidence of continuing bias in the labor market, those findings require some critical comment here.[16]

In Chicago black and white testers were treated the same way by employers 86 percent of the time—either both were offered the job or neither was. Whites were favored over blacks 10 percent of the time, and blacks were favored over whites in almost 5 percent of the tests. In light of the small sample size (197 cases) and other methodological flaws, it is hard to take that small differential seriously. If it is attributable to discrimination at all, rather than chance variation, it is discrimination at a level that can barely be detected.

In Washington, D.C., the white member of a testing pair was favored over his black partner almost a fifth of the time, while the African American was preferred only one out of twenty times. This seems a sizable, though not a huge, difference. What to make of it, however, is complicated by the fact that Washington, D.C., is quite atypical of large American cities in one crucial respect: it is a company town, with the federal government by far the most important local employer. Despite that, the Urban Institute chose to focus its attention solely on private businesses in the area; none of its testers applied for federal jobs to see if they would be treated on a color-neutral basis. Since the federal government is very strongly committed to affirmative action hiring, an investigation of the District of Columbia labor

**TABLE 2   Racial Preferences Shown by Employers to Matched Pairs of Testers in Three Cities, 1990 and 1991**

| | PERCENT OF CASES SHOWING | | |
| --- | --- | --- | --- |
| | *No racial difference* | *White preferred* | *Black preferred* |
| Chicago, 1990 | 85.8 | 9.6 | 4.5 |
| Washington, 1990 | 75.1 | 19.1 | 5.8 |
| Denver, 1991 | 77.9 | 11.7 | 10.3 |

SOURCE: Data as summarized in tables 5.1 and 5.3 of James J. Heckman and Peter Siegelman, "The Urban Institute Audit Studies: Their Methods and Findings," in Michael Fix and Raymond J. Struyk, eds., *Clear and Convincing Evidence: Measurement of Discrimination in America* (Washington, D.C.: Urban Institute Press, 1993).

market that did not exclude its dominant employer would very likely have yielded different results. Since the largest employer in town probably would have offered white testers fewer jobs than black testers, the overall results might have shown a pattern opposite to the one reported — with employers favoring blacks over whites by a margin of 15 points or even more. We cannot know this for sure, but the failure to include the federal government among the D.C. employers severely limits the generalizations that can be drawn from this study.[17]

Other important methodological questions can be raised about the Urban Institute's audit studies.[18] The most significant involves the motivations of the testers. Employers may place a very high premium on finding job applicants who truly want to work for them. An effective tester thus would have to be one who successfully deceived his interviewers. Did all testers try equally hard to do so? College student testers who devoted a summer to working on studies like these might have had political and ideological beliefs that influenced what they *hoped* to find. Given the study design, the real finding was perhaps a self-fulfilling prophecy. The white testers may have been trying very hard to elicit job offers, while black testers could have been conveying in subtle, even unconscious, ways that they weren't really all that keen on getting it. The training given to the testers may have exacerbated this problem. As economists Heckman and Siegelman have observed, "an explicit part of the training" was instruction about "the pervasive problem of discrimination in the United States," with the result that "they may have inadvertently been motivated to find it."[19]

The results of the 1991 Denver study have received far less publicity than the others, perhaps because of its unexpected findings — namely, that black and white testers had met with the same reception 78 percent of the time. The African American was favored over the white in 10 percent of the cases; the white was favored in 12 percent, yielding no statistically significant discrimination against blacks at all. The study also found that more employers discriminated in favor of Hispanics over whites than vice versa.

In short, the "audit studies" of hiring decisions that have been done thus far cannot bear the heavy burden that proponents of preferential policies have placed upon them. Two of the three major studies show hardly any discrimination or none whatever, and the third — in Washington — is problematic on a number of counts. We are left with the conclusion suggested by the several studies examining racial differences in income controlled for cognitive skill: that the racial differences that remain today are primarily the result of differences in what the economists call "pre-market factors" — differences in what was learned in school (and home and community) before the first job was sought.

## NOTES

1. Louis Freedberg, "The Enforcer," *San Francisco Chronicle*, 4 June 1995, 1. The Office of Federal Contract Compliance Programs (OFCCP) has the power to conduct a "compliance review" — an investigation into a corporation's hiring record — which can be either a random audit or the consequence of a complaint. The settlements in the Marriott Hotel and UC–San Diego cases were the result of just such compliance reviews. In congressional testimony in 1995, OFCCP director Shirley Wilcher stated that the agency was then finding violations in 73 percent of the more than 4,000 compliance reviews it conducted each year; James Bovard, "Here Comes the Goon Squad," *American Spectator,* July 1996, 36. Our research assistant, Kevin Marshall, prepared a first draft of portions of this section.

2. Christopher Edley, Jr., and George Stephanopoulos, "Affirmative Action Review: Report to the President," 19 July 1995, 67, n. 85.

3. "Minority Enterprise: Fat White Wallets," *Economist,* 27 November 1993, 29.

4. Tim W. Ferguson, "Race (etc.) Preferences on the Line," *Wall Street Journal,* 14 March 1995, A16.

5. Peter Behr, "Crucial Break or Unjustified Crutch?" *Washington Post,* 10 March 1995, 1.

6. The media covered the Viacom story extensively; see, e.g., Jeffrey H. Birnbaum, "Turning Back the Clock," *Time,* 20 March 1995, 36; Terry Eastland, "Powell Preferred," *National Review,* 12 February 1996, 20.

7. Jonathan Rauch, "Color TV," *New Republic,* 19 December 1994, 9.

8. Selwyn Raab, "12 Charged in Minority Businesses Scheme," *New York Times,* 19 May 1995, B2.

9. Speech by President Clinton at the National Archives, 19 July 1995, extended excerpts from which were reprinted in the *Washington Post,* 20 July 1995, A12.

10. U.S. Bureau of the Census, Current Population Reports, P-20-480, *The Black Population in the United States: March 1994 and 1993* (Washington, D.C.: U.S. Government Printing Office, 1995), table 7.

11. George Farkas and Keven Vicknair, "Appropriate Tests of Racial Wage Discrimination Require Controls for Cognitive Skills: Comment on Cancio, Evans, and Maume," *American Sociological Review* 61 (August 1996), 557–560. This is a critique of A. Silvia Cancio, T. David Evans, and David J. Maume, "Reconsidering the Declining Significance of Race: Racial Differences in Early Career Wages" in the same issue of the *American Sociological Review,* 541–556, which had measured education crudely by levels of schooling completed. The authors' rejoinder to this critique in the same issue, 561–564, argues that it is inappropriate to control for education by using tests of cognitive skills because those tests are biased, and really only test "exposure to the values and experiences of the White middle class" (561). Employers are apparently guilty of class and racial bias if they want employees to be able to read a training manual or to calculate how many bags of grass seed and fertilizer the customer will need to make a lawn that is 60 feet long and 40 feet wide.

12. This approach grows out of James S. Coleman's pioneering work suggesting that researchers should assess the effects of education not in terms of "inputs" (how many years spent in school?) but in terms of "outputs" (how much do students

know when they come out of school?). This insight of Coleman's was appealing to economists, most of them associated with the University of Chicago, who were interested in the role of "human capital" — investment in education and training — in economic growth. The first systematic examination of racial differences in income that controlled for cognitive skills, by Eric Hanushek in 1978, used the 1965 Coleman report results and 1970 census data from the Public Use Sample; it found, like the Farkas study cited in the previous note, that black males were actually better paid than white males with comparable education — they received "higher returns per year of quality-equivalent schooling [years of schooling adjusted by test scores] than comparable whites"; Eric Hanushek, "Ethnic Income Variations: Magnitudes and Explanations," in Thomas Sowell, ed., *Essays and Data on American Ethnic Groups* (Washington, D.C.: Urban Institute, 1978), 139–166. More than a decade elapsed before other researchers pursued these issues, but several important studies pointing in the same direction have appeared in the 1990s. These include June O'Neill, "The Role of Human Capital in Earnings Differences between Black and White Men," *Journal of Economic Perspectives* 4 (Fall 1990), 25–45; Ronald F. Ferguson, "New Evidence on the Growing Value of Skill and Consequences for Racial Disparity and Returns to Schooling" (Cambridge: Malcolm Wiener Center for Social Policy, H-93-10, Harvard University, 1993); Ferguson, "Shifting Challenges: Fifty Years of Economic Change toward Black-White Earnings Equality," *Daedalus* 124 (Winter 1995), 37–76; Derek A. Neal and William R. Johnson, "The Role of Pre-Market Factors in Black-White Wage Differences," *Journal of Political Economy* 104 (October 1996), 869–896. Not all of these studies showed an earnings advantage for black males. In O'Neill's sample the hourly earnings of black men in their twenties were 17.1 percent below those of whites in 1987 without adjusting for any characteristics. When she controlled for region, years of schooling, and test scores, the differential shrank by three-quarters, to 4.5 percent, and it virtually disappeared when years of work experience were controlled. Ferguson's point of departure was the growth in the racial wage gap for 18-to-28-year-old males from 6 percent in 1976 to 16 percent in 1989. He found that the reason was an increase in the value of basic reading and math skills. Had the value of skills to employers not increased as it did, "the long-term patterns of convergence toward parity between young black and white males would have continued through the 1980s." The one exception was in the case of men with twelve or fewer years of schooling living in the North Central Region after the mid-1980s. Neal and Johnson found that applying an educational control that included test scores cut the wage gap between black and white males by three-quarters, to just 27 cents per hour in 1990–1991, and reversed it among women, so that black women earned 3 cents more per hour. No studies of this type can measure the extent of discrimination with much precision, but together they certainly challenge the premise upon which current preferential policies rest — that racial discrimination in employment is severe and pervasive.

13. Richard J. Murnane and Frank Levy, *Teaching the New Basic Skills: Principles for Educating Children to Thrive in a Changing Economy* (New York: Free Press, 1996), 32. A more detailed technical version of the analysis is available in Richard Murnane, John Willett, and Frank Levy, "The Growing Importance of Cognitive Skills in Wage Determination," *Review of Economics and Statistics* 77 (1995), 251–266.

14. Murnane and Levy, *Teaching the New Basic Skills,* 41–44.

15. Ibid., 34–35; National Center for Education Statistics, *Data Compendium*

*for the NAEP 1992 Mathematics Assessment of the Nation and the States,* Report No. 23-ST04 (Washington, D.C.: U.S. Government Printing Office, 1993), 744 [percent above 300 anchor level]; National Center for Education Statistics, *NAEP 1994 Reading Report Card for the Nation and the States* (Washington, DC: U.S. Department of Education, 1996), 48 [percent reading at or above proficient level].

16. The findings of the Urban Institute Washington and Chicago studies are reported in Margaret Turner, Michael Fix, and John Yinger, *Opportunities Denied, Opportunities Diminished: Discrimination in Hiring* (Washington, D.C.: Urban Institute Press, 1991). The Denver study is described in Franklin L. James and Steve W. DelCastillo, "Measuring Job Discrimination by Private Employers against Young Black and Hispanic Males Seeking Entry Level Work in the Denver Metropolitan Area," unpublished report (Denver: University of Colorado, 1991). The key findings of the three studies are conveniently summarized in James J. Heckman and Peter Siegelman, "The Urban Institute Audit Studies: Their Methods and Findings," in Michael Fix and Raymond J. Struyk, eds., *Clear and Convincing Evidence: Measurement of Discrimination in America* (Washington, D.C.: Urban Institute Press, 1993), tables 5.1 and 5.3. Justice Ginsberg cites this research approvingly in her dissent in *Adarand Constructors, Inc. v. Pena,* 115 S.Ct 2097 (1995) at 2135.

17. The special character of the District of Columbia could have skewed the results for another reason as well. Private employers in a labor market so dominated by a single employer known to follow strong preferential policies in hiring might as a result have been inclined to be suspicious of black job applicants who looked attractive, reasoning that "if they're as good as they seem, why aren't they applying for a better-paid, more secure post in the Department of Transportation?"

18. For example, whether the "matched" pairs were truly matched in every important respect can be debated. Did the researchers have sufficient knowledge of the cognitive skills and other traits employers value most in making hiring decisions? People who seemed a perfect match to the researchers might not have appeared so to employers. The difference in perception would not be chalked up as an error by the researchers; it would be interpreted as employer bias. Heckman and Siegelman provide a searching and, we think, quite devastating critique in *Clear and Convincing Evidence,* 187–258. A rejoinder by John Yinger and a further set of comments by Heckman and Siegelman appear on 259–275.

19. Heckman and Siegelman in *Clear and Convincing Evidence,* 216, 272.

# Part 4: Primary Sources

In the United States, federal laws can be made by all three branches of government: the executive branch, the legislature, and the judiciary. Presidents can sign executive orders. Congress can pass statutes. The courts can make law when they rule on matters brought before them. The judicial branch determines whether given practices conform to the law of the land; the judicial branch is also empowered to determine whether executive orders and statutes are constitutional and consistent with established legal doctrine.

The federal judiciary has three levels. At the bottom is the district level. Next comes the appellate level (also known as the circuit level). At the highest level is the nine-member Supreme Court. A circuit court can uphold or reverse any district court decision within its jurisdiction, and its pronouncements about what is or is not legal are binding for people in its territory. Altogether, the United States is divided into eleven circuits, each of which is responsible for all the district courts in its territory. The Supreme Court can uphold or reverse any district court decision and any appellate (circuit) court decision. Supreme Court decisions are binding for the entire nation. Supreme Court decisions are determined by votes, and a simple majority wins. Each decision is written up by one of the justices in such a way as to make clear the reasoning behind the decision as well as the decision itself. Minority opinions are written up by one or more of the justices who disagree with the majority vote. Even when justices concur with the majority decision, they may disagree with the reasoning behind it. In such instances, justices can present their own reasoning in a separate statement.

All three branches of the federal government have weighed in on the topic of affirmative action. The term *affirmative action* appeared in the Civil Rights Law of 1964. Title VII of that law appears here in its entirety. Then, on September 24, 1965, President Johnson signed Executive Order 11246, which mandated that all federal contractors take actions to make sure that they do not discriminate. The 1965 version of Executive Order 11246 appears here in its entirety. The order was amended in subsequent years, but the spirit of the order remains the same.

Since the passage of the Civil Rights Act and the signing of Executive Order 11246, individuals and organizations have challenged the legality, indeed, the constitutionality, of some affirmative action programs. A representative sample of the most important Supreme Court decisions on affirmative action and one appellate court decision (*Adarand*) are presented here, in excerpted form.

In all of the Supreme Court cases since *Griggs,* the justices exhibit differences of opinion, sometimes in the extreme. According to Newman (1989), disagreements among Supreme Court justices appear to be greater on issues of affirmative action than on most issues before the Court.

Why is there so much judicial controversy? One reason may be that the legal system of the United States has been designed to be reactive, not proactive. Generally the judiciary is supposed to become involved in correcting bad situations or in punishing wrongdoers. The legal system is supposed to become involved in people's problems only after an aggrieved party has come forward asking for a remedy. Generally, for someone to bring a case to court, he or she must have "standing," which is to say a legitimate interest in the situation at hand. As a result, preventative measures such as affirmative action must strike a delicate legal balance. As Newman (1989) points out, affirmative action programs that are remedial in nature — designed to remedy a particular discriminatory system — are more likely than others to withstand legal challenge.

Another reason for special controversy concerns the peculiar and shameful place of racism, and particularly anti-black racism, in the United States. Less than 150 years ago some people in the country were slaves. After the Civil War, the passage of the Fourteenth Amendment made it unconstitutional to divide life's riches and opportunities along racial lines. Given the long suffering of people of color, it seemed to many legal minds entirely proper to take compensatory measures with the aim of equalizing opportunities in fact as well as in word. Several famous justices, including Justice Brennan, noted that to move beyond racial imbalances into greater racial neutrality, it is first necessary to take notice of race. Similarly, under the leadership of Justice Powell, whose opinion in the *Bakke* case has become legal doctrine, many judges and lawyers see a useful distinction between benign racial distinctions (those that help the underdog) and malevolent racial distinctions (those that keep the underdog downtrodden). In recent years, as the Court has become more conservative, the sentiment is that the time has come to abandon the distinction between benign and malevolent categorical distinctions. Now, all distinctions based on immutable features like skin color or gender are suspect.

A word about the excerpting process is needed here. Title VII and Executive Order 11246 are included unabridged. So is the *Griggs* decision. All the other decisions have been excerpted, sometimes quite a bit. We have tried in every instance to preserve the line of reasoning, but we have left out details such as the references to other legal cases and many details of fact. Ellipses ( . . . ) denote missing text. If a whole paragraph or more has been omitted, the ellipses appear at the left margin. If a portion of the text within a paragraph has been omitted, the ellipses appear within the text.

# Title VII —
# Equal Employment Opportunity

Laws are divided into sections called titles. Reprinted here is the full text of Title VII of the 1964 Civil Rights Act.

There are several points of similarity between this law and any other law. Lawmakers need to pay close attention to specific issues of wording, to be certain to limit the powers of the law, to be careful that the current law does not contradict existing laws, to be certain about enforcement, and to give clear starting dates. Therefore, many parts of Title VII are very detailed and specific. In addition, sections 703 (a) through 703 (d) and section 705 (a) give the very heart of the law. Also, immediately after spelling out how far the law reaches, in sections 703 (a) through (d), the statute makes clear — in section 703 (e) — some of the limitations of the new rules.

Some aspects of this law may differ from many other laws about employment: for instance, the emphasis placed upon intentions. As indicated in sections 703 (h) and 706 (g) the 1964 Civil Rights Act was more concerned with behaviors and intentions than with unintentional outcomes. Legal scholars make a distinction between disparate treatment and disparate outcomes. If an employer intentionally treats women differently than men, then that employer is guilty of disparate treatment and is breaking the law according to Title VII. But an employer might also appear to treat men and women the same but do so in a way that produces disparate outcomes. A thoughtless employer, for example, might install in factories restrooms that each have many urinals but only one toilet. The impact of such treatment on women employees would be very different than on men employees, despite identical treatment. The 1964 Civil Rights Law is silent on the issue of disparate impact, even as it renders illegal intentionally disparate treatment.

An additional important point is that the law requires organizations to keep good records and allows the judiciary to order "affirmative action" on the part of an employer if there is clear evidence of unlawful employment practices. The details appear in sections 706 (g) and 709 (c). This is thus a reactive position. In marked contrast are the practices required by the federal code of regulations that implements Executive Order 11246, President Johnson's order establishing affirmative action. With affirmative action, good records are to be kept, even without any finding of discrimination. The good records are thought to be a major way that organizations can patrol their own behavior.

Finally, one might note how hard it is to find the words "preferential treatment" in 703 (j).

## DEFINITIONS

SEC. 701. For the purposes of this title—

(a) The term "person" includes one or more individuals, labor unions, partnerships, associations, corporations, legal representatives, mutual companies, joint-stock companies, trusts, unincorporated organizations, trustees, trustees in bankruptcy, or receivers.

(b) The term "employer" means a person engaged in an industry affecting commerce who has twenty-five or more employees for each working day in each of twenty or more calendar weeks in the current or preceding calendar year, and any agent of such a person, but such term does not include (1) the United States, a corporation wholly owned by the Government of the United States, an Indian tribe, or a State or political subdivision thereof, (2) a bona fide private membership club (other than a labor organization) which is exempt from taxation under section 501 (c) of the Internal Revenue Code of 1954: *Provided,* That during the first year after the effective date prescribed in subsection (a) of section 716, persons having fewer than one hundred employees (and their agents) shall not be considered employers, and, during the second year after such date, persons having fewer than seventy-five employees (and their agents) shall not be considered employers, and, during the third year after such date, persons having fewer than fifty employees (and their agents) shall not be considered employers: *Provided further,* That it shall be the policy of the United States to insure equal employment opportunities for Federal employees without discrimination because of race, color, religion, sex or national origin and the President shall utilize his existing authority to effectuate this policy.

(c) The term "employment agency" means any person regularly undertaking with or without compensation to procure employees for an employer or to procure for employees opportunities to work for an employer and includes an agent of such a person; but shall not include an agency of the United States, or an agency of a State or political subdivision of a State, except that such term shall include the United States Employment Service and the system of State and local employment services receiving Federal assistance.

(d) The term "labor organization" means a labor organization engaged in an industry affecting commerce, and any agent of such an organization, and includes any organization of any kind, any agency, or employee representation committee, group, association, or plan so engaged in which employees participate and which exists for the purposes, in whole or in part, of dealing with employers concerning grievances, labor disputes, wages, rates of pay, hours, or other terms or conditions of employment, and any conference, general committee, joint or system board, or joint council so engaged which is subordinate to a national or international labor organization.

(e) A labor organization shall be deemed to be engaged in an industry affecting commerce if (1) it maintains or operates a hiring hall or hiring office which procures employees for an employer or procures for employees opportunities to work for an employer, or (2) the number of its members (or, where it is a labor organization composed of other labor organizations or their representatives, if the aggregate number of the members of such other labor organization) is (A) one hundred or more during the first year after the effective date prescribed in subsection (a) of section 716, (B) seventy-five or more during the second year after such date or fifty or more during the third year, or (C) twenty-five or more thereafter, and such labor organization —

(1) is the certified representative of employees under the provisions of the National Labor Relations Act, as amended, or the Railway Labor Act, as amended;

(2) although not certified, is a national or international labor organization or a local labor organization recognized or acting as the representative of employees of an employer or employers engaged in an industry affecting commerce; or

(3) has chartered a local labor organization or subsidiary body which is representing or actively seeking to represent employees of employers within the meaning of paragraph (1) or (2); or

(4) has been chartered by a labor organization representing or actively seeking to represent employees within the meaning of paragraph (1) or (2) as the local or subordinate body through which such employees may enjoy membership or become affiliated with such labor organization; or

(5) is a conference, general committee, joint or system board, or joint council subordinate to a national or international labor organization, which includes a labor organization engaged in an industry affecting commerce within the meaning of any of the preceding paragraphs of this subsection.

(f) The term "employee" means an individual employed by an employer.

(g) The term "commerce" means trade, traffic, commerce, transportation, transmission, or communication among the several States; or between a State and any place outside thereof; or within the District of Columbia, or a possession of the United States; or between points in the same State but through a point outside thereof.

(h) The term "industry affecting commerce" means any activity, business, or industry in commerce or in which a labor dispute would hinder or obstruct commerce or the free flow of commerce and includes any activity or industry "affecting commerce" within the meaning of the Labor-Management Reporting and Disclosure Act of 1959.

(i) The term "State" includes a State of the United States, the District of Columbia, Puerto Rico, the Virgin Islands, American Samoa, Guam, Wake Island, the Canal Zone, and Outer Continental Shelf lands defined in the Outer Continental Shelf Lands Act.

## EXEMPTION

SEC. 702. This title shall not apply to an employer with respect to the employment of aliens outside any State, or to a religious corporation, association, or society with respect to the employment of individuals of a particular religion to perform work connected with the carrying on by such corporation, association, or society of its religious activities or to an educational institution with respect to the employment of individuals to perform work connected with the educational activities of such institution.

## DISCRIMINATION BECAUSE OF RACE, COLOR, RELIGION, SEX, OR NATIONAL ORIGIN

SEC. 703. (a) It shall be an unlawful employment practice for an employer—

(1) to fail or refuse to hire or to discharge any individual, or otherwise to discriminate against any individual with respect to his compensation, terms, conditions, or privileges of employment, because of such individual's race, color, religion, sex, or national origin; or

(2) to limit, segregate, or classify his employees in any way which would deprive or tend to deprive any individual of employment opportunities or otherwise adversely affect his status as an employee, because of such individual's race, color, religion, sex, or national origin.

(b) It shall be an unlawful employment practice for an employment agency to fail or refuse to refer for employment, or otherwise to discriminate against, any individual because of his race, color, religion, sex, or national origin, or to classify or refer for employment any individual on the basis of his race, color, religion, sex, or national origin.

(c) It shall be an unlawful employment practice for a labor organization—

(1) to exclude or to expel from its membership, or otherwise to discriminate against, any individual because of his race, color, religion, sex, or national origin;

(2) to limit, segregate, or classify its membership, or to classify or

fail or refuse to refer for employment any individual, in any way which would deprive or tend to deprive any individual of employment opportunities, or would limit such employment opportunities or otherwise adversely affect his status as an employee or as an applicant for employment, because of such individual's race, color, religion, sex, or national origin; or

(3) to cause or attempt to cause an employer to discriminate against an individual in violation of this section.

(d) It shall be an unlawful employment practice for any employer, labor organization, or joint labor-management committee controlling apprenticeship or other training or retraining, including on-the-job training programs to discriminate against any individual because of his race, color, religion, sex, or national origin in admission to, or employment in, any program established to provide apprenticeship or other training.

(e) Notwithstanding any other provisions of this title, (1) it shall not be an unlawful employment practice for an employer to hire and employ employees, for an employment agency to classify, or refer for employment any individual, for a labor organization to classify its membership or to classify or refer for employment any individual, or for an employer, labor organization, or joint labor-management committee controlling apprenticeship or other training or retraining programs to admit or employ any individual in any such program, on the basis of his religion, sex, or national origin in those certain instances where religion, sex, or national origin is a bona fide occupational qualification reasonably necessary to the normal operation of that particular business or enterprise, and (2) it shall not be an unlawful employment practice for a school, college, university, or other educational institution or institution of learning to hire and employ employees of a particular religion if such school, college, university, or other educational institution or institution of learning is, in whole or in substantial part, owned, supported, controlled, or managed by a particular religion or by a particular religious corporation, association, or society, or if the curriculum of such school, college, university, or other educational institution or institution of learning is directed toward the propagation of a particular religion.

(f) As used in this title, the phrase "unlawful employment practice" shall not be deemed to include any action or measure taken by an employer, labor organization, joint labor-management committee, or employment agency with respect to an individual who is a member of the Communist Party of the United States or of any other organization required to register as a Communist-action or Communist-front organization by final order of the Subversive Activities Control Board pursuant to the Subversive Activities Control Act of 1950.

(g) Notwithstanding any other provision of this title, it shall not be an unlawful employment practice for an employer to fail or refuse to hire and employ any individual for any position, for an employer to discharge any individual from any position, or for an employment agency to fail or refuse to refer any individual for employment in any position or for a labor organization to fail or refuse to refer any individual for employment in any position, if—

(1) the occupancy of such position, or access to the premises in or upon which any part of the duties of such position is performed or is to be performed, is subject to any requirement imposed in the interest of the national security of the United States under any security program in effect pursuant to or administered under any statute of the United States or any Executive order of the President, and

(2) such individual has not fulfilled or has ceased to fulfill that requirement.

(h) Notwithstanding any other provision of this title, it shall not be an unlawful employment practice for an employer to apply different standards of compensation, or different terms, conditions, or privileges of employment pursuant to a bona fide seniority or merit system, or a system which measures earnings by quantity or quality of production or to employees who work in different locations, provided that such differences are not the result of an intention to discriminate because of race, color, religion, sex or national origin, nor shall it be an unlawful employment practice for an employer to give and to act upon the results of any professionally developed ability test provided that such test, its administration or action upon the results is not designed, intended or used to discriminate because of race, color, religion, sex or national origin. It shall not be an unlawful employment practice under this title for any employer to differentiate upon the basis of sex in determining the amount of the wages or compensation paid or to be paid to employees of such employer if such differentiation is authorized by the provisions of section 6 (d) of the Fair Labor Standards Act of 1938, as amended (29 U.S.C. 206 (d)).

(i) Nothing contained in this title shall apply to any business or enterprise on or near an Indian reservation with respect to any publicly announced employment practice of such business or enterprise under which a preferential treatment is given to any individual because he is an Indian living on or near a reservation.

(j) Nothing contained in this title shall be interpreted to require any employer, employment agency, labor organization, or joint labor-management committee subject to this title to grant preferential treatment to any individual or to any group because of the race, color, religion, sex, or national origin of such individual or group on account of an imbalance which may exist with respect to the total number or percentage of persons of any race, color, religion, sex, or national origin employed by any employer, referred or classified for employment by any employment agency or labor organization, admitted to membership or classified by any labor organization, or admitted to, or employed in, any apprenticeship or other training program, in comparison with the total number or percentage of persons of such race, color, religion, sex, or national origin in any community, State, section, or other area, or in the available work force in any community, State, section, or other area.

## OTHER UNLAWFUL EMPLOYMENT PRACTICES

SEC. 704. (a) It shall be an unlawful employment practice for an employer to discriminate against any of his employees or applicants for employment, for an employment agency to discriminate against any individual, or for a labor organization to discriminate against any member thereof or applicant for membership, because he has opposed any practice made an unlawful employment practice by this title, or because he has made a charge, testified, assisted, or participated in any manner in an investigation, proceeding, or hearing under this title.

(b) It shall be an unlawful employment practice for an employer, labor organization, or employment agency to print or publish or cause to be printed or published any notice or advertisement relating to employment by such an employer or membership in or any classification or referral for employment by such a labor organization, or relating to any classification or referral for employment by such an employment agency, indicating any preference, limitation, specification, or discrimination, based on race, color, religion, sex, or national origin, except that such a notice or advertisement may indicate a preference, limitation, specification, or discrimination based on religion, sex, or national origin when religion, sex, or national origin is a bona fide occupational qualification for employment.

## EQUAL EMPLOYMENT OPPORTUNITY COMMISSION

SEC. 705. (a) There is hereby created a Commission to be known as the Equal Employment Opportunity Commission, which shall be composed of five members, not more than three of whom shall be members of the same political party, who shall be appointed by the President by and with the advice and consent of the Senate. One of the original members shall be appointed for a term of one year, one for a term of two years, one for a term of three years, one for a term of four years, and one for a term of five years, beginning from the date of enactment of this title, but their successors shall be appointed for terms of five years each, except that any individual chosen to fill a vacancy shall be appointed only for the unexpired term of the member whom he shall succeed. The President shall designate one member to serve as Chairman of the Commission, and one member to serve as Vice Chairman. The Chairman shall be responsible on behalf of the Commission for the administrative operations of the Commission, and shall appoint, in accordance with the civil service laws, such officers, agents, attorneys, and employees as it deems necessary to assist it in the performance of its functions and to fix their compensation in accordance with the Classification Act of 1949, as amended. The Vice Chairman shall act as Chairman in the absence or disability of the Chairman or in the event of a vacancy in that office.

(b) A vacancy in the Commission shall not impair the right of the remaining members to exercise all the powers of the Commission and three members thereof shall constitute a quorum.

(c) The Commission shall have an official seal which shall be judicially noticed.

(d) The Commission shall at the close of each fiscal year report to the Congress and to the President concerning the action it has taken; the names, salaries, and duties of all individuals in its employ and the moneys it has disbursed; and shall make such further reports on the cause of and means of eliminating discrimination and such recommendations for further legislation as may appear desirable.

(e) The Federal Executive Pay Act of 1956, as amended (5 U.S.C. 2201–2209), is further amended —

(1) by adding to section 105 thereof (5 U.S.C. 2204) the following clause: "(32) Chairman, Equal Employment Opportunity Commission"; and

(2) by adding to clause (45) of section 106 (a) thereof (5 U.S.C. 2205 (a)) the following: "Equal Employment Opportunity Commission (4)."

(f) The principal office of the Commission shall be in or near the District of Columbia, but it may meet or exercise any or all its powers at any other place. The Commission may establish such regional or State offices as it deems necessary to accomplish the purpose of this title.

(g) The Commission shall have power —

(1) to cooperate with and, with their consent, utilize regional, State, local, and other agencies, both public and private, and individuals;

(2) to pay to witnesses whose depositions are taken or who are summoned before the Commission or any of its agents the same witness and mileage fees as are paid to witnesses in the courts of the United States;

(3) to furnish to persons subject to this title such technical assistance as they may request to further their compliance with this title or an order issued thereunder;

(4) upon the request of (i) any employer, whose employees or some of them, or (ii) any labor organization, whose members or some of them, refuse or threaten to refuse to cooperate in effectuating the provisions of this title, to assist in such effectuation by conciliation or such other remedial action as is provided by this title;

(5) to make such technical studies as are appropriate to effectuate the purposes and policies of this title and to make the results of such studies available to the public;

(6) to refer matters to the Attorney General with recommendations for intervention in a civil action brought by an aggrieved party under section 706, or for the institution of a civil action by the Attorney General under section 707, and to advise, consult, and assist the Attorney General on such matters.

(h) Attorneys appointed under this section may, at the direction of the Commission, appear for and represent the Commission in any case in court.

(i) The Commission shall, in any of its educational or promotional activities, cooperate with other departments and agencies in the performance of such educational and promotional activities.

(j) All officers, agents, attorneys, and employees of the Commission shall be subject to the provisions of section 9 of the Act of August 2, 1939, as amended (the Hatch Act), notwithstanding any exemption contained in such section.

## PREVENTION OF UNLAWFUL
## EMPLOYMENT PRACTICES

SEC. 706. (a) Whenever it is charged in writing under oath by a person claiming to be aggrieved, or a written charge has been filed by a member of the Commission where he has reasonable cause to believe a violation of this title has occurred (and such charge sets forth the facts upon which it is based) that an employer, employment agency, or labor organization has engaged in an unlawful employment practice, the Commission shall furnish such employer, employment agency, or labor organization (hereinafter referred to as the "respondent") with a copy of such charge and shall make an investigation of such charge, provided that such charge shall not be made public by the Commission. If the Commission shall determine, after such investigation, that there is reasonable cause to believe that the charge is true, the Commission shall endeavor to eliminate any such alleged unlawful employment practice by informal methods of conference, conciliation, and persuasion. Nothing said or done during and as a part of such endeavors may be made public by the Commission without the written consent of the parties, or used as evidence in a subsequent proceeding. Any officer or employee of the Commission, who shall make public in any manner whatever any information in violation of this subsection shall be deemed guilty of a misdemeanor and upon conviction thereof shall be fined not more than $1,000 or imprisoned not more than one year.

(b) In the case of an alleged unlawful employment practice occurring in a State, or political subdivision of a State, which has a State or local law prohibiting the unlawful employment practice alleged and establishing or authorizing a State or local authority to grant or seek relief from such practice or to institute criminal proceedings with respect thereto upon receiving notice thereof, no charge may be filed under subsection (a) by the person aggrieved before the expiration of sixty days after proceedings have been commenced under the State or local law, unless such proceedings have been earlier terminated, provided that such sixty-day period shall be extended to one hundred and twenty days during the first year after the effective date of such State or local law. If any requirement for the commencement of such proceedings is imposed by a State or local authority other than a requirement of the filing of a written and signed statement of the facts upon which the proceeding is based, the proceeding shall be deemed to have been commenced for the purposes of this subsection at the time such statement is sent by registered mail to the appropriate State or local authority.

(c) In the case of any charge filed by a member of the Commission alleging an unlawful employment practice occurring in a State or political subdivision of a State, which has a State or local law prohibiting the practice alleged and establishing or authorizing a State or local authority to grant or seek relief from such practice or to institute criminal proceedings with respect thereto upon receiving notice thereof, the Commission shall, before taking any action with respect to such charge, notify the appropriate State or local officials and, upon request, afford them a reasonable time, but not less than sixty days (provided that such sixty-day period shall be extended to one hundred and twenty days during the first year after the effective day of such State or local law), unless a shorter period is requested, to act under such State or local law to remedy the practice alleged.

(d) A charge under subsection (a) shall be filed within ninety days after the alleged unlawful employment practice occurred, except that in the case of an unlawful employment practice with respect to which the person aggrieved has followed the procedure set out in subsection (b), such charge shall be filed by the person aggrieved within two hundred and ten days after the alleged unlawful employment practice occurred, or within thirty days after receiving notice that the State or local agency has terminated the proceedings under the State or local law, whichever is earlier, and a copy of such charge shall be filed by the Commission with the State or local agency.

(e) If within thirty days after a charge is filed with the Commission or within thirty days after expiration of any period of reference under subsection (c) (except that in either case such period may be extended to not more than sixty days upon a determination by the Commission that further efforts to secure voluntary compliance are warranted), the Commission has been unable to obtain voluntary compliance with this title, the Commission shall so notify the person aggrieved and a civil action may, within thirty days thereafter, be brought against the respondent named in the charge (1) by the person claiming to be aggrieved, or (2) if such charge was filed by a member of the Commission, by any person whom the charge alleges was aggrieved by the alleged unlawful employment practice. Upon application by the complainant and in such circumstances as the court may deem just, the court may appoint an attorney for such complainant and may authorize the commencement of the action without the payment of fees, costs, or security. Upon timely application, the court may, in its discretion, permit the Attorney General to intervene in such civil action if he certifies that the case is of general public importance. Upon request, the court may, in its discretion, stay further proceedings for not more than sixty days pending the termination of State or local proceedings described in subsection (b) or the efforts of the Commission to obtain voluntary compliance.

(f) Each United States district court and each United States court of a place subject to the jurisdiction of the United States shall have jurisdiction of actions brought under this title. Such an action may be brought in any judicial district in the State in which the unlawful employment practice is alleged to have been committed, in the judicial district in which the employment records relevant to such practice are maintained and administered, or in the judicial district in which the plaintiff would have worked but for the alleged unlawful employment practice, but if the respondent is not found within any such district, such an action may be brought within the judicial district in which the respondent has his principal office. For purposes of sections 1404 and 1406 of title 28 of the United States Code, the judicial district in which the respondent has his principal office shall in all cases be considered a district in which the action might have been brought.

(g) If the court finds that the respondent has intentionally engaged in or is intentionally engaging in an unlawful employment practice charged in the complaint, the court may enjoin the respondent from engaging in such unlawful employment practice, and order such affirmative action as may be appropriate, which may include reinstatement or hiring of employees, with or without back pay (payable by the employer, employment agency, or labor organization, as the case may be, responsible for the unlawful employment practice). Interim earnings or amounts earnable with reasonable diligence by the person or persons discriminated against shall operate to reduce the back pay otherwise allowable. No order of the court shall require the admission or reinstatement of an individual as a member of a union or the hiring, reinstatement, or promotion of an individual as an employee, or the payment to him of any back pay, if such individual was refused admission, suspended, or expelled or was refused employment or advancement or was suspended or discharged for any reason other than discrimination on account of race, color, religion, sex or national origin or in violation of section 704 (a).

(h) The provisions of the Act entitled "An Act to amend the Judicial Code and to define and limit the jurisdiction of courts sitting in equity, and for other purposes," approved March 23, 1932 (29 U.S.C. 101–115), shall not apply with respect to civil actions brought under this section.

(i) In any case in which an employer, employment agency, or labor organization fails to comply with an order of a court issued in a civil action brought under subsection (e), the Commission may commence proceedings to compel compliance with such order.

(j) Any civil action brought under subsection (e) and any proceedings brought under subsection (i) shall be subject to appeal as provided in sections 1291 and 1292, title 28, United States Code.

(k) In any action or proceeding under this title the court, in its discretion, may allow the prevailing party, other than the Commission or the United States, a reasonable attorney's fee as part of the costs, and the Commission and the United States shall be liable for costs the same as a private person.

SEC. 707. (a) Whenever the Attorney General has reasonable cause to believe that any person or group of persons is engaged in a pattern or practice of resistance to the full enjoyment of any of the rights secured by this title, and that the pattern or practice is of such a nature and is intended to deny the full exercise of the rights herein described, the Attorney General may bring a civil action in the appropriate district court of the United States by filing with it a complaint (1) signed by him (or in his absence the Acting Attorney General), (2) setting forth facts pertaining to such pattern or practice, and (3) requesting such relief, including an application for a permanent or temporary injunction, restraining order or other order against the person or persons responsible for such pattern or practice, as he deems necessary to insure the full enjoyment of the rights herein described.

(b) The district courts of the United States shall have and shall exercise jurisdiction of proceedings instituted pursuant to this section, and in any such proceeding the Attorney General may file with the clerk of such court a request that a court of three judges be convened to hear and determine the case. Such request by the Attorney General shall be accompanied by a certificate that, in his opinion, the case is of general public importance. A copy of the certificate and request for a three-judge court shall be immediately furnished by such clerk to the chief judge of the circuit (or in his absence, the presiding circuit judge of the circuit) in which the case is pending. Upon receipt of such request it shall be the duty of the chief judge of the circuit or the presiding circuit judge, as the case may be, to designate immediately three judges in such circuit, of whom at least one shall be a circuit judge and another of whom shall be a district judge of the court in which the proceeding was instituted, to hear and determine such case, and it shall be the duty of the judges so designated to assign the case for hearing at the earliest practicable date, to participate in the hearing and determination thereof, and to cause the case to be in every way expedited. An appeal from the final judgment of such court will lie to the Supreme Court.

In the event the Attorney General fails to file such a request in any such proceeding, it shall be the duty of the chief judge of the district (or in his absence, the acting chief judge) in which the case is pending immediately to designate a judge in such district to hear and determine the case. In the event that no judge in the district is available to hear and determine the case, the chief judge of the district, or the acting chief judge, as the case may be, shall certify this fact to the chief judge of the circuit (or in his absence, the acting chief judge) who shall then designate a district or circuit judge of the circuit to hear and determine the case.

It shall be the duty of the judge designated pursuant to this section to assign the case for hearing at the earliest practicable date and to cause the case to be in every way expedited.

## EFFECT ON STATE LAWS

SEC. 708. Nothing in this title shall be deemed to exempt or relieve any person from any liability, duty, penalty, or punishment provided by any present or future law of any State or political subdivision of a State, other than any such law which purports to require or permit the doing of any act which would be an unlawful employment practice under this title.

## INVESTIGATIONS, INSPECTIONS, RECORDS, STATE AGENCIES

SEC. 709. (a) In connection with any investigation of a charge filed under section 706, the Commission or its designated representative shall at all reasonable times have access to, for the purposes of examination, and the right to copy any evidence of any person being investigated or proceeded against that relates to unlawful employment practices covered by this title and is relevant to the charge under investigation.

(b) The Commission may cooperate with State and local agencies charged with the administration of State fair employment practices laws and, with the consent of such agencies, may for the purpose of carrying out its functions and duties under this title and within the limitation of funds appropriated specifically for such purpose, utilize the services of such agencies and their employees and, notwithstanding any other provision of law, may reimburse such agencies and their employees for services rendered to assist the Commission in carrying out this title. In furtherance of such cooperative efforts, the Commission may enter into written agreements with such State or local agencies and such agreements may include provisions under which the Commission shall refrain from processing a charge in any cases or class of cases specified in such agreements and under which no person may bring a civil action under section 706 in any cases or class of cases so specified, or under which the Commission shall relieve any person or class of persons in such State or locality from requirements imposed under this section. The Commission shall rescind any such agreement whenever it determines that the agreement no longer serves the interest of effective enforcement of this title.

(c) Except as provided in subsection (d), every employer, employment agency, and labor organization subject to this title shall (1) make and keep such records relevant to the determinations of whether unlawful employment practices have been or are being committed, (2) preserve such records for such periods, and (3) make such reports therefrom, as the Commission shall prescribe by regulation or order, after public hearing, as reasonable, necessary, or appropriate for the enforcement of this title or the regulations or orders thereunder. The Commission shall, by regulation, require each employer, labor organization, and joint labor-management committee subject to this title which controls an apprenticeship or other training program to maintain such records as are reasonably necessary to carry out the purpose of this title, including, but not limited to, a list of applicants who wish to participate in such program, including the chronological order in which such applicants were received, and shall furnish to the Commission, upon request, a detailed description of the manner in which persons are selected to participate in the apprenticeship or other training program. Any employer, employment agency, labor organization, or joint labor-management committee which believes that the application to it of any regulation or order issued under this section would result in undue hardship may (1) apply to the Commission for an exemption from the application of such regulation or order, or (2) bring a civil action in the United States district court for the district where such records are kept. If the Commission or the court, as the case may be, finds that the application of the regulation or order to the employer, employment agency, or labor organization in question would impose an undue hardship, the Commission or the court, as the case may be, may grant appropriate relief.

(d) The provisions of subsection (c) shall not apply to any employer, employment agency, labor organization, or joint labor-management committee with respect to matters occurring in any State or political subdivision thereof which has a fair employment practice law during any period in which such employer, employment agency, labor organization, or joint labor-management committee is subject to such law, except that the Commission may require such notations on records which such employer, employment agency, labor organization, or joint labor-management committee keeps or is required to keep as are necessary because of differences in coverage or methods of enforcement between the State or local law and the provisions of this title. Where an employer is required by Executive Order 10925, issued March 6, 1961, or by any other Executive order prescribing fair employment practices for Government contractors and subcontractors, or by rules or regulations issued thereunder, to file reports relating to his employment practices with any Federal agency or committee, and he is substantially in compliance with such requirements, the Commission shall not require him to file additional reports pursuant to subsection (c) of this section.

(e) It shall be unlawful for any officer or employee of the Commission to make public in any manner whatever any information obtained by the Commission pursuant to its authority under this section prior to the institution of any proceeding under this title involving such information. Any officer or employee of the Commission who shall make public in any manner whatever any information in violation of this subsection shall be guilty of a misdemeanor and upon conviction thereof, shall be fined not more than $1,000, or imprisoned not more than one year.

## INVESTIGATORY POWERS

SEC. 710. (a) For the purposes of any investigation of a charge filed under the authority contained in section 706, the Commission shall have authority to examine witnesses under oath and to require the production of documentary evidence relevant or material to the charge under investigation.

(b) If the respondent named in a charge filed under section 706 fails or refuses to comply with a demand of the Commission for permission to examine or to copy evidence in conformity with the provisions of section 709 (a), or if any person required to comply with the provisions of section 709 (c) or (d) fails or refuses to do so, or if any person fails or refuses to comply with a demand by the Commission to give testimony under oath, the United States district court for the district in which such person is found, resides, or transacts business, shall, upon application of the Commission, have jurisdiction to issue to such person an order requiring him to comply with the provisions of section 709 (c) or (d) or to comply with the demand of the Commission, but the attendance of a witness may not be required outside the State where he is found, resides, or transacts business and the production of evidence may not be required outside the State where such evidence is kept.

(c) Within twenty days after the service upon any person charged under section 706 of a demand by the Commission for the production of documentary evidence or for permission to examine or to copy evidence in conformity with the provisions of section 709 (a), such person may file in the district court of the United States for the judicial district in which he resides, is found, or transacts business, and serve upon the Commission a petition for an order of such court modifying or setting aside such demand. The time allowed for compliance with the demand in whole or in part as deemed proper and ordered by the court shall not run during the pendency of such petition in the court. Such petition shall specify each ground upon which the petitioner relies in seeking such relief, and may be based upon any failure of such demand to comply with the provisions of this title or with the limitations generally applicable to compulsory process or upon any constitutional or other legal right or privilege of such person. No objection which is not raised by such a petition may be urged in the defense to a proceeding initiated by the Commission under subsection (b) for enforcement of such a demand unless such proceeding is commenced by the Commission prior to the expiration of the twenty-day period, or unless the court determines that the defendant could not reasonably have been aware of the availability of such ground of objection.

(d) In any proceeding brought by the Commission under subsection (b), except as provided in subsection (c) of this section, the defendant may petition the court for an order modifying or setting aside the demand of the Commission.

## NOTICES TO BE POSTED

SEC. 711. (a) Every employer, employment agency, and labor organization, as the case may be, shall post and keep posted in conspicuous places upon its premises where notices to employees, applicants for employment, and members are customarily posted a notice to be prepared or approved by the Commission setting forth excerpts from or, summaries of, the pertinent provisions of this title and information pertinent to the filing of a complaint.

(b) A willful violation of this section shall be punishable by a fine of not more than $100 for each separate offense.

## VETERANS' PREFERENCE

SEC. 712. Nothing contained in this title shall be construed to repeal or modify any Federal, State, territorial, or local law creating special rights or preference for veterans.

## RULES AND REGULATIONS

SEC. 713. (a) The Commission shall have authority from time to time to issue, amend, or rescind suitable procedural regulations to carry out the provisions of this title. Regulations issued under this section shall be in conformity with the standards and limitations of the Administrative Procedure Act.

(b) In any action or proceeding based on an alleged unlawful employment practice, no person shall be subject to any liability or punishment for or on account of (1) the commission by such person of an unlawful employment practice if he pleads and proves that the act or omission complained of was in good faith, in conformity with, and in reliance on any written interpretation or opinion of the Commission, or (2) the failure of such person to publish and file any information required by any provision of this title if he pleads and proves that he failed to publish and file such information in good faith, in conformity with the instructions of the Commission issued under this title regarding the filing of such information. Such a defense, if established, shall be a bar to the action or proceeding, notwithstanding that (A) after such act or omission, such interpretation or opinion is modified or rescinded or is determined by judicial authority to be invalid or of no legal effect, or (B) after publishing or filing the description and annual reports, such publication or filing is determined by judicial authority not to be in conformity with the requirements of this title.

## FORCIBLY RESISTING THE COMMISSION OR ITS REPRESENTATIVES

SEC. 714. The provisions of section 111, title 18, United States Code, shall apply to officers, agents, and employees of the Commission in the performance of their official duties.

## SPECIAL STUDY BY SECRETARY OF LABOR

SEC. 715. The Secretary of Labor shall make a full and complete study of the factors which might tend to result in discrimination in employment because of age and of the consequences of such discrimination on the economy and individuals affected. The Secretary of Labor shall make a report to the Congress not later than June 30, 1965, containing the results of such study and shall include in such report such recommendations for legislation to prevent arbitrary discrimination in employment because of age as he determines advisable.

## EFFECTIVE DATE

SEC. 716. (a) This title shall become effective one year after the date of its enactment.

(b) Notwithstanding subsection (a), sections of this title other than sections 703, 704, 706, and 707 shall become effective immediately.

(c) The President shall, as soon as feasible after the enactment of this title, convene one or more conferences for the purpose of enabling the leaders of groups whose members will be affected by this title to become familiar with the rights afforded and obligations imposed by its provisions, and for the purpose of making plans which will result in the fair and effective administration of this title when all of its provisions become effective. The President shall invite the participation in such conference or conferences of (1) the members of the President's Committee on Equal Employment Opportunity, (2) the members of the Commission on Civil Rights, (3) representatives of State and local agencies engaged in furthering equal employment opportunity, (4) representatives of private agencies engaged in furthering equal employment opportunity, and (5) representatives of employers, labor organizations, and employment agencies who will be subject to this title.

# Executive Order 11246: Equal Employment Opportunity

Executive Order 11246 is generally regarded as the law that established affirmative action. This executive order is part of Lyndon Johnson's plan for the Great Society and is seen as a central part of his legacy.

Several aspects of the executive order merit comment or explanation.

1. The law applies to the federal government, to all federal contractors, and to construction companies that obtain government assistance. A federal contractor is an organization that provides the U.S. government with goods or services in exchange for payment. Imagine that an organization sells airplane parts to the army. That would make the organization a federal contractor. If the contractor does not believe in affirmative action, all that is necessary is to stop doing business with (i.e., stop selling airplane parts to) the army. But if the contractor wants to keep the contract, it must play by the rules. The choice is up to the contractor. In other words, affirmative action is not required of every organization; it is required only of those that choose to do business with the government. If an organization is found to have an inadequate or illegal program, the only sanction is loss of business. No one is fined. No one is put in jail.

2. Part I states that the Civil Service Commission is charged with enforcement of the law for federal workers. Thus, the Civil Service Commission is like the Equal Employment Opportunity Commission set up by the 1964 Civil Rights Act for civilian workers.

3. Parts II and III state that some organizations (contractors and assisted construction companies) must take affirmative actions to assure nondiscrimination. The executive order generally leaves to the Department of Labor the task of specifying what counts as proper action. In the decades since the passage of EO 11246, the Office of Federal Contract Compliance Programs (OFCCP) has been created as a unit within the Department of Labor. The OFCCP helps organizations devise and operate legal programs and generally supervises matters that relate to affirmative action in organizations

above a minimum size. With less than one thousand employees nationwide, the OFCCP oversees compliance of over 100,000 organizations that do business with the U.S. government.

4. The essence of the affirmative action programs established by EO 11246 is to monitor hiring, retention, and promotion. Following well developed rules, each contractor must match the utilization of employees in designated classes (e.g., women) against the known availability of qualified workers in those same designated classes. If utilization falls short of availability, remedies must be devised.

5. One way in which affirmative action differs from the nondiscrimination mandated by the 1964 Civil Rights Act concerns documentation. According to the 1964 law, organizations must produce documents *only if* there is a preliminary finding of wrongdoing. According to the executive order, organizations must produce documentation of their employment practices whenever the government asks to see the documents, even if there is no presumption of wrongdoing. Part II, Subpart B, Section 5 spells out this responsibility.

---

Under and by virtue of the authority vested in me as President of the United States by the Constitution and statutes of the United States, it is ordered as follows:

## PART I — NONDISCRIMINATION IN GOVERNMENT EMPLOYMENT

Section 101. It is the policy of the Government of the United States to provide equal opportunity in Federal employment for all qualified persons, to prohibit discrimination in employment because of race, creed, color, or national origin, and to promote the full realization of equal employment opportunity through a positive, continuing program in each executive department and agency. The policy of equal opportunity applies to every aspect of Federal employment policy and practice.

Sec. 102. The head of each executive department and agency shall establish and maintain a positive program of equal employment opportunity for all civilian employees and applicants for employment within his jurisdiction in accordance with the policy set forth in Section 101.

Sec. 103. The Civil Service Commission shall supervise and provide leadership and guidance in the conduct of equal employment opportunity programs for the civilian employees of and application for employment within the executive departments and agencies and shall review agency program accomplishments periodically. In order to facilitate the achievement of a model program for equal employment opportunity in the Federal service, the Commission may consult from time to time with such individuals, groups, or organizations as may be of assistance in improving the Federal program and realizing the objectives of this Part.

SEC. 104. The Civil Service Commission shall provide for the prompt, fair, and impartial consideration of all complaints of discrimination in Federal employment on the basis of race, creed, color, or national origin. Procedures for the consideration of complaints shall include at least one impartial review within the executive department or agency and shall provide for appeal to the Civil Service Commission.

SEC. 105. The Civil Service Commission shall issue such regulations, orders, and instructions as it deems necessary and appropriate to carry out its responsibility under this Part, and the head of each executive department and agency shall comply with the regulations, orders, and instructions issued by the Commission under this Part.

## PART II — NONDISCRIMINATION IN EMPLOYMENT BY GOVERNMENT CONTRACTORS AND SUBCONTRACTORS

### SUBPART A — DUTIES OF THE SECRETARY OF LABOR

SEC. 201. The Secretary of Labor shall be responsible for the administration of Parts II and III of this Order and shall adopt such rules and regulations and issue such orders as he deems necessary and appropriate to achieve the purposes thereof.

### SUBPART B — CONTRACTORS' AGREEMENTS

SEC. 202. Except in contracts exempted in accordance with Section 204 of this Order, all Government contracting agencies shall include in every Government contract hereafter entered into the following provisions:

"During the performance of this contract, the contractor agrees as follows:

"(1) The contractor will not discriminate against any employee or applicant for employment because of race, creed, color, or national origin. The contractor will take affirmative action to ensure that applicants are employed, and that employees are treated during employment, without regard to their race, creed, color, or national origin. Such action shall include, but not be limited to the following: employment, upgrading, demotion, or transfer; recruitment or recruitment advertising; layoff or termination; rates of pay or other forms of compensation; and selection for training, including apprenticeship. The contractor agrees to post in conspicuous places, available to employees and applicants for employment, notices to be provided by the contracting officer setting forth the provisions of this nondiscrimination clause.

"(2) The contractor will, in all solicitations or advertisements for employees placed by or on behalf of the contractor, state that all qualified applicants will receive consideration for employment without regard to race, creed, color, or national origin.

"(3) The contractor will send to each labor union or representative of workers with which he has a collective bargaining agreement or other contract or understanding, a notice, to be provided by the agency contracting officer, advising the labor union or workers' representative of the contractor's commitments under Section 202 of Executive Order No. 11246 of September 24, 1965, and shall post copies of the notice in conspicuous places available to employees and applicants for employment.

"(4) The contractor will comply with all provisions of Executive Order No. 11246 of Sept. 24, 1965, and of the rules, regulations, and relevant orders of the Secretary of Labor.

"(5) The contractor will furnish all information and reports required by Executive Order No. 11246 of September 24, 1965, and by the rules, regulations, and orders of the Secretary of Labor, or pursuant thereto, and will permit access to his books, records, and accounts by the contracting agency and the Secretary of Labor for purposes of investigation to ascertain compliance with such rules, regulations, and orders.

"(6) In the event of the contractor's noncompliance with the non-discrimination clauses of this contract or with any of such rules, regulations, or orders, this contract may be cancelled, terminated or suspended in whole or in part and the contractor may be declared ineligible for further Government contracts in accordance with procedures authorized in Executive Order No. 11246 of Sept. 24, 1965, and such other sanctions may be imposed and remedies invoked as provided in Executive Order No. 11246 of September 24, 1965, or by rule, regulation, or order of the Secretary of Labor, or as otherwise provided by law.

"(7) The contractor will include the provisions of Paragraphs (1) through (7) in every subcontract or purchase order unless exempted by rules, regulations, or orders of the Secretary of Labor issued pursuant to Section 204 of Executive Order No. 11246 of Sept. 24, 1965, so that such provisions will be binding upon each subcontractor or vendor. The contractor will take such action with respect to any subcontract or purchase order as the contracting agency may direct as a means of enforcing such provisions including sanctions for noncompliance: *Provided, however,* that in the event the contractor becomes involved in, or is threatened with, litigation with a subcontractor or vendor as a result of such direction by the contracting agency, the contractor may request the United States to enter into such litigation to protect the interests of the United States."

SEC. 203. (a) Each contractor having a contract containing the provisions prescribed in Section 202 shall file, and shall cause each of his subcontractors to file, Compliance Reports with the contracting agency or the Secretary of Labor as may be directed. Compliance Reports shall be filed within such times and shall contain such information as to the practices, policies, programs, and employment policies, programs, and employment statistics of the contractor and each subcontractor, and shall be in such form, as the Secretary of Labor may prescribe.

(b) Bidders or prospective contractors or subcontractors may be required to state whether they have participated in any previous contract subject to the provisions of this Order, or any preceding similar Executive order, and in that event to submit, on behalf of themselves and their proposed subcontractors, Compliance Reports prior to or as an initial part of their bid or negotiation of a contract.

(c) Whenever the contractor or subcontractor has a collective bargaining agreement or other contract or understanding with a labor union or an agency referring workers or providing or supervising apprenticeship or training for such workers, the Compliance Report shall include such information as to such labor union's or agency's practices and policies affecting compliance as the Secretary of Labor may prescribe: *Provided,* That to the extent such information is within the exclusive possession of a labor union or an agency referring workers or providing or supervising apprenticeship or training and such labor union or agency shall refuse to furnish such information to the contractor, the contractor shall so certify to the contracting agency as part of its Compliance Report and shall set forth what efforts he has made to obtain such information.

(d) The contracting agency or the Secretary of Labor may direct that any bidder or prospective contractor or subcontractor shall submit, as part of his Compliance Report, a statement in writing, signed by an authorized officer or agent on behalf of any labor union or any agency referring workers or providing or supervising apprenticeship or other training, with which the bidder or prospective contractor deals, with supporting information, to the effect that the signer's practices and policies do not discriminate on the grounds of race, color, creed, or national origin, and that the signer either will affirmatively cooperate in the implementation of the policy and provisions of this Order or that it consents and agrees that recruitment, employment, and the terms and conditions of employment under the proposed contract shall be in accordance with the purposes and provisions of the Order. In the event that the union, or the agency shall refuse to execute such a statement, the Compliance Report shall so certify and set forth what efforts have been made to secure such a statement and such additional factual material as the contracting agency or the Secretary of Labor may require.

SEC. 204. The Secretary of Labor may, when he deems that special circumstances in the national interest so require, exempt a contracting agency from the requirement of including any or all of the provisions of Section 202 of this Order in any specific contract, subcontract, or purchase order. The Secretary of Labor may, by rule or regulation, also exempt certain classes of contracts, subcontracts, or purchase orders (1) whenever work is to be or has been performed outside the United States and no recruitment of workers within the limits of the United States is involved;

(2) for standard commercial supplies or raw materials; (3) involving less than specified amounts of money or specified numbers of workers; or (4) to the extent that they involve subcontracts below a specified tier. The Secretary of Labor may also provide, by rule, regulation, or order, for the exemption of facilities of a contractor which are in all respects separate and distinct from activities of the contractor related to the performance of the contract: *Provided,* That such an exemption will not interfere with or impede the effectuation of the purposes of this Order: *And provided further,* That in the absence of such an exemption all facilities shall be covered by the provisions of this Order.

### SUBPART C — POWERS AND DUTIES OF THE SECRETARY OF LABOR AND THE CONTRACTING AGENCIES

SEC. 205. Each contracting agency shall be primarily responsible for obtaining compliance with the rules, regulations, and orders of the Secretary of Labor with respect to contracts entered into by such agency or its contractors. All contracting agencies shall comply with the rules of the Secretary of Labor in discharging their primary responsibility for securing compliance with the provisions of contracts and otherwise with the terms of this Order and of the rules, regulations, and orders of the Secretary of Labor issued pursuant to this Order. They are directed to cooperate with the Secretary of Labor and to furnish the Secretary of Labor such information and assistance as he may require in the performance of his functions under this Order. They are further directed to appoint or designate, from among the agency's personnel, compliance officers. It shall be the duty of such officers to seek compliance with the objectives of this Order by conference, conciliation, mediation, or persuasion.

SEC. 206. (a) The Secretary of Labor may investigate the employment practices of any Government contractor or subcontractor, or initiate such investigation by the appropriate contracting agency, to determine whether or not the contractual provisions specified in Section 202 of this Order have been violated. Such investigation shall be conducted in accordance with the procedures established by the Secretary of Labor and the investigating agency shall report to the Secretary of Labor any action taken or recommended.

(b) The Secretary of Labor may receive and investigate or cause to be investigated complaints by employees or prospective employees of a Government contractor or subcontractor which allege discrimination contrary to the contractual provisions specified in Section 202 of this Order. If this investigation is conducted for the Secretary of Labor by a contracting agency, that agency shall report to the Secretary what action has been taken or is recommended with regard to such complaints.

SEC. 207. The Secretary of Labor shall use his best efforts, directly and through contracting agencies, other interested Federal, state, and local agencies, contractors, and all other available instrumentalities to cause any labor union engaged in work under Government contracts or any agency referring workers or providing or supervising apprenticeship or training for or in the course of such work to cooperate in the implementation of the purposes of this Order. The Secretary of Labor shall, in appropriate cases, notify the Equal Employment Opportunity Commission, the Department of Justice, or other appropriate Federal agencies whenever it has reason to believe that the practices of any such labor organization or agency violate Title VI or Title VII of the Civil Rights Act of 1964 or other provision of Federal law.

SEC. 208. (a) The Secretary of Labor, or any agency, officer, or employee in the executive branch of the Government designated by rule, regulation, or order of the Secretary, may hold such hearings, public or private, as the Secretary may deem advisable for compliance, enforcement, or educational purposes.

(b) The Secretary of Labor may hold, or cause to be held, hearings in accordance with Subsection (a) of this Section prior to imposing, ordering, or recommending the imposition of penalties and sanctions under this Order. No order for debarment of any contractor from further Government contracts under Section 209 (a) (6) shall be made without affording the contractor an opportunity for a hearing.

SUBPART D — SANCTIONS AND PENALTIES

SEC. 209. (a) In accordance with such rules, regulations, or orders as the Secretary of Labor may issue or adopt, the Secretary or the appropriate contracting agency may:

(1) Publish, or cause to be published, the names of contractors or unions which it has concluded have complied or have failed to comply with the provisions of this Order or of the rules, regulations, and orders of the Secretary of Labor.

(2) Recommend to the Department of Justice that, in cases in which there is substantial or material violation or the threat of substantial or material violation of the contractual provisions set forth in Section 202 of this Order, appropriate proceedings be brought to enforce those provisions, including the enjoining, within the limitations of applicable law, of organizations, individuals, or groups who prevent directly or indirectly, or seek to prevent directly or indirectly, compliance with the provisions of this Order.

(3) Recommend to the Equal Employment Opportunity Commission or the Department of Justice that appropriate proceedings be instituted under Title VII of the Civil Rights Act of 1964.

(4) Recommend to the Department of Justice that criminal proceedings be brought for the furnishing of false information to any contracting agency or to the Secretary of Labor as the case may be.

(5) Cancel, terminate, suspend, or cause to be cancelled, terminated, or suspended, any contract, or any portion or portions thereof,

for failure of the contractor or subcontractor to comply with the non-discrimination provisions of the contract. Contracts may be cancelled, terminated, or suspended absolutely or continuance of contracts may be conditioned upon a program for future compliance approved by the contracting agency.

(6) Provide that any contracting agency shall refrain from entering into further contracts or extensions or other modifications of existing contracts, with any noncomplying contractor, until such contractor has satisfied the Secretary of Labor that such contractor has established and will carry out personnel and employment policies in compliance with the provisions of this Order.

(b) Under rules and regulations prescribed by the Secretary of Labor, each contracting agency shall make reasonable efforts within a reasonable time limitation to secure compliance with the contract provisions of this Order by methods of conference, conciliation, mediation, and persuasion before proceedings shall be instituted under Subsection (a) (2) of this Section, or before a contract shall be cancelled or terminated in whole or in part under Subsection (a) (5) of this Section for failure of a contractor or subcontractor to comply with the contract provisions of this Order.

SEC. 210. Any contracting agency taking any action authorized by this Subpart, whether on its own motion, or as directed by the Secretary of Labor, or under the rules and regulations of the Secretary, shall promptly notify the Secretary of such action. Whenever the Secretary of Labor makes a determination under this Section, he shall promptly notify the appropriate contracting agency of the action recommended. The agency shall take such action and shall report the results thereof to the Secretary of Labor within such time as the Secretary shall specify.

SEC. 211. If the Secretary shall so direct, contracting agencies shall not enter into contracts with any bidder or prospective contractor unless the bidder or prospective contractor has satisfactorily complied with the provisions of this Order or submits a program for compliance acceptable to the Secretary of Labor or, if the Secretary so authorizes, to the contracting agency.

SEC. 212. Whenever a contracting agency cancels or terminates a contract, or whenever a contractor has been debarred from further Government contracts, under Section 209 (a) (6) because of noncompliance with the contract provisions with regard to nondiscrimination, the Secretary of Labor, or the contracting agency involved, shall promptly notify the Comptroller General of the United States. Any such debarment may be rescinded by the Secretary of Labor or by the contracting agency which imposed the sanction.

SUBPART E — CERTIFICATES OF MERIT

SEC. 213. The Secretary of Labor may provide for issuance of a United States Government Certificate of Merit to employers or labor unions, or other agencies which are or may hereafter be engaged in work under Government contracts, if the Secretary is satisfied that the personnel and employment practices of the employer, or that the personnel, training, apprenticeship, membership, grievance and representation, upgrading, and other practices and policies of the labor union or other agency conform to the purposes and provisions of this Order.

SEC. 214. Any Certificate of Merit may at any time be suspended or revoked by the Secretary of Labor if the holder thereof, in the judgment of the Secretary, has failed to comply with the provisions of this Order.

SEC. 215. The Secretary of Labor may provide for the exemption of any employer, labor union, or other agency from any reporting requirements imposed under or pursuant to this Order if such employer, labor union, or other agency has been awarded a Certificate of Merit which has not been suspended or revoked.

## PART III — NONDISCRIMINATION PROVISIONS IN FEDERALLY ASSISTED CONSTRUCTION CONTRACTS

SEC. 301. Each executive department and agency which administers a program involving Federal financial assistance shall require as a condition for the approval of any grant, contract, loan, insurance, or guarantee thereunder, which may involve a construction contract, that the applicant for Federal assistance undertake and agree to incorporate, or cause to be incorporated, into all construction contracts paid for in whole or in part with funds obtained from the Federal Government or borrowed on the credit of the Federal Government pursuant to such grant, contract, loan, insurance, or guarantee, or undertaken pursuant to any Federal program involving such grant, contract, loan, insurance, or guarantee, the provisions prescribed for Government contracts by Section 202 of this Order or such modification thereof, preserving in substance the contractor's obligations thereunder, as may be approved by the Secretary of Labor, together with such additional provisions as the Secretary deems appropriate to establish and protect the interest of the United States in the enforcement of those obligations. Each such applicant shall also undertake and agree (1) to assist and cooperate actively with the administering department or agency and the Secretary of Labor in obtaining the compliance of contractors and subcontractors with those contract provisions and with the rules, regulations, and relevant orders of the Secretary, (2) to obtain and to furnish to the administering department or agency and to the Secretary of Labor such information as they may require for the supervision of such compliance, (3) to carry out sanctions and penalties for violation of such obligations imposed upon contractors and subcontractors by the Secretary of Labor or the administering department or agency pursuant to Part II, Subpart D, of this Order, and (4) to refrain from entering into any contract subject to this

Order, or extension or other modification of such a contract with a contractor debarred from Government contracts under Part II, Subpart D, of this Order.

SEC. 302. (a) "Construction contract" as used in the Order means any contract for the construction, rehabilitation, alteration, conversion, extension, or repair of buildings, highways, or other improvements to real property.

(b) The provisions of Part II of this Order shall apply to such construction contracts, and for purposes of such application the administering department or agency shall be considered the contracting agency referred to therein.

(c) The term "applicant" as used in this Order means an applicant for Federal assistance or, as determined by agency regulation, other program participant, with respect to whom an application for any grant, contract, loan, insurance, or guarantee is not finally acted upon prior to the effective date of this Part, and it includes such an applicant after he becomes a recipient of such Federal assistance.

SEC. 303. (a) Each administering department and agency shall be responsible for obtaining the compliance of such applicants with their undertakings under this Order. Each administering department and agency is directed to cooperate with the Secretary of Labor, and to furnish the Secretary such information and assistance as he may require in the performance of his functions under this Order.

(b) In the event an applicant fails and refuses to comply with his undertakings, the administering department or agency may take any or all of the following actions: (1) cancel, terminate, or suspend in whole or in part the agreement, contract, or other arrangement with such applicant with respect to which the failure and refusal occurred; (2) refrain from extending any further assistance to the applicant under the program with respect to which the failure or refusal occurred until satisfactory assurance of future compliance has been received from such applicant; and (3) refer the case to the Department of Justice for appropriate legal proceedings.

(c) Any action with respect to an applicant pursuant to Subsection (b) shall be taken in conformity with Section 602 of the Civil Rights Act of 1964 (and the regulations of the administering department or agency issued thereunder), to the extent applicable. In no case shall action be taken with respect to an applicant pursuant to Clause (1) or (2) of Subsection (b) without notice and opportunity for hearing before the administering department or agency.

SEC. 304. Any executive department or agency which imposes by rule, regulation, or order requirements of nondiscrimination in employment, other than requirements imposed pursuant to this Order, may delegate to the Secretary of Labor by agreement such responsibilities with respect to compliance standards, reports, and procedures as would tend to bring the administration of such requirements into conformity with the administration of requirements imposed under this Order: *Provided,* That actions to effect compliance by recipients of Federal financial assistance with requirements imposed pursuant to Title VI of the Civil Rights Act of 1964 shall be taken in conformity with the procedures and limitations prescribed in Section 602 thereof and the regulations of the administering department or agency issued thereunder.

## PART IV — MISCELLANEOUS

SEC. 401. The Secretary of Labor may delegate to any officer, agency, or employee in the Executive branch of the Government, any function or duty of the Secretary under Parts II and III of this Order, except authority to promulgate rules and regulations of a general nature.

SEC. 402. The Secretary of Labor shall provide administrative support for the execution of the program known as the "Plans for Progress."

SEC. 403. (a) Executive Orders Nos. 10590 (January 19, 1955), 10722 (August 5, 1957), 10925 (March 6, 1961), 11114 (June 22, 1963), and 11162 (July 28, 1964), are hereby superseded and the President's Committee on Equal Employment Opportunity established by Executive Order No. 10925 is hereby abolished. All records and property in the custody of the Committee shall be transferred to the Civil Service Commission and the Secretary of Labor, as appropriate.

(b) Nothing in this Order shall be deemed to relieve any person of any obligation assumed or imposed under or pursuant to any Executive Order superseded by this Order. All rules, regulations, orders, instructions, designations, and other directives issued by the President's Committee on Equal Employment Opportunity and those issued by the heads of various departments or agencies under or pursuant to any of the Executive orders superseded by this Order, shall, to the extent that they are not inconsistent with this Order, remain in full force and effect unless and until revoked or superseded by appropriate authority. References in such directives to provisions of the superseded orders shall be deemed to be references to the comparable provisions of this Order.

SEC. 404. The General Services Administration shall take appropriate action to revise the standard Government contract forms to accord with the provisions of this Order and of the rules and regulations of the Secretary of Labor.

SEC. 405. This Order shall become effective thirty days after the date of this Order.

LYNDON B. JOHNSON
THE WHITE HOUSE
*September 24, 1965.*

# Proposition 209

On November 5, 1996, the citizens of California passed Proposition 209 into law. Fifty-four percent of the voters were in favor of the proposition. The media portrayed the vote as signaling the end of affirmative action.

Following is the text of the initiative as it appeared on the ballot. The words *affirmative action* never appear in the initiative. Item (c) is also of interest: Translation? Let's keep enforcing Executive Order 11246!

---

## AMENDMENT TO ARTICLE I

Section 31 is added to Article I of the California Constitution as follows:

SEC. 31. (a) The state shall not discriminate against, or grant preferential treatment to, any individual or group on the basis of race, sex, color, ethnicity, or national origin in the operation of public employment, public education, or public contracting.

(b) This section shall apply only to action taken after the section's effective date.

(c) Nothing in this section shall be interpreted as prohibiting bona fide qualifications based on sex which are reasonably necessary to the normal operation of public employment, public education, or public contracting.

(d) Nothing in this section shall be interpreted as invalidating any court order or consent decree which is in force as of the effective date of this section.

(e) Nothing in this section shall be interpreted as prohibiting action which must be taken to establish or maintain eligibility for any federal program, where ineligibility would result in a loss of federal funds to the state.

(f) For the purposes of this section, "state" shall include, but not necessarily be limited to, the state itself, any city, county, city and county, public university system, including the University of California, community college district, school district, special district, or any other political subdivision or governmental instrumentality of or within the state.

(g) The remedies available for violations of this section shall be the same, regardless of the injured party's race, sex, color, ethnicity, or national origin, as are otherwise available for violations of then-existing California antidiscrimination law.

(h) This section shall be self-executing. If any part or parts of this section are found to be in conflict with federal law or the United States Constitution, the section shall be implemented to the maximum extent that federal law and the United States Constitution permit. Any provision held invalid shall be severable from the remaining portions of this section.

# Griggs et al. *v.* Duke Power Co.

As noted in the introduction to Part 4, there are three levels to the federal judiciary: district, appellate, and supreme. Decisions of the district court can be upheld or overturned by the circuit court. If the Supreme Court agrees to hear a case, it may uphold or overrule the circuit court judgment. When giving decisions, the Supreme Court makes law. In *Griggs,* the Court established the doctrine of disparate impact. Practices that are applied equally to all but that affect one group negatively cannot be sustained without a pressing reason. "Good intent . . . does not redeem employment procedures . . . that operate as 'built-in headwinds' for minority groups."

---

CERTIORARI TO THE UNITED STATES COURT OF
APPEALS FOR THE FOURTH CIRCUIT

No. 124. Argued December 14, 1970–Decided March 8, 1971

. . .

BURGER, C. J., delivered the opinion of the Court, in which all members joined except BRENNAN, J., who took no part in the consideration or decision of the case.

MR. CHIEF JUSTICE BURGER delivered the opinion of the Court.

We granted the writ in this case to resolve the question whether an employer is prohibited by the Civil Rights Act of 1964, Title VII, from requiring a high school education or passing of a standardized general intelligence test as a condition of employment in or transfer to jobs when (a) neither standard is shown to be significantly related to successful job performance, (b) both requirements operate to disqualify Negroes at a substantially higher rate than white applicants, and (c) the jobs in question formerly had been filled only by white employees as part of a longstanding practice of giving preference to whites.

Congress provided, in Title VII of the Civil Rights Act of 1964, for class actions for enforcement of provisions of the Act and this proceeding was brought by a group of incumbent Negro employees against Duke

Power Company. All the petitioners are employed at the Company's Dan River Steam Station, a power generating facility located at Draper, North Carolina. At the time this action was instituted, the Company had 95 employees at the Dan River Station, 14 of whom were Negroes; 13 of these are petitioners here.

The District Court found that prior to July 2, 1965, the effective date of the Civil Rights Act of 1964, the Company openly discriminated on the basis of race in the hiring and assigning of employees at its Dan River plant. The plant was organized into five operating departments: (1) Labor, (2) Coal Handling, (3) Operations, (4) Maintenance, and (5) Laboratory and Test. Negroes were employed only in the Labor Department where the highest paying jobs paid less than the lowest paying jobs in the other four "operating" departments in which only whites were employed. Promotions were normally made within each department on the basis of job seniority. Transferees into a department usually began in the lowest position.

In 1955 the Company instituted a policy of requiring a high school education for initial assignment to any department except Labor, and for transfer from the Coal Handling to any "inside" department (Operations, Maintenance, or Laboratory). When the Company abandoned its policy of restricting Negroes to the Labor Department in 1965, completion of high school also was made a prerequisite to transfer from Labor to any other department. From the time the high school requirement was instituted to the time of trial, however, white employees hired before the time of the high school education requirement continued to perform satisfactorily and achieve promotions in the "operating" departments. Findings on this score are not challenged.

The Company added a further requirement for new employees on July 2, 1965, the date on which Title VII became effective. To qualify for placement in any but the Labor Department it became necessary to register satisfactory scores on two professionally prepared aptitude tests, as well as to have a high school education. Completion of high school alone continued to render employees eligible for transfer to the four desirable departments from which Negroes had been excluded if the incumbent had been employed prior to the time of the new requirement. In September 1965 the Company began to permit incumbent employees who lacked a high school education to qualify for transfer from Labor or Coal Handling to an "inside" job by passing two tests — the Wonderlic Personnel Test, which purports to measure general intelligence, and the Bennett Mechanical Comprehension Test. Neither was directed or intended to measure the ability to learn to perform a particular job or category of jobs. The requisite scores used for both initial hiring and transfer approximated the national median for high school graduates.

The District Court had found that while the Company previously followed a policy of overt racial discrimination in a period prior to the Act, such conduct had ceased. The District Court also concluded that

Title VII was intended to be prospective only and, consequently, the impact of prior inequities was beyond the reach of corrective action authorized by the Act.

The Court of Appeals was confronted with a question of first impression, as are we, concerning the meaning of Title VII. After careful analysis a majority of that court concluded that a subjective test of the employer's intent should govern, particularly in a close case, and that in this case there was no showing of a discriminatory purpose in the adoption of the diploma and test requirements. On this basis, the Court of Appeals concluded there was no violation of the Act.

The Court of Appeals reversed the District Court in part, rejecting the holding that residual discrimination arising from prior employment practices was insulated from remedial action. The Court of Appeals noted, however, that the District Court was correct in its conclusion that there was no showing of a racial purpose or invidious intent in the adoption of the high school diploma requirement or general intelligence test and that these standards had been applied fairly to white and Negroes alike. . . .

The objective of Congress in the enactment of Title VII is plain from the language of the statute. It was to achieve equality of employment opportunities and remove barriers that have operated in the past to favor an identifiable group of white employees over other employees. Under the Act, practices, procedures, or tests neutral on their face, and even neutral in terms of intent, cannot be maintained if they operate to "freeze" the status quo of prior discriminatory employment practices.

The Court of Appeals' opinion, and the partial dissent, agreed that, on the record in the present case, "whites register far better on the Company's alternative requirements" than Negroes. 420 F. 2d 1225, 1239 n. 6. This consequence would appear to be directly traceable to race. Basic intelligence must have the means of articulation to manifest itself fairly in a testing process. Because they are Negroes, petitioners have long received inferior education in segregated schools and this Court expressly recognized these differences in *Gaston County* v. *United States,* 395 U. S. 285 (1969). There, because of the inferior education received by Negroes in North Carolina, this Court barred the institution of a literacy test for voter registration on the ground that the test would abridge the right to vote indirectly on account of race. Congress did not intend by Title VII, however, to guarantee a job to every person regardless of qualifications. In short, the Act does not command that any person be hired simply because he was formerly the subject of discrimination, or because he is a member of a minority group. Discriminatory preference for any group, minority or majority, is precisely and only what Congress has proscribed. What is required by Congress is the removal of artificial, arbitrary, and unnecessary barriers to employment when the barriers operate invidiously to discriminate on the basis of racial or other impermissible classification.

. . .

The evidence, however, shows that employees who have not completed high school or taken the tests have continued to perform satisfactorily and make progress in departments for which the high school and test criteria are now used. The promotion record of present employees who would not be able to meet the new criteria thus suggests the possibility that the requirements may not be needed even for the limited purpose of preserving the avowed policy of advancement within the Company. . . .

The Court of Appeals held that the Company had adopted the diploma and test requirements without any "intention to discriminate against Negro employees." 420 F. 2d, at 1232. We do not suggest that either the District Court or the Court of Appeals erred in examining the employer's intent; but good intent or absence of discriminatory intent does not redeem employment procedures or testing mechanisms that operate as "built-in headwinds" for minority groups and are unrelated to measuring job capability.

The Company's lack of discriminatory intent is suggested by special efforts to help the undereducated employees through Company financing of two-thirds the cost of tuition for high school training. But Congress directed the thrust of the Act to the *consequences* of employment practices, not simply the motivation. More than that, Congress has placed on the employer the burden of showing that any given requirement must have a manifest relationship to the employment in question.

. . .

The judgment of the Court of Appeals is, as to that portion of the judgment appealed from, reversed.

# Regents of the University of California *v.* Bakke

## CERTIORARI TO THE SUPREME COURT OF CALIFORNIA

The Supreme Court of the United States can agree to hear a case that has made its way through a state system. In 1977, the Supreme Court heard arguments in the famous *Bakke* case. The Medical School at UC Davis had denied admission to a white applicant, Allan Bakke, and had granted admission to some students of color who had lower scores than Bakke. Bakke sued, claiming racial discrimination because the Medical School used two separate lists in selecting applicants: one for whites and one for other people. The five-person majority opinion in *Bakke* was that the Medical School (called here "the petitioner") had erred and had violated the legal rights of Allan Bakke. Five members of the court (Chief Justice Burger and Justices Powell, Stewart, Rehnquist, and Stevens) voted to uphold the decision of the California Supreme Court (forbidding quotas and directing Bakke to be admitted), while four members (Justices Brennan, Blackmun, Marshall, and White) disagreed with the decision of the majority.

There are six separate opinions. Thus, even when the justices agreed with one another's conclusions, they disagreed about the reasoning behind the conclusions. There is a great deal of difference of opinion about this case, especially relative to *Griggs*. Each person seems to see something different in the situation. In the excerpts presented here, we have tried to be true to the reasoning of each justice or each group of justices. The sequence of roman numerals and capital letters (also present in the original decisions) shows the structure of each argument in outline form.

The arguments of Justice Powell are extremely eloquent. His opinion is structured as follows. He first gives the background facts (Section I). Then in Sections II through VI, Justice Powell presents prior arguments on specific issues (generally in Part A), the core of his own opinion on the issue (Part B), and additional observations (Parts C and D). Especially influential are the arguments presented in Parts IIB, IVD, and VB. In Part VA there is a reference to the Harvard University admission plan that was appended to the original decision. Justice Powell commented favorably on using race as a "plus factor" along with many other factors in determining admission. This point of view is very different than the point of view that says that race may never be a factor noticed in admissions or hiring. Different too is the opinion of Justices Stevens, Burger, Stewart, and Rehnquist, who say, "[T]he question whether race can ever be used as a factor in an admissions decision is not an issue in this case."

All six opinions in the *Bakke* case represent distinct approaches to the issues at hand, but one opinion presents a highly unusual approach. That is the opinion of Justice Marshall, the one African American on the court at the time. A small portion of his opinion is excerpted here. Essentially, Justice Marshall argues here that the long sad history of racism requires strong corrective actions today.

---

No. 76-811. Argued October 12, 1977 — Decided June 28, 1978

. . .

MR. JUSTICE POWELL announced the judgment of the Court.

This case presents a challenge to the special admissions program of the petitioner, the Medical School of the University of California at Davis, which is designed to assure the admission of a specified number of students from certain minority groups. The Superior Court of California sustained respondent's [Bakke's] challenge, holding that petitioner's [UC Davis's] program violated the California Constitution, Title VI of the Civil Rights Act of 1964, 42 U.S.C. § 2000d *et seq.*, and the Equal Protection Clause of the Fourteenth Amendment. The court enjoined petitioner [UC Davis] from considering respondent's race or the race of any other applicant in making admissions decisions. It refused, however, to order respondent's admission to the Medical School holding that he had not carried his burden of proving that he would have been admitted but for the constitutional and statutory violations. The Superior Court of California affirmed those portions of the trial court's judgment declaring the special admissions program unlawful and enjoining petitioner [UC Davis] from considering the race of any applicant. It modified that portion of the judgment denying respondent's [Bakke's] requested injunction and directed the trial court to order his admission.

For the reasons stated in the following opinion, I believe that so much of the judgment of the California court as holds petitioner's [UC Davis's] special admissions program unlawful and directs that respondent be admitted to the Medical School must be affirmed. For the reasons expressed in a separate opinion, my Brothers THE CHIEF JUSTICE, MR. JUSTICE STEWART, MR. JUSTICE REHNQUIST, and MR. JUSTICE STEVENS concur in this judgment.

. . .

I

The Medical School of the University of California at Davis opened in 1968 with an entering class of 50 students. In 1971, the size of the entering class was increased to 100 students, a level at which it remains. No admissions program for disadvantaged or minority students existed when the school opened, and the first class contained three Asians but no blacks, no Mexican-Americans, and no American Indians. Over the next two years, the faculty devised a special admissions program to increase the representation of "disadvantaged" students in each Medical School class. The special program consisted of a separate admissions system operating in coordination with the regular admissions process.

. . . While the overall class size was still 50, the prescribed number was 8; in 1973 and 1974, when the class size had doubled to 100, the prescribed number of special admissions also doubled, to 16.

. . .

Allan Bakke is a white male who applied to the Davis Medical School in both 1973 and 1974. In both years Bakke's application was considered under the general admissions program. . . . [Bakke was denied admission in 1973 and 1974. He then sued.]

. . . The trial court found that the special program operated as a racial quota, because minority applicants in the special program were rated only against one another . . . and 16 places in the class of 100 were reserved for them. . . . Declaring that the University could not take race into account in making admissions decisions, the trial court held the challenged program violative of the Federal Constitution, the State Constitution, and Title VI. The court refused to order Bakke's admission, however, holding that he had failed to carry his burden of proving that he would have been admitted but for the existence of the special program.

Bakke appealed from the portion of the trial court judgment denying him admission, and the University appealed from the decision that its special admissions program was unlawful and the order enjoining it from considering race in the processing of applications. The Supreme Court of California transferred the case directly from the trial court, "because of the importance of the issues involved." . . . The California court accepted the findings of the trial court with respect to the University's program. Because the special admissions program involved a racial classification, the Supreme Court held itself bound to apply strict scrutiny. . . . It then turned to the goals the University presented as justifying the special program. Although the court agreed that the goals of integrating the medical profession and increasing the number of physicians willing to serve members of minority groups were compelling state interests, . . . it concluded that the special admissions program was not the least intrusive means of achieving those goals. Without passing on the state constitutional or the federal statutory grounds cited in the trial court's judgment, the California court held that the Equal Protection Clause of the Fourteenth

Amendment required that "no applicant may be rejected because of his race, in favor of another who is less qualified, as measured by standards applied without regard to race." . . .

Turning to Bakke's appeal, the court ruled that since Bakke had established that the University had discriminated against him on the basis of his race, the burden of proof shifted to the University to demonstrate that he would not have been admitted even in the absence of the special admissions program.

. . .

## II

In this Court the parties neither briefed nor argued the applicability of Title VI of the Civil Rights Act of 1964. Rather . . . they focused exclusively upon . . . the Equal Protection Clause. . . . [W]e requested supplementary briefing on the statutory issue. . . .

### A

At the outset we face the question of whether a right of action for private parties exists under Title VI.

. . .

### B

The language of § 601, 78 Stat. 252, like that of the Equal Protection Clause, is majestic in its sweep:

> "No person in the United States shall, on the ground of race, color, or national origin, be excluded from participation in, be denied the benefits of, or be subjected to discrimination under any program or activity receiving Federal financial assistance."

The concept of "discrimination," like the phrase "equal protection of the laws," is susceptible of varying interpretations, for as Mr. Justice Holmes declared, "[a] word is not a crystal, transparent and unchanged, it is the skin of a living thought and may vary greatly in color and content according to the circumstances and the time in which it is used." . . . We must, therefore, seek whatever aid is available in determining the precise meaning of the statute before us. . . . Examination of the voluminous legislative history of Title VI reveals a congressional intent to halt federal funding of entities that violate a prohibition of racial discrimination similar to that of the Constitution. Although isolated statements of various legislators, taken out of context, can be marshaled in support of the proposition that § 601 enacted a purely colorblind scheme, without regard to the reach of the Equal Protection Clause, these comments must be read against the background of both the problem that Congress was addressing and the broader view of the statute that emerges from a full examination of the legislative debates.

The problem confronting Congress was discrimination against Negro citizens at the hands of recipients of federal moneys. . . . Over and over again, proponents of the bill detailed the plight of Negroes seeking equal treatment in such programs. There simply was no reason for Congress to consider the validity of hypothetical preferences that might be accorded minority citizens; the legislators were dealing with the real and pressing problem of how to guarantee those citizens equal treatment.
. . .

## III

Petitioner does not deny that decisions based on race or ethnic origin by faculties and administrations of state universities are reviewable under the Fourteenth Amendment.
. . .

The guarantees of the Fourteenth Amendment extend to all persons. Its language is explicit: "No State shall . . . deny to any person within its jurisdiction the equal protection of the laws." It is settled beyond question that the "rights created by the first section of the Fourteenth Amendment are, by its terms, guaranteed to the individual. The rights established are personal rights." . . . The guarantee of equal protection cannot mean one thing when applied to one individual and something else when applied to a person of another color. If both are not accorded the same protection then it is not equal.

Nevertheless, petitioner argues that the court below erred in applying strict scrutiny to the special admissions program because white males, such as respondent, are not a "discrete and insular minority" requiring extraordinary protection from the majoritarian political process. . . . This rationale, however, has never been invoked in our decisions as a prerequisite to subjecting racial or ethnic distinctions to strict scrutiny. Nor has this Court held that discreteness and insularity constitute necessary preconditions to a holding that a particular classification is invidious. . . . The court has never questioned the validity of those pronouncements. Racial and ethnic distinctions of any sort are inherently suspect and thus call for the most exacting scrutiny.

### B

This perception of racial and ethnic distinctions is rooted in our Nation's constitutional and demographic history. The Court's initial view of the Fourteenth Amendment was that its "one pervading purpose" was "freedom of the slave race, the security and firm establishment of that freedom, and the protection of the newly-made freeman and citizen from the oppressions of those who had formerly exercised dominion over him." . . .
. . .

. . . Because the landmark decisions in this area arose in response to the continued exclusion of Negroes from the mainstream of American society, they could be characterized as involving discrimination by the "majority" white race against the Negro minority. But they need not be read as depending upon that characterization for their results. It suffices to say that "[o]ver the years, this Court has consistently repudiated '[d]istinctions between citizens solely because of their ancestry' as being 'odious to a free people whose institutions are founded upon the doctrine of equality.' " . . .

Petitioner urges us to adopt for the first time a more restrictive view of the Equal Protection Clause and hold that discrimination against members of the white "majority" cannot be suspect if its purpose can be characterized as "benign." The clock of our liberties, however, cannot be turned back to 1868. . . . It is far too late to argue that the guarantee of equal protection to *all* persons permits the recognition of special wards entitled to a degree of protection greater than that accorded others. "The Fourteenth Amendment is not directed solely against discrimination due to a 'two-class theory' — that is, based upon differences between 'white' and Negro." . . .

Once the artificial line of a "two-class theory" of the Fourteenth Amendment is put aside, the difficulties entailed in varying the level of judicial review according to a perceived "preferred" status of a particular racial or ethnic minority are intractable. The concepts of "majority" and "minority" necessarily reflect temporary arrangements and political judgments. The white "majority" itself is composed of various minority groups, most of which can lay claim to a history of poor discrimination at the hands of the State and private individuals. Not all of these groups can receive preferential treatment and corresponding judicial tolerance of distinctions drawn in terms of race and nationality, for then the only "majority" left would be a new minority of white Anglo-Saxon Protestants. There is no principled basis for deciding which groups would merit "heightened judicial solicitude" and which would not. Courts would be asked to evaluate the extent of the prejudice and consequent harm suffered by various minority groups. Those whose societal injury is thought to exceed some arbitrary level of tolerability then would be entitled to preferential classifications at the expense of individuals belonging to other groups. Those classifications would be free from exacting judicial scrutiny. As these preferences began to have their desired effect, and the consequences of past discrimination were undone, new judicial rankings would be necessary. The kind of variable sociological and political analysis necessary to produce such rankings simply does not lie within the judicial competence — even if they otherwise were politically feasible and socially desirable.

Moreover, there are serious problems of justice connected with the idea of preference itself. First, it may not always be clear that a so-called preference is in fact benign. Courts may be asked to validate burdens imposed upon individual members of a particular group in order to advance the group's general interest. . . . Nothing in the Constitution supports the notion that individuals may be asked to suffer otherwise impermissible burdens in order to enhance the societal standing of their ethnic groups. Second, preferential programs may only reinforce common stereotypes holding that certain groups are unable to achieve success without special protection based on a factor having no relationship to individual worth. . . . Third, there is a measure of inequity in forcing innocent persons in respondent's position to bear the burdens of redressing grievances not of their making.

. . .

### C

Petitioner contends that on several occasions this Court has approved preferential classifications without applying the most exacting scrutiny. Most of the cases upon which petitioner relies are drawn from three areas: school desegregation, employment discrimination, and sex discrimination. Each of the cases cited presented a situation materially different from the facts of this case.

The school desegregation cases are inapposite. . . .

The employment discrimination cases also do not advance the petitioner's cause. . . .

Nor is petitioner's view as to the applicable standard supported by the fact that gender-based classifications are not subjected to this level of scrutiny.

. . .

### IV

We have held that "in order to justify the use of a suspect classification, a State must show that its purpose or interest is both constitutionally permissible and substantial, and that its use of the classification is 'necessary . . . to the accomplishment' of its purpose or the safeguarding of its interest." . . .

### A

If petitioner's purpose is to assure within its student body some specified percentage of a particular group merely because of its race or ethnic origin, such a preferential purpose must be rejected not as insubstantial but as facially invalid. Preferring members of any one group for no reason other than race or ethnic origin is discrimination for its own sake. This the Constitution forbids.

### B

The State certainly has a legitimate and substantial interest in ameliorating, or eliminating where feasible, the disabling effects of identified discrimination. The line of school desegregation cases, commencing with *Brown,* attests to the importance of this state goal and the commitment of the judiciary to affirm all lawful means toward its attainment.

In the school cases, the States were required by court order to redress the wrongs worked by specific instances of racial discrimination. That goal was far more focused than the remedying of the effects of "societal discrimination," an amorphous concept of injury that may be ageless in its reach into the past.

We have never approved a classification that aids persons perceived as members of relatively victimized groups at the expense of other innocent individuals in the absence of judicial, legislative, or administrative findings of constitutional or statutory violations.

. . . Also, the remedial action usually remains subject to continuing oversight to assure that it will work the least harm possible to other innocent persons competing for the benefit. Without such findings of constitutional or statutory violations, it cannot be said that the government has any greater interest in helping one individual than in refraining from harming another. Thus, the government has no compelling justification for inflicting such harm.

Petitioner does not purport to have made, and is in no position to make, such findings.

. . .

C

Petitioner identifies, as another purpose of its program, improving the delivery of health-care services to communities currently underserved. It may be assumed that in some situations a State's interest in facilitating the health care of its citizens is sufficiently compelling to support the use of a suspect classification. But there is virtually no evidence in the record indicating that petitioner's special admissions program is either needed or geared to promote that goal. The court below addressed this failure of proof:

> "The University concedes it cannot assure that minority doctors who entered under the program, all of whom expressed an 'interest' in practicing in a disadvantaged community, will actually do so. It may be correct to assume that some of them will carry out this intention, and that it is more likely they will practice in minority communities than the average white doctor. . . . Nevertheless, there are more precise and reliable ways to identify applicants who are genuinely interested in the medical problems of minorities than by race. An applicant of whatever race who has demonstrated his concern for disadvantaged minorities in the past and who declares that practice in such a community is his primary professional goal would be more likely to contribute to alleviation of the medical shortage than one who is chosen entirely on the basis of race and disadvantage. In short, there is no empirical data to demonstrate that any one race is more selflessly socially oriented or by contrast that another is more selfishly acquisitive.". . .

Petitioner simply has not carried its burden of demonstrating that it must prefer members of particular ethnic groups over all other individuals in order to promote better health-care delivery to deprived citizens. Indeed, petitioner has not shown that its preferential classification is likely to have any significant effect on the problem.

D

The fourth goal asserted by petitioner is the attainment of a diverse student body. This clearly is a constitutionally permissible goal for an institution of higher education. Academic freedom, though not a specifically enumerated constitutional right, long has been viewed as a special concern of the First Amendment. The freedom of a university to make its own judgments as to education includes the selection of its student body. . . .

Thus, in arguing that its universities must be accorded the right to select those students who will contribute the most to the "robust exchange of ideas," petitioner invokes a countervailing constitutional interest, that of the First Amendment. In this light, petitioner must be viewed as seeking to achieve a goal that is of paramount importance in the fulfillment of its mission.

It may be argued that there is greater force to these views at the undergraduate level than in a medical school where the training is centered primarily on professional competency. But even at the graduate level, our tradition and experience lend support to the view that the contribution of diversity is substantial. . . .

Ethnic diversity, however, is only one element in a range of factors a university properly may consider in attaining the goal of a heterogeneous student body. Although a university must have wide discretion in making the sensitive judgments as to who should be admitted, constitutional limitations protecting individual rights may not be disregarded. Respondent urges — and the courts below have held — that petitioner's dual admissions program is a racial classification that impermissibly infringes his rights under the Fourteenth Amendment. As the interest of diversity is compelling in the context of a university's admissions program, the question remains whether the program's racial classification is necessary to promote this interest.

V

A

It may be assumed that the reservation of a specified number of seats in each class for individuals from the preferred ethnic groups would contribute to the attainment of considerable ethnic diversity in the student body. But petitioner's argument that this is the only effective means of serving the interest of diversity is seriously flawed. In a most fundamental sense the argument misconceives the nature of the state interest that would justify consideration of race or ethnic background. It is not an interest in simple ethnic diversity, in which a specified percentage of the student body is in effect guaranteed to be members of selected ethnic groups, with the remaining percentage an undifferentiated aggregation of students. The diversity that furthers a compelling state interest encompasses a far broader array of qualifications and characteristics of which racial or ethnic origin is but a single though important element. Petitioner's special admissions program, focused *solely* on ethnic diversity, would hinder rather than further attainment of genuine diversity.

. . .

In such an admissions program [as Harvard's], race or ethnic background may be deemed a "plus" in a particular applicant's file, yet it does not insulate the individual from comparison with all other candidates for the available seats. The file of a particular black applicant may be examined for his potential contribution to diversity without the factor of race being decisive when compared, for example, with that of an applicant identified as an Italian-American if the latter is thought to exhibit qualities more likely to promote beneficial educational pluralism. Such qualities could include exceptional personal talents, unique work or service experience, leadership potential, maturity, demonstrated compassion, a history of overcoming disadvantage, ability to communicate with the poor, or other qualifications deemed important. In short, an admissions program operated in this way is flexible enough to consider all pertinent elements of diversity in light of the particular qualifications of each applicant, and to place them on the same footing for consideration, although not necessarily according them the same weight. Indeed, the weight attributed to a particular quality may vary from year to year depending upon the "mix" both of the student body and the applicants for the incoming class.

This kind of program treats each applicant as an individual in the admissions process. The applicant who loses out on the last available seat to another candidate receiving a "plus" on the basis of ethnic background will not have been foreclosed from all consideration for that seat simply because he was not the right color or had the wrong surname. It would mean only that his combined qualifications, which may have included similar nonobjective factors, did not outweigh those of the other applicant. His qualifications would have been weighed fairly and competitively, and he would have no basis to complain of unequal treatment under the Fourteenth Amendment.

It has been suggested that an admissions program which considers race only as one factor is simply a subtle and more sophisticated — but no less effective — means of according racial preference than the Davis program. A facial intent to discriminate, however, is evident in petitioner's preference program and not denied in this case. No such facial infirmity exists in an admissions program where race or ethnic background is simply one element — to be weighed fairly against other elements — in the selection process. "A boundary line," as Mr. Justice Frankfurter remarked in another connection, "is none the worse for being narrow." . . . And a court would not assume that a university, professing to employ a facially nondiscriminatory admissions policy, would operate it as a cover for the functional equivalent of a quota system. In short, good faith would be presumed in the absence of a showing to the contrary in the manner permitted by our cases. . . .

### B

In summary, it is evident that the Davis special admissions program involves the use of an explicit racial classification never before countenanced by this Court. It tells applicants who are not Negro, Asian, or Chicano that they are totally excluded from a specific percentage of the seats in an entering class. No matter how strong their qualifications, quantitative and extracurricular, including their own potential for contribution to educational diversity, they are never afforded the chance to compete with applicants from the preferred groups for the special admissions seats. At the same time, the preferred applicants have the opportunity to compete for every seat in the class.

The fatal flaw in petitioner's preferential program is its disregard of individual rights as guaranteed by the Fourteenth Amendment. . . . Such rights are not absolute. But when a State's distribution of benefits or imposition of burdens hinges on ancestry or the color of a person's skin, that individual is entitled to a demonstration that the challenged classification is necessary to promote a substantial state interest. Petitioner has failed to carry this burden. For this reason, that portion of the California court's judgment holding petitioner's special admissions program invalid under the Fourteenth Amendment must be affirmed.

### C

In enjoining petitioner from ever considering the race of any applicant, however, the courts below failed to recognized that the State has a substantial interest that legitimately may be served by a properly devised admissions program involving the competitive consideration of race and ethnic origin. For this reason, so much of the California court's judgment as enjoins petitioner from any consideration of the race of any applicant must be reversed.

### VI

With respect to respondent's entitlement to an injunction directing his admission to the Medical School, petitioner has conceded that it could not carry its burden of proving that, but for the existence of its unlawful special admissions program, respondent still would not have been admitted.

Hence, respondent is entitled to the injunction, and that portion of the judgment must be affirmed.

. . .

Opinion of MR. JUSTICE BRENNAN, MR. JUSTICE WHITE, MR. JUSTICE MARSHALL, and MR. JUSTICE BLACKMUN, concurring in the judgment in part and dissenting in part.

The Court today, in reversing in part the judgment of the Supreme Court of California, affirms the constitutional power of Federal and State Governments to act affirmatively to achieve equal opportunity for all. The difficulty of the issue presented — whether government may use race-conscious programs to redress the continuing effects of past discrimination — and the mature consideration which each of our Brethren has brought to it have resulted in many opinions, no single one speaking for the Court. But this should not and must not mask the central meaning of today's opinions: Government may take race into account when it acts not to demean or insult any racial group, but to remedy disadvantages cast on minorities by past racial prejudice, at least when appropriate findings have been made by judicial, legislative, or administrative bodies with competence to act in this area.

. . .

I

Our Nation was founded on the principle that "all Men are created equal." Yet candor requires acknowledgment that the Framers of our Constitution, to forge the 13 Colonies into one Nation, openly compromised this principle of equality with its antithesis: slavery. The consequences of this compromise are well known and have aptly been called our "American Dilemma." Still, it is well to recount how recent the time has been, if it has yet come, when the promise of our principles has flowered into the actuality of equal opportunity for all regardless of race or color.

. . . And a glance at our docket and at dockets of lower courts will show that even today officially sanctioned discrimination is not a thing of the past.

Against this background, claims that law must be "colorblind" or that the datum of race is no longer relevant to public policy must be seen as aspiration rather than as description of reality.

. . .

MR. JUSTICE WHITE.

I write separately concerning the question of whether Title VI of the Civil Rights Act of 1964, 42 U. S. C. § 2000d et seq., provides for a private cause of action. Four Justices are apparently of the view that such a private cause of action exists, and four Justices assume it for purposes of this case. I am unwilling merely to assume an affirmative answer. If in fact no private cause of action exists, this Court and the lower courts as well are without jurisdiction to consider respondent's Title VI claim. As I see it, if we are not obliged to do so, it is at least advisable to address this threshold jurisdictional issue. . . . Furthermore, just as it is inappropriate to address constitutional issues without determining whether statutory grounds urged before us are dispositive, it is at least questionable practice to adjudicate a novel and difficult statutory issue without first considering whether we have jurisdiction to decide it. Consequently I address the question of whether respondent may bring suit under Title VI.

A private cause of action under Title VI, in terms both of the Civil Rights Act as a whole and that Title, would not be "consistent with the underlying purposes of the legislative scheme" and would be contrary to the legislative intent.

. . .

Because each of my colleagues either has a different view or assumes a private cause of action, however, the merits of the Title VI issue must be addressed. My views in that regard, as well as my views with respect to the equal protection issue, are included in the joint opinion that my Brothers BRENNAN, MARSHALL, and BLACKMUN and I have filed.

MR. JUSTICE MARSHALL.

I agree with the judgment of the Court only insofar as it permits a university to consider the race of an applicant in making admissions decisions. I do not agree that petitioner's admissions program violates the Constitution. For it must be remembered that, during most of the past 200 years, the Constitution as interpreted by this Court did not prohibit the most ingenious and pervasive forms of discrimination against the Negro. Now, when a State acts to remedy the effects of that legacy of discrimination, I cannot believe that this same Constitution stands as a barrier.

I

A

Three hundred and fifty years ago, the Negro was dragged to this country in chains to be sold into slavery.

. . .

II

The position of the Negro today in America is the tragic but inevitable consequence of centuries of unequal treatment. Measured by any benchmark of comfort or achievement, meaningful equality remains a distant dream for the Negro.

A Negro child today has a life expectancy which is shorter by more than five years than that of a white child. The Negro child's mother is over three times more likely to die of complications in childbirth, and the infant mortality rate for Negroes is nearly twice that for whites. The median income of the Negro family is only 60% that of the median of a white family, and the percentage of Negroes who live in families with incomes below the poverty line is nearly four times greater than that of whites.

When the Negro child reaches working age, he finds that America offers him significantly less than it offers his white counterpart. For Negro adults, the unemployment rate is twice that of whites, and the unemployment rate for Negro teenagers is nearly three times that of white teenagers. A Negro male who completes four years of college can expect a median annual income of merely $110 more than a white male who has only a high school diploma. Although Negroes represent 11.5% of the population, they are only 1.2% of the lawyers and judges, 2% of the physicians, 2.3% of the dentists, 1.1% of the engineers and 2.6% of the college and university professors.

The relationship between those figures and the history of unequal treatment afforded to the Negro cannot be denied. At every point from birth to death the impact of the past is reflected in the still disfavored position of the Negro.

In light of the sorry history of discrimination and its devastating impact on the lives of Negroes, bringing the Negro into the mainstream of American life should be a state interest of the highest order. To fail to do so is to ensure that America will forever remain a divided society.

### III

I do not believe that the Fourteenth Amendment requires us to accept that fate.

. . .

### IV

While I applaud the judgment of the Court that a university may consider race in its admissions process, it is more than a little ironic that, after several hundred years of class-based discrimination against Negroes, the Court is unwilling to hold that a class-based remedy for that discrimination is permissible.

It is because of a legacy of unequal treatment that we now must permit the institutions of this society to give consideration to race in making decisions about who will hold the positions of influence, affluence, and prestige in America. For far too long, the doors to those positions have been shut to Negroes. If we are ever to become a fully integrated society, one in which the color of a person's skin will not determine the opportunities available to him or her, we must be willing to take steps to open those doors. I do not believe that anyone can truly look into America's past and still find that a remedy for the effects of that past is impermissible.

It has been said that this case involves only the individual, Bakke, and this University. I doubt, however, that there is a computer capable of determining the number of persons and institutions that may be affected by the decision in this case. For example, we are told by the Attorney General of the United States that at least 27 federal agencies have adopted regulations requiring recipients of federal funds to take " *'affirmative action'* to overcome the effects of conditions which resulted in limiting participation . . . by persons of a particular race, color, or national origin." . . . I cannot even guess the number of state and local governments that have set up affirmative-action programs, which may be affected by today's decision.

I fear that we have come full circle. After the Civil War our Government started several "affirmative action" programs. This Court in the *Civil Rights Cases* and *Plessy* v. *Ferguson* destroyed the movement toward complete equality. For almost a century no action was taken, and this nonaction was with the tacit approval of the courts. Then we had *Brown* v. *Board of Education* and the Civil Rights Acts of Congress, followed by numerous affirmative-action programs. *Now,* we have this Court again stepping in, this time to stop affirmative-action programs of the type used by the University of California.

Mr. Justice Blackmun.

I participate fully, of course, in the opinion that bears the names of my Brothers Brennan, White, Marshall, and myself. I add only some general observations that hold particular significance for me, and then a few comments on equal protection.

I

. . .

It is somewhat ironic to have us so deeply disturbed over a program where race is an element of consciousness, and yet to be aware of the fact, as we are, that institutions of higher learning, albeit more on the undergraduate than the graduate level, have given conceded preferences up to a point to those possessed of athletic skills, to the children of alumni, to the affluent who may bestow their largess on the institutions, and to those having connections with celebrities, the famous, and the powerful.

Programs of admission to institutions of higher learning are basically a responsibility for academicians and for administrators and the specialists they employ. The judiciary, in contrast, is ill-equipped and poorly trained for this. The administration and management of educational institutions are beyond the competence of judges and are within the special competence of educators, provided always that the educators perform within legal and constitutional bounds. For me, therefore, interference by the judiciary must be the rare exception and not the rule.

II

I, of course, accept the propositions that (a) Fourteenth Amendment rights are personal; (b) racial and ethnic distinctions where they are stereotypes are inherently suspect and call for exacting judicial scrutiny; (c) academic freedom is a special concern of the First Amendment; and (d) the

Fourteenth Amendment has expanded beyond its original 1868 concept and now is recognized to have reached a point where, as MR. JUSTICE POWELL states, . . . it embraces a "broader principle."

. . .

It is worth noting, perhaps, that governmental preference has not been a stranger to our legal life. We see it in veterans' preferences. We see it in the aid-to-the-handicapped programs. We see it in the progressive income tax. We see it in the Indian programs. We may excuse some of these on the ground that they have specific constitutional protection or, as with Indians, that those benefited are wards of the Government. Nevertheless, these preferences exist and may not be ignored. And in the admissions field, as I have indicated, educational institutions have always used geography, athletic ability, anticipated financial largess, alumni pressure, and other factors of that kind.

I add these only as additional components on the edges of the central question as to which I join my Brothers BRENNAN, WHITE, and MARSHALL in our more general approach.

. . .

MR. JUSTICE STEVENS, with whom THE CHIEF JUSTICE, MR. JUSTICE STEWART, and MR. JUSTICE REHNQUIST join, concurring in the judgment in part and dissenting in part.

It is always important at the outset to focus precisely on the controversy before the Court. It is particularly important to do so in this case because correct identification of the issues will determine whether it is necessary or appropriate to express any opinion about the legal status of any admissions program other than petitioner's.

I

This is not a class action. The controversy is between two specific litigants.

. . .

The California Supreme Court, in a holding that is not challenged, ruled that the trial court incorrectly placed the burden on Bakke of showing that he would have been admitted in the absence of discrimination. The University then conceded "that it [could] not meet the burden of proving that the special admissions program did not result in Mr. Bakke's failure to be admitted." Accordingly, the California Supreme Court directed the trial court to enter judgment ordering Bakke's admission. Since that order superseded paragraph 2 of the trial court's judgment, there is no outstanding injunction forbidding any consideration of racial criteria in processing applications.

It is therefore perfectly clear that the question whether race can ever be used as a factor in an admissions decision is not an issue in this case, and that discussion of that issue is inappropriate.

. . .

# United Steelworkers of America, AFL-CIO-CLC *v.* Weber et al.

The *Weber* case is one of the clearest victories for affirmative action. The five-person majority opinion states that employers are allowed to create affirmative action programs to correct existing wrongs. Written by Justice Brennan, the opinion proceeds in a logical fashion. Part I sets out the issues. Part II asks, Does the 1964 Civil Rights Act permit employers to develop affirmative action plans? The answer is yes. Part III then asks, Is the particular plan in question legal? Again the answer is yes. Brennan is at pains to emphasize that the majority opinion is "narrow" — it is not intended to legitimate all affirmative action programs.

The dissent by Chief Justice Burger is scathing. The chief justice accuses the majority of ignoring the written law in favor of legislative history. Most dissenting opinions are not so strongly worded.

---

CERTIORARI TO THE UNITED STATES COURT OF
APPEALS FOR THE FIFTH CIRCUIT

No. 78-432. Argued March 28, 1979 — Decided June 27, 1979

BRENNAN, J., delivered the opinion of the Court, in which STEWART, WHITE, MARSHALL, and BLACKMUN, JJ., joined. BLACKMUN, J., filed a concurring opinion. BURGER, C. J., filed a dissenting opinion. REHNQUIST, J., filed a dissenting opinion, in which BURGER, C. J., joined. POWELL and STEVENS, JJ., took no part in the consideration or decision of the cases. . . .

MR. JUSTICE BRENNAN delivered the opinion of the Court.

Challenged here is the legality of an affirmative action plan — collectively bargained by an employer and a union — that reserves for black employees 50% of the openings in an in-plant craft-training program until the percentage of black craftworkers in the plant is commensurate with the percentage of blacks in the local labor force. The question for decision is whether Congress, in Title VII of the Civil Rights Act of 1964, 78 Stat. 253, as amended, 42 U. S. C. § 2000e *et seq.,* left employers and unions in the private sector free to take such race-conscious steps to eliminate manifest racial imbalances in traditionally segregated job categories. We hold that Title VII does not prohibit such race-conscious affirmative action plans.

I

In 1974, petitioner United Steelworkers of America (USWA) and petitioner Kaiser Aluminum & Chemical Corp. (Kaiser) entered into a master collective-bargaining agreement covering terms and conditions of employment at 15 Kaiser plants. The agreement contained *inter alia,* an affirmative action plan designed to eliminate conspicuous racial imbalances in Kaiser's then almost exclusively white craftwork forces. Black crafthiring goals were set for each Kaiser plant equal to the percentage of blacks in the respective local labor forces. To enable plants to meet these goals on-the-job training programs were established to teach unskilled production workers — black and white — the skills necessary to become craftworkers. The plan reserved for black employees 50% of the openings in these newly created in-plant training programs.

This case arose from the operation of the plan at Kaiser's plant in Gramercy, La. Until 1974, Kaiser hired as craftworkers for that plant only persons who had had prior craft experience. Because blacks had long been excluded from craft unions, few were able to present such credentials. As a consequence, prior to 1974 only 1.83% (5 out of 273) of the skilled craftworkers at the Gramercy plant were black even though the work force in the Gramercy area was approximately 39% black.

Pursuant to the national agreement Kaiser altered its crafthiring practice in the Gramercy plant. Rather than hiring already trained outsiders, Kaiser established a training program to train its production workers to fill craft openings. Selection of craft trainees was made on the basis of seniority, with the proviso that at least 50% of the new trainees were to be black until the percentage of black skilled craftworkers in the Gramercy plant approximated the percentage of blacks in the local labor force. See 415 F. Supp. 761, 764.

During 1974 the first year of the operation of the Kaiser-USWA affirmative action plan, 13 craft trainees were selected from Gramercy's production work force. Of these, seven were black and six white. The most senior black selected into the program had less seniority than several white production workers whose bids for admission were rejected. Thereafter one of those white production workers, respondent Brian Weber (hereafter respondent), instituted this class action in the United States District Court for the Eastern District of Louisiana.

. . .

II

We emphasize at the outset the narrowness of our inquiry. Since the Kaiser-USWA plan does not involve state action, this case does not present an alleged violation of the Equal Protection Clause of the Fourteenth Amendment. Further, since the Kaiser-USWA plan was adopted voluntarily, we are not concerned with what Title VII requires or with what a court might order to remedy a past provided violation of the Act. The only question before us is the narrow statutory issue of whether Title VII *forbids* private employers and unions from voluntarily agreeing upon bona fide affirmative action plans that accord racial preferences in the manner and for the purpose provided in the Kaiser-USWA plan.

. . .

It plainly appears from the House Report accompanying the Civil Rights Act that Congress did not intend wholly to prohibit private and voluntary affirmative action efforts as one method of solving this problem. The Report provides:

"No bill can or should lay claim to eliminating all of the causes and consequences of racial and other types of discrimination against minorities. There is reason to believe, however, that national leadership provided by the enactment of Federal legislation dealing with the most troublesome problems *will create an atmosphere conducive to voluntary or local resolution of other forms of discrimination.*" H. R. Rep. No. 914, 88th Cong., 1st Sess., pt. 1, p. 18 (1963). (Emphasis supplied.)

Given this legislative history, we cannot agree with respondent that Congress intended to prohibit the private sector from taking effective steps to accomplish the goal that Congress designed Title VII to achieve.

. . .

. . . In view of this legislative history and in view of Congress' desire to avoid undue federal regulation of private businesses, use of the word "require" rather than the phrase "require or permit" in § 703 (j) fortifies the conclusion that Congress did not intend to limit traditional business freedom to such a degree as to prohibit all voluntary, race-conscious affirmative action.

We therefore hold that Title VII's prohibition in §§ 703 (a) and (d) against racial discrimination does not condemn all private, voluntary, race-conscious affirmative action plans.

## III

We need not today define in detail the line of demarcation between permissible and impermissible affirmative action plans. It suffices to hold that the challenged Kaiser-USWA affirmative action plan falls on the permissible side of the line. The purposes of the plan mirror those of the statute. Both were designed to break down old patterns of racial segregation and hierarchy. Both were structured to "open employment opportunities for Negroes in occupations which have been traditionally closed to them." 110 Cong. Rec. 6548 (1964) (remarks of Sen. Humphrey).

At the same time, the plan does not unnecessarily trammel the interests of the white employees. The plan does not require the discharge of white workers and their replacement with new black hirees. . . . Nor does the plan create an absolute bar to the advancement of white employees; half of those trained in the program will be white. Moreover, the plan is a temporary measure; it is not intended to maintain racial balance, but simply to eliminate a manifest racial imbalance. Preferential selection of craft trainees at the Gramercy plant will end as soon as the percentage of black skilled craftworkers in the Gramercy plant approximates the percentage of blacks in the local labor force. . . .

We conclude, therefore, that the adoption of the Kaiser-USWA plan for the Gramercy plant falls within the area of discretion left by Title VII to the private sector voluntarily to adopt affirmative action plans designed to eliminate conspicuous racial imbalance in traditionally segregated job categories. Accordingly, the judgment of the Court of Appeals for the Fifth Circuit is *Reversed.*

MR. JUSTICE POWELL and MR. JUSTICE STEVENS took no part in the consideration or decision of these cases.

MR. JUSTICE BLACKMUN, concurring.

While I share some of the misgivings expressed in MR. JUSTICE REHNQUIST's dissent concerning the extent to which the legislative history of Title VII clearly supports the result the Court reaches today, I believe that additional considerations, practical and equitable, only partially perceived, if perceived at all, by the 88th Congress, support the conclusion reached by the Court today, and I therefore join its opinion as well as its judgment.

. . .

## II

. . .

Strong considerations of equity support an interpretation of Title VII that would permit private affirmative action to reach where Title VII itself does not. The bargain struck in 1964 with the passage of Title VII guaranteed equal opportunity for white and black alike, but where Title VII provides no remedy for blacks, it should not be construed to foreclose private affirmative action from supplying relief. It seems unfair for respondent Weber to argue as he does, that the asserted scarcity of black craftsmen in Louisiana, the product of historic discrimination, makes Kaiser's training program illegal because it ostensibly absolves Kaiser of all Title VII liability. . . . Absent compelling evidence of legislative intent, I would not interpret Title VII itself as a means of "locking in" the effects of segregation for which Title VII provides no remedy. Such a construction, as the Court points out, . . . would be "ironic," given the broad remedial purposes of Title VII.

. . .

## III

. . . And if the Court has misperceived the political will, it has the assurance that because the question is statutory Congress may set a different course if it so chooses.

MR. CHIEF JUSTICE BURGER, dissenting.

The Court reaches a result I would be inclined to vote for were I a Member of Congress considering a proposed amendment of Title VII. I cannot join the Court's judgment, however, because it is contrary to the explicit language of the statute and arrived at by means wholly incompatible with long-established principles of separation of powers. Under the guise of statutory "construction," the Court effectively rewrites Title VII to achieve what it regards as a desirable result. It "amends" the statute to do precisely what both its sponsors and its opponents agreed the statute was *not* intended to do.

When Congress enacted Title VII after long study and searching debate, it produced a statute of extraordinary clarity, which speaks directly to the issue we consider in this case. In § 703 (d) Congress provided:

> "It shall be an unlawful employment practice for any employer, labor organization, or joint labor-management committee controlling apprenticeship or other training or retraining, including on-the-job training programs to discriminate against any individual because of his race, color, religion, sex, or national origin in admission to, or employment in, any program established to provide apprenticeship or other training." 42 U. S. C. § 2000e-2 (d).

Often we have difficulty interpreting statutes either because of imprecise drafting or because legislative compromises have produced genuine ambiguities. But here there is no lack of clarity, no ambiguity. The quota embodied in the collective-bargaining agreement between Kaiser and the Steelworkers unquestionably discriminates on the basis of race against individual employees seeking admission to on-the-job training programs. And, under the plain language of § 703 (d), that is "an *unlawful* employment practice."

Oddly, the Court seizes upon the very clarity of the statute almost as a justification for evading the unavoidable impact of its language. The Court blandly tells us that Congress could not really have meant what it said, for a "literal construction" would defeat the "purpose" of the statute — at least the congressional "purpose" as five Justices divine it today. But how are judges supposed to ascertain the *purpose* of a statute except through the words Congress used and the legislative history of the statute's evolution? . . .

It is often observed that hard cases make bad law. I suspect there is some truth to that adage, for the "hard" cases always tempt judges to exceed the limits of their authority, as the Court does today by totally rewriting a crucial part of Title VII to reach a "desirable" result. Cardozo no doubt had this type of case in mind when he wrote:

> "The judge, even when he is free, is still not wholly free. He is not to innovate at pleasure." . . .

What Cardozo tells us is beware the "good result," achieved by judicially unauthorized or intellectually dishonest means on the appealing notion that the desirable ends justify the improper judicial means. For there is always the danger that the seeds of precedent sown by good men for the best of motives will yield a rich harvest of unprincipled acts of others also aiming at "good ends."

MR. JUSTICE REHNQUIST, with whom THE CHIEF JUSTICE joins, dissenting.

In a very real sense, the Court's opinion is ahead of its time: it could more appropriately have been handed down five years from now, in 1984, a year coinciding with the title of a book from which the Court's opinion borrows, perhaps subconsciously, at least one idea. . . .

. . .

We have never wavered in our understanding that Title VII "prohibits all racial discrimination in employment, without exception for any group of particular employees." . . . In *Griggs* v. *Duke Power Co.,* 401 U. S. 424, 431 (1971), our first occasion to interpret Title VII, a unanimous Court observed that "[d]iscriminatory preference for any group, minority or majority, is precisely and only what Congress has proscribed." And in our most recent discussion of the issue, we uttered words seemingly dispositive of this case: "It is clear beyond cavil that the obligation imposed by Title VII is to provide an equal opportunity for *each* applicant regardless of race, without regard to whether members of the applicant's race are already proportionately represented in the work force." . . .

Today, however, the Court behaves much like the Orwellian speaker earlier described, as if it had been handed a note indicating that Title VII would lead to a result unacceptable to the Court if interpreted here as it was in our prior decisions. Accordingly, without even a break in syntax, the Court rejects "a literal construction of § 703 (a)" in favor of newly discovered "legislative history," which leads it to a conclusion directly contrary to that compelled by the "uncontradicted legislative history" unearthed in *McDonald* and our other prior decisions. Now we are told that the legislative history of Title VII shows that employers are free to discriminate on the basis of race: an employer may, in the Court's words, "trammel the interests of the white employees" in favor of black employees in order to eliminate "racial imbalance."

. . .

# H. Earl Fullilove et al., Petitioners *v.* Philip M. Klutznick, Secretary of Commerce of the United States, et al.

In 1997 a law required that 10 percent of federal construction grants were to go to minority owned businesses, unless a waiver was granted. Several associations of contractors and subcontractors challenged the law on the grounds that it violated the Fourteenth Amendment and also the equal protection clause of the Fifth Amendment. The majority opinion held that the law was constitutional because it was narrowly tailored and of finite duration and, in view of the possibility of a waiver, did not impose an undue burden on white people. Note the dissenting opinion by Justice Stewart, a small portion of which is included here. This dissenting opinion foreshadows much of the current climate of the Court.

---

No. 701007. Argued Nov. 27, 1979. Decided July 2, 1980.

. . .

MR. CHIEF JUSTICE BURGER announced the judgment of the Court and delivered an opinion, in which MR. JUSTICE WHITE and MR. JUSTICE POWELL joined.

We granted certiorari to consider a facial constitutional challenge to a requirement in a congressional spending program that, absent an administrative waiver, 10% of the federal funds granted for local public works projects must be used by the state or local grantee to procure services or supplies from businesses owned and controlled by members of statutorily identified minority groups. 441 U.S. 960, 99 S.Ct. 2403, 60 L.Ed.2d 1064 (1979).

I

In May 1977, Congress enacted the Public Works Employment Act of 1977. . . . The 1977 amendments authorized an additional $4 billion appropriation for federal grants to be made . . . to state and local governmental entities for use in local public works projects. Among the changes made was the addition of the provision that has become the focus of this litigation. Section 103(f)(2) of the 1977 Act, referred to as the "minority business enterprise" or "MBE" provision, requires that:

"Except to the extent that the Secretary determines otherwise, no grant shall be made under this Act for any local public works project unless the applicant gives satisfactory assurance to the Secretary that at least 10 per centum of the amount of each grant shall be expended for minority business enterprises. For purposes of this paragraph, the term 'minority business enterprise' means a business at least 50 per centum of which is owned by minority group members or, in case of a publicly owned business, at least 51 per centum of the stock of which is owned by minority group members. For the purposes of the preceding sentence minority group members are citizens of the United States who are Negroes, Spanish-speaking, Orientals, Indians, Eskimos, and Aleuts."

In late May 1977, the Secretary promulgated regulations governing administration of the grant program. . . .

On November 30, 1977, petitioners filed a complaint. . . . Petitioners . . . alleged that they had sustained economic injury due to enforcement of the 10% MBE requirement and that the MBE provision on its face violated the Equal Protection Clause of the Fourteenth Amendment, the equal protection component of the Due Process Clause of the Fifth Amendment, and various antidiscrimination provisions.

. . . On December 19, 1977, the District Court issued a memorandum opinion upholding the validity of the MBE program and denying the injunction relief sought. . . .

The United States Court of Appeals for the Second Circuit affirmed . . . holding that "even under the most exacting standard of review the MBE provision passes constitutional muster." . . .

## II

### A

The MBE provision was enacted as part of the Public Works Employment Act of 1977, which made various amendments to Title I of the Local Public Works Capital Development and Investment Act of 1976. The 1976 Act was intended as a short-term measure to alleviate the problem of national unemployment and to stimulate the national economy. . . .

. . .

The origin of the provision was an amendment to the House version of the 1977 Act, H.R. 11, offered on the floor of the House on February 23, 1977, by Representative Mitchell of Maryland. . . .

. . .

The sponsor stated that the objective of the amendment was to direct funds into the minority business community, a sector of the economy sorely

in need of economic stimulus but which, on the basis of past experience with Government procurement programs, could not be expected to benefit significantly from the public works program as then formulated.
. . .

The amendment was put forward not as a new concept, but rather one building upon prior administrative practice. In his introductory remarks, the sponsor rested his proposal squarely on the ongoing program under § 8(a) of the Small Business Act, Pub.L. 85-536 § 2, 72 Stat. 389. . . .
. . .

The device of a 10% MBE participation requirement, subject to administrative waiver, was thought to be required to assure minority business participation; otherwise it was thought that repetition of the prior experience could be expected, with participation by minority business accounting for an inordinately small percentage of government contracting. The causes of this disparity were perceived as involving the longstanding existence and maintenance of barriers impairing access by minority enterprises to public contracting opportunities, or sometimes as involving more direct discrimination, but not as relating to lack — as Senator Brooke put it — "of capable and qualified minority enterprises who are ready and willing to work." In the words of its sponsor, the MBE provision was "designed to begin to redress this grievance that has been extant for so long."

B

The legislative objectives of the MBE provision must be considered against the background of ongoing efforts directed toward deliverance of the century-old promise of equality of economic opportunity. The sponsors of the MBE provision in the House and the Senate expressly linked the provision to the existing administrative programs promoting minority opportunity in government procurement, particularly those related to § 8(a) of the Small Business Act of 1953. . . .

At the time the MBE provision was enacted, the regulations governing the § 8(a) program defined "social or economic disadvantage" as follows:

> "An applicant concern must be owned and controlled by one or more persons who have been deprived of the opportunity to develop and maintain a competitive position in the economy because of social or economic disadvantage. Such disadvantage may arise from cultural, social, chronic economic circumstances or background, or other similar cause. Such persons include, but are not limited to, black Americans, American Indians, Spanish-Americans, oriental Americans, Eskimos, and Aleuts. . . ."

The guidelines accompanying these regulations provided that a minority business could not be maintained in the program, even when owned and controlled by members of the identified minority groups, if it appeared that the business had not been deprived of the opportunity to develop and maintain a competitive position in the economy because of social or economic disadvantage.

As the Congress began consideration of the Public Works Employment Act of 1977, the House Committee on Small Business issued a lengthy Report summarizing its activities. . . . The . . . Report . . . observed:

"The subcommittee is acutely aware that the economic policies of this Nation must function within and be guided by our constitutional system which guarantees 'equal protection of the laws.' The effects of past inequities stemming from racial prejudice have not remained in the past. The Congress has recognized the reality that past discriminatory practices have, to some degree, adversely affected our present economic system.

"While minority persons comprise about 16 percent of the Nation's population, of the 13 million businesses in the United States, only 382,000, or approximately 3.0 percent, are owned by minority individuals. The most recent data from the Department of Commerce also indicates that the gross receipts of all businesses in this country totals about $2,540.8 billion, and of this amount only $16.6 billion, or about 0.65 percent was realized by minority business concerns.

"These statistics are not the result of random choice. The presumption must be made that past discriminatory systems have resulted in present economic inequities. In order to right this situation the Congress has formulated certain remedial programs designed to uplift those socially or economically disadvantaged persons to a level where they may effectively participate in the business mainstream of our economy."

. . .

Against this backdrop of legislative and administrative programs, it is inconceivable that Members of both Houses were not fully aware of the objectives of the MBE provision and of the reasons prompting its enactment.

C

Although the statutory MBE provision itself outlines only the bare bones of the federal program, it makes a number of critical determinations: the decision to initiate a limited racial and ethnic preference; the specification of a minimum level for minority business participation; the identification of the minority groups that are to be encompassed by the program; and the provision for an administrative waiver where application of the program is not feasible. Congress relied on the administrative agency to flesh out this skeleton, pursuant to delegated rulemaking authority, and to develop an administrative operation consistent with legislative intentions and objectives. . . .

. . .

The EDA guidelines also outline the projected administration of applications for waiver of the 10% MBE requirement, which may be sought by the grantee either before or during the bidding process. The Technical Bulletin issued by EDA discusses in greater detail the processing of waiver requests, clarifying certain issues left open by the guidelines. It specifies that waivers may be total or partial, depending on the circumstances, and it illustrates the projected operation of the waiver procedure by posing hypothetical questions with projected administrative responses. . . .

Th[e] announced policy makes clear the administrative understanding that a waiver or partial waiver is justified (and will be granted) to avoid subcontracting with a minority business enterprise at an "unreasonable" price, i.e, a price above competitive levels which cannot be attributed to the minority firm's attempt to cover costs inflated by the present effects of disadvantage or discrimination.

This administrative approach is consistent with the legislative intention. It will be recalled that in the Report of the House Subcommittee on SBA Oversight and Minority Enterprise the Subcommittee took special care to note that when using the term "minority" it intended to include "only such minority individuals as are considered to be economically or socially disadvantaged." . . .

The EDA Technical Bulletin provides other elaboration of the MBE provision. It clarifies the definition of "minority group members." It also indicates EDA's intention "to allow credit for utilization of MBEs only for those contracts in which involvement constitutes a basis for strengthening the long-term and continuing participation of the MBE in the construction and related industries." Finally, the Bulletin outlines a procedure for the processing of complaints of "unjust participation by an enterprise or individuals in the MBE program," or of improper administration of the MBE requirement.

### III

. . .

When we are required to pass on the constitutionality of an Act of Congress, we assume "the gravest and most delicate duty that this Court is called on to perform." . . . A program that employs racial or ethnic criteria, even in a remedial context, calls for close examination; yet we are bound to approach our task with appropriate deference to the Congress, a co-equal branch charged by the Constitution with the power to "provide for the . . . general Welfare of the United States" and "to enforce, by appropriate legislation," the equal protection guarantees of the Fourteenth Amendment. . . . [W]e accorded "great weight to the decisions of Congress" even though the legislation implicated fundamental constitutional rights guaranteed by the First Amendment. The rule is not different when a congressional program raises equal protection concerns. . . .

. . .

The clear objective of the MBA provision is disclosed by our necessarily extended review of its legislative and administrative background. The program was designed to ensure that, to the extent federal funds were granted under the Public Works Employment Act of 1977, grantees who elect to participate would not employ procurement practices that Congress had decided might result in perpetuation of the effects of prior discrimination which had impaired or foreclosed access by minority businesses to public contracting opportunities. The MBE program does not mandate the allocation of federal funds according to inflexible percentages solely based on race or ethnicity.

Our analysis proceeds in two steps. At the outset, we must inquire whether the objectives of this legislation are within the power of Congress. If so, we must go on to decide whether the limited use of racial and ethnic criteria, in the context presented, is a constitutionally permissible means for achieving the congressional objectives and does not violate the equal protection component of the Due Process Clause of the Fifth Amendment.

A

*(1)*

In enacting the MBE provision, it is clear that Congress employed an amalgam of its specifically delegated powers. The Public Works Employment Act of 1977, by its very nature, is primarily an exercise of the Spending Power. . . . Congress has frequently employed the Spending Power to further broad policy objectives by conditioning receipt of federal moneys upon compliance by the recipient with federal statutory and administrative directives. This Court has repeatedly upheld against constitutional challenge the use of this technique to induce governments and private parties to cooperate voluntarily with federal policy. . . .

The MBE program is structured within this familiar legislative pattern. The program conditions receipt of public works grants upon agreement by the state or local government grantee that at least 10% of the federal funds will be devoted to contracts with minority businesses, to the extent this can be accomplished by overcoming barriers to access and by awarding contracts to bona fide MBE's. It is further conditioned to require that MBE bids on these contracts are competitively priced, or might have been competitively priced but for the present effects of prior discrimination. Admittedly, the problems of administering this program with respect to these conditions may be formidable. . . .

Here we need not explore the outermost limitations on the objectives attainable through such an application of the Spending Power. The reach of the Spending Power, within its sphere, is at least as broad as the regulatory powers of Congress. . . .

*(2)*

. . . Had Congress chosen to do so, it could have drawn on the Commerce Clause to regulate the practices of prime contractors on federally funded

public works projects. . . . The legislative history of the MBE provision
shows that there was a rational basis for Congress to conclude that the
subcontracting practices of prime contractors could perpetuate the prevailing impaired access by minority businesses to public contracting opportunities, and that this inequity has an effect on interstate commerce. Thus Congress could take necessary and proper action to remedy the situation. Ibid.

It is not necessary that these prime contractors be shown responsible
for any violation of antidiscrimination laws. . . . We conclude that in this
respect the objectives of the MBE provision are within the scope of the
Spending Power.

### (3)

In certain contexts, there are limitations on the reach of the Commerce
Power to regulate the actions of state and local governments. . . . A review
of our cases persuades us that the objectives of the MBE program are
within the power of Congress under § 5 "to enforce, by appropriate legislation," the equal protection guarantees of the Fourteenth Amendment. . . .
. . .

### B

We now turn to the question whether, as a *means* to accomplish these
plainly constitutional objectives, Congress may use racial and ethnic criteria, in this limited way, as a condition attached to a federal grant. . . .
Congress may employ racial or ethnic classifications in exercising its Spending or other legislative powers only if those classifications do not violate the
equal protection component of the Due Process Clause of the Fifth Amendment. We recognize the need for careful judicial evaluation to assure that
any congressional program that employs racial or ethnic criteria to accomplish the objective of remedying the present effects of past discrimination is
narrowly tailored to the achievement of that goal.

Again, we stress the limited scope of our inquiry. Here we are not
dealing with a remedial decree of a court but with the legislative authority
of Congress. Furthermore, petitioners have challenged the constitutionality of the MBE provision on its face; they have not sought damages or other
specific relief for injury allegedly flowing from specific applications of the
program; nor have they attempted to show that as applied in identified
situations the MBE provision violated the constitutional or statutory rights
of any party to this case. In these circumstances, given a reasonable construction and in light of its projected administration, if we find the MBE
program on its face to be free of constitutional defects, it must be upheld as
within congressional power. . . .

Our review of the regulations and guidelines governing administration
of the MBE provision reveals that Congress enacted the program as a
strictly remedial measure; moreover, it is a remedy that functions prospec-
tively, in the manner of an injunctive decree.
. . .

*(1)*

. . . As a threshold matter, we reject the contention that in the remedial context the Congress must act in a wholly "color-blind" fashion. . . . And in North Carolina Board of Education v. Swann, . . . [W]e invalidated a state law that absolutely forbade assignment of any student on account of race because it foreclosed implementation of desegregation plans that were designed to remedy constitutional violations. We held that "[j]ust as the race of students must be considered in determining whether a constitutional violation has occurred, so also must race be considered in formulating a remedy." . . .

. . .

When we have discussed the remedial powers of a federal court, we have been alert to the limitation that "[t]he power of the federal courts to restructure the operation of local and state governmental entities 'is not plenary. . . .' [A] federal court is required to tailor 'the scope of the remedy' to fit the nature and extent of the . . . violation." . . .

. . . Here we deal, as we noted earlier, not with the limited remedial powers of a federal court, for example, but with the broad remedial powers of Congress. It is fundamental that in no organ of government, state or federal, does there repose a more comprehensive remedial power than in the Congress, expressly charged by the Constitution with competence and authority to enforce equal protection guarantees. Congress not only may induce voluntary action to assure compliance with existing federal statutory or constitutional antidiscrimination provisions, but also, where Congress has authority to declare certain conduct unlawful, it may, as here, authorize and induce state action to avoid such conduct. . . .

*(2)*

A more specific challenge to the MBE program is the charge that it impermissibly deprives nonminority businesses of access to at least some portion of the government contracting opportunities generated by the Act. It must be conceded that by its objective of remedying the historical impairment of access, the MBE provision can have the effect of awarding some contracts to MBE's which otherwise might be awarded to other businesses, who may themselves be innocent of any prior discriminatory actions. . . .

. . . It is not a constitutional defect in this program that it may disappoint the expectations of nonminority firms. When effectuating a limited and properly tailored remedy to cure the effects of prior discrimination, such "a sharing of the burden" by innocent parties is not impermissible. . . . The actual "burden" shouldered by nonminority firms is relatively light in this connection when we consider the scope of this public works program as compared with overall construction contracting opportunities. Moreover, although we may assume that the complaining parties are innocent of any discriminatory conduct, it was within congressional power to act on the assumption that in the past some nonminority businesses may have reaped competitive benefit over the years from the virtual exclusion of minority firms from these contracting opportunities.

### (3)

Another challenge to the validity of the MBE program is the assertion that it is underinclusive — that it limits its benefit to specified minority groups rather than extending its remedial objectives to all businesses whose access to government contracting is impaired by the effects of disadvantages or discrimination. Such an extension would, of course, be appropriate for Congress to provide; it is not a function for the courts.

. . .

The Congress has not sought to give select minority groups a preferred standing in the construction industry, but has embarked on a remedial program to place them on a more equitable footing with respect to public contracting opportunities. . . . But on this record we find no basis to hold that Congress is without authority to undertake the kind of limited remedial effort represented by the MBE program. Congress, not the courts, has the heavy burden of dealing with a host of intractable economic and social problems.

### (4)

It is also contended that the MBE program is overinclusive — that it bestows a benefit on businesses identified by racial or ethnic criteria which cannot be justified on the basis of competitive criteria or as a remedy for the present effects of identified prior discrimination. It is conceivable that a particular application of the program may have this effect; however, the peculiarities of specific applications are not before us in this case. We are not presented here with a challenge involving a specific award of a construction contract or the denial of a waiver request; such questions of specific application must await future cases.

This does not mean that the claim of overinclusiveness is entitled to no consideration in the present case. The history of governmental tolerance of practices using racial or ethnic criteria for the purpose or with the effect of imposing an invidious discrimination must alert us to the deleterious effects of even benign racial or ethnic classifications when they stray from narrow remedial justifications. Even in the context of a facial challenge such as presented in this case, the MBE provision cannot pass muster unless, with due account for its administrative program, it provides a reasonable assurance that application of racial or ethnic criteria will be limited to accomplishing the remedial objectives of Congress and that misapplications of the program will be promptly and adequately remedied administratively.

It is significant that the administrative scheme provides for waiver and exemption. Two fundamental congressional assumptions underlie the MBE program: (1) that the present effects of past discrimination have impaired the competitive position of businesses owned and controlled by members of minority groups; and (2) that affirmative efforts to eliminate barriers to minority-firm access, and to evaluate bids with adjustment for the present effects of past discrimination, would assure that at least 10% of the federal funds granted under the Public Works Employment Act of 1977 would be accounted for by contracts with available, qualified, bona fide minority business enterprises. Each of these assumptions may be rebutted in the administrative process.

. . .

There is administrative scrutiny to identify and eliminate from participation in the program MBE's who are not "bona fide" within the regulations and guidelines; for example, spurious minority-front entities can be exposed. A significant aspect of this surveillance is the complaint procedure available for reporting "unjust participation by an enterprise or individuals in the MBE program." And even as to specific contract awards, waiver is available to avoid dealing with an MBE who is attempting to exploit the remedial aspects of the program by charging an unreasonable price, i.e., a price not attributable to the present effects of past discrimination. We must assume that Congress intended close scrutiny of false claims and prompt action on them.

Grantees are given the opportunity to demonstrate that their best efforts will not succeed or have not succeeded in achieving the statutory 10% target for minority firm participation within the limitations of the program's remedial objectives. In these circumstances a waiver or partial waiver is available once compliance has been demonstrated. A waiver may be sought and granted at any time during the contracting process, or even prior to letting contracts if the facts warrant.

. . .

. . . The MBE provision may be viewed as a pilot project, appropriately limited in extent and duration, and subject to reassessment and reevaluation by the Congress prior to any extension or re-enactment. Miscarriages of administration could have only a transitory economic impact on businesses not encompassed by the program, and would not be irremediable.

## IV

Congress, after due consideration, perceived a pressing need to move forward with new approaches in the continuing effort to achieve the goal of equality of economic opportunity. In this effort, Congress has necessary latitude to try new techniques such as the limited use of racial and ethnic criteria to accomplish remedial objectives; this is especially so in programs where voluntary cooperation with remedial measures is induced by placing conditions on federal expenditures. That the program may press the outer limits of congressional authority affords no basis for striking it down.

Petitioners have mounted a facial challenge to a program developed by the politically responsive branches of Government. For its part, the Congress must proceed only with programs narrowly tailored to achieve its objectives, subject to continuing evaluation and reassessment; administration of the programs must be vigilant and flexible; and, when such a program comes under judicial review, courts must be satisfied that the legislative objectives and projected administration give reasonable assurance that the program will function within constitutional limitations. . . .

. . .

. . . Any preference based on racial or ethnic criteria must necessarily receive a most searching examination to make sure that it does not conflict with constitutional guarantees. This case is one which requires, and which has received, that kind of examination. This opinion does not adopt, either expressly or implicitly, the formulas of analysis articulated in such cases as *University of California Regents v. Bakke.* . . . However, our analysis demonstrates that the MBE provision would survive judicial review under either "test" articulated in the several Bakke opinions. The MBE provision of the Public Works Employment Act of 1977 does not violate the Constitution.
    *Affirmed.*

. . .

MR. JUSTICE POWELL, concurring.
    Although I would place greater emphasis than THE CHIEF JUSTICE on the need to articulate judicial standards of review in conventional terms, I view his opinion announcing the judgment as substantially in accord with my own views. Accordingly, I join that opinion and write separately to apply the analysis set forth by my opinion in *University of California Regents v. Bakke.* . . .
    The question in this case is whether Congress may enact the requirement in 103(f)(2) of the Public Works Employment Act of 1977 (PWEA), that 10% of federal grants for local public work projects funded by the Act be set aside for minority business enterprises. Section 103(f)(2) employs a racial classification that is constitutionally prohibited unless it is a necessary means of advancing a compelling governmental interest.

. . .

    The Equal Protection Clause, and the equal protection component of the Due Process Clause of the Fifth Amendment, demand that any governmental distinction among groups must be justifiable. . . . Racial classifications must be assessed under the most stringent level of review because immutable characteristics, which bear no relation to individual merit or need, are irrelevant to almost every governmental decision. See, e. g., *Anderson v. Martin,* 375 U.S. 399, 402, 404, 84 S.Ct. 454, 455, 456, 11 L.Ed.2d 430 (1964). In this case, however, I believe that § 103(f)(2) is justified as a remedy that serves the compelling governmental interest in eradicating the continuing effects of past discrimination identified by Congress.

I

    Racial preference never can constitute a compelling state interest. " 'Distinctions between citizens solely because of their ancestry' [are] 'odious to a free people whose institutions are founded upon the doctrine of equality.' " *Loving v. Virginia.* . . . Thus, if the set-aside merely expresses a congressional desire to prefer one racial or ethnic group over another, § 103(f)(2) violates the equal protection component in the Due Process Clause of the Fifth Amendment. . . .

The Government does have a legitimate interest in ameliorating the disabling effects of identified discrimination. . . . The existence of illegal discrimination justifies the imposition of a remedy that will "make persons whole for injuries suffered on account of unlawful . . . discrimination." A critical inquiry, therefore, is whether § 103(f)(2) was enacted as a means of redressing such discrimination. But this Court has never approved race-conscious remedies absent judicial, administrative, or legislative findings of constitutional or statutory violations. . . .

Because the distinction between permissible remedial action and impermissible racial preference rests on the existence of a constitutional or statutory violation, the legitimate interest in creating a race-conscious remedy is not compelling unless an appropriate governmental authority has found that such a violation has occurred. In other words, two requirements must be met. First, the governmental body that attempts to impose a race-conscious remedy must have the authority to act in response to identified discrimination. . . . Second, the governmental body must make findings that demonstrate the existence of illegal discrimination. . . .
. . .

In reviewing the constitutionality of § 103(f)(2), we must decide: (i) whether Congress is competent to make findings of unlawful discrimination; (ii) if so, whether sufficient findings have been made to establish that unlawful discrimination has affected adversely minority business enterprises; and (iii) whether the 10% set-aside is a permissible means for redressing identifiable past discrimination. None of these questions may be answered without explicit recognition that we are reviewing an Act of Congress.

## II

The history of this Court's review of congressional action demonstrates beyond question that the National Legislature is competent to find constitutional and statutory violations. Unlike the Regents of the University of California, Congress properly may — and indeed must — address directly the problems of discrimination in our society. . . .
. . .

Congress' authority to find and provide for the redress of constitutional violations also has been confirmed in cases construing the Enforcement Clause of the Fifteenth Amendment. . . .

It is beyond question, therefore, that Congress has the authority to identify unlawful discriminatory practices, to prohibit those practices, and to prescribe remedies to eradicate their continuing effects. The next inquiry is whether Congress has made findings adequate to support its determination that minority contractors have suffered extensive discrimination.

## III

### A

The petitioners contend that the legislative history of § 103(f)(2) reflects no congressional finding of statutory or constitutional violations. Crucial to that contention is the assertion that a reviewing court may not look beyond the legislative history of the PWEA itself for evidence that Congress believed it was combating invidious discrimination. But petitioners' theory would erect an artificial barrier to full understanding of the legislative process.

. . .

Acceptance of petitioners' argument would force Congress to make specific factual findings with respect to each legislative action. Such a requirement would mark an unprecedented imposition of adjudicatory procedures upon a coordinate branch of Government. Neither the Constitution nor our democratic tradition warrants such a constraint on the legislative process. I therefore conclude that we are not confined in this case to an examination of the legislative history of § 103(f)(2) alone. Rather, we properly may examine the total contemporary record of congressional action dealing with the problems of racial discrimination against minority business enterprises.

### B

In my view, the legislative history of § 103(f)(2) demonstrates that Congress reasonably concluded that private and governmental discrimination had contributed to the negligible percentage of public contracts awarded minority contractors. The opinion of THE CHIEF JUSTICE provides a careful overview of the relevant legislative history . . . to which only a few words need be added.

. . .

In light of these legislative materials and the discussion of legislative history contained in THE CHIEF JUSTICE's opinion, I believe that a court must accept as established the conclusion that purposeful discrimination contributed significantly to the small percentage of federal contracting funds that minority business enterprises have received. . . . Although the discriminatory activities were not identified with the exactitude expected in judicial or administrative adjudication, it must be remembered that "Congress may paint with a much broader brush than may this Court. . . ." . . .

## IV

Under this Court's established doctrine, a racial classification is suspect and subject to strict judicial scrutiny. As noted in Part I, the government may employ such a classification only when necessary to accomplish a compelling governmental purpose. . . . The conclusion that Congress found a compelling governmental interest in redressing identified discrimination against minority contractors therefore leads to the inquiry whether use of a 10% set-aside is a constitutionally appropriate means of serving that interest. In the past, this "means" test has been virtually impossible to satisfy. . . . [T]he failure of legislative action to survive strict scrutiny has led some to wonder whether our review of racial classifications has been strict in theory, but fatal in fact. See Gunther, The Supreme Court, 1971 Term — Foreword: In Search of Evolving Doctrine on a Changing Court: A Model for a Newer Equal Protection, 86 Harv.L. Rev. 1, 8 (1972).

A

Application of the "means" test necessarily demands an understanding of the type of congressional action at issue. This is not a case in which Congress has employed a racial classification solely as a means to confer a racial preference. Such a purpose plainly would be unconstitutional. . . . Nor has Congress sought to employ a racially conscious means to further a nonracial goal. In such instances, a nonracial means should be available to further the legitimate governmental purpose. . . .

Enactment of the set-aside is designed to serve the compelling governmental interest in redressing racial discrimination. As this Court has recognized, the implementation of any affirmative remedy for redress of racial discrimination is likely to affect persons differently depending upon their race. . . .

I believe that the Enforcement Clauses of the Thirteenth and Fourteenth Amendments give Congress a similar measure of discretion to choose a suitable remedy for the redress of racial discrimination. . . .

. . .

I conclude, therefore, that the Enforcement Clauses of the Thirteenth and Fourteenth Amendments confer upon Congress the authority to select reasonable remedies to advance the compelling state interest in repairing the effects of discrimination. But that authority must be exercised in a manner that does not erode the guarantees of these Amendments. The Judicial Branch has the special responsibility to make a searching inquiry into the justification for employing a race-conscious remedy. Courts must be sensitive to the possibility that less intrusive means might serve the compelling state interest equally as well. I believe that Congress' choice of a remedy should be upheld, however, if the means selected are equitable and reasonably necessary to the redress of identified discrimination. Such a test allows the Congress to exercise necessary discretion but preserves the essential safeguard of judicial review of racial classifications.

B

When reviewing the selection by Congress of a race-conscious remedy, it is instructive to note the factors upon which the Courts of Appeals have relied in a closely analogous area. Courts reviewing the proper scope of race-conscious hiring remedies have considered (i) the efficacy of alternative remedies, . . . (ii) the planned duration of the remedy, . . . (iii) the relationship between the percentage of minority workers to be employed and the percentage of minority group members in the relevant population or work force, . . . and (iv) the availability of waiver provisions if the hiring plan could not be met. . . .

By the time Congress enacted § 103(f)(2) in 1977, it knew that other remedies had failed to ameliorate the effects of racial discrimination in the construction industry. . . . Section 103(f)(2) was enacted as part of a bill designed to stimulate the economy by appropriating $4 billion in federal funds for new public construction. . . . Moreover, Congress understood that any effective remedial program had to provide minority contractors the experience necessary for continued success without federal assistance. . . .

The § 103(f)(2) set-aside is not a permanent part of federal contracting requirements. As soon as the PWEA program concludes, this set-aside program ends. The temporary nature of this remedy ensures that a race-conscious program will not last longer than the discriminatory effects it is designed to eliminate. . . .

The percentage chosen for the set-aside is within the scope of congressional discretion. . . .

Although the set-aside is pegged at a reasonable figure, its effect might be unfair if it were applied rigidly in areas of the country where minority group members constitute a small percentage of the population. To meet this concern, Congress enacted a waiver provision into § 103(f)(2). . . .

C

A race-conscious remedy should not be approved without consideration of an additional crucial factor — the effect of the set-aside upon innocent third parties. . . . In this case, the petitioners contend with some force that they have been asked to bear the burden of the set-aside even though they are innocent of wrongdoing. I do not believe, however, that their burden is so great that the set-aside must be disapproved. . . .

. . .

V

In the history of this Court and this country, few questions have been more divisive than those arising from governmental action taken on the basis of race. Indeed, our own decisions played no small part in the tragic legacy of government-sanctioned discrimination. . . . At least since the decision in *Brown v. Board of Education*, . . . the Court has been resolute in its dedication to the principle that the Constitution envisions a Nation where race is irrelevant. The time cannot come too soon when no governmental decision will be based upon immutable characteristics of pigmentation or origin. But in our quest to achieve a society free from racial classification, we cannot ignore the claims of those who still suffer from the effects of identifiable discrimination.

Distinguishing the rights of all citizens to be free from racial classifications from the rights of some citizens to be made whole is a perplexing, but necessary, judicial task. When we first confronted such an issue in *Bakke,* I concluded that the Regents of the University of California were not competent to make, and had not made, findings sufficient to uphold the use of the race-conscious remedy they adopted. As my opinion made clear, I believe that the use of racial classifications, which are fundamentally at odds with the ideals of a democratic society implicit in the Due Process and Equal Protection Clauses, cannot be imposed simply to serve transient social or political goals, however worthy they may be. But the issue here turns on the scope of congressional power, and Congress has been given a unique constitutional role in the enforcement of the post–Civil War Amendments. In this case, where Congress determined that minority contractors were victims of purposeful discrimination and where Congress chose a reasonably necessary means to effectuate its purpose, I find no constitutional reason to invalidate § 103(f)(2).

MR. JUSTICE MARSHALL, with whom MR. JUSTICE BRENNAN and MR. JUSTICE BLACKMUN join, concurring in the judgment.

My resolution of the constitutional issue in this case is governed by the separate opinion I coauthored in *University of California Regents v. Bakke. . . .* In my view, the 10% minority set-aside provision of the Public Works Employment Act of 1977 passes constitutional muster under the standard announced in that opinion.

I

In *Bakke,* I joined my Brothers BRENNAN, WHITE, and BLACKMUN in articulating the view that "racial classifications are not per se invalid under [the Equal Protection Clause of] the Fourteenth Amendment." . . .

We recognized, however, that these principles outlawing the irrelevant or pernicious use of race were inapposite to racial classifications that provide benefits to minorities for the purpose of remedying the present effects of past racial discrimination. . . . Because the consideration of race is relevant to remedying the continuing effects of past racial discrimination, and because governmental programs employing racial classifications for remedial purposes can be crafted to avoid stigmatization, we concluded that such programs should not be subjected to conventional "strict scrutiny" — scrutiny that is strict in theory, but fatal in fact. . . .

We recognized that race has often been used to stigmatize politically powerless segments of society, and that efforts to ameliorate the effects of past discrimination could be based on paternalistic stereotyping, not on a careful consideration of modern social conditions. In addition, we acknowledged that governmental classification on the immutable characteristic of race runs counter to the deep national belief that state-sanctioned benefits and burdens should bear some relationship to individual merit and responsibility. Id., at 360–61, 98 S.Ct., at 2784.

We concluded, therefore, that because a racial classification ostensibly designed for remedial purposes is susceptible to misuse, it may be justified only by showing "an important and articulated purpose for its use." Id, at 361, 98 S.Ct., at 2785. "In addition any statute must be stricken that stigmatizes any group or that singles out those least well represented in the political process to bear the brunt of a benign program." . . .

## II

Judged under this standard, the 10% minority set-aside provision at issue in this case is plainly constitutional. Indeed, the question is not even a close one.

. . .

In sum, it is clear to me that the racial classifications employed in the set-aside provision are substantially related to the achievement of the important and congressionally articulated goal of remedying the present effects of past racial discrimination. The provision, therefore, passes muster under the equal protection standard I adopted in *Bakke.*

## III

In my separate opinion in *Bakke,* . . . I recounted the "ingenious and pervasive forms of discrimination against the Negro" long condoned under the Constitution and concluded that "[t]he position of the Negro today in America is the tragic but inevitable consequence of centuries of unequal treatment." . . .

. . .

Congress recognized these realities when it enacted the minority set-aside provision at issue in this case. Today, by upholding this race-conscious remedy, the Court accords Congress the authority necessary to undertake the task of moving our society toward a state of meaningful equality of opportunity, not an abstract version of equality in which the effects of past discrimination would be forever frozen into our social fabric. I applaud this result. Accordingly, I concur in the judgment of the Court.

Mr. Justice Stewart, with whom Mr. Justice Rehnquist joins, dissenting.

"Our Constitution is color-blind, and neither knows nor tolerates classes among citizens. . . . The law regards man as man, and takes no account of his surroundings or of his color. . . ." . . . His colleagues disagreed with him, and held that a statute that required the separation of people on the basis of their race was constitutionally valid because it was a "reasonable" exercise of legislative power and had been "enacted in good faith for the promotion [of] the public good. . . ." . . . Today, the Court upholds a statute that accords a preference to citizens who are "Negroes, Spanish-speaking, Orientals, Indians, Eskimos, and Aleuts," for much the same reasons. I think today's decision is wrong for the same reason that *Plessy v. Ferguson* was wrong, and I respectfully dissent.

A

The equal protection standard of the Constitution has one clear and central meaning—it absolutely prohibits invidious discrimination by government. That standard must be met by every State under the Equal Protection Clause of the Fourteenth Amendment. . . .

. . .

The rule cannot be any different when the persons injured by a racially biased law are not members of a racial minority. The guarantee of equal protection is "universal in [its] application, to all persons . . . without regard to any differences of race, of color, or of nationality." . . . [T]he benefits afforded by the Equal Protection Clause "are, by its terms, guaranteed to the individual. [They] are personal rights." From the perspective of a person detrimentally affected by a racially discriminatory law, the arbitrariness and unfairness is entirely the same, whatever his skin color and whatever the law's purpose, be it purportedly "for the promotion of the public good" or otherwise.

No one disputes the self-evident proposition that Congress has broad discretion under its spending power to disburse the revenues of the United States as it deems best and to set conditions on the receipt of the funds disbursed. No one disputes that Congress has the authority under the Commerce Clause to regulate contracting practices on federally funded public works projects, or that it enjoys broad powers under § 5 of the Fourteenth Amendment "to enforce by appropriate legislation" the provisions of that Amendment. But these self-evident truisms do not begin to answer the question before us in this case. For in the exercise of its powers, Congress must obey the Constitution just as the legislatures of all the States must obey the Constitution in the exercise of their powers. If a law is unconstitutional, it is no less unconstitutional just because it is a product of the Congress of the United States.

B

On its face, the minority business enterprise (MBE) provision at issue in this case denies the equal protection of the law. . . .

The Court's attempt to characterize the law as a proper remedial measure to counteract the effects of past or present racial discrimination is remarkably unconvincing.

. . .

But even assuming that Congress has the power, under § 5 of the Fourteenth Amendment or some other constitutional provision, to remedy previous illegal racial discrimination, there is no evidence that Congress has in the past engaged in racial discrimination in its disbursement of federal contracting funds. . . .

. . .

. . . Since the MBE provision was in whole or in part designed to effectuate objectives other than the elimination of the effects of racial discrimination, it cannot stand as a remedy that comports with the strictures of equal protection, even if it otherwise could.

C

The Fourteenth Amendment was adopted to ensure that every person must be treated equally by each State regardless of the color of his skin. . . .

. . .

There are those who think that we need a new Constitution, and their views may someday prevail. But under the Constitution we have, one practice in which government may never engage is the practice of racism — not even "temporarily" and not even as an "experiment."

For these reasons, I would reverse the judgment of the Court of Appeals.

Mr. Justice Stevens, dissenting.

The 10% set-aside contained in the Public Works Employment Act of 1977 (Act), 91 Stat. 116, creates monopoly privileges in a $400 million market for a class of investors defined solely by racial characteristics. The direct beneficiaries of these monopoly privileges are the relatively small number of persons within the racial classification who represent the entrepreneurial subclass — those who have, or can borrow, working capital.

History teaches us that the costs associated with a sovereign's grant of exclusive privileges often encompass more than the high prices and shoddy workmanship that are familiar handmaidens of monopoly; they engender animosity and discontent as well. . . .

. . . When government accords different treatment to different persons, there must be a reason for the difference. Because racial characteristics so seldom provide a relevant basis for disparate treatment, and because classifications based on race are potentially so harmful to the entire body politic, it is especially important that the reasons for any such classification be clearly identified and unquestionably legitimate.

The statutory definition of the preferred class includes "citizens of the United States who are Negroes, Spanish-speaking, Orientals, Indians, Eskimos, and Aleuts." All aliens and all nonmembers of the racial class are excluded. No economic, social, geographical, or historical criteria are relevant for exclusion or inclusion. There is not one word in the remainder of the Act or in the legislative history that explains why any Congressman or Senator favored this particular definition over any other or that identifies the common characteristics that every member of the preferred class was believed to share. Nor does the Act or its history explain why 10% of the total appropriation was the proper amount to set aside for investors in each of the six racial subclasses.

Four different, though somewhat interrelated, justifications for the racial classification in this Act have been advanced: first that the 10% set-aside is a form of reparation for past injuries to the entire membership of the class; second, that it is an appropriate remedy for past discrimination against minority business enterprises that have been denied access to public contracts; third, that the members of the favored class have a special entitlement to "a piece of the action" when government is distributing benefits; and, fourth, that the program is an appropriate method of fostering greater minority participation in a competitive economy. Each of these asserted justifications merits separate scrutiny.

I

Racial characteristics may serve to define a group of persons who have suffered a special wrong and who, therefore, are entitled to special reparations. Congress has recognized, for example, that the United States has treated some Indian tribes unjustly and has created procedures for allowing members of the injured classes to obtain classwide relief. . . . But as I have formerly suggested, if Congress is to authorize a recovery for a class of similarly situated victims of a past wrong, it has an obligation to distribute that recovery among the members of the injured class in an evenhanded way. . . .

. . .

Even if we assume that each of the six racial subclasses has suffered its own special injury at some time in our history, surely it does not necessarily follow that each of those subclasses suffered harm of identical magnitude. Although "the Negro was dragged to this country in chains to be sold in slavery," . . . the "Spanish-speaking" subclass came voluntarily, frequently without invitation, and the Indians, the Eskimos and the Aleuts had an opportunity to exploit America's resources before the ancestors of most American citizens arrived. There is no reason to assume, and nothing in the legislative history suggests, much less demonstrates, that each of these subclasses is equally entitled to reparations from the United States Government.

. . .

Although I do not dispute the validity of the assumption that each of the subclasses identified in the Act has suffered a severe wrong at some time in the past, I cannot accept this slapdash statute as a legitimate method of providing classwide relief.

II

The Act may also be viewed as a much narrower remedial measure — one designed to grant relief to the specific minority business enterprises that have been denied access to public contracts by discriminatory practices.

The legislative history of the Act does not tell us when, or how often, any minority business enterprise was denied such access. . . .

. . .

## III

The legislative history of the Act discloses that there is a group of legislators in Congress identified as the "Black Caucus" and that members of that group argued that if the Federal Government was going to provide $4 billion of new public contract business, their constituents were entitled to "a piece of the action."

It is neither unusual nor reprehensible for Congressmen to promote the authorization of public construction in their districts. . . .

. . .

The legislators' interest in providing their constituents with favored access to benefits distributed by the Federal Government is, in my opinion, a plainly impermissible justification for this racial classification.

## IV

The interest in facilitating and encouraging the participation by minority business enterprises in the economy is unquestionably legitimate. . . .

. . .

This Act has a character that is fundamentally different from a carefully drafted remedial measure like the Voting Rights Act of 1965. A consideration of some of the dramatic differences between these two legislative responses to racial injustice reveals not merely a difference in legislative craftsmanship but a difference of constitutional significance. Whereas the enactment of the Voting Rights Act was preceded by exhaustive hearings and debates concerning discriminatory denial of access to the electoral process, and became effective in specific States only after specific findings were made, this statute authorizes an automatic nationwide preference for all members of diverse racial class regardless of their possible interest in the particular geographic areas where the public contracts are to be performed. . . .

. . .

. . . Preferences based on characteristics acquired at birth foster intolerance and antagonism against the entire membership of the favored classes. For this reason, I am firmly convinced that this "temporary measure" will disserve the goal of equal opportunity.

## V

A judge's opinion that a statute reflects a profoundly unwise policy determination is an insufficient reason for concluding that it is unconstitutional. Congress has broad power to spend money to provide for the "general Welfare of the United States," to "regulate Commerce . . . among the several States," to enforce the Civil War Amendments, and to discriminate between aliens and citizens. . . .

. . .

In both its substantive and procedural aspects this Act is markedly different from the normal product of the legislative decisionmaking process. The very fact that Congress for the first time in the Nation's history has created a broad legislative classification for entitlement to benefits based solely on racial characteristics identifies a dramatic difference between this Act and the thousands of statutes that preceded it. This dramatic point of departure is not even mentioned in the statement of purpose of the Act or in the Reports of either the House or the Senate Committee that processed the legislation, and was not the subject of any testimony or inquiry in any legislative hearing on the bill that was enacted.

. . .

In all events, rather than take the substantive position expressed in MR. JUSTICE STEWART's dissenting opinion, I would hold this statute unconstitutional on a narrower ground. It cannot fairly be characterized as a "narrowly tailored" racial classification because it simply raises too many serious questions that Congress failed to answer or even to address in a responsible way. The risk that habitual attitudes toward classes of persons, rather than analysis of the relevant characteristics of the class, will serve as a basis for a legislative classification is present when benefits are distributed as well as when burdens are imposed. . . .

When Congress creates a special preference, or a special disability, for a class of persons, it should identify the characteristic that justifies the special treatment. When the classification is defined in racial terms, I believe that such particular identification is imperative.

In this case, only two conceivable bases for differentiating the preferred classes from society as a whole have occurred to me: (1) that they were the victims of unfair treatment in the past and (2) that they are less able to compete in the future. Although the first of these factors would justify an appropriate remedy for past wrongs, for reasons that I have already stated, this statute is not such a remedial measure. The second factor is simply not true. Nothing in the record of this case, the legislative history of the Act, or experience that we may notice judicially provides any support for such a proposition. It is up to Congress to demonstrate that its unique statutory preference is justified by a relevant characteristic that is shared by the members of the preferred class. In my opinion, because it has failed to make that demonstration, it has also failed to discharge its duty to govern impartially embodied in the Fifth Amendment to the United States Constitution.

I respectfully dissent.

# City of Richmond
# *v.* J. A. Croson Co.

In *Croson,* there is a lot of complexity. Each justice seems to take an individual route to arrive at either the majority or minority opinion.

Part I of the plurality opinion, written by Justice O'Connor, lays out the facts of the situation in a clear way.

Then Justice O'Connor's opinion seems to take a number of unexpected twists, wandering slightly and making reference to legal specifics that are not familiar to many citizens. One reason that her opinion presents challenges on first reading is that much of it argues against the dissenting opinion of Justice Marshall. So, until one has also read Marshall's opinion, it is hard to understand some aspects of O'Connor's opinion. Here in a nutshell is what O'Connor argues: If the city of Richmond had based its affirmative action program on a careful study in which it had documented the extent of discrimination, then the program would have been legal. But the city appeared to pick numbers from the air, so its program is illegal.

While O'Connor criticizes the city of Richmond for the seeming arbitrariness of the 30 percent rule, Justice Marshall criticizes O'Connor for her unwillingness to see the extent of present discrimination. "The majority's perfunctory dismissal of the testimony of Richmond's appointed and elected leaders," says Justice Marshall, "is also deeply disturbing." In *Croson,* as in *Weber,* Marshall maintains that current racial distinctions that benefit those who have been oppressed historically are qualitatively different than current racial distinctions that benefit those who have historically been the oppressors.

Justice Scalia's opinion is the exact opposite of Justice Marshall's opinion. Scalia sees virtually any categorization by race as unconstitutional. The third paragraph of his abridged opinion presented here contains a brief but eloquent argument against what others call "reverse discrimination."

APPEAL FROM THE UNITED STATES COURT OF
APPEALS FOR THE FOURTH CIRCUIT

No. 87-998. Argued October 5, 1988—Decided January 23, 1989

. . .

JUSTICE O'CONNOR announced the judgment of the Court and delivered the opinion of the Court with respect to Parts I, III-B, and IV, an opinion with respect to Part II, in which THE CHIEF JUSTICE and JUSTICE WHITE join, and an opinion with respect to Parts III-A and V, in which THE CHIEF JUSTICE, JUSTICE WHITE, and JUSTICE KENNEDY join.

In this case, we confront once again the tension between the Fourteenth Amendment's guarantee of equal treatment to all citizens, and the use of race-based measures to ameliorate the effects of past discrimination on the opportunities enjoyed by members of minority groups in our society. In *Fullilove* v. *Klutznick,* 448 U. S. 448 (1980), we held that a congressional program requiring that 10% of certain federal construction grants be awarded to minority contractors did not violate the equal protection principles embodied in the Due Process Clause of the Fifth Amendment. Relying largely on our decision in *Fullilove,* some lower federal courts have applied a similar standard of review in assessing the constitutionality of state and local minority set-aside provisions under the Equal Protection Clause of the Fourteenth Amendment. . . .

I

On April 11, 1983, the Richmond City Council adopted the Minority Business Utilization Plan (the Plan). The Plan required prime contractors to whom the city awarded construction contracts to subcontract at least 30% of the dollar amount of the contract to one or more Minority Business Enterprises (MBE's). Ordinance No. 83-69-59, codified in Richmond, Va., City Code, § 12-156(a) (1985). The 30% set-aside did not apply to city contracts awarded to minority-owned prime contractors. *Ibid.*

The Plan defined an MBE as "[a] business at least fifty-one (51) percent of which is owned and controlled . . . by minority group members." § 12-23, p. 941. "Minority group members" were defined as "[c]itizens of the United States who are Blacks, Spanish-speaking, Orientals, Indians, Eskimos, or Aleuts." *Ibid.* There was no geographic limit to the Plan; an otherwise qualified MBE from anywhere in the United States could avail itself of the 30% set-aside. The Plan declared that it was "remedial" in nature, and enacted "for the purpose of promoting wider participation by minority business enterprises in the construction of public projects." § 12-158(a). The Plan expired on June 30, 1988, and was in effect for approximately five years. *Ibid.*

The Plan authorized the Director of the Department of General Services to promulgate rules which "shall allow waivers in those individual situations where a contractor can prove to the satisfaction of the director that the requirements herein cannot be achieved." . . .

. . .

The Plan was adopted by the Richmond City Council after a public hearing. App. 9-50. Seven members of the public spoke to the merits of the ordinance: five were in opposition, two in favor. Proponents of the set-aside provision relied on a study which indicated that, while the general population of Richmond was 50% black, only 0.67% of the city's prime construction contracts had been awarded to minority businesses in the 5-year period from 1978 to 1983. It was also established that a variety of contractors' associations, whose representatives appeared in opposition to the ordinance, had virtually no minority businesses within their membership. . . .

. . .

There was no direct evidence of race discrimination on the part of the city in letting contracts or any evidence that the city's prime contractors had discriminated against minority-owned subcontractors. . . .

On September 6, 1983, the city of Richmond issued an invitation to bid on a project for the provision and installation of certain plumbing fixtures at the city jail. On September 30, 1983, Eugene Bonn, the regional manager of J. A. Croson Company (Croson), a mechanical plumbing and heating contractor, received the bid forms. The project involved the installation of stainless steel urinals and water closets in the city jail. Products of either of two manufacturers were specified, Acorn Engineering Company (Acorn) or Bradley Manufacturing Company (Bradley). Bonn determined that to meet the 30% set-aside requirement, a minority contractor would have to supply the fixtures. The provision of the fixtures amounted to 75% of the total contract price. . . .

. . . [Croson tried to find a qualified minority subcontractor, but was unable. Croson requested a waiver.]

. . . The city denied both Croson's request for a waiver and its suggestion that the contract price be raised. The city informed Croson that it had decided to rebid the project. On December 9, 1983, counsel for Croson wrote the city asking for a review of the waiver denial. The city's attorney responded that the city had elected to rebid the project, and that there is no appeal of such a decision. Shortly thereafter Croson brought this action under 42 U. S. C. § 1983 in the Federal District Court for the Eastern District of Virginia, arguing that the Richmond ordinance was unconstitutional on its face and as applied in this case.

The District Court upheld the Plan in all respects. . . . In its original opinion, a divided panel of the Fourth Circuit Court of Appeals affirmed. . . . Both courts applied a test derived from "the common concerns articulated by the various Supreme Court opinions" in *Fullilove* v. *Klutznick,* 448 U. S. 448 (1980), and *University of California Regents* v. *Bakke,* 438 U. S. 265 (1978). . . .

. . .

Croson sought certiorari from this Court. We granted the writ, vacated the opinion of the Court of Appeals, and remanded the case for further consideration in light of our intervening decision in *Wygant* v. *Jackson Board of Education,* 476 U. S. 267 (1986). . . . [Note: To remand means to send back to the lower court for reconsideration.]

On remand, a divided panel of the Court of Appeals struck down the Richmond set-aside program as violating both prongs of strict scrutiny under the Equal Protection Clause of the Fourteenth Amendment. . . . [Note: Whenever there is consideration of race or sex, there must be "strict scrutiny" of the situation. One "prong" of strict scrutiny states that race-based and sex-based distinctions are allowed only if there is a compelling state reason. Another "prong" states that distinctions must be finely tailored, not general or gross.] The majority found that the "core" of this Court's holding in *Wygant* was that "[t]o show that a plan is justified by compelling governmental interest, a municipality that wishes to employ a racial preference cannot rest on broad-brush assumptions of historical discrimination." 822 F. 2d, at 1357. As the court read this requirement, "[f]indings of *societal* discrimination will not suffice; the findings must concern 'prior discrimination *by the government unit involved.*' " . . .

In this case, the debate at the city council meeting "revealed no record of prior discrimination by the city in awarding public contracts. . . ." . . .

The Court of Appeals went on to hold that even if the city had demonstrated a compelling interest in the use of a race-based quota, the 30% set-aside was not narrowly tailored to accomplish a remedial purpose. The court found that the 30% figure was "chosen arbitrarily" and was not tied to the number of minority subcontractors in Richmond or to any other relevant number. *Ibid.* The dissenting judge argued that the majority had "misconstrue[d] and misapplie[d]" our decision in *Wygant.* 822 F. 2d, at 1362. We noted probable jurisdiction of the city's appeal, . . . and we now affirm the judgment.

## II

The parties and their supporting *amici* fight an initial battle over the scope of the city's power to adopt legislation designed to address the effects of past discrimination. Relying on our decision in *Wygant,* appellee argues that the city must limit any race-based remedial efforts to eradicating the effects of its own prior discrimination. This is essentially the position taken by the Court of Appeals below. Appellant argues that our decision in *Fullilove* is controlling, and that as a result the city of Richmond enjoys sweeping legislative power to define and attack the effects of prior discrimination in its local construction industry. We find that neither of these two rather stark alternatives can withstand analysis.

. . .

We do not, as JUSTICE MARSHALL's dissent suggests, find in § 5 of the Fourteenth Amendment some form of federal pre-emption in matters of race. We simply note what should be apparent to all — § 1 of the Fourteenth Amendment stemmed from a distrust of state legislative enactments based on race; § 5 is, as the dissent notes, " 'a *positive* grant of legislative power' " to Congress. . . . Thus, our treatment of an exercise of congressional power in *Fullilove* cannot be dispositive here. In the *Slaughter-House Cases,* 16 Wall. 36 (1873), cited by the dissent, the Court noted that the Civil War Amendments granted "additional powers to the Federal government," and laid "additional restraints upon those of the States." . . .

It would seem equally clear, however, that a state or local subdivision (if delegated the authority from the State) has the authority to eradicate the effects of private discrimination within its own legislative jurisdiction. This authority must, of course, be exercised within the constraints of § 1 of the Fourteenth Amendment. Our decision in *Wygant* is not to the contrary. . . .

Thus, if the city could show that it had essentially become a "passive participant" in a system of racial exclusion practiced by elements of the local construction industry, we think it clear that the city could take affirmative steps to dismantle such a system. It is beyond dispute that any public entity, state or federal, has a compelling interest in assuring that public dollars, drawn from the tax contributions of all citizens, do not serve to finance the evil of private prejudice. . . .

## III

### A

The Equal Protection Clause of the Fourteenth Amendment provides that "[n]o State shall . . . deny to *any person* within its jurisdiction the equal protection of the laws." . . .

Absent searching judicial inquiry into the justification for such race-based measures, there is simply no way of determining what classifications are "benign" or "remedial" and what classifications are in fact motivated by illegitimate notions of racial inferiority or simple racial politics. . . .

Classifications based on race carry a danger of stigmatic harm. Unless they are strictly reserved for remedial settings, they may in fact promote notions of racial inferiority and lead to a politics of racial hostility. See *University of California Regents* v. *Bakke,* 438 U. S., at 298 (opinion of Powell, J.) ("[P]referential programs may only reinforce common stereotypes holding that certain groups are unable to achieve success without special protection based on a factor having no relation to individual worth"). We thus reaffirm the view expressed by the plurality in *Wygant* that the standard of review under the Equal Protection Clause is not dependent on the race of those burdened or benefited by a particular classification. . . .

Our continued adherence to the standard of review employed in *Wygant* does not, as Justice Marshall's dissent suggests, indicate that we view "racial discrimination as largely a phenomenon of the past" or that "government bodies need no longer preoccupy themselves with rectifying racial injustice." As we indicate, States and their local subdivisions have many legislative weapons at their disposal both to punish and prevent present discrimination and to remove arbitrary barriers to minority advancement. Rather, our interpretation of § 1 stems from our agreement with the view expressed by Justice Powell in *Bakke* that "[t]he guarantee of equal protection cannot mean one thing when applied to one individual and something else when applied to a person of another color." . . .

Under the standard proposed by JUSTICE MARSHALL's dissent, "race-conscious classifications designed to further remedial goals" are forthwith subject to a relaxed standard of review. How the dissent arrives at the legal conclusion that a racial classification is "designed to further remedial goals," without first engaging in an examination of the factual basis for its enactment and the nexus between its scope and that factual basis, we are not told. However, once the "remedial" conclusion is reached, the dissent's standard is singularly deferential, and bears little resemblance to the close examination of legislative purpose we have engaged in when reviewing classifications based either on race or gender. . . . ("[T]he mere recitation of a benign, compensatory purpose is not an automatic shield which protects against any inquiry into the actual purposes underlying a statutory scheme"). The dissent's watered-down version of equal protection review effectively assures that race will always be relevant in American life, and that the "ultimate goal" of "eliminat[ing] entirely from governmental decisionmaking such irrelevant factors as a human being's race," . . . will never be achieved.

Even were we to accept a reading of the guarantee of equal protection under which the level of scrutiny varies according to the ability of different groups to defend their interests in the representative process, heightened scrutiny would still be appropriate in the circumstances of this case. One of the central arguments for applying a less exacting standard to "benign" racial classifications is that such measures essentially involve a choice made by dominant racial groups to disadvantage themselves. If one aspect of the judiciary's role under the Equal Protection Clause is to protect "discrete and insular minorities" from majoritarian prejudice or indifference, . . . some maintain that these concerns are not implicated when the "white majority" places burdens upon itself. . . .

In this case, blacks constitute approximately 50% of the population of the city of Richmond. Five of the nine seats on the city council are held by blacks. The concern that a political majority will more easily act to the disadvantage of a minority based on unwarranted assumptions or incomplete facts would seem to militate for, not against, the application of heightened judicial scrutiny in this case. . . .

. . .

B

We think it clear that the factual predicate offered in support of the Richmond Plan suffers from the same two defects identified as fatal in *Wygant*. The District Court found the city council's "findings sufficient to ensure that, in adopting the Plan, it was remedying the present effects of past discrimination in the *construction industry.*" . . . Like the "role model" theory employed in *Wygant,* a generalized assertion that there has been past discrimination in an entire industry provides no guidance for a legislative body to determine the precise scope of the injury it seeks to remedy. It "has no logical stopping point." . . . "Relief" for such an ill-defined wrong could extend until the percentage of public contracts awarded to MBE's in Richmond mirrored the percentage of minorities in the population as a whole.

Appellant [City of Richmond] argues that it is attempting to remedy various forms of past discrimination that are alleged to be responsible for the small number of minority businesses in the local contracting industry. Among these the city cites the exclusion of blacks from skilled construction trade unions and training programs. This past discrimination has prevented them "from following the traditional path from laborer to entrepreneur." . . . The city also lists a host of nonracial factors which would seem to face a member of any racial group attempting to establish a new business enterprise, such as deficiencies in working capital, inability to meet bonding requirements, unfamiliarity with bidding procedures, and disability caused by an inadequate track record. . . .

While there is no doubt that the sorry history of both private and public discrimination in this country has contributed to a lack of opportunities for black entrepreneurs, this observation, standing alone, cannot justify a rigid racial quota in the awarding of public contracts in Richmond, Virginia. Like the claim that discrimination in primary and secondary schooling justifies a rigid racial preference in medical school admissions, an amorphous claim that there has been past discrimination in a particular industry cannot justify the use of an unyielding racial quota.

It is sheer speculation how many minority firms there would be in Richmond absent past societal discrimination, just as it was sheer speculation how many minority medical students would have been admitted to the medical school at Davis absent past discrimination in educational opportunities. . . .

. . .

The city and the District Court also relied on evidence that MBE membership in local contractors' associations was extremely low. Again, standing alone this evidence is not probative of any discrimination in the local construction industry. There are numerous explanations for this dearth of minority participation, including past societal discrimination in education and economic opportunities as well as both black and white career and entrepreneurial choices. . . .

For low minority membership in these associations to be relevant, the city would have to link it to the number of local MBE's eligible for membership. If the statistical disparity between eligible MBE's and MBE membership were great enough, an inference of discriminatory exclusion could arise. In such a case, the city would have a compelling interest in preventing its tax dollars from assisting these organizations in maintaining a racially segregated construction market. . . .

. . .

JUSTICE MARSHALL apparently views the requirement that Richmond identify the discrimination it seeks to remedy in its own jurisdiction as "a mere administrative headache, an onerous documentary obligatio[n]." We cannot agree. In this regard, we are in accord with JUSTICE STEVENS' observation in *Fullilove,* that "[b]ecause racial characteristics so seldom provide a relevant basis for disparate treatment, and because classifications based on race are potentially so harmful to the entire body politic, it is especially important that the reasons for any such classification be clearly identified and unquestionably legitimate." . . . The "evidence" relied upon by the dissent, the history of school desegregation in Richmond and numerous congressional reports, does little to define the scope of any injury to minority contractors in Richmond or the necessary remedy. The factors relied upon by the dissent could justify a preference of any size or duration.

Moreover, JUSTICE MARSHALL's suggestion that findings of discrimination may be "shared" from jurisdiction to jurisdiction in the same manner as information concerning zoning and property values is unprecedented. . . .

. . .

The foregoing analysis applies only to the inclusion of blacks within the Richmond set-aside program. There is *absolutely no evidence* of past discrimination against Spanish-speaking, Oriental, Indian, Eskimo, or Aleut persons in any aspect of the Richmond construction industry. The District Court took judicial notice of the fact that the vast majority of "minority" persons in Richmond were black. Supp. App. 207. It may well be that Richmond has never had an Aleut or Eskimo citizen. The random inclusion of racial groups that, as a practical matter, may never have suffered from discrimination in the construction industry in Richmond suggests that perhaps the city's purpose was not in fact to remedy past discrimination.

If a 30% set-aside was "narrowly tailored" to compensate black contractors for past discrimination, one may legitimately ask why they are forced to share this "remedial relief" with an Aleut citizen who moves to Richmond tomorrow? The gross overinclusiveness of Richmond's racial preference strongly impugns the city's claim of remedial motivation. . . .

IV

As noted by the court below, it is almost impossible to assess whether the Richmond Plan is narrowly tailored to remedy prior discrimination since it is not linked to identified discrimination in any way. We limit ourselves to two observations in this regard.

First, there does not appear to have been any consideration of the use of race-neutral means to increase minority business participation in city contracting. . . .

. . .

Second, the 30% quota cannot be said to be narrowly tailored to any goal, except perhaps outright racial balancing. It rests upon the "completely unrealistic" assumption that minorities will choose a particular trade in lockstep proportion to their representation in the local population. . . .

. . .

Given the existence of an individualized procedure, the city's only interest in maintaining a quota system rather than investigating the need for remedial action in particular cases would seem to be simple administrative convenience. But the interest in avoiding the bureaucratic effort necessary to tailor remedial relief to those who truly have suffered the effects of prior discrimination cannot justify a rigid line drawn on the basis of a suspect classification. . . .

## V

Nothing we say today precludes a state or local entity from taking action to rectify the effects of identified discrimination within its jurisdiction. If the city of Richmond had evidence before it that nonminority contractors were systematically excluding minority businesses from subcontracting opportunities, it could take action to end the discriminatory exclusion. Where there is a significant statistical disparity between the number of qualified minority contractors willing and able to perform a particular service and the number of such contractors actually engaged by the locality or the locality's prime contractors, an inference of discriminatory exclusion could arise. . . .

Nor is local government powerless to deal with individual instances of racially motivated refusals to employ minority contractors. Where such discrimination occurs, a city would be justified in penalizing the discriminator and providing appropriate relief to the victim of such discrimination. . . .

Even in the absence of evidence of discrimination, the city has at its disposal a whole array of race-neutral devices to increase the accessibility of city contracting opportunities to small entrepreneurs of all races. Simplification of bidding procedures, relaxation of bonding requirements, and training and financial aid for disadvantaged entrepreneurs of all races would open the public contracting market to all those who have suffered the effects of past societal discrimination or neglect. Many of the formal barriers to new entrants may be the product of bureaucratic inertia more than actual necessity, and may have a disproportionate effect on the opportunities open to new minority firms. Their elimination or modification would have little detrimental effect on the city's interests and would serve to increase the opportunities available to minority business without classifying individuals on the basis of race. The city may also act to prohibit discrimination in the provision of credit or bonding by local suppliers and banks. Business as usual should not mean business pursuant to the unthinking exclusion of certain members of our society from its rewards.

. . .

Proper findings in this regard are necessary to define both the scope of the injury and the extent of the remedy necessary to cure its effects. Such findings also serve to assure all citizens that the deviation from the norm of equal treatment of all racial and ethnic groups is a temporary matter, a measure taken in the service of the goal of equality itself. Absent such findings, there is a danger that a racial classification is merely the product of unthinking stereotypes or a form of racial politics. . . . Accordingly the judgment of the Court of Appeals for the Fourth Circuit is *Affirmed.*

JUSTICE STEVENS, concurring in part and concurring in the judgment.

A central purpose of the Fourteenth Amendment is to further the national goal of equal opportunity for all our citizens. In order to achieve that goal we must learn from our past mistakes, but I believe the Constitution requires us to evaluate our policy decisions — including those that govern the relationships among different racial and ethnic groups — primarily by studying their probable impact on the future. I therefore do not agree with the premise that seems to underlie today's decision, as well as the decision in *Wygant* v. *Jackson Board of Education,* 476 U. S. 267 (1986), that a governmental decision that rests on a racial classification is never permissible except as a remedy for a past wrong. I do, however, agree with the Court's explanation of why the Richmond ordinance cannot be justified as a remedy for past discrimination, and therefore join Parts I, III-B, and IV of its opinion. I write separately to emphasize three aspects of the case that are of special importance to me.

First, the city makes no claim that the public interest in the efficient performance of its construction contracts will be served by granting a preference to minority-business enterprises. This case is therefore completely unlike *Wygant,* in which I thought it quite obvious that the school board had reasonably concluded that an integrated faculty could provide educational benefits to the entire student body that could not be provided by an all-white, or nearly all-white, faculty. . . .

Second, this litigation involves an attempt by a legislative body, rather than a court, to fashion a remedy for a past wrong. Legislatures are primarily policymaking bodies that promulgate rules to govern future conduct. The constitutional prohibitions against the enactment of *ex post facto* laws and bills of attainder reflect a valid concern about the use of the political process to punish or characterize past conduct of private citizens. It is the judicial system, rather than the legislative process, that is best equipped to identify past wrongdoers and to fashion remedies that will create the conditions that presumably would have existed had no wrong been committed. . . .

Third, instead of engaging in a debate over the proper standard of review to apply in affirmative-action litigation, I believe it is more constructive to try to identify the characteristics of the advantaged and disadvantaged classes that may justify their disparate treatment. . . .

. . .

Accordingly, I concur in Parts I, III-B, and IV of the Court's opinion, and in the judgment.

JUSTICE KENNEDY, concurring in part and concurring in the judgment.

I join all but Part II of JUSTICE O'CONNOR's opinion and give this further explanation.

. . .

The moral imperative of racial neutrality is the driving force of the Equal Protection Clause. JUSTICE SCALIA's opinion underscores that proposition, quite properly in my view. The rule suggested in his opinion, which would strike down all preferences which are not necessary remedies to victims of unlawful discrimination, would serve important structural goals, as it would eliminate the necessity for courts to pass upon each racial preference that is enacted. Structural protections may be necessities if moral imperatives are to be obeyed. His opinion would make it crystal clear to the political branches, at least those of the States, that legislation must be based on criteria other than race.

. . .

JUSTICE SCALIA, concurring in the judgment.

I agree with much of the Court's opinion, and, in particular, with JUSTICE O'CONNOR's conclusion that strict scrutiny must be applied to all governmental classification by race, whether or not its asserted purpose is "remedial" or "benign." . . . I do not agree, however, with JUSTICE O'CONNOR's dictum suggesting that, despite the Fourteenth Amendment, state and local governments may in some circumstances discriminate on the basis of race in order (in a broad sense) "to ameliorate the effects of past discrimination." . . . The benign purpose of compensating for social disadvantages, whether they have been acquired by reason of prior discrimination or otherwise, can no more be pursued by the illegitimate means of racial discrimination than can other assertedly benign purposes we have repeatedly rejected. . . .

. . .

In my view there is only one circumstance in which the States may act *by race* to "undo the effects of past discrimination": where that is necessary to eliminate their own maintenance of a system of unlawful racial classification. If, for example, a state agency has a discriminatory pay scale compensating black employees in all positions at 20% less than their nonblack counterparts, it may assuredly promulgate an order raising the salaries of "all black employees" to eliminate the differential. . . .

. . .

It is plainly true that in our society blacks have suffered discrimination immeasurably greater than any directed at other racial groups. But those who believe that racial preferences can help to "even the score" display, and reinforce, a manner of thinking by race that was the source of the injustice and that will, if it endures within our society, be the source of more injustice still. The relevant proposition is not that it was blacks, or Jews, or Irish who were discriminated against, but that it was individual men and women, "created equal," who were discriminated against. And the relevant resolve is that that should never happen again. Racial preferences appear to "even the score" (in some small degree) only if one embraces the proposition that our society is appropriately viewed as divided into races, making it right that an injustice rendered in the past to a black man should be compensated for by discriminating against a white. Nothing is worth that embrace. . . .

Since I believe that the appellee [Cronson] here had a constitutional right to have its bid succeed or fail under a decisionmaking process uninfected with racial bias, I concur in the judgment of the Court.

JUSTICE MARSHALL, with whom JUSTICE BRENNAN and JUSTICE BLACKMUN join, dissenting.

It is a welcome symbol of racial progress when the former capital of the Confederacy acts forthrightly to confront the effects of racial discrimination in its midst. In my view, nothing in the Constitution can be construed to prevent Richmond, Virginia, from allocating a portion of its contracting dollars for businesses owned or controlled by members of minority groups. Indeed, Richmond's set-aside program is indistinguishable in all meaningful respects from — and in fact was patterned upon — the federal set-aside plan which this Court upheld in *Fullilove* v. *Klutznick,* 448 U. S. 448 (1980).

A majority of this Court holds today, however, that the Equal Protection Clause of the Fourteenth Amendment blocks Richmond's initiative. The essence of the majority's position is that Richmond has failed to catalog adequate findings to prove that past discrimination has impeded minorities from joining or participating fully in Richmond's construction contracting industry. I find deep irony in second-guessing Richmond's judgment on this point. . . .

More fundamentally, today's decision marks a deliberate and giant step backward in this Court's affirmative-action jurisprudence. Cynical of one municipality's attempt to redress the effects of past racial discrimination in a particular industry, the majority launches a grapeshot attack on race-conscious remedies in general. The majority's unnecessary pronouncements will inevitably discourage or prevent governmental entities, particularly States and localities, from acting to rectify the scourge of past discrimination. This is the harsh reality of the majority's decision, but it is not the Constitution's command.

. . .

Richmond's reliance on localized, industry-specific findings is a far cry from the reliance on generalized "societal discrimination" which the majority decries as a basis for remedial action. . . . But characterizing the plight of Richmond's minority contractors as mere "societal discrimination" is not the only respect in which the majority's critique shows an unwillingness to come to grips with why construction-contracting in Richmond is essentially a whites-only enterprise. The majority also takes the disingenuous approach of disaggregating Richmond's local evidence, attacking it piecemeal, and thereby concluding that no *single* piece of evidence adduced by the city, "standing alone," . . . suffices to prove past discrimination. But items of evidence do not, of course, "stan[d] alone" or exist in alien juxtaposition; they necessarily work together, reinforcing or contradicting each other.

In any event, the majority's criticisms of individual items of Richmond's evidence rest on flimsy foundations. The majority states, for example, that reliance on the disparity between the share of city contracts awarded to minority firms (0.67%) and the minority population of Richmond (approximately 50%) is "misplaced." . . . It is true that, when the factual predicate needed to be proved is one of *present* discrimination, we have generally credited statistical contrasts between the racial composition of a work force and the general population as proving discrimination only where this contrast revealed "gross statistical disparities." . . . But this principle does not impugn Richmond's statistical contrast, for two reasons. First, considering how miniscule the share of Richmond public construction contracting dollars received by minority-owned businesses is, it is hardly unreasonable to conclude that this case involves a "gross statistical disparit[y]." . . . There are roughly equal numbers of minorities and nonminorities in Richmond — yet minority-owned businesses receive *one-seventy-fifth* of the public contracting funds that other businesses receive. . . .

Second, and more fundamentally, where the issue is not present discrimination but rather whether *past* discrimination has resulted in the *continuing exclusion* of minorities from a historically tight-knit industry, a contrast between population and work force is entirely appropriate to help gauge the degree of the exclusion. . . .

The majority's perfunctory dismissal of the testimony of Richmond's appointed and elected leaders is also deeply disturbing. These officials — including councilmembers, a former mayor, and the present city manager — asserted that race discrimination in area contracting had been widespread, and that the set-aside ordinance was a sincere and necessary attempt to eradicate the effects of this discrimination. The majority, however, states that where racial classifications are concerned, "simple legislative assurances of good intention cannot suffice." . . .

. . .

## III

### A

Today for the first time, a majority of this Court has adopted strict scrutiny as its standard of Equal Protection Clause review of race-conscious remedial measures. . . . This is an unwelcome development. A profound difference separates governmental actions that themselves are racist, and governmental actions that seek to remedy the effects of prior racism or to prevent neutral governmental activity from perpetuating the effects of such racism. . . .

Racial classifications "drawn on the presumption that one race is inferior to another or because they put the weight of government behind racial hatred and separatism" warrant the strictest judicial scrutiny because of the very irrelevance of these rationales. . . . By contrast, racial classifications drawn for the purpose of remedying the effects of discrimination that itself was race based have a highly pertinent basis: the tragic and indelible fact that discrimination against blacks and other racial minorities in this Nation has pervaded our Nation's history and continues to scar our society. . . .

JUSTICE BLACKMUN, with whom JUSTICE BRENNAN joins, dissenting.

I join JUSTICE MARSHALL's perceptive and incisive opinion revealing great sensitivity toward those who have suffered the pains of economic discrimination in the construction trades for so long.

I never thought that I would live to see the day when the city of Richmond, Virginia, the cradle of the Old Confederacy, sought on its own, within a narrow confine, to lessen the stark impact of persistent discrimination. But Richmond, to its great credit, acted. Yet this Court, the supposed bastion of equality, strikes down Richmond's efforts as though discrimination had never existed or was not demonstrated in this particular litigation. JUSTICE MARSHALL convincingly discloses the fallacy and the shallowness of that approach. History is irrefutable, even though one might sympathize with those who—though possibly innocent in themselves—benefit from the wrongs of past decades.

So the Court today regresses. I am confident, however, that, given time, it one day again will do its best to fulfill the great promises of the Constitution's Preamble and of the guarantees embodied in the Bill of Rights—a fulfillment that would make this Nation very special.

# Adarand Constructors, Inc. *v.* Pena, Secretary of Transportation, et al.

The Supreme Court announced its decision in *Adarand* just as the Clinton administration was about to set forth its policy on affirmative action. The *Adarand* decision did not change Clinton's "mend it, don't end it" stance, but it did serve to strengthen the resolve of those who wished to restore affirmative action to the kind of monitoring policy established by Executive Order 11246 and to eliminate set-asides.

As with earlier cases, this one is marked by much dissension. The justices do not speak with one voice. Even when they agree with each other in their conclusions, they disagree about the means for reaching their conclusions.

Justice O'Connor's opinion is noteworthy in a few respects. First, it shows clearly the harvest of previous vacillations by the Court. Much of her argument is meant to show why the present decision can go against the Court's decision in the *Metro Broadcasting* case. When prior cases conflict, the Justices must pick and choose among earlier decisions to find one that seems to fit the present situation, and so it is with the *Adarand* case. The second notable aspect of Justice O'Connor's opinion is that some of it is an argument against Justice Stevens's dissent and not an argument in favor of any precedent. This approach is similar to that used in O'Connor's opinion in *Croson,* where a great deal of effort was devoted to arguing why Justice Marshall's views were faulty. Third, as the final paragraph of III-D shows, Justice O'Connor took pains to note that narrowly tailored racial distinctions might sometimes be in the state's interests. Finally, and most importantly, O'Connor's decision rests almost entirely on the claims that strict scrutiny must be applied to any program that makes racial distinctions and that the program challenged here fails to meet the criteria of strict scrutiny. As discussed in *Croson,* there are two aspects to strict scrutiny. First, the distinction must serve a strong or compelling interest of the state (e.g., that educators reflect the racial mix of students). Second, the distinction must be narrowly tailored (e.g., if it is blacks who are excluded now, the program must be aimed at increasing the representation of blacks, not the representation of all ethnic minority groups). No one could claim that the Department of Transportation plan satisfied the criteria of strict scrutiny, and so Justice O'Connor did not dwell on that point. Where she put all the energy was into stating why strict scrutiny is needed.

The Court is very divided. O'Connor's opinion walks the thin line between two extremes. At the far right are Justices Scalia and Thomas, who think that the state can never have a compelling interest in making distinctions on the basis of race. At the far left are Justices Souter and Ginsburg. Justice Stevens resembles Justices Souter and Ginsburg. For these justices, the spirit of the Constitution is as important as the letter of the Constitution. The plain fact that whites are the privileged people in the United States—a fact that the conservative justices do not dispute—leads Justices Souter, Ginsburg, and Stevens to question the honesty of so-called race neutral policies.

---

## CERTIORARI TO THE UNITED STATES COURT OF APPEALS FOR THE TENTH CIRCUIT

No. 93-1841. Argued January 17, 1995—Decided June 12, 1995

. . .

JUSTICE O'CONNOR announced the judgment of the Court and delivered an opinion with respect to Parts I, II, III-A, III-B, III-D, and IV, which is for the Court except insofar as it might be inconsistent with the views expressed in JUSTICE SCALIA's concurrence, and an opinion with respect to Part III-C in which JUSTICE KENNEDY joins.

Petitioner Adarand Constructors, Inc., claims that the Federal Government's practice of giving general contractors on Government projects a financial incentive to hire subcontractors controlled by "socially and economically disadvantaged individuals," and in particular, the Government's use of race-based presumptions in identifying such individuals, violates the equal protection component of the Fifth Amendment's Due Process Clause. The Court of Appeals rejected Adarand's claim. We conclude, however, that courts should analyze cases of this kind under a different standard of review than the one the Court of Appeals applied. We therefore vacate the Court of Appeals' judgment and remand the case for further proceedings.

I

In 1989, the Central Federal Lands Highway Division (CFLHD), which is part of the United States Department of Transportation (DOT), awarded the prime contract for a highway construction project in Colorado

to Mountain Gravel & Construction Company. Mountain Gravel then solic-
ited bids from subcontractors for the guardrail portion of the contract.
Adarand, a Colorado-based highway construction company specializing in
guardrail work, submitted the low bid. Gonzales Construction Company
also submitted a bid.

The prime contract's terms provide that Mountain Gravel would receive additional compensation if it hired subcontractors certified as small
businesses controlled by "socially and economically disadvantaged individuals." . . . Gonzales is certified as such a business; Adarand is not. Mountain Gravel awarded the subcontract to Gonzales, despite Adarand's low
bid, and Mountain Gravel's Chief Estimator has submitted an affidavit
stating that Mountain Gravel would have accepted Adarand's bid, had it
not been for the additional payment it received by hiring Gonzales instead. . . . Federal law requires that a subcontracting clause similar to the
one used here must appear in most federal agency contracts, and it also
requires the clause to state that "[t]he contractor shall presume that socially
and economically disadvantaged individuals include Black Americans, Hispanic Americans, Native Americans, Asian Pacific Americans, and other
minorities, or any other individual found to be disadvantaged by the [Small
Business] Administration pursuant to section 8(a) of the Small Business
Act." 15 U. S. C. §§ 637(d)(2), (3). Adarand claims that the presumption
set forth in that statute discriminates on the basis of race in violation of the
Federal Government's Fifth Amendment obligation not to deny anyone
equal protection of the laws.
. . .

## II

Adarand, in addition to its general prayer for "such other and further
relief as to the Court seems just and equitable," specifically seeks declaratory and injunctive relief against any *future* use of subcontractor compensation clauses. . . . Before reaching the merits of Adarand's challenge, we
must consider whether Adarand has standing [i.e., is entitled] to seek
forward-looking relief. Adarand's allegation that it has lost a contract in
the past because of a subcontractor compensation clause of course entitles
it to seek damages for the loss of that contract. . . . But as we explained in
*Los Angeles* v. *Lyons,* . . . the fact of past injury, "while presumably affording [the plaintiff] standing to claim damages . . . , does nothing to establish
a real and immediate threat that he would again" suffer similar injury in the
future. . . .

If Adarand is to maintain its claim for forward-looking relief, our cases
require it to allege that the use of subcontractor compensation clauses in the
future constitutes "an invasion of a legally protected interest which is (a)
concrete and particularized, and (b) actual or imminent, not conjectural or
hypothetical." *Lujan* v. *Defenders of Wildlife,* 504 U. S. 555, 560 (1992)
(footnote, citations, and internal quotation marks omitted). Adarand's

claim that the Government's use of subcontractor compensation clauses denies it equal protection of the laws of course alleges an invasion of a legally protected interest, and it does so in a manner that is "particularized" as to Adarand. We note that, contrary to respondents' suggestion, . . . Adarand need not demonstrate that it has been, or will be, the low bidder on a Government contract. The injury in cases of this kind is that a "discriminatory classification prevent[s] the plaintiff from competing on an equal footing." . . . The aggrieved party "need not allege that he would have obtained the benefit but for the barrier in order to establish standing." . . .

It is less clear, however, that the future use of subcontractor compensation clauses will cause Adarand "imminent" injury. We said in *Lujan* that "[a]lthough 'imminence' is concededly a somewhat elastic concept, it cannot be stretched beyond its purpose, which is to ensure that the alleged injury is not too speculative for Article III purposes — that the injury is *'certainly* impending.' " . . . We therefore must ask whether Adarand has made an adequate showing that sometime in the relatively near future it will bid on another Government contract that offers financial incentives to a prime contractor for hiring disadvantaged subcontractors.

We conclude that Adarand has satisfied this requirement. Adarand's general manager said in a deposition that his company bids on every guardrail project in Colorado. . . . According to documents produced in discovery, the CFLHD let 14 prime contracts in Colorado that included guardrail work between 1983 and 1990. . . . Two of those contracts do not present the kind of injury Adarand alleges here. In one, the prime contractor did not subcontract out the guardrail work; in another, the prime contractor was itself a disadvantaged business, and in such cases the contract generally does not include a subcontractor compensation clause. . . . Thus, statistics from the years 1983 through 1990 indicate that the CFLHD lets on average 1-1/2 contracts per year that could injure Adarand in the manner it alleges here. Nothing in the record suggests that the CFLHD has altered the frequency with which it lets contracts that include guardrail work. And the record indicates that Adarand often must compete for contracts against companies certified as small disadvantaged businesses. . . . Because the evidence in this case indicates that the CFLHD is likely to let contracts involving guardrail work that contain a subcontractor compensation clause at least once per year in Colorado, that Adarand is very likely to bid on each such contract, and that Adarand often must compete for such contracts against small disadvantaged businesses, we are satisfied that Adarand has standing to bring this lawsuit.

III

. . .

Adarand's claim arises under the Fifth Amendment to the Constitution, which provides that "No person shall . . . be deprived of life, liberty, or property, without due process of law." Although this Court has always understood that Clause to provide some measure of protection against *arbitrary* treatment by the Federal Government, it is not as explicit a guarantee of *equal* treatment as the Fourteenth Amendment, which provides that "No *State* shall . . . deny to any person within its jurisdiction the equal protection of the laws" (emphasis added). Our cases have accorded varying degrees of significance to the difference in the language of those two Clauses. We think it necessary to revisit the issue here.

A

Through the 1940's, this Court had routinely taken the view in non-race-related cases that, "[u]nlike the Fourteenth Amendment, the Fifth contains no equal protection clause and it provides no guaranty against discriminatory legislation by Congress." . . .

. . .

In *Bolling* v. *Sharpe,* 347 U. S. 497 (1954), the Court for the first time explicitly questioned the existence of any difference between the obligations of the Federal Government and the States to avoid racial classifications. . . .

B

Most of the cases discussed above involved classifications burdening groups that have suffered discrimination in our society. In 1978, the Court confronted the question whether race-based governmental action designed to *benefit* such groups should also be subject to "the most rigid scrutiny." . . .

Two years after *Bakke,* the Court faced another challenge to remedial race-based action, this time involving action undertaken by the Federal Government. In *Fullilove* v. *Klutznick,* 448 U. S. 448 (1980), the Court upheld Congress' inclusion of a 10% set-aside for minority-owned businesses in the Public Works Employment Act of 1977. . . .

In *Wygant* v. *Jackson Bd. of Ed.,* 476 U. S. 267 (1986), the Court considered a Fourteenth Amendment challenge to another form of remedial racial classification. The issue in *Wygant* was whether a school board could adopt race-based preferences in determining which teachers to lay off. Justice Powell's plurality opinion observed that "the level of scrutiny does not change merely because the challenged classification operates against a group that historically has not been subject to governmental discrimination." . . . In other words, "racial classifications of any sort must be subjected to 'strict scrutiny.' " . . .

The Court's failure to produce a majority opinion in *Bakke, Fullilove,* and *Wygant* left unresolved the proper analysis for remedial race-based governmental action. . . .

The Court resolved the issue, at least in part, in 1989. *Richmond* v. *J. A. Croson Co.,* 488 U. S. 469 (1989), concerned a city's determination that 30% of its contracting work should go to minority-owned businesses. A majority of the Court in *Croson* held that "the standard of review under the Equal Protection Clause is not dependent on the race of those burdened or benefited by a particular classification," and that the single standard of review for racial classifications should be "strict scrutiny." . . .

With *Croson*, the Court finally agreed that the Fourteenth Amendment requires strict scrutiny of all race-based action by state and local governments. [For an explanation of strict scrutiny, see p. 283.] But *Croson* of course had no occasion to declare what standard of review the Fifth Amendment requires for such action taken by the Federal Government. . . .

. . . Despite lingering uncertainty in the details, however, the Court's cases through *Croson* had established three general propositions with respect to governmental racial classifications. First, skepticism: " 'Any preference based on racial or ethnic criteria must necessarily receive a most searching examination.' " . . .

A year later, however, the Court took a surprising turn. *Metro Broadcasting, Inc.* v. *FCC, supra,* involved a Fifth Amendment challenge to two race-based policies of the Federal Communications Commission (FCC). In *Metro Broadcasting,* the Court repudiated the long-held notion that "it would be unthinkable that the same Constitution would impose a lesser duty on the Federal Government" than it does on a State to afford equal protection of the laws. . . . It did so by holding that "benign" federal racial classifications need only satisfy intermediate scrutiny, even though *Croson* had recently concluded that such classifications enacted by a State must satisfy strict scrutiny. "[B]enign" federal racial classifications, the Court said, " — even if those measures are not 'remedial' in the sense of being designed to compensate victims of past governmental or societal discrimination — are constitutionally permissible to the extent that they serve *important* governmental objectives within the power of Congress and are *substantially related* to achievement of those objectives." *Metro Broadcasting,* 497 U. S., at 564–565 (emphasis added). The Court did not explain how to tell whether a racial classification should be deemed "benign," other than to express "confiden[ce] that an 'examination of the legislative scheme and its history' will separate benign measures from other types of racial classifications." . . .

Applying this test, the Court first noted that the FCC policies at issue did not serve as a remedy for past discrimination. . . . Proceeding on the assumption that the policies were nonetheless "benign," it concluded that they served the "important governmental objective" of "enhancing broadcast diversity," . . . and that they were "substantially related" to that objective. . . . It therefore upheld the policies.

By adopting intermediate scrutiny as the standard of review for congressionally mandated "benign" racial classifications, *Metro Broadcasting* departed from prior cases in two significant respects. First, it turned its back on *Croson*'s explanation of why strict scrutiny of all governmental racial classifications is essential. . . .

Second, *Metro Broadcasting* squarely rejected one of the three propositions established by the Court's earlier equal protection cases, namely, congruence between the standards applicable to federal and state racial classifications, and in so doing also undermined the other two — skepticism of all racial classifications and consistency of treatment irrespective of the race of the burdened or benefited group. Under *Metro Broadcasting,* certain racial classifications ("benign" ones enacted by the Federal Government) should be treated less skeptically than others; and the race of the benefited group is critical to the determination of which standard of review to apply. *Metro Broadcasting* was thus a significant departure from much of what had come before it.

The three propositions undermined by *Metro Broadcasting* all derive from the basic principle that the Fifth and Fourteenth Amendments to the Constitution protect *persons,* not *groups.* It follows from that principle that all governmental action based on race — a *group* classification long recognized as "in most circumstances irrelevant and therefore prohibited," . . . — should be subjected to detailed judicial inquiry to ensure that the *personal* right to equal protection of the laws has not been infringed. These ideas have long been central to this Court's understanding of equal protection, and holding "benign" state and federal racial classifications to different standards does not square with them. "[A] free people whose institutions are founded upon the doctrine of equality," *ibid.,* should tolerate no retreat from the principle that government may treat people differently because of their race only for the most compelling reasons. Accordingly, we hold today that all racial classifications, imposed by whatever federal, state, or local governmental actor, must be analyzed by a reviewing court under strict scrutiny. In other words, such classifications are constitutional only if they are narrowly tailored measures that further compelling governmental interests. To the extent that *Metro Broadcasting* is inconsistent with that holding, it is overruled.

In dissent, JUSTICE STEVENS criticizes us for "deliver[ing] a disconcerting lecture about the evils of governmental racial classifications." . . . With respect, we believe his criticisms reflect a serious misunderstanding of our opinion.

JUSTICE STEVENS concurs in our view that courts should take a skeptical view of all governmental racial classifications. *Ibid.* He also allows that "[n]othing is inherently wrong with applying a single standard to fundamentally different situations, as long as that standard takes relevant differences into account." What he fails to recognize is that strict scrutiny *does* take "relevant differences" into account — indeed, that is its fundamental purpose. The point of carefully examining the interest asserted by the government in support of a racial classification, and the evidence offered to show that the classification is needed, is precisely to distinguish legitimate from illegitimate uses of race in governmental decisionmaking. . . . And JUSTICE STEVENS concedes that "some cases may be difficult to classify," . . . ; all the more reason, in our view, to examine all racial classifications carefully. Strict scrutiny does not "trea[t] dissimilar race-based decisions as though they were equally objectionable," . . . ; to the contrary, it evaluates carefully all governmental race-based decisions *in order to decide* which are constitutionally objectionable and which are not. By requiring strict scrutiny of racial classifications, we require courts to make sure that a governmental classification based on race, which "so seldom provide[s] a relevant basis for disparate treatment," . . . is legitimate, before permitting unequal treatment based on race to proceed.

JUSTICE STEVENS chides us for our "supposed inability to differentiate between 'invidious' and 'benign' discrimination," because it is in his view sufficient that "people understand the difference between good intentions and bad." . . . But, as we have just explained, the point of strict scrutiny is to "differentiate between" permissible and impermissible governmental use of race. And JUSTICE STEVENS himself has already explained in his dissent in *Fullilove* why "good intentions" alone are not enough to sustain a supposedly "benign" racial classification: "[E]ven though it is not the actual predicate for this legislation, a statute of this kind inevitably is perceived by many as resting on an assumption that those who are granted this special preference are less qualified in some respect that is identified purely by their race. Because that perception — *especially when fostered by the Congress of the United States* — can only exacerbate rather than reduce racial prejudice, it will delay the time when race will become a truly irrelevant, or at least insignificant, factor. *Unless Congress clearly articulates the need and basis* for a racial classification, *and also tailors the classification to its justification,* the Court should not uphold this kind of statute." . . .

. . .

C

"Although adherence to precedent is not rigidly required in constitutional cases, any departure from the doctrine of *stare decisis* demands special justification." . . . In deciding whether this case presents such justification, we recall Justice Frankfurter's admonition that "*stare decisis* is a principle of policy and not a mechanical formula of adherence to the latest decision, however recent and questionable, when such adherence involves collision with a prior doctrine more embracing in its scope, intrinsically sounder, and verified by experience." . . . Remaining true to an "intrinsically sounder" doctrine established in prior cases better serves the values of *stare decisis* than would following a more recently decided case inconsistent with the decisions that came before it; the latter course would simply compound the recent error and would likely make the unjustified break from previously established doctrine complete. In such a situation, "special justification" exists to depart from the recently decided case.

As we have explained, *Metro Broadcasting* undermined important principles of this Court's equal protection jurisprudence, established in a line of cases stretching back over 50 years. . . . This case therefore presents precisely the situation described by Justice Frankfurter in *Helvering:* We cannot adhere to our most recent decision without colliding with an accepted and established doctrine. We also note that *Metro Broadcasting*'s application of different standards of review to federal and state racial classifications has been consistently criticized by commentators. . . .

. . .

"The real problem," Justice Frankfurter explained, "is whether a principle shall prevail over its later misapplications." . . . *Metro Broadcasting*'s untenable distinction between state and federal racial classifications lacks support in our precedent, and undermines the fundamental principle of equal protection as a personal right. In this case, as between that principle and "its later misapplications," the principle must prevail.

D

Our action today makes explicit what JUSTICE POWELL thought implicit in the *Fullilove* lead opinion: Federal racial classifications, like those of a State, must serve a compelling governmental interest, and must be narrowly tailored to further that interest. . . .

Some have questioned the importance of debating the proper standard of review of race-based legislation. . . . But we agree with JUSTICE STEVENS that, "[b]ecause racial characteristics so seldom provide a relevant basis for disparate treatment, and because classifications based on race are potentially so harmful to the entire body politic, it is especially important that the reasons for any such classification be clearly identified and unquestionably legitimate," and that "[r]acial classifications are simply too pernicious to permit any but the most exact connection between justification and classification." *Fullilove* (dissenting opinion) (footnotes omitted). We think that requiring strict scrutiny is the best way to ensure that courts will consistently give racial classifications that kind of detailed examination, both as to ends and as to means. . . .

Finally, we wish to dispel the notion that strict scrutiny is "strict in theory, but fatal in fact." . . . The unhappy persistence of both the practice and the lingering effects of racial discrimination against minority groups in this country is an unfortunate reality, and government is not disqualified from acting in response to it. As recently as 1987, for example, every Justice of this Court agreed that the Alabama Department of Public Safety's "pervasive, systematic, and obstinate discriminatory conduct" justified a narrowly tailored race-based remedy. . . . When race-based action is necessary to further a compelling interest, such action is within constitutional constraints if it satisfies the "narrow tailoring" test this Court has set out in previous cases.

. . .

Because our decision today alters the playing field in some important respects, we think it best to remand the case to the lower courts for further consideration in light of the principles we have announced. . . .

. . .

Accordingly, the judgment of the Court of Appeals is vacated, and the case is remanded for further proceedings consistent with this opinion.

*It is so ordered.*

JUSTICE SCALIA, concurring in part and concurring in the judgment.

I join the opinion of the Court, except Part III-C, and except insofar as it may be inconsistent with the following: In my view, government can never have a "compelling interest" in discriminating on the basis of race in order to "make up" for past racial discrimination in the opposite direction. See *Richmond* v. *J. A. Croson Co.,* 488 U. S. 469, 520 (1989) (SCALIA, J., concurring in judgment). Individuals who have been wronged by unlawful racial discrimination should be made whole; but under our Constitution there can be no such thing as either a creditor or a debtor race. That concept is alien to the Constitution's focus upon the individual, see Amdt. 14, § 1 ("[N]or shall any State . . . deny to *any person*" the equal protection of the laws) (emphasis added), and its rejection of dispositions based on race, see Amdt. 15, § 1 (prohibiting abridgment of the right to vote "on account of race"), or based on blood, see Art. III, § 3 ("[N]o Attainder of Treason shall work Corruption of Blood"); Art. I, § 9, cl. 8 ("No Title of Nobility shall be granted by the United States"). To pursue the concept of racial entitlement—even for the most admirable and benign of purposes—is to reinforce and preserve for future mischief the way of thinking that produced race slavery, race privilege and race hatred. In the eyes of government, we are just one race here. It is American.

It is unlikely, if not impossible, that the challenged program would survive under this understanding of strict scrutiny, but I am content to leave that to be decided on remand.

JUSTICE THOMAS, concurring in part and concurring in the judgment.

I agree with the majority's conclusion that strict scrutiny applies to *all* government classifications based on race. I write separately, however, to express my disagreement with the premise underlying JUSTICE STEVENS' and JUSTICE GINSBURG's dissents: that there is a racial paternalism exception to the principle of equal protection. I believe that there is a "moral [and] constitutional equivalence," . . . between laws designed to subjugate a race and those that distribute benefits on the basis of race in order to foster some current notion of equality. Government cannot make us equal; it can only recognize, respect, and protect us as equal before the law.

That these programs may have been motivated, in part, by good intentions cannot provide refuge from the principle that under our Constitution, the government may not make distinctions on the basis of race. . . .
. . .

In my mind, government-sponsored racial discrimination based on benign prejudice is just as noxious as discrimination inspired by malicious prejudice. In each instance, it is racial discrimination, plain and simple.

JUSTICE STEVENS, with whom JUSTICE GINSBURG joins, dissenting.

Instead of deciding this case in accordance with controlling precedent,

the Court today delivers a disconcerting lecture about the evils of governmental racial classifications. . . .

. . .

## II

The Court's concept of "consistency" assumes that there is no significant difference between a decision by the majority to impose a special
burden on the members of a minority race and a decision by the majority to
provide a benefit to certain members of that minority notwithstanding its
incidental burden on some members of the majority. In my opinion that
assumption is untenable. There is no moral or constitutional equivalence
between a policy that is designed to perpetuate a caste system and one that
seeks to eradicate racial subordination. Invidious discrimination is an en-
gine of oppression, subjugating a disfavored group to enhance or maintain
the power of the majority. Remedial race-based preferences reflect the
opposite impulse: a desire to foster equality in society. No sensible conception of the Government's constitutional obligation to "govern impartially" . . . should ignore this distinction.

. . .

The consistency that the Court espouses would disregard the difference between a "No Trespassing" sign and a welcome mat. It would treat a
Dixiecrat Senator's decision to vote against Thurgood Marshall's confirma-
tion in order to keep African Americans off the Supreme Court as on a par
with President Johnson's evaluation of his nominee's race as a positive
factor. It would equate a law that made black citizens ineligible for military
service with a program aimed at recruiting black soldiers. An attempt by
the majority to exclude members of a minority race from a regulated market is fundamentally different from a subsidy that enables a relatively small
group of newcomers to enter that market. An interest in "consistency"
does not justify treating differences as though they were similarities.

The Court's explanation for treating dissimilar race-based decisions as
though they were equally objectionable is a supposed inability to differentiate between "invidious" and "benign" discrimination. . . . But the term
"affirmative action" is common and well understood. Its presence in everyday parlance shows that people understand the difference between good
intentions and bad. As with any legal concept, some cases may be difficult
to classify, but our equal protection jurisprudence has identified a critical
difference between state action that imposes burdens on a disfavored few
and state action that benefits the few "in spite of" its adverse effects on the
many. . . .

. . .

Moreover, the Court may find that its new "consistency" approach to
race-based classifications is difficult to square with its insistence upon rigidly
separate categories for discrimination against different classes of individuals. For example, as the law currently stands, the Court will apply "inter-

mediate scrutiny" to cases of invidious gender discrimination and "strict scrutiny" to cases of invidious race discrimination, while applying the same standard for benign classifications as for invidious ones. If this remains the law, then today's lecture about "consistency" will produce the anomalous result that the Government can more easily enact affirmative-action programs to remedy discrimination against women than it can enact affirmative-action programs to remedy discrimination against African Americans — even though the primary purpose of the Equal Protection Clause was to end discrimination against the former slaves. . . . When a court becomes preoccupied with abstract standards, it risks sacrificing common sense at the altar of formal consistency.

. . .

## III

The Court's concept of "congruence" assumes that there is no significant difference between a decision by the Congress of the United States to adopt an affirmative-action program and such a decision by a State or a municipality. In my opinion that assumption is untenable. It ignores important practical and legal differences between federal and state or local decisionmakers.

. . .

An additional reason for giving greater deference to the National Legislature than to a local law-making body is that federal affirmative-action programs represent the will of our entire Nation's elected representatives, whereas a state or local program may have an impact on nonresident entities who played no part in the decision to enact it. Thus, in the state or local context, individuals who were unable to vote for the local representatives who enacted a race-conscious program may nonetheless feel the effects of that program. This difference recalls the goals of the Commerce Clause, U. S. Const., Art. I, § 8, cl. 3, which permits Congress to legislate on certain matters of national importance while denying power to the States in this area for fear of undue impact upon out-of-state residents. See *Southern Pacific Co.* v. *Arizona ex rel. Sullivan,* 325 U. S. 761, 767–768, n. 2 (1945) ("[T]o the extent that the burden of state regulation falls on interests outside the state, it is unlikely to be alleviated by the operation of those political restraints normally exerted when interests within the state are affected").

Ironically, after all of the time, effort, and paper this Court has expended in differentiating between federal and state affirmative action, the majority today virtually ignores the issue. . . .

. . .

In my judgment, the Court's novel doctrine of "congruence" is seriously misguided. Congressional deliberations about a matter as important as affirmative action should be accorded far greater deference than those of a State or municipality.

. . .

## IV

. . .

This is the third time in the Court's entire history that it has considered the constitutionality of a federal affirmative-action program. On each of the two prior occasions, the first in 1980, *Fullilove* v. *Klutznick,* 448 U. S. 448, and the second in 1990, *Metro Broadcasting, Inc.* v. *FCC,* 497 U. S. 547, the Court upheld the program. Today the Court explicitly overrules *Metro Broadcasting* (at least in part), and undermines *Fullilove* by recasting the standard on which it rested and by calling even its holding into question. By way of explanation, JUSTICE O'CONNOR advises the federal agencies and private parties that have made countless decisions in reliance on those cases that "we do not depart from the fabric of the law; we restore it." A skeptical observer might ask whether this pronouncement is a faithful application of the doctrine of *stare decisis.* A brief comment on each of the two ailing cases may provide the answer.

In the Court's view, our decision in *Metro Broadcasting* was inconsistent with the rule announced in *Richmond* v. *J. A. Croson Co.* . . . But two decisive distinctions separate those two cases. First, *Metro Broadcasting* involved a federal program, whereas *Croson* involved a city ordinance. *Metro Broadcasting* thus drew primary support from *Fullilove,* which predated *Croson* and which *Croson* distinguished on the grounds of the federal-state dichotomy that the majority today discredits. Although Members of today's majority trumpeted the importance of that distinction in *Croson,* they now reject it in the name of "congruence." It is therefore quite wrong for the Court to suggest today that overruling *Metro Broadcasting* merely restores the *status quo ante,* for the law at the time of that decision was entirely open to the result the Court reached. *Today's* decision is an unjustified departure from settled law.

Second, *Metro Broadcasting*'s holding rested on more than its application of "intermediate scrutiny." Indeed, I have always believed that, labels notwithstanding, the Federal Communications Commission (FCC) program we upheld in that case would have satisfied any of our various standards in affirmative-action cases—including the one the majority fashions today. What truly distinguishes *Metro Broadcasting* from our other affirmative-action precedents is the distinctive goal of the federal program in that case. Instead of merely seeking to remedy past discrimination, the FCC program was intended to achieve future benefits in the form of broadcast diversity. Reliance on race as a legitimate means of achieving diversity was first endorsed by Justice Powell in *Regents of Univ. of Cal.* v. *Bakke.* . . . Later, in *Wygant* v. *Jackson Bd. of Ed.* . . . , I also argued that race is not always irrelevant to governmental decisionmaking, . . . in response, JUSTICE O'CONNOR correctly noted that, although the school board had relied on an interest in providing black teachers to serve as role models for black students, that interest "should not be confused with the very different goal of promoting racial diversity among the faculty." . . . She then added that, because the school board had not relied on an interest in diversity, it was not "necessary to discuss the magnitude of that interest or its applicability in this case." . . .

Thus, prior to *Metro Broadcasting,* the interest in diversity had been mentioned in a few opinions, but it is perfectly clear that the Court had not yet decided whether that interest had sufficient magnitude to justify a racial classification. *Metro Broadcasting,* of course, answered that question in the affirmative. The majority today overrules *Metro Broadcasting* only insofar as it is "inconsistent with [the] holding" that strict scrutiny applies to "benign" racial classifications promulgated by the Federal Government. . . . The proposition that fostering diversity may provide a sufficient interest to justify such a program is *not* inconsistent with the Court's holding today — indeed, the question is not remotely presented in this case — and I do not take the Court's opinion to diminish that aspect of our decision in *Metro Broadcasting.*

. . .

If the 1977 program of race-based set-asides satisfied the strict scrutiny dictated by Justice Powell's vision of the Constitution — a vision the Court expressly endorses today — it must follow as night follows the day that the Court of Appeals' judgment upholding this more carefully crafted program should be affirmed.

. . .

## VI

. . .

JUSTICE SOUTER, with whom JUSTICE GINSBURG and JUSTICE BREYER join, dissenting.

As this case worked its way through the federal courts prior to the grant of certiorari that brought it here, petitioner Adarand Constructors, Inc., was understood to have raised only one significant claim: that before a federal agency may exceed the goals adopted by Congress in implementing a race-based remedial program, the Fifth and Fourteenth Amendments require the agency to make specific findings of discrimination, as under *Richmond* v. *J. A. Croson Co.* . . . sufficient to justify surpassing the congressional objective. . . .

. . .

In these circumstances, I agree with JUSTICE STEVENS's conclusion that *stare decisis* compels the application of *Fullilove.* Although *Fullilove* did not reflect doctrinal consistency, its several opinions produced a result on shared grounds that petitioner does not attack: that discrimination in the construction industry had been subject to government acquiescence, with effects that remain and that may be addressed by some preferential treatment falling within the congressional power under § 5 of the Fourteenth Amendment.

. . .

. . . The Court has long accepted the view that constitutional authority to remedy past discrimination is not limited to the power to forbid its continuation, but extends to eliminating those effects that would otherwise persist and skew the operation of public systems even in the absence of current intent to practice any discrimination. . . . ("Where racial discrimination is concerned, 'the [district] court has not merely the power but the duty to render a decree which will so far as possible eliminate the discriminatory effects of the past as well as bar like discrimination in the future' "). . . . this is so whether the remedial authority is exercised by a court, . . . the Congress . . . or some other legislature. . . . Indeed, a majority of the Court today reiterates that there are circumstances in which Government may, consistently with the Constitution, adopt programs aimed at remedying the effects of past invidious discrimination. . . .

When the extirpation of lingering discriminatory effects is thought to require a catchup mechanism, like the racially preferential inducement under the statutes considered here, the result may be that some members of the historically favored race are hurt by that remedial mechanism, however innocent they may be of any personal responsibility for any discriminatory conduct. When this price is considered reasonable, it is in part because it is a price to be paid only temporarily; if the justification for the preference is eliminating the effects of a past practice, the assumption is that the effects will themselves recede into the past, becoming attenuated and finally disappearing. Thus, Justice Powell wrote in his concurring opinion in *Fullilove* that the "temporary nature of this remedy ensures that a race-conscious program will not last longer than the discriminatory effects it is designed to eliminate." . . .

. . .

JUSTICE GINSBURG, with whom JUSTICE BREYER joins, dissenting.

For the reasons stated by JUSTICE SOUTER, and in view of the attention the political branches are currently giving the matter of affirmative action, I see no compelling cause for the intervention the Court has made in this case. I further agree with JUSTICE STEVENS that, in this area, large deference is owed by the Judiciary to "Congress' institutional competence and constitutional authority to overcome historical racial subjugation." . . . I write separately to underscore not the differences the several opinions in this case display, but the considerable field of agreement — the common understandings and concerns — revealed in opinions that together speak for a majority of the Court.

I

The statutes and regulations at issue, as the Court indicates, were adopted by the political branches in response to an "unfortunate reality": "[t]he unhappy persistence of both the practice and the lingering effects of racial discrimination against minority groups in this country." . . . The

United States suffers from those lingering effects because, for most of our Nation's history, the idea that "we are just one race," . . . was not embraced. For generations, our lawmakers and judges were unprepared to say that there is in this land no superior race, no race inferior to any other. In *Plessy* v. *Ferguson*, . . . not only did this Court endorse the oppressive practice of race segregation, but even Justice Harlan, the advocate of a "color-blind" Constitution, stated:

> "The white race deems itself to be the dominant race in this country. And so it is, in prestige, in achievements, in education, in wealth and in power. So, I doubt not, it will continue to be for all time, if it remains true to its great heritage and holds fast to the principles of constitutional liberty." . . .

Not until *Loving* v. *Virginia*, . . . which held unconstitutional Virginia's ban on interracial marriages, could one say with security that the Constitution and this Court would abide no measure "designed to maintain White Supremacy." . . .

The divisions in this difficult case should not obscure the Court's recognition of the persistence of racial inequality and a majority's acknowledgment of Congress' authority to act affirmatively, not only to end discrimination, but also to counteract discrimination's lingering effects. . . . Those effects, reflective of a system of racial caste only recently ended, are evident in our workplaces, markets, and neighborhoods. Job applicants with identical resumes, qualifications, and interview styles still experience different receptions, depending on their race. White and African-American consumers still encounter different deals. People of color looking for housing still face discriminatory treatment by landlords, real estate agents, and mortgage lenders. Minority entrepreneurs sometimes fail to gain contracts though they are the low bidders, and they are sometimes refused work even after winning contracts. Bias both conscious and unconscious, reflecting traditional and unexamined habits of thought, keeps up barriers that must come down if equal opportunity and nondiscrimination are ever genuinely to become this country's law and practice.

Given this history and its practical consequences, Congress surely can conclude that a carefully designed affirmative action program may help to realize, finally, the "equal protection of the laws" the Fourteenth Amendment has promised since 1868.

. . .

# Cheryl Hopwood *v.* University of Texas

This case was decided in the Fifth Circuit. It was heard, in other words, in the appellate court that includes Texas. The decision in Hopwood was extreme. The Court decided that race can never be used as a factor in admissions decisions. Section III A 2 states this explicitly.

---

FIFTH CIRCUIT, 1996 BEFORE SMITH, WIENER AND DEMOSS, CIRCUIT JUDGES. JERRY E. SMITH, CIRCUIT JUDGE:

With the best of intentions, in order to increase the enrollment of certain favored classes of minority students, the University of Texas School of Law ("the law school") discriminates in favor of those applicants by giving substantial racial preferences in its admissions program. The beneficiaries of this system are blacks and Mexican Americans, to the detriment of whites and non-preferred minorities. The question we decide today in No. 94-50664 is whether the Fourteenth Amendment permits the school to discriminate in this way.

We hold that it does not. The law school has presented no compelling justification, under the Fourteenth Amendment or Supreme Court precedent, that allows it to continue to elevate some races over others, even for the wholesome purpose of correcting perceived racial imbalance in the student body. "Racial preferences appear to 'even the score' . . . only if one embraces the proposition that our society is appropriately viewed as divided into races, making it right that an injustice rendered in the past to a black man should be compensated for by discriminating against a white." . . .

As a result of its diligent efforts in this case, the district court concluded that the law school may continue to impose racial preferences. . . . In No. 94-50664, we reverse and remand, concluding that the law school may not use race as a factor in law school admissions. Further, we instruct the court to reconsider the issue of damages in accordance with the legal standards we now explain. In No. 94-50569, regarding the denial of intervention by two black student groups, we dismiss the appeal for want of jurisdiction.

I

A

The University of Texas School of Law is one of the nation's leading law schools, consistently ranking in the top twenty. . . .

Of course, the law school did not rely upon numbers alone. The admissions office necessarily exercised judgment in interpreting the individual scores of applicants, taking into consideration factors such as the strength of a student's undergraduate education, the difficulty of his major, and significant trends in his own grades and the undergraduate grades at his respective college (such as grade inflation). Admissions personnel also considered what qualities each applicant might bring to his law school class. Thus, the law school could consider an applicant's background, life experiences, and outlook. Not surprisingly, these hard-to-quantify factors were especially significant for marginal candidates.

Because of the large number of applicants and potential admissions factors, the TI's [Texas Index's] administrative usefulness was its ability to sort candidates. For the class entering in 1992 — the admissions group at issue in this case — the law school placed the typical applicant in one of three categories according to his TI scores: "presumptive admit," "presumptive deny," or a middle "discretionary zone." An applicant's TI category determined how extensive a review his application would receive.
. . .

Applicants in the presumptive denial category also received little consideration. . . .

Applications in the middle range were subjected to the most extensive scrutiny. . . .

Blacks and Mexican Americans were treated differently from other candidates, however. First, compared to whites and non-preferred minorities, the TI ranges that were used to place them into the three admissions categories were lowered to allow the law school to consider and admit more of them. In March 1992, for example, the presumptive TI admission score for resident whites and non-preferred minorities was 199. Mexican Americans and blacks needed a TI of only 189 to be presumptively admitted. The difference in the presumptive-deny ranges is even more striking. The presumptive denial score for "nonminorities" was 192; the same score for blacks and Mexican Americans was 179.
. . .

These disparate standards greatly affected a candidate's chance of admission. For example, by March 1992, because the presumptive *denial* score for whites was a TI of 192 or lower, and the presumptive *admit* TI for minorities was 189 or higher, a minority candidate with a TI of 189 or above almost certainly would be *admitted,* even though his score was considerably below the level at which a white candidate almost certainly would be *rejected.* Out of the pool of resident applicants who fell within this range

(189–192 inclusive), 100% of blacks and 90% of Mexican Americans, but only 6% of whites, were offered admission.

The stated purpose of this lowering of standards was to meet an "aspiration" of admitting a class consisting of 10% Mexican Americans and 5% blacks, proportions roughly comparable to the percentages of those races graduating from Texas colleges. The law school found meeting these "goals" difficult, however, because of uncertain acceptance rates and the variable quality of the applicant pool. In 1992, for example, the entering class contained 41 blacks and 55 Mexican Americans, respectively 8% and 10.7% of the class.

In addition to maintaining separate presumptive TI levels for minorities and whites, the law school ran a segregated application evaluation process. Upon receiving an application form, the school color-coded it according to race. If a candidate failed to designate his race, he was presumed to be in a nonpreferential category. Thus, race was always an overt part of the review of any applicant's file.

. . .

B

Cheryl Hopwood, Douglas Carvell, Kenneth Elliott, and David Rogers (the "plaintiffs") applied for admission to the 1992 entering law school class. All four were white residents of Texas and were rejected.

The plaintiffs were considered as discretionary zone candidates. . . .

II

. . .

After a bench trial, the district court held that the school had violated the plaintiffs' equal protection rights. . . . The plaintiff's victory was pyrrhic at best, however, as the court refused to enjoin the law school from using race in admissions decisions or to grant damages beyond a one-dollar nominal award to each plaintiff. The district court, however, did grant declaratory relief and ordered that the plaintiffs be allowed to apply again without paying the requisite fee. . . .

The district court began by recognizing the proper constitutional standard under which to evaluate the admissions program: strict scrutiny. . . . As it was undisputed that the school had treated applicants disparately based upon the color of their skin, the court asked whether the law school process (1) served a compelling government interest and (2) was narrowly tailored to the achievement of that goal. Under the first prong of the test, the court held that two of the law school's five proffered reasons met constitutional muster: (1) "obtaining the educational benefits that flow from a racially and ethnically diverse student body" and (2) "the objective of overcoming past effects of discrimination." . . .

Significantly, on the second justification, the court rejected the plaintiffs' argument that the analysis of past discrimination should be limited to that of the law school; instead, the court held that the State of Texas's "institutions of higher education are inextricably linked to the primary and secondary schools in the system." . . . Accordingly, the court found that Texas's long history of racially discriminatory practices in primary and secondary schools in its not-too-distant past had the following present effects at UT law: "the law school's lingering reputation in the minority community, particularly with prospective students, as a 'white' school; an underrepresentation of minorities in the student body; and some perception that the law school is a hostile environment for minorities." . . . The court also noted that "were the Court to limit its review to the University of Texas, the Court would still find a 'strong evidentiary basis for concluding that remedial action is necessary.' " . . .

The court next evaluated whether the Texas program was narrowly tailored to further these goals. . . . Thus, the court struck down the school's use of separate admissions committees for applications in the discretionary zone . . . and in *dictum* speculated that presumptive denial lines would not pass muster, as many white candidates would get no review, while similarly situated minorities would. . . .

Though it declared that the law school's 1992 admissions program violated the plaintiffs' equal protection rights, the court granted little relief. First, the court did not order that the plaintiffs be admitted to the law school. Instead, it used what it saw as analogous title VII caselaw on burden-shifting to hold that while the state had committed a constitutional violation, the plaintiffs had the ultimate burden of proving damages. . . . The court then found that the defendants had proffered a legitimate, non-discriminatory reason for denying the plaintiffs admission and that the plaintiffs had not met their burden of showing that they would have been admitted but for the unlawful system. . . .

Moreover, the court held that the plaintiffs were not entitled to prospective injunctive relief, because "of the law school's voluntary change to a procedure, which on paper and from the testimony, appears to remedy the defects the Court has found in the 1992 procedure." . . .

Finally, the court determined that the only appropriate relief was a declaratory judgment and an order allowing the plaintiffs to reapply to the school without charge. . . . No compensatory or punitive damages, the court reasoned, could be awarded where the plaintiffs had proven no harm. Moreover, the court reasoned that as the law school had promised to change its admissions program by abandoning the two-committee system, no prospective injunctive relief was justified.

## III

The central purpose of the Equal Protection Clause "is to prevent the States from purposefully discriminating between individuals on the basis of race." . . .

. . .

Strict scrutiny is necessary because the mere labeling of a classification by the government as "benign" or "remedial" is meaningless. . . .

Under the strict scrutiny analysis, we ask two questions: (1) Does the racial classification serve a compelling government interest, and (2) is it narrowly tailored to the achievement of that goal? . . .

. . .

## A

### 1

Justice Powell's separate opinion in *Bakke* provided the original impetus for recognizing diversity as a compelling state interest in higher education. In that case, Allan Bakke, a white male, was denied admission to the Medical School of the University of California at Davis, a state-run institution. Claiming that the State had discriminated against him impermissibly because it operated two separate admissions programs for the medical school, he brought suit under the state constitution, title VI, and the Equal Protection Clause.

. . .

Notably, because the first step in reviewing an affirmative action program is a determination of the state's interests at stake, it often is the determinative step. Justice Powell outlined the four state interests proffered by the *Bakke* defendants:

> The special admissions program purports to serve the purposes of:
> (i) "reducing the historic deficit of traditionally disfavored minorities in medical schools and in the medical profession"; (ii) countering the effects of societal discrimination; (iii) increasing the number of physicians who will practice in communities currently underserved; and (iv) *obtaining the educational benefits that flow from an ethnically diverse student body. . . .*

Justice Powell reasoned that the second and third justifications — remedying societal discrimination and providing role models — were never appropriate. He determined that any remedial justification was limited to eliminating "identified discrimination" with "disabling effects." . . . He specifically emphasized that a particularized finding of a constitutional or statutory violation must be present before a remedy is justified. He determined not only that such findings were not present in *Bakke,* but that the medical school was not even in a position to make such findings. . . .

Justice Powell further reasoned that diversity is a sufficient justification for limited racial classification. . . . "[The attainment of a diverse student body] clearly is a constitutionally permissible goal for an institution of higher education." . . . He argued that diversity of minorities' viewpoints furthered "academic freedom," an interest under the Constitution. While acknowledging that "academic freedom" does not appear as a constitutional right, he argued that it had "long . . . been viewed as a special concern of the First Amendment." . . .

Justice Powell presented this "special concern" as in tension with the Fourteenth Amendment. . . .

Justice Powell speculated that a program in which "race or ethnic background may be deemed a 'plus' in a particular applicant's file, yet does not insulate the individual from comparison with all the other candidates for the available seats," might pass muster. . . .

Under this conception of the Fourteenth Amendment, a program that considered a host of factors that include race would be constitutional, even if an applicant's race "tipped the scales" among qualified applicants. . . .

*2*

Here, the plaintiffs [Hopwood and the other white applicants] argue that diversity is not a compelling governmental interest under superseding Supreme Court precedent. Instead, they believe that the Court finally has recognized that only the *remedial* use of race is compelling. In the alternative, the plaintiffs assert that the district court misapplied Justice Powell's *Bakke* standard, as the law school program here uses race as a strong determinant rather than a mere "plus" factor and, in any case, the preference is not narrowly applied. The law school maintains, on the other hand, that Justice Powell's formulation in *Bakke* is law and must be followed — at least in the context of higher education.

We agree with the plaintiffs that any consideration of race or ethnicity by the law school for the purpose of achieving a diverse student body is not a compelling interest under the Fourteenth Amendment. Justice Powell's argument in *Bakke* garnered only his own vote and has never represented the view of a majority of the Court in *Bakke* or any other case. Moreover, subsequent Supreme Court decisions regarding education state that non-remedial state interests will never justify racial classifications. Finally, the classification of persons on the basis of race for the purpose of diversity frustrates, rather than facilitates, the goals of equal protection.
. . .

Within the general principles of the Fourteenth Amendment, the use of race in admissions for diversity in higher education contradicts, rather than furthers, the aims of equal protection. Diversity fosters, rather than minimizes, the use of race. It treats minorities as a group, rather than as individuals. It may further remedial purposes but, just as likely, may promote improper racial stereotypes, thus fueling racial hostility.

The use of race, in and of itself, to choose students simply achieves a student body that looks different. Such a criterion is no more rational on its own terms than would be choices based upon the physical size or blood type of applicants. Thus, the Supreme Court has long held that governmental actors cannot justify their decisions solely because of race. . . .

Accordingly, we see the caselaw as sufficiently established that the use of ethnic diversity simply to achieve racial heterogeneity, even as part of the consideration of a number of factors, is unconstitutional. Were we to decide otherwise, we would contravene precedent that we are not authorized to challenge.

While the use of race *per se* is proscribed, state-supported schools may reasonably consider a host of factors — some of which may have some correlation with race — in making admissions decisions. The federal courts have no warrant to intrude on those executive and legislative judgments unless the distinctions intrude on specific provisions of federal law or the Constitution.

A university may properly favor one applicant over another because of his ability to play the cello, make a downfield tackle, or understand chaos theory. An admissions process may also consider an applicant's home state or relationship to school alumni. Law schools specifically may look at things such as unusual or substantial extracurricular activities in college, which may be atypical factors affecting undergraduate grades. Schools may even consider factors such as whether an applicant's parents attended college or the applicant's economic and social background.

For this reason, race often is said to be justified in the diversity context, not on its own terms, but as a proxy for other characteristics that institutions of higher education value but that do not raise similar constitutional concerns. Unfortunately, this approach simply replicates the very harm that the Fourteenth Amendment was designed to eliminate.

The assumption is that a certain individual possesses characteristics by virtue of being a member of a certain racial group. This assumption, however, does not withstand scrutiny. . . .

To believe that a person's race controls his point of view is to stereotype him. . . .

Instead, individuals, with their own conceptions of life, further diversity of viewpoint. Plaintiff Hopwood is a fair example of an applicant with a unique background. She is the now-thirty-two-year-old wife of a member of the Armed Forces stationed in San Antonio and, more significantly, is raising a severely handicapped child. Her circumstance would bring a different perspective to the law school. The school might consider this an advantage to her in the application process, or it could decide that her family situation would be too much of a burden on her academic performance.
. . .

The Court also has recognized that government's use of racial classifications serves to stigmatize. . . .

Finally, the use of race to achieve diversity undercuts the ultimate goal of the Fourteenth Amendment: the end of racially-motivated state action. Justice Powell's conception of race as a "plus" factor would allow race always to be a potential factor in admissions decisionmaking. While Justice Blackmun recognized the tension inherent in using race-conscious remedies to achieve a race-neutral society, he nevertheless accepted it as necessary. . . . Several Justices who, unlike Justices Powell and Blackmun, are still on the Court, have now renounced toleration of this tension, however. . . . ("The dissent's watered down version of equal protection review effectively assures that race will always be relevant in American life, and that the 'ultimate goal' of 'eliminat[ing] entirely from government decisionmaking such irrelevant factors as a human being's race . . . will never be achieved.' ") (quoting *Wygant,* 476 U.S. at 320, 106 S.Ct. at 1871 (Stevens, J., dissenting)).

In sum, the use of race to achieve a diverse student body, whether as a proxy for permissible characteristics, simply cannot be a state interest compelling enough to meet the steep standard of strict scrutiny. These latter factors may, in fact, turn out to be substantially correlated with race, but the key is that race itself not be taken into account. Thus, that portion of the district court's opinion upholding the diversity rationale is reversibly flawed.

B

We now turn to the district court's determination that "the remedial purpose of the law school's affirmative action program is a compelling government objective." . . .

. . .

Because a state does not have a compelling state interest in remedying the present effects of past *societal* discrimination, however, we must examine the district court's legal determination that the relevant governmental entity is the system of education within the state as a whole. Moreover, we also must review the court's identification of what types of present effects of past discrimination, if proven, would be sufficient under strict scrutiny review. Finally, where the state actor puts forth a remedial justification for its racial classifications, the district court must make a "factual determination" as to whether remedial action is necessary. . . . We review such factual rulings for clear error.

. . .

Applying the teachings of *Croson* and *Wygant,* we conclude that the district court erred in expanding the remedial justification to reach all public education within the State of Texas. The Supreme Court repeatedly has warned that the use of racial remedies must be carefully limited, and a remedy reaching all education within a state addresses a putative injury that is vague and amorphous. It has "no logical stopping point." . . .

The district court's holding employs no viable limiting principle. If a state can "remedy" the present effects of past discrimination in its primary and secondary schools, it also would be allowed to award broad-based preferences in hiring, government contracts, licensing, and any other state activity that in some way is affected by the educational attainment of the applicants. . . .

No one disputes that in the past, Texas state actors have discriminated against some minorities in public schools. In this sense, some lingering effects of such discrimination is not "societal," if that term is meant to exclude all state action. But the very program at issue here shows how remedying such past wrongs may be expanded beyond any reasonable limits.

Even if, *arguendo,* the state is the proper government unit to scrutinize, the law school's admissions program would not withstand our review. For the admissions scheme to pass constitutional muster, the State of Texas, through its legislature, would have to find that past segregation has present effects; it would have to determine the magnitude of those present effects; and it would need to limit carefully the "plus" given to applicants to remedy that harm. A broad program that sweeps in all minorities with a remedy that is in no way related to past harms cannot survive constitutional scrutiny. Obviously, none of those predicates has been satisfied here.

. . .

In sum, for purposes of determining whether the law school's admissions system properly can act as a remedy for the present effects of past discrimination, we must identify the law school as the relevant alleged past discriminator. The fact that the law school ultimately may be subject to the directives of others, such as the board of regents, the university president, or the legislature, does not change the fact that the relevant putative discriminator in this case is still the law school. In order for any of these entities to direct a racial preference program at the law school, it must be because of past wrongs at the school.

. . .

As a legal matter, the district court erred in concluding that the first and third effects it identified — bad reputation and hostile environment — were sufficient to sustain the use of race in the admissions process. The Fourth Circuit examined similar arguments in *Podberesky,* a recent case that struck down the use of race-based scholarships. The university in that case sought, in part, to justify a separate scholarship program based solely upon race because of the university's "poor reputation within the African-American community" and because "the atmosphere on campus [was] perceived as being hostile to African-American students." . . .

The *Podberesky* court rejected the notion that either of these rationales could support the single-race scholarship program. . . .

. . .

By the late 1960's, the school had implemented its first program designed to recruit minorities, *id.* at 557, and it now engages in an extensive minority recruiting program that includes a significant amount of scholarship money. The vast majority of the faculty, staff, and students at the law school had absolutely nothing to do with any discrimination that the law school practiced in the past.

. . .

Even if the law school's alleged current lingering reputation in the minority community — and the perception that the school is a hostile environment for minorities — were considered to be the present effects of past discrimination, rather than the result of societal discrimination, they could not constitute compelling state interests justifying the use of racial classifications in admissions. A bad reputation within the minority community is alleviated not by the consideration of race in admissions, but by school action designed directly to enhance its reputation in that community.

. . .

The law school wisely concentrates only on the second effect the district court identified: underrepresentation of minorities because of past discrimination. The law school argues that we should consider the prior discrimination by the State of Texas and its educational system rather than of the law school. The school contends that this prior discrimination by the state had a direct effect on the educational attainment of the pool of minority applicants and that the discriminatory admissions program was implemented partially to discharge the school's duty of eliminating the vestiges of past segregation.

As we have noted, the district court accepted the law school's argument that past discrimination on the part of the Texas school system (including primary and secondary schools), reaching back perhaps as far as the education of the parents of today's students, justifies the current use of racial classifications. No one disputes that Texas has a history of racial discrimination in education. We have already discussed, however, that the *Croson* Court unequivocally restricted the proper scope of the remedial interest to the state actor that had previously discriminated. 488 U.S. at 499, 109 S.Ct. at 724–25. The district court squarely found that "[i]n recent history, there is no evidence of overt officially sanctioned discrimination at the University of Texas." . . . As a result, past discrimination in education, other than at the law school, cannot justify the present consideration of race in law school admissions.

. . .

## IV

While the district court declared the admissions program unconstitutional, it granted the plaintiffs only limited relief. They had requested injunctive relief ordering that they be admitted to law school, compensatory and punitive damages, and prospective injunctive relief preventing the school from using race as a factor in admissions.

### A

We must decide who bears the burden of proof on the damages issue. The district court refused to order the plaintiffs' admission (or award any compensatory damages), as it found that they had not met their burden of persuasion in attempting to show that they would have been admitted absent the unconstitutional system. . . . The law school now argues that the plaintiffs had the burden of persuasion on the issue of damages and that the district court's findings are not clearly erroneous. The plaintiffs maintain, as they did in the district court, that once they had shown a constitutional violation, the burden of persuasion shifted to the school to show that the denial of admission was not caused by that violation.

The well-established rule is that in order to collect money damages, plaintiffs must prove that they have been injured. . . .

. . .

Obviously, if the school proves that a plaintiff would not have gained admittance to the law school under a race-blind system, that plaintiff would not be entitled to an injunction admitting him to the school. On the other hand, the law school's inability to establish a plaintiff's non-admission — if that occurs on remand — opens a panoply of potential relief, depending in part upon what course that plaintiff's career has taken since trial in mid-1994. It then would be up to the district court, in its able discretion, to decide whether money damages can substitute for an order of immediate admission — relief that would ring hollow for a plaintiff for whom an education at the law school now is of little or no benefit.

Additionally, the district court erred in holding that plaintiffs did not prove that defendants had committed intentional discrimination under title VI. "Intentional discrimination," as used in this context, means that a plaintiff must prove "that the governmental actor, in adopting or employing the challenged practices or undertaking the challenged action, *intended* to treat similarly situated persons differently on the basis of race." . . . While we agree with the district court's conclusion that the various defendants acted in good faith, there is no question that they intended to treat the plaintiffs differently on account of their race.

. . .

B

. . .

According to the district court, the school had abandoned the admissions procedure — consisting of the separate minority subcommittee — that was used in 1992, 1993 and 1994. The court reasoned that, as a new procedure was developed for 1995, a prospective injunction against the school was inappropriate. We conclude, however, that, while the district court may have been correct in deciding that the new procedure eliminates the constitutional flaws that the district court identified in the 1992 system, there is no indication that the new system will cure the additional constitutional defects we now have explained.

The new system utilizes a small "administrative admissions group" and does not use presumptive admission and denial scores. . . . Most significantly, there is no indication that in employing the new plan, the law school will cease to consider race *per se* in making its admissions decisions. To the contrary, as the district court recognized, the law school continues to assert that overt racial preferences are necessary to the attainment of its goals. . . .

The district court has already granted some equitable relief: It directed that the plaintiffs be permitted to re-apply to the law school without incurring further administrative costs. In accordance with this opinion, the plaintiffs are entitled to apply under a system of admissions that will not discriminate against anyone on the basis of race. Moreover, the plaintiffs have shown that it is likely that the law school will continue to take race into account in admissions unless it receives further judicial instruction to the effect that it may not do so for the purpose of (1) obtaining a diverse student body; (2) altering the school's reputation in the community; (3) combating the school's perceived hostile environment toward minorities; or (4) remedying the present effects of past discrimination by actors other than the law school.

It is not necessary, however, for us to order at this time that the law school be enjoined, as we are confident that the conscientious administration at the school, as well as its attorneys, will heed the directives contained in this opinion. If an injunction should be needed in the future, the district court, in its discretion, can consider its parameters without our assistance. Accordingly, we leave intact that court's refusal to enter an injunction.

C

The plaintiffs contend that the district court's application of the wrong standard causes it to deny punitive damages. The plaintiffs aver that the court applied an animus standard, when it should have asked whether the school acted with "reckless indifference" to their constitutional rights. They ask for a remand on this issue.

It is not apparent, from the record, what standard the district court applied in considering the punitive damages issue. The court did determine, however, that the law school had always acted in good faith. This is a difficult area of the law, in which the law school erred with the best of intentions. As a result, the plaintiffs have not met the federal standard for punitive damages as stated in *Smith* v. *Wade,* 461 U.S. 30, 56, 103 S.Ct. 1625, 1640, 75 L.Ed.2d 632 (1983). Thus, we agree with the district court that punitive damages are not warranted. We note, however, that if the law school continues to operate a disguised or overt racial classification system in the future, its actors could be subject to actual and punitive damages. . . .

# References

Affirmative action on the line. 1995. *Chronicle of Higher Education,* April 28.

*Amherst Student.* 1991. April 3, pp. 1–2.

Arthur, W., Jr., D. Doverspike, and R. Fuentes. 1992. Recipients' affective responses to affirmative action interventions: A cross-cultural perspective. *Behavioral Sciences and the Law* 10:229–43.

Ayers, L. R. 1992. Perceptions of affirmative action among its beneficiaries. *Social Justice Research* 5:223–38.

Becker, G. S. 1971. *A theory of discrimination.* 2d ed. Chicago: University of Chicago Press.

Behr, P. 1995. Crucial break or unjustified crutch? *Washington Post,* March 10, p. 1.

Belkin, L. 1989. Bars to equality of sexes seen as eroding, slowly. *New York Times,* August 20, pp. 1, 26.

Bell, D. 1987. Whites make big gains under broadened selection criteria. *Los Angeles Daily Journal,* September 1, p. 4.

Bendick, M., Jr. 1997. *Declaration.* Statement submitted to the Supreme Court of California in response to Proposition 209, September 26.

Birnbaum, J. H. 1995. Turning back the clock. *Time,* March 20, 36.

Birt, C. M., and K. L. Dion. 1987. Relative deprivation theory and responses to discrimination in a gay male and lesbian sample. *British Journal of Social Psychology* 26:139–45.

Biskupic, J. 1992. After nineteen years, racial job-bias case isn't over yet. *Washington Post,* November 23, pp. 1, 12.

Blair-Loy, M. 1996. Career patterns of executive women in finance: An optimal matching analysis. Manuscript, Department of Sociology, University of Chicago.

Bovard, J. 1996. Here comes the goon squad. *American Spectator,* July, 36.

Brimelow, P. 1992. Spiral of silence. *Forbes,* May 25, 76–77.

Brimelow, P., and L. Spencer. 1993. When quotas replace merit, everybody suffers. *Forbes,* February 15, 80–102.

Brimmer, A. F. 1995. The economic cost of discrimination against black Americans. In *Economic perspectives on affirmative action,* ed. M. C. Simms, 11–29. Washington, DC: Joint Center for Political and Economic Studies.

Browne, I., ed. 1998. *Latinas and African American women at work: Race, gender, and economic inequality.* New York: Russell Sage Foundation.

Bruno, A. 1995. *CRS Report for Congress: Affirmative action in employment.* Washington, DC: Congressional Research Service, Library of Congress, January 17.

Bryan, K. 1996. Mend it, don't end it: The affirmative action debate. *Outlook* 90:8–11.

Bunzel, J. H. 1992. *Race relations on campus: Stanford students speak.* Stanford: Stanford Alumni Association.

Burd, S. 1995. Private colleges try to keep a low profile. *Chronicle of Higher Education,* April 28, p. A19.

Bureau of National Affairs. 1986. *Affirmative action today: A legal and practical analysis.* BNA special report. Washington, DC: Bureau of National Affairs.

Cage, M. C. 1990. Government officials urged to create incentives for colleges to increase minority enrollment. *Chronicle of Higher Education,* December 12, p. A17.

Cancio, S., T. D. Evans, and D. J. Maume. 1996. Reconsidering the declining significance of race: Racial differences in early career wages. *American Sociological Review* 61 (August): 541–56; and rejoinder to comment by G. Farknas and K. Vicknair, 561–64.

Carter, S. L. 1991. *Reflections of an affirmative action baby.* New York: Basic Books.

Cassirer, N. R., and B. F. Reskin. 1998. The effect of organizational context on women's and men's attachment to their jobs. Manuscript, Department of Sociology, Notre Dame University, South Bend, IN.

Catalyst. 1996. *Women in corporate leadership.* New York: Catalyst.

———. 1998. *Women of color in corporate management: Dynamics of career advancement.* New York: Catalyst.

Chan, S., and L. Wang. 1991. Racism and the model minority: Asian-Americans in higher education. In *The racial crisis in American higher education,* ed. P. G. Altbach and K. Lomotey. Albany: State University of New York.

Chávez, L. 1991. *Out of the barrio.* New York: Basic Books.

Clayton, S. D. 1989. The recognition of discrimination in a minimal-information format. Paper presented at the eighty-seventh meeting of the American Psychological Association, New Orleans, LA, August.

Clayton, S. D., and F. J. Crosby. 1992. *Justice, gender, and affirmative action.* Ann Arbor: University of Michigan Press.

Clayton, S. D., and S. S. Tangri. 1989. The justice of affirmative action. In *Affirmative action in perspective,* ed. F. Blanchard and F. Crosby, 177–92. New York: Springer-Verlag.

*Congressional Record.* 1995. Senate: Act to end unfair preferential treatment, March 3.

Connerly, W. 1995. UC must end affirmative action. *San Francisco Chronicle,* May 3.

Conrad, C. 1995. The economic cost of affirmative action. In *Economic perspectives on affirmative action,* ed. M. C. Simms, 33–53. Washington, DC: Joint Center for Political and Economic Studies.

Cox, T. H., and S. Blake. 1991. Managing cultural diversity: Implications for organizational competitiveness. *Academy of Management Executive* 5:45–56.

Crocker, J., and B. Major. 1989. Social stigma and self-esteem: The self-protective properties of stigma. *Psychological Review* 96:608–30.

Crosby, F. J. 1982. *Relative deprivation and working women.* New York: Oxford University Press.

———. 1984. The denial of personal discrimination. *American Behavioral Scientist* 27:371–86.

————. 1994. Understanding affirmative action. *Basic and Applied Social Psychology* 15:13–41.

————. 1995. The psychology of affirmative action. Presentation at the McCormack Institute of Public Policy, Boston, MA, December.

————. 1996. A rose by any other name. In *Affirmative action: Quotas and equality,* ed. K. Arioli, 151–67. Zurich, Switzerland: Swiss National Science Foundation.

Crosby, F. J., S. D. Clayton, K. Hemker, and O. Alksnis. 1986. Cognitive biases in the perception of discrimination: The importance of format. *Sex Roles* 14:637–46.

Crosby, F. J., and S. D. Herzberger. 1996. For affirmative action. In *Affirmative action: Pros and cons of policy and practice,* ed. R. J. Simon, 3–109. Washington, DC: American University Press.

Dale, C. V. 1995. *Congressional Research Service Report to Robert Dole: Compilation and overview of federal laws and regulations establishing affirmative action goals or other preferences based on race, gender, and ethnicity.* Washington, DC: Congressional Research Service, Library of Congress, February 17.

Dass, P., and B. Parker. 1999. Strategies for managing human resource diversity: From resistance to learning. *Academy of Management Executive* 13 (2): 68–80.

Deaux, K., and J. C. Ullman. 1983. *Women of steel.* New York: Praeger.

D'Emilio, J. 1983. *Sexual politics, sexual communities: The making of a homosexual minority in the U.S., 1940–1970.* Chicago: University of Chicago Press.

Dionne, E. J., Jr. 1989. Struggle for work and family fueling women's movement. *New York Times,* August 22, pp. A1, A18.

Donohue, J. J. 1986. Is Title VII efficient? *University of Pennsylvania Law Review* 134:1411–31.

Donohue, J. J., III, and J. Heckman. 1991. Continuous versus episodic change: The impact of civil rights policy on the economic status of blacks. *Journal of Economic Literature* 29 (December): 1603–43.

D'Souza, D. 1991. *Illiberal education: The politics of race and sex on campus.* New York: Free Press.

————. 1991. Illiberal education: Current controversies in American higher education. *Atlantic* 267 (3): 51–72.

Eastland, T. 1996. Powell preferred. *National Review,* February 12, 20.

*Economic Report of the President* 1995. Washington, DC: U.S. Government Printing Office.

Edsall, T., and M. Edsall. 1991. Race. *Atlantic,* May, 73.

Farkas, G., and K. Vicknair. 1996. Appropriate tests of racial wage discrimination require controls for cognitive skills: Comment on Cancio, Evans, and Maume. *American Sociological Review* 61 (August): 557–60.

Ferdman, B. M. 1997. Values about fairness in the ethnically diverse workplace. *Business and Contemporary World* 9:191–208.

Ferdman, B. M., and S. E. Brody. 1996. Models of diversity training. In *Handbook of intercultural training,* 2d ed., ed. D. Landis and R. Bhagat, 282–303. Thousand Oaks, CA: Sage.

Ferguson, R. F. 1993. *New evidence on the growing value of skill and consequences for racial disparity and returns to schooling.* No. H-93-106 Cambridge, MA: Malcolm Wiener Center for Social Policy, Harvard University.

————. 1995. Shifting challenges: Fifty years of economic change toward black-white earnings equality. *Daedalus* 124 (winter): 37–76.

Ferguson, T. W. 1995. Race (etc.) preferences on the line. *Wall Street Journal,* March 14, p. A16.

Fisher, A. B. 1985. Businessmen like to hire by the numbers. *Fortune,* September 16, 26, 28–30.

Ford, D. L. 1988. Minority and non-minority MBA progress in business. In *Ensuring minority success in corporate management,* ed. D. E. Thompson and N. DiTomaso, 57–69. New York: Plenum.

Freedberg, L. 1995. The enforcer. *San Francisco Chronicle,* June 4, p. 1.

Freeman, R. B. 1973. Changes in the labor market for black Americans, 1948–1972. In *Brookings Papers on Economic Activity,* ed. A. Okun and G. Perry, 67–132. Washington, DC: Brookings Institution.

Gallup Short Subjects. 1995. *Gallup Poll Monthly* 358 (July): 34–61.

Garcia, L. T., N. Erskine, K. Hawn, and S. R. Casmay. 1981. The effect of affirmative action on attributions about minority group members. *Journal of Personality* 49:427–37.

Glazer, N. 1988. The future of preferential affirmative action. In *Eliminating racism: Profiles in controversy,* ed. P. A. Katz and D. A. Taylor. New York: Plenum.

Gould, S. J. 1981. *The mismeasure of man.* New York: W. W. Norton.

Gross, E. 1968. *Plus ça change . . . ?* The sexual structure of occupations over time. *Social Problems* 16:198–208.

Groups at odds over affirmative action revisions. 1995. *San Diego Union-Tribune,* September 13, p. AA-2.

Guimond, S., and L. Dubé. 1983. Relative deprivation theory and the Quebec Nationalist Movement: On the cognitive-emotion distinction and the personal-group deprivation issue. *Journal of Personality and Social Psychology* 44:526–35.

Hafer, C. L., and J. M. Olson. 1989. Beliefs in a just world and reactions to personal deprivation. *Journal of Personality* 57:799–823.

Hanushek, E. 1978. Ethnic income variations: Magnitudes and explanations. In *Essays and data on American ethnic groups,* ed. T. Sowell, 139–66. Washington, DC: Urban Institute.

*The harassed staffer's guide to employment and training policy.* 1995. Baltimore: Johns Hopkins University, Sar Levitan Center for Social Policy Studies.

Harwood, R. 1995. The new elite in American society. *Cosmos,* 13–19.

Heckman, J., and B. Paynor. 1989. Determining the impact of federal anti-discrimination policy on the economic status of blacks: A study of South Carolina. *American Economic Review* 79 (1): 138–77.

Heckman, J. J., and P. Siegelman. 1993. The urban institute audit studies: Their methods and findings. In *Clear and convincing evidence: Measurement of discrimination in America,* ed. M. Fix and R. J. Struyk. Washington, DC: Urban Institute.

Heilman, M. E. 1994. Affirmative action: Some unintended consequences for working women. In *Research in organizational behavior,* ed. B. Staw and L. Cummings, 125–69. Greenwich, CT: JAI Press.

———. 1996. Affirmative action's contradictory consequences. *Journal of Social Issues* 52:105–9.

Heilman, M. E., C. J. Block, and J. A. Lucas. 1992. Presumed incompetent? Stigmatization and affirmative action efforts. *Journal of Applied Psychology* 77:536–44.

Heilman, M. E., C. Block, and P. Stathatos. 1997. The affirmative action stigma of incompetence: Effects of performance information ambiguity. *Academy of Management Journal* 40 (3): 603–25.

Heilman, M. E., J. A. Lucas, and S. R. Kaplow. 1990. Self-derogating consequences of preferential selection: The moderating role of initial self-confidence. *Organizational Behavior and Human Decision Process* 46:202–16.

Heilman, M. E., W. F. McCullough, and D. Gilbert. 1996. The other side of affirmative action: Reactions of non-beneficiaries to sex-based preferential selection. *Journal of Applied Psychology* 81:346–57.

Heilman, M. E., J. C. Rivero, and J. F. Brett. 1991. Skirting the competence issue: Effects of sex-based preferential selection on task choices of women and men. *Journal of Applied Psychology* 76:99–105.

Heilman, M. E., M. C. Simon, and D. P. Repper. 1987. Intentionally favored, unintentionally harmed? The impact of gender-based preferential selection on self-perceptions and self-evaluations. *Journal of Applied Psychology* 72: 62–68.

Hellerstein, J. K., D. Neumark, and K. R. Troske. 1998. Market forces and sex discrimination. Manuscript, Department of Sociology, University of Maryland, College Park.

Henry, W. A., III. 1991. What price preference? *Time,* September 30, 30–31.

Hernandez, R. 1990. Diversity: Don't go to work without it. *Hispanic Business,* September, 18–22.

Herrnstein, R. J., and C. Murray. 1994. *The bell curve: Intelligence and class structure in American life.* New York: Free Press.

Hersch, J. 1991. Equal employment opportunity law and firm profitability. *Journal of Human Resources* 26:139–53.

Hochschild, J. 1995. *Facing up to the American dream.* Princeton, NJ: Princeton University Press.

Holmes, S. A. 1991. When grass looks greener on this side of the fence. *New York Times,* April 21, p. E6.

Holzer, H. J., and D. Neumark. 1999. Are affirmative action hires less qualified? Evidence from employer-employee data on new hires. *Journal of Labor Economics* 17:534–69.

Huckle, P. 1983. A decade's difference: Mid-level managers and affirmative action. *Public Personnel Management Journal* 12 (3): 249–57.

Jacobs, J. A. 1989. Long-term trends in occupational segregation by sex. *American Journal of Sociology* 95:16–73.

Jacobson, M. B., and W. Koch. 1977. Women as leaders: Performance evaluation as a function of method of leader selection. *Organizational Behavior and Human Performance* 20:149–57.

James, F. L., and S. W. DelCastillo. 1991. Measuring job discrimination by private employers against young black and Hispanic males seeking entry level work in the Denver metropolitan area. Report, University of Colorado.

Jeffries, J. C., Jr. 1994. *Justice Lewis F. Powell, Jr.* New York: Charles Scribner's Sons.

Jones, J. M. 1998. Psychological knowledge and the new American dilemma of race. *Journal of Social Issues* 54:641–62.

Juhn C., K. M. Murphy, and B. Pierce. 1991. Accounting for the slowdown in black-white convergence. In *Workers and their wages: Changing patterns in the*

*United States,* ed. M. Kosters, 107–45. Washington, DC: American Enterprise Institute Press.

Kanter, R. M. 1977. *Men and women of the corporation.* New York: Basic Books.

Kern, L. 1996. Hiring and seniority: Issues in policing in the post-judicial intervention period. Manuscript, Department of Sociology, Ohio State University, Columbus.

Klitgaard, R. 1985. *Choosing elites.* New York: Basic Books.

Kluegel, J. R., and E. R. Smith. 1982. White's beliefs about black's opportunity. *American Sociological Review* 47:518–32.

Komaromy, M., K. Grumbach, M. Drake, K. Vranizan, N. Lurie, D. Keane, and A. Bindman. 1996. The role of black and Hispanic physicians in providing health care for underserved populations. *New England Journal of Medicine* 334:1305–10.

Konrad, A. M., and F. Linnehan. 1999. Affirmative action: History, effects, and attitudes. In *Handbook of gender and work,* ed. G. N. Powell, 429–52. Thousand Oaks, CA: Sage.

Kravitz, D. A., D. A. Harrison, M. E. Turner, E. L. Levine, W. Chaves, M. T. Brannick, D. L. Denning, C. J. Russell, and M. A. Conrad. 1997. *Affirmative action: A review of psychological and behavioral research.* Bowling Green, OH: Society for Industrial and Organizational Psychology.

Kravitz, D., and J. Platania. 1993. Attitudes and beliefs about affirmative action: Effects of target and of respondent sex and ethnicity. *Journal of Applied Psychology* 78:928–38.

Krester, E. 1993. Germany prepares kids for good jobs: We are preparing ours for Wendy's. *Smithsonian* 23 (March): 44–50.

Labor letter: A special news report on people and their jobs in offices, fields, and factories: Affirmative action is accepted by most corporate chiefs. 1979. *Wall Street Journal,* April 3, p. 1.

LaFraniere, S. 1991. Testers to probe bias by landlords. *Washington Post,* November 5, p. A19.

Lamar, J. 1991. Whose legacy is it, anyway? *New York Times,* October 9, p. A15.

Leonard, J. S. 1984a. Anti-discrimination or reverse discrimination: The impact of changing demographics, Title VII, and affirmative action on productivity. *Journal of Human Resources* 19:145–74.

———. 1984b. Employment and occupational advances under affirmative action. *Review of Economics and Statistics* 66:377–85.

———. 1984c. Impact of affirmative action on employment. *Journal of Labor Economics* 2 (4): 439–63.

———. 1985. Affirmative action as earnings redistribution: The targeting of compliance reviews. *Journal of Labor Economics* 3 (July): 363–84.

———. 1994. Use of enforcement techniques in eliminating glass ceiling barriers. Report to the Glass Ceiling Commission, U.S. Department of Labor. Washington, DC, April.

Lerner, M. J. 1971. Observer's evaluation of a victim: Justice, guilt, and veridical perception. *Journal of Personality and Social Psychology* 20:127–35.

Lind, M. 1995. *The next American nation.* New York: Free Press.

Loury, G. C. 1990. The salience of race. *Second Thoughts* 1 (3).

———. 1992. Incentive effects of affirmative action. *Annals of the American Academy of Political and Social Science* 523 (September): 19–29.

Lovrich, N. P., B. S. Steel, and D. Hood. 1986. Equity versus productivity:

Affirmative action and municipal police services. *Public Productivity Review* 39:61–72.

Major, B., J. Feinstein, and J. Crocker. 1994. Attributional ambiguity of affirmative action. *Basic and Applied Social Psychology* 15:113–41.

Markham, W. T., S. L. Harlan, and E. J. Hackett. 1987. Promotion opportunity in organizations: Causes and consequences. *Research in Personnel and Human Resources Management* 5:223–87.

Martin, S. E. 1991. The effectiveness of affirmative action: The case of women in policing. *Justice Quarterly* 8:489–504.

Mayhew, L. 1968. *Law and equal opportunity: A study of Massachusetts Commission against Discrimination.* Cambridge, MA: Harvard University Press.

Mays, V., and S. Cochran. 1986. Relationship experience and the perception of discrimination of black lesbians. Paper presented at the eighty-fourth annual meeting of the American Psychological Association, Washington, DC, August.

McConahay, J. B. 1983. Modern racism and modern discrimination: The effects of race, racial attitudes, and context on simulated hiring decisions. *Personality and Social Psychology Bulletin* 9:551.

McMillen, L. 1995. [Affirmative action] Policies said to help companies hire qualified workers at no extra cost. *Chronicle of Higher Education,* November 17, p. A7.

Miller, F. A., and M. A. Clark. 1997. Looking toward the future: Young people's attitudes about affirmative action and the American dream. *American Behavioral Scientist* 41:262–71.

Miller, F. A., and J. H. Katz. 1995. Cultural diversity as a developmental process: The path from monocultural club to inclusive organization. In *The 1995 Annual,* ed. J. W. Pfeiffer. Vol. 2, *Consulting,* 267–81. San Diego: Pfeiffer and Co.

Minority enterprise: Fat white wallets. 1993. *Economist,* November 27, 29.

Molyneux, G. 1996. Recent public opinion research on race and affirmative action. Paper presented at GSS Conference on "Beyond Black and White: Multiculturalism and the General Social Survey," Washington, DC.

Moore, D. W. 1995. Americans today are dubious about affirmative action. *Gallup Poll Monthly,* March, 36–38.

Murnane, R. J., and F. Levy. 1996. *Teaching the new basic skills: Principles for educating children to thrive in a changing economy.* New York: Free Press.

Murnane, R. J., J. Willett, and F. Levy. 1995. The growing importance of cognitive skills in wage determination. *Review of Economics and Statistics* 77:251–66.

Nacoste, R. B. 1987. But do they care about fairness? The dynamics of preferential treatment and minority interest. *Basic and Applied Social Psychology* 8:117–91.

———. 1990. Sources of stigma: Analyzing the psychology of affirmative action. *Law and Policy* 12:175–95.

———. 1994. If empowerment is the goal . . . : Affirmative action and social interaction. *Basic and Applied Social Psychology* 15:87–112.

Nacoste, R. W. 1985. Selection procedure and responses to affirmative action: The case of favorable treatment. *Law and Human Behavior* 9:225–42.

National Center for Education Statistics. 1993. *Data compendium for the NAEP 1992 mathematics assessment of the nation and the states.* Report 23-ST04. Washington, DC: U.S. Government Printing Office.

————. 1996. *NAEP 1994 reading report card for the nation and the states.* Washington, DC: U.S. Department of Education.

National Commission on Testing and Public Policy. 1990. *From gatekeeper to gateway: Transforming testing in America.* Chestnut Hill, MA: National Commission on Testing and Public Policy.

National Research Council. 1989. *Fairness in employment testing.* Washington, DC: National Academy Press.

Neal, D. A., and W. R. Johnson. 1996. The role of pre-market factors in black-white wage differences. *Journal of Political Economy* 104 (October): 869–96.

Newman, J. D. 1989. Affirmative action and the courts. In *Affirmative action in perspective,* ed. F. A. Blanchard and F. J. Crosby, 31–49. New York: Springer-Verlag.

Noble, K. 1986. Employers are split on affirmative goals. *New York Times,* March 3, p. B4.

Northrup, H. R., and J. A. Larson. 1979. The impact of the AT&T-EEO consent decrees. Labor Relations and the Public Policy Series 20, University of Pennsylvania, Industrial Research Unit, Philadelphia.

O'Neill, D. M., and J. O'Neill. 1992. Affirmative action in the labor market. *Annals of the American Academy of Political and Social Science* 523:88–103.

O'Neill, J. 1990. The role of human capital in earnings differences between black and white men. *Journal of Economic Perspectives* 4 (4): 25–45.

O'Neill, J., J. Cunningham, A. Sparks, and H. Sider. 1986. *Economic progress of black men in America.* Clearing House Publication 91. Washington, DC: Commission on Civil Rights, October.

O'Neill, J., and S. Polachek. 1993. Why the gender gap in wages narrowed in the 1980s. *Journal of Labor Economics* 11 (1): 205–28.

Ozawa, K., M. Crosby, and F. Crosby. 1996. Individualism and resistance to affirmative action: A comparison of Japanese and American samples. *Journal of Applied Social Psychology* 26:1138–52.

Penn, N. E., P. J. Russell, and H. J. Simon. 1986. Affirmative action at work: A survey of graduates of the University of California at San Diego Medical School. *American Journal of Public Health* 76:1144–46.

Pettigrew, T., and J. Martin. 1987. Shaping the organizational context for black American inclusion. *Journal of Social Issues* 43:41–78.

Pole, J. R. 1978. *The pursuit of equality in American history.* Berkeley: University of California Press.

Potts, J. 1994. White men can help—but it's hard. In *The promise of diversity: Over forty voices discuss strategies for eliminating discrimination in organizations,* ed. E. Y. Cross, J. H. Katz, F. A. Miller, and E. W. Seashore, 165–69. Burr Ridge, IL: Irwin.

Pratkanis, A. R., and M. E. Turner. 1996. The proactive removal of discriminatory barriers: Affirmative action policy. *Journal of Social Issues* 52 (4): 111–32.

Raab, S. 1995. Twelve charged in minority businesses scheme. *New York Times,* May 19, p. B2.

Ramphele, M. 1996. Equity and excellence—strange bedfellows? A case study of South African higher education. Paper presented at the Princeton Conference on Higher Education, March.

Rand, A. B. 1996. Diversity in corporate America. In *The affirmative action debate,* ed. G. Curry, 65–76. Reading, MA: Addison-Wesley.

Rauch, J. 1994. Color TV. *New Republic,* December 19, 9.

Reskin, B. F., and H. Hartmann. 1986. *Women's work, men's work: Sex segregation on the job.* Washington, DC: National Academy Press.

Reskin, B. F., M. Hickey, and A. Wheeler. 1998. Trends in the effects of sex and race on intergroup occupational contact. Manuscript, Department of Sociology, Harvard University.

Reskin, B. F., and P. Roos. 1990. *Job queues, gender queues.* Philadelphia: Temple University Press.

Rhode, D. 1989. *Justice and gender: Sex discrimination and the law.* Cambridge, MA: Harvard University Press.

Salwen, K. G. 1993. The cutting edge: German-owned maker of power tools finds job training pays off. *Wall Street Journal,* April 19, p. 1.

Schmermund, A., R. Sellers, B. Mueller, and F. Crosby. 1998. Attitudes toward affirmative action as a function of racial identity among black college students. Manuscript.

Smith, J. P., and F. Welch. 1984. Affirmative action and labor markets. *Journal of Labor Economics* 2:269–301.

Sowell, T. 1990. *Preferential policies: An international perspective.* New York: Morrow.

———. 1994. *Race and culture: A world view.* New York: Basic Books.

Spangler, E., M. A. Gordon, and R. M. Pipkin. 1978. Token women: An empirical test of Kanter's hypothesis. *American Journal of Sociology* 84:160.

Steel, B. S., and N. P. Lovrich. 1987. Equality and efficiency tradeoffs in affirmative action—real or imagined? The case of women in policing. *Social Science Journal* 24:53–70.

Steele, S. 1990. *The content of our character: A new vision of race in America.* New York: St. Martin's Press.

Stephanopoulos, G., and C. Edley, Jr. 1995. *Affirmative action review: Report to the president.* Washington, DC: U.S. Government Printing Office.

Taylor, D. A. 1989. Affirmative action and presidential executive orders. In *Affirmative action in perspective,* ed. F. A. Blanchard and F. J. Crosby, 21–29. New York: Springer-Verlag.

Taylor, M. C. 1994. Impact of affirmative action on beneficiary groups: Evidence from the 1990 General Social Survey. *Basic and Applied Social Psychology* 15:143–78.

Theodore, A. 1986. *The campus troublemakers: Academic women in protest.* Houston: Cap and Gown Press.

Thernstrom, A. 1992. The drive for racially inclusive schools. *Annals of the American Academy of Political and Social Science* 523 (June): 131–43.

Thomas, R. R., Jr. 1990. From affirmative action to affirming diversity. *Harvard Business Review* 68 (2): 107–17.

Truax, K., D. I. Cordova, A. Wood, E. Wright, and F. Crosby. 1998. Undermined? Affirmative action from the targets' point of view. In *Prejudice: The target's perspective,* ed. J. Swim and C. Stangor, 171–87. New York: Academic Press.

Turner, M. A., M. Fix, and R. J. Struyk. 1991. Opportunities denied, opportunities diminished. Report 91-9, Urban Institute, Washington, DC.

Turner, M., M. Fix, and J. Yinger. 1991. *Opportunities denied, opportunities diminished: Discrimination in hiring.* Washington, DC: Urban Institute.

Turner, M. E., and A. R. Pratkanis. 1994. Affirmative action as help: A review of recipient reactions to preferential selection and affirmative action. *Basic and Applied Social Psychology* 15:43–69.

Turner, M. E., A. R. Pratkanis, and T. J. Hardaway. 1991. Sex differences in reactions to preferential selection: Towards a model of preferential selection as help. *Journal of Social Behavior and Personality* 6:797–814.

Turner, S. 1996. Barriers to a better break: Wages, race, and space in metropolitan Detroit. Manuscript, Department of Sociology, Wayne State University, Detroit, MI.

U.S. Bureau of the Census. 1963. *Census of the population and housing, 1960: Subject report, occupational characteristics.* PC(2)-7A. Washington, DC: U.S. Government Printing Office.

———. 1972. *Census of the population and housing, 1970.* Public Use Microsamples (MRDF). Washington, DC: U.S. Bureau of the Census (producer).

———. 1983. *Census of population and housing, 1980.* Public Use Microsamples (MRDF). Washington, DC: U.S. Bureau of the Census (producer).

———. 1992. *Census of population and housing, 1990.* Public Use Microsamples (MRDF). Washington, DC: U.S. Bureau of the Census (producer).

———. 1995a. *Income, poverty, and valuation of non-cash benefits: 1993.* Current Population Reports, P60-188. Washington, DC: U.S. Government Printing Office.

———. 1995b. *The black population in the United States: March 1994 and 1993.* Current Population Reports, P-20-480. Washington, DC: U.S. Government Printing Office.

———. 1996. *The black population in the United States: March 1995.* Current Population Reports, PPL-45. Washington, DC: U.S. Government Printing Office.

U.S. Bureau of Labor Statistics. 1971. *Employment and earnings* 18 (January). Washington, DC: U.S. Government Printing Office.

———. 1991. *Employment and earnings* 38 (January). Washington, DC: U.S. Government Printing Office.

U.S. Department of Labor. 1995. *Fact sheet no. ESA 95-17: Executive Order 11246.* Washington, DC: U.S. Government Printing Office.

———. 1996. The facts on Executive Order 11246: Affirmative Action. Washington, DC: Office of Federal Contract Compliance Programs.

U.S. Department of Labor, Employment Standards Administration, Office of Federal Contract Compliance Programs (cited as OFCCP). n.d. The rhetoric and the reality about federal affirmative action at the OFCCP, Washington, DC: U.S. Department of Labor.

U.S. Department of Labor, OFCCP, Glass Ceiling Commission. 1995. *Good for business: Making full use of the nation's human capital/the environmental scar.* Washington, DC: U.S. Government Printing Office.

U.S. Senate, Committee on Labor and Human Resources. 1995. *Federal job training programs: The need for overhaul: Hearings before the Committee on Labor and Human Resources.* Washington, DC: U.S. Government Printing Office.

Verhovek, S. H. 1997. In poll, Americans reject means but not ends of racial diversity. *New York Times,* December 14, pp. 1, 32.

Watson, W. E., K. Kumar, and L. K. Michaelsen. 1993. Cultural diversity's impact on interaction process and performance: Comparing homogeneous and diverse task groups. *Academy of Management Journal* 36:590–602.

Wegener, B. 1990. Equity, relative deprivation, and the value-consensus paradox. *Social Justice Research* 4:65–86.

Werner, D. 1988. College admissions: Shaky ethics. *New York Times,* June 4.

Wheeler, M. L. 1994. *Diversity training: A research report.* Report R-1083, Conference Board, 845 Third Avenue, New York, NY 10022.

———. 1995. *Diversity: Business rationale and strategies: A research report.* Report 1130-95-RR, Conference Board, 845 Third Avenue, New York, NY 10022.

Williams, J. B. 1992. Affirmative action at Harvard. *Annals of the American Academy of Political and Social Science* 523 (September): 207–20.

Wilson, W. J. 1987. *The truly disadvantaged.* Chicago: University of Chicago Press.

Wright, P., S. P. Ferris, J. S. Hiller, and M. Kroll. 1995. Competitiveness through management of diversity: Effects on stock price valuation. *Academy of Management Journal* 38:272–87.

Zanna, M. P., F. J. Crosby, and G. Loewenstein. 1987. Male reference groups and discontent among female professionals. In *Women's career development,* ed. B. A. Gutek and L. Larwood, 28–41. Newbury Park, CA: Sage.

Zanna, M. P., G. Goethals, and J. Hill. 1975. Evaluating a sex-related ability: Social comparison with a similar other and standard setters. *Journal of Experimental Social Psychology* 11:86–93.

## ADDITIONAL READINGS

Allina, A. 1987. *Beyond standardized tests: Admissions alternatives that work.* Cambridge, MA: Fair Test.

Arthur, J., and A. Shapiro, eds. 1995. *Campus wars: Multiculturalism and the politics of difference.* Boulder, CO: Westview Press.

Beckwith, F. J., and T. E. Jones, eds. 1997. *Affirmative action: Social justice or reverse discrimination?* Amherst, NY: Prometheus Books.

Belz, H. 1991. *Equality transformed: A quarter-century of affirmative action.* New Brunswick, NJ: Transaction Publishers.

Bergmann, B. R. 1996. *In defense of affirmative action.* New York: Basic Books.

Blanchard, F. A., and F. J. Crosby, eds. 1989. *Affirmative action in perspective.* New York: Springer-Verlag.

Bolick, C. 1996. *The affirmative action fraud: Can we restore the American civil rights vision?* Washington, DC: Cato Institute.

Bowen, W. G., and D. Bok. 1998. *The shape of the river: Long-term consequences of considering race in college and university admissions.* Princeton, NJ: Princeton University Press.

Brown, W., Jr., and W. Connerly. 1995. Choosing sides. *Black Enterprise* 26 (4): 156–57.

Burstein, P. 1993. Affirmative action and the rhetoric of reaction. *American Prospect* 14 (summer): 138–47.

Caplan, L. 1997. *Up against the law: Affirmative action and the Supreme Court.* New York: Twentieth Century Fund Press.

Carter, S. L. 1991. *Reflections of an affirmative action baby.* New York: Basic Books.

Chávez, L. 1992. Hispanics, affirmative action, and voting. *Annals of the American Academy of Political and Social Science* 523 (September): 75–87.

———. 1998. *The color bind: California's battle to end affirmative action.* Berkeley: University of California Press.

Clayton, S. D., and F. J. Crosby. 1992. *Justice, gender, and affirmative action.* Ann Arbor: University of Michigan Press.

Cohen, M. N. 1998. *Culture of intolerance: Chauvinism, class, and racism in the United States.* New Haven, CT: Yale University Press.

Cornell, D. 1991. *Beyond accommodation: Ethical feminism, deconstruction, and the law.* New York: Routledge.

Crosby, F. J. 1993. Affirmative action is worth it. *Chronicle of Higher Education,* December 15, B1.

———. 1994. Understanding affirmative action. Special Issue: Social psychological perspectives on affirmative action. *Basic and Applied Social Psychology* 15 (1–2): 13–41.

Crosby, F., and S. Clayton. 1990. Affirmative action and the issue of expectancies. (Expectancies and Social Issues). *Journal of Social Issues* 46 (2): 61.

Curry, G. E., ed. 1996. *The affirmative action debate.* Reading, MA: Addison-Wesley.

Delgado, R. 1996. *The coming race war? And other apocalyptic tales of America after affirmative action and welfare.* New York: New York University Press.

Drake, W. A., and R. D. Holsworth. 1996. *Affirmative action and the stalled quest for black progress.* Urbana: University of Illinois Press.

Duster, T. 1991. They're taking over! And other myths about race on campus. *Mother Jones* 16 (5): 30–35.

Eastland, T. 1996. *Ending affirmative action: The case for colorblind justice.* New York: Basic Books.

Eberhardt, J. L., and S. T. Fiske. 1994. Affirmative action in theory and practice: Issues of power, ambiguity, and gender versus race. Special Issue: Social psychological perspectives on affirmative action. *Basic and Applied Social Psychology* 15 (1–2): 201–20.

Edley, C. F. 1996. *Not all black and white: Affirmative action, race, and American values.* New York: Hill and Wang.

Edwards, S., ed. 1985. *Gender, sex, and the law.* London; Dover, NH: Croom Helm.

Eisenstein, Z. 1991. Privatizing the state: Reproductive rights, affirmative action, and the problem of democracy. *Basic and Applied Social Psychology* 12 (1): 98–125.

Fair, B. K. 1997. *Notes of a racial caste baby: Color blindness and the end of affirmative action.* New York: New York University Press.

Feinberg, W. 1998. *On higher ground: Education and the case for affirmative action.* New York: Teachers College Press.

Foner, E. 1995. Hiring quotas for white males only. *Nation* 260 (25): 924–25.

Gabel, P. 1995. Affirmative action and racial harmony. *Tikkun* 10 (3): 33–36.

Garcia, M., ed. 1997. *Affirmative action's testament of hope: Strategies for a new era in higher education.* Albany: State University of New York Press.

Graham, H. D. 1992. The origins of affirmative action: Civil rights and the regulatory state. *Annals of the American Academy of Political and Social Science* 52 (September): 50–62.

Greenwood, M. R. C. 1996. Dancing with wolves. *Science* 271 (5257): 1787.

Guinier, L., M. Fine, and J. Balin. 1997. *Becoming gentlemen: Women, law school, and institutional change.* Boston: Beacon Press.

———. 1994. *The tyranny of the majority: Fundamental fairness in representative democracy.* New York: Free Press.

————. 1998. *Lift every voice: Turning a civil rights setback into a new vision of social justice.* New York: Simon and Schuster.

Hacker, A. 1995. The drive to end affirmative action: The perils of class-based preferences. *Chronicle of Higher Education,* July 14, p. B2.

Hill, A. F., and E. C. Jordan. 1995. *Race, gender, and power in America: The legacy of the Hill-Thomas hearings.* New York: Oxford University Press.

Horner, C. 1995. Reclaiming the vision: What should we do after affirmative action? *Current,* no. 377:3–7.

Jordan, J. 1996. Justice at risk. *Progressive* 60 (4): 18–19.

————. 1998. *Affirmative acts: Political essays.* New York: Anchor Books/ Doubleday.

Jung, D., C. Wadia, and M. J. Haberman. 1996. *Affirmative action and the courts.* Sacramento: California Research Bureau, California State Library.

Karst, K. L. 1993. *Law's promise, law's expression: Visions of power in the politics of race, gender, and religion.* New Haven, CT: Yale University Press.

Kirp, D. L., M. G. Yudolf, and M. S. Franks. 1986. *Gender justice.* Chicago: University of Chicago Press.

Kravitz, D. A., et al., eds. 1997. *Affirmative action: A review of psychological and behavioral research.* Bowling Green, OH: Society for Industrial and Organizational Psychology.

Laham, N. 1998. *The Reagan presidency and the politics of race: In pursuit of colorblind justice and limited government.* Westport, CT: Praeger.

Lawrence, C., and M. J. Matsuda. 1997. *We won't go back: Making the case for affirmative action.* Boston: Houghton Mifflin.

Lawson, W. E. 1992. *The underclass question.* Philadelphia: Temple University Press.

Levine, A., ed. 1993. *Higher learning in America, 1980–2000.* Baltimore, MD: Johns Hopkins University Press.

Maschke, K. J., ed. 1997. *Educational equity.* New York: Garland.

Matsuda, M. J. 1996. *Where is your body? And other essays on race, gender, and the law.* Boston: Beacon Press.

McLean, S., and N. Burrows, eds. 1988. *The legal relevance of gender: Some aspects of sex-based discrimination.* Atlantic Highlands, NJ: Humanities Press International.

McWhirter, D. A. 1996. *The end of affirmative action: Where do we go from here?* New York: Carol Publishing Group.

Mills, N., ed. 1994. *Debating affirmative action: Race, gender, ethnicity, and the politics of inclusion.* New York: Delta Trade Paperbacks.

————. 1995. Affirmative action on the ropes. *Dissent* 42 (2): 189–90.

Mosley, A. G., and N. Capaldi. 1996. *Affirmative action: Social justice or unfair preference?* Lanham, MD: Rowman and Littlefield.

Myers, S. L., ed. 1977. *Civil rights and race relations in the post Reagan-Bush era.* Westport, CT: Praeger.

Oakes, J. 1985. *Keeping track: How schools structure inequality.* New Haven, CT: Yale University Press.

Omi, M., and D. Takagi. 1996. Situating Asian Americans in the political discourse on affirmative action. *Representations* 55 (summer): 155–62.

Ong, P., et al., eds. 1997. *The impact of affirmative action on public-sector employment and contracting in California.* Berkeley: California Policy Seminar, University of California.

Post, R., and M. Rogin, eds. 1998. *Race and representation: Affirmative action.* New York: Zone Books.

Pratkanis, A., and M. Turner. 1996. The proactive removal of discriminatory barriers: Affirmative action as effective help. *Journal of Social Issues* 52 (4): 111–32.

Reskin, B. 1998. *The realities of affirmative action in employment.* Washington, DC: American Sociological Association.

Rhode, D. L. 1989. *Justice and gender: Sex discrimination and the law.* Cambridge, MA: Harvard University Press.

Rodriguez, R. 1995. Coalition: Black/brown relations fused by anti–affirmative action policies. *Black Issues in Higher Education* 12 (15): 8–17.

Skedsvold, P., and T. Mann, eds. 1996. The affirmative action debate: What's fair in policy and programs? *Journal of Social Issues* 52 (4).

Skrentny, J. D. 1996. *The ironies of affirmative action: Politics, culture, and justice in America.* Chicago: University of Chicago Press.

Stein, N. 1995. Affirmative action and the persistence of racism. *Social Justice* 22 (3): 28–44.

Takagi, D. 1992. *The retreat from race: Asian-American admissions and racial politics.* New Brunswick, NJ: Rutgers University Press.

———. 1993. Asian Americans and racial politics: A postmodern paradox. *Social Justice* 20 (1–2): 115–28.

Tomasson, R. F., F. J. Crosby, and S. D. Herzberger. 1996. *Affirmative acton: The pros and cons of policy and practice.* Lanham, MD: American University Press.

Truax, K., D. I. Cordova, A. Wood, E. Wright, and F. J. Crosby. 1998. Undermined? Affirmative action from the target's point of view. In *Prejudice: The target's perspective,* ed. J. K. Swim and C. Stangor. San Diego: Academic Press.

Turner, M., and A. Pratkanis. 1994. Affirmative action: Insights from social psychological and organization research. *Basic and Applied Social Psychology* 15 (1–2): 1–11.

U.S. Congress. Senate. Committee on the Judiciary. Subcommittee on the Constitution, Federalism, and Property Rights. 1996. *An overview of affirmative action.* Washington, DC: U.S. Government Printing Office.

Weiss, R. J. 1997. *"We want jobs": A history of affirmative action.* New York: Garland.

Welch, S., and J. Gruhl. 1998. *Affirmative action and minority enrollments in medical and law schools.* Ann Arbor: University of Michigan Press.

West, C. 1993. *Race matters.* Boston: Beacon Press.

Williams, P. J. 1991. *The alchemy of race and rights.* Cambridge, MA: Harvard University Press.

Winston, K., and M. J. Bane, eds. 1993. *Gender and public policy: Cases and comments.* Boulder, CO: Westview Press.

Wolf-Devine, C. 1997. *Diversity and community in the academy: Affirmative action in faculty appointments.* Lanham, MD: Rowman and Littlefield.

Yoder, J. D. 1991. Rethinking tokenism: Looking beyond numbers. *Gender and Society* 5 (2): 178–92.

Zelnick, B. 1996. *Backfire: A reporter's look at affirmative action.* Washington, DC: Regnery.

## WEB SITES

### Anti–Affirmative Action

*Campaign for a Color-Blind America*
<http://www.equalrights.com/>.
Sponsored by the Campaign for a Color-Blind America, Legal Defense, and Educational Foundation, which challenges race-based public policies. Provides database of political office candidates' opinions regarding race-based public policy, newspaper editorials, information on litigation of cases involving racial preference, and press releases.

*AADAP—Daily news concerning affirmative action, race, gender, and ethnicity*
<http://www.aadap.org/>.
Sponsored by Americans against Discrimination and Preference. Provides daily updates of news, events, and commentaries regarding affirmative action. Also includes archive of articles posted in previous days.

### Neutral

*Washingtonpost.com: Affirmative Action Special Report*
<http://www.washingtonpost.com/wp-srv/politics/special/affirm/affirm.htm>.
Provides a thorough review of affirmative action, including overview, news stories and noteworthy events from the *Post* and the Associated Press, opinion pieces and editorials, and links to other affirmative action web sites.

*Affirmative Action and Diversity Page*
<http://humanitas.ucsb.edu/aa.html>.
Sponsored by the University of California, Santa Barbara. Presents diverse opinions regarding topics in affirmative action in the form of articles, theoretical analyses, policy documents, current legislative updates, and bibliography of research and teaching materials.

*Policy.com—Issue of the Week: Affirmative Action in Focus*
<http://www.policy.com/issuewk/1999/0222_58/index.html>.
Sponsored by Policy.com, a policy news and information service. Provides information on the effects of minority status, evaluating and regulating affirmative action compliance, effectiveness of affirmative action, federal and state affirmative action law and enforcement, legal challenges to affirmative action, debating affirmative action, and additional resources.

*Affirmative Action Review: Report to the President*
<http://www.whitehouse.gov/WH/EOP/OP/html/aa/aa-index.html>.
Investigation and report completed by George Stephanopoulous and Christopher Edley, Jr., for the president in 1995 regarding federal affirmative action programs. Also provides background, summary of empirical research, and justifications for affirmative action.

**Pro–Affirmative Action**

*Americans United for Affirmative Action (AUAA)*
<http://www.auaa.org/>.
Sponsored by the AUAA, a national organization dedicated to maintaining affirmative action and equal opportunity. Provides updated information on issues related to affirmative action concerning the executive, legislative, and judicial branches of the government as well as state legislation.

*Affirmative Action Information Center*
<http://www.feminist.org/other/ccri/cahome.html>.
Sponsored by the Feminist Majority Foundation. Focuses on affirmative action's role in expanding women's opportunities in employment and education. Also provides information on the origins of affirmative action for women, answers to commonly asked questions regarding Proposition 209, and news stories and press releases.